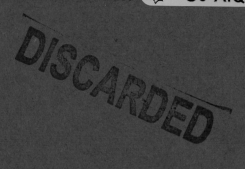

DATE DUE

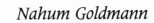

Nahum Goldmann

JUDAIC STUDIES SERIES
Leon J. Weinberger, General Editor

Nahum Goldmann

His Missions to the Gentiles

RAPHAEL PATAI

The University of Alabama Press

Library of Congress Cataloging in Publication Data

Patai, Raphael, 1910–
    Nahum Goldmann: his missions to the Gentiles.

    (Judaic studies series)
    Bibliography: p.
    Includes index.
    1. Goldmann, Nahum, 1895–1982. 2. Zionists—Biography.
3. Jewish-Arab relations—1917– . 4. Restitution
and indemnification claims (1933–)—Germany, West.
5. Jews—Legal status, laws, etc.—Germany, West.
I. Title. II. Series.
DS151.G585P38   1987   956.94′001′0924 [B] 85-24518
ISBN 0-8173-0294-8

Contents

Acknowledgments

I wish to express my thanks to several libraries for their help in locating documents and other source material that were invaluable in writing this book. My gratitude is extended to Miss Esther Togman, director of the Zionist Archives and Library of New York; Dr. Leonard S. Gold, head of the Jewish Division of the New York Public Library; Mr. Christian Filstrup, chief of the Oriental Division of the New York Public Library; Mr. Myron Weinstein, head of the Hebraic Section of the Library of Congress, Washington, D.C.; Melle Madeleine Neige, supervisor of the Service Hébraique of the Bibliothèque Nationale, in Paris; Dr. David Goldstein, keeper, Hebrew Section, Department of Oriental Manuscripts and Printed Books, the British Library, London; and the staffs of all these institutions. Their courtesy and bibliographical expertise were immensely helpful in connection with my research for this volume.

My thanks are due also to several publishers for their courtesy, to wit:

Deutsche Verlagsanstalt, Stuttgart, and Hachette, Paris, for permission to quote from Konrad Adenauer, *Erinnerungen,* 1966.

Dufour Editions, Chester Springs, Pennsylvania, for permission to quote from Rolf Vogel, *The German Path to Israel,* 1969.

Holt, Rinehart and Winston, New York, for permission to quote from *The Autobiography of Nahum Goldmann,* translated by Helen Sebba, 1969.

Propyläen Verlag and Ullstein Verlag, Berlin, for permission to quote from Herbert Blankenhorn, *Verständnis und Verständigung,* 1980.

Raphael Patai

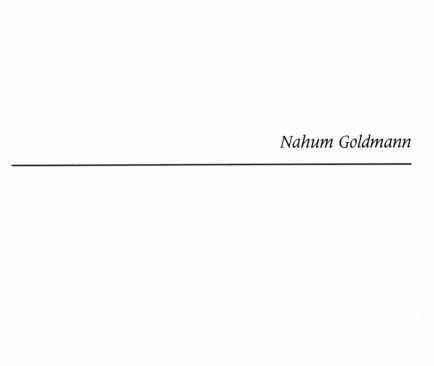

Nahum Goldmann

Dr. Nahum Goldmann addressing a luncheon meeting in honor of the tenth anniversary of the establishment of the Herzl Press, held on May 20, 1964, at the Jewish Agency headquarters, 515 Park Avenue, New York. *Left to right:* Raphael Patai, Nahum Goldmann (standing), Emanuel Neuman, Judah Shapiro, Rose Halprin.

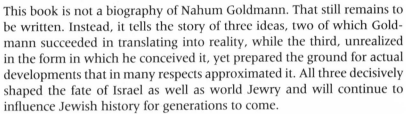

This book is not a biography of Nahum Goldmann. That still remains to be written. Instead, it tells the story of three ideas, two of which Goldmann succeeded in translating into reality, while the third, unrealized in the form in which he conceived it, yet prepared the ground for actual developments that in many respects approximated it. All three decisively shaped the fate of Israel as well as world Jewry and will continue to influence Jewish history for generations to come.

Chronologically, the first of these ideas was the partition of Palestine, which made the establishment of the State of Israel possible. Goldmann fought long and hard to have the idea of partition accepted by the Zionist leadership on the one hand, and, on the other, by the leaders of the nations whose voices carried the most weight in having the UN General Assembly vote for it. It is likely that without Goldmann's work the State of Israel could not have been born on May 14, 1948.

The second idea was the approval by the German government of monetary reparations to Israel and individual Jews. In this, Goldmann's role was crucial. The effect of the reparations on Israel's development and on the lives of thousands of individual Jews cannot be overestimated.

The third idea, to which Goldmann also devoted considerable thought, time, and effort, has not materialized. It comprised a proposed meeting with Gamal Abdel Nasser of Egypt, the establishment of a confederation between Israel and the Arab states, and the neutralization of Israel. Goldmann never met Nasser; no Israeli-Arab or Near Eastern Confederation exists; nor has Israel been neutralized. But in 1977 Nasser's successor, President Anwar Sadat, did journey to Israel and met her leaders as well as Goldmann, and it is not too farfetched to assume that this historic step was facilitated by Sadat's knowledge of the willingness of Nasser to meet Goldmann. Likewise, though no Israeli-Arab confederation has been established, formal peace prevails between Egypt and Israel as well as *de facto* open or semiopen borders between Israel and Jordan and Lebanon so that the isolation that had characterized Israel's position in the early years has definitely been breached. And, finally, even though Israel is not neutralized and no international treaties guarantee her existence as Goldmann had advocated for decades, she does, in fact, rely more and more on the UN presence along her borders to keep the peace with her neighbors.

To be able to penetrate, at least to some extent, the sources of Nahum Goldmann's ability to function as the Jewish people's spokesman vis-à-vis the Gentiles, to negotiate as an equal with some of the most powerful men of his times despite the fact that he was a statesman without a state, a representative without any power base, and a leader who had to create much of his own international organizational basis, I felt it was necessary to study his childhood and youth. Hence, I placed five brief chapters at the head of the book that discuss his childhood, youth, early steps in the Gentile world, and the ideologies to which he was exposed during his formative years. Those early influences were to remain with him all his life and were major factors that went into the formation of his unique personality, which was characterized, over and above his wit, charm, talent, and extraordinary mental agility, by a supreme self-confidence and self-assurance as well as the conviction that he possessed a superior capacity of achieving results, and, in particular, that he could fulfill any diplomatic task better than anyone else.

The search for early childhood impressions and experiences as the formative influences on the personality, attitudes, reactions, and relations to the human environment of the adult into whom the child eventually develops has become commonplace during recent decades. Moreover, this view of the child as the father of the man has jumped the traditional barriers separating the historical from the psychological sciences, and as a result psychologically oriented historical and biographical studies have proliferated. In fact, psychology has become by now so much a part of history, or, to put it differently, history has become so much psychologically oriented, that it is practically no longer possible to write anything historical without giving due place to psychological considerations.

It therefore goes without saying that the present study of Nahum Goldmann had to be strongly psychologically oriented. What does need to be pointed out is that rarely does one encounter an individual caught up and immersed in manifold public activities, facing so many and diverse challenges and carrying such a heavy burden of responsibilities who would be as fully conscious as Goldmann of the childhood conditioning that, once and for all, implanted into his psyche the guidelines along which proceeded all his approaches and reactions to people, tasks, and situations. This came through strongly in the interviews I conducted with him during the course of writing this book.

Goldmann was always fully aware of the importance of his role in Jewish life. He was proud, and rightly so, of his achievements for the Jewish people to whom he had an absolute commitment. Throughout his life he was engaged in the most diverse spheres of Jewish activity. He began his lifelong service of the Zionist cause as an adolescent. His oratorical talent soon became apparent. However, political work could never fully satisfy him. His dynamism had to have other outlets as well. In 1925, at the age of thirty, he co-founded the Eschkol Publishing House in Berlin, and from 1928 was co-publisher of the German *Encyclopaedia Judaica*, of which ten volumes were issued until the Nazi regime put a stop to it. In 1933 he became chairman of the Comité des Délégations Juives and in 1935 representative of the Jewish Agency in the League of Nations. In 1936 he organized, together with Rabbi Stephen Wise, the World Jewish Congress and was its chairman and president for almost forty years. After the outbreak of World War II he established in New York the Zionist Emergency Council. He was for twelve years president of the World Zionist Organization. In 1951 he became president of the Conference of Jewish Material Claims Against Germany, in which capacity he led the negotiations with the German government that resulted in the German payments of reparations to Israel and indemnification for Nazi victims (see chapter 7). In 1955 he created the Conference of Presidents of Major American Jewish Organizations, which became the representative body of practically all of American Jewry vis-à-vis the Government. In 1965 he founded the Memorial Foundation for Jewish Culture, which has since become an influential factor in Jewish cultural life. It was he who, through an allocation obtained from the German reparation fund, made possible the publication of the sixteen-volume English *Encyclopaedia Judaica*. In the last decade of his life he created, on the campus of Tel Aviv University, the Museum of the Jewish Diaspora as a memorial for East and Central European Jewry annihilated by Hitler, and as a means of deepening the psychological and intellectual relationship between Israel and the Diaspora. Subsequently this unique museum was named after him.[1] Of all this, except for Goldmann's contacts with

German Chancellor Adenauer, nothing will be said in the present book.

This impressive list of accomplishments should make the reader aware that a book dealing only with Nahum Goldmann's missions to the Gentiles presents only part of his lifework. But it so happened that, after publishing in 1977 my book *The Jewish Mind*,[2] I was conditioned to be interested in that aspect of his work in particular. A major part of *The Jewish Mind* is devoted to an analysis of six great historical-cultural encounters between the Jews and the Gentile world. This left me with a residual wish to supplement the general, large-scale study of Jewish-Gentile encounters with a case study of the encounters between one representative modern Jewish individual and Gentile personages. Goldmann wrote of himself, "I, more than many other Jewish personalities, represent this unique [Jewish] generation."[3] Long before I read this statement, I had felt that his relations with the Gentiles, more than those of any other Jewish leader I knew, could be for me the most attractive and instructive subject to study and to serve as a test case for the applicability to a modern individual of the insights I gained in writing *The Jewish Mind*. Goldmann's missions to the Gentiles seemed to be a highly suitable subject to treat in the light of my thesis that Jewish culture evolved and progressed by selectively adopting cultural features from the Gentile environment and adapting them to the basic traditional tenets and values of Judaism.

Goldmann was, I knew, an *Europäer* through and through, fluent in several Western languages, a man of strong European culture, a connoisseur of European art and literature, and a master in the European art of diplomacy. Yet, though having absorbed all this from his European environment, he remained deeply rooted in Judaism, spoke Hebrew and Yiddish fluently, knew and loved Jewish literature as well as tradition, and firmly believed in and fought for Zionism, Jewish rights, and Jewish values. As such, he was a worthy present-day counterpart and successor of the great figures in Jewish history whose vignettes dot the pages of *The Jewish Mind*. He differed from these giants in that he felt it was his mission to influence the Gentiles, and, unlike St. Paul, to do this solely for the benefit of the Jews.

I had known Goldmann for more than half a century. I first saw and heard him speak in the summer of 1929 at the Sixteenth Zionist Congress, in Zurich, and the founding conference of the expanded Jewish Agency for Palestine that followed it, both of which I attended as a young student member of the audience. At those meetings, the thirty-four-year-old Goldmann was as yet no more than a rising star on the Zionist horizon, a member of the Zionist Actions Committee, and known chiefly as cofounder with Jacob Klatzkin of the Eschkol publishing house in Berlin as well as one of those responsible for the German and Hebrew *Encyclopaedia Judaica,* which began to appear in 1928. The only reason I remember Goldmann from that congress is that at one point he and my father carried on a lengthy discussion in my presence about what could be done to further Zionism in Hungary.[4]

Over the ensuing years, as Goldmann rose in the Zionist hierarchy, he maintained contact with my father, who was the founder (in 1927) and the moving spirit of the Pro Palestine Association of Hungarian Jews. Goldmann visited Budapest several times and was a guest in my parents' house more than once. Because I did not keep a diary in my youth, a long hiatus exists in my recollections concerning occasional meetings with Goldmann until 1948. Then, on May 8, I was invited by him and his wife to a party given in their home on Central Park West, in New York, at which two quartets, both consisting of students of the violinist Emil Hauser, performed.

During my fifteen years as director of research of the Herzl Institute and editor of the Herzl Press (1956–71), my office and that of Goldmann were in the same building in New York, and my work required us to meet from time to time. On one of those occasions, he told me that he had just read, and enjoyed, my book *Sex and Family in the Bible and the Middle East,* which was published in 1959 by Doubleday. In 1960, in my capacity as editor of the Herzl Press, I accepted for publication a manuscript by Goldmann's son Guido on Zionism in Soviet Russia. The publication of this first book by his son gave deep satisfaction to Goldmann. On another occasion I consulted him about a few details in his biographical sketch that was being prepared for inclusion in the *Encyclopaedia of Zionism and Israel,* of which I was editor and which was published in 1971 by the Herzl Press and the McGraw-Hill Book Company. On a few occasions, Goldmann and I sat next to each other on the dais during public gatherings, as on May 20, 1964, when a luncheon was held in the lecture hall of the Jewish Agency building at 515 Park Avenue, New York, in honor of the tenth anniversary of the foundation of the Herzl Press.

So much for my occasional contact with Nahum Goldmann before 1979. On April 11 of that year I had to write to him in connection with several literary and editorial matters. One of the issues I mentioned was my intention to dedicate my book *The Messiah Texts,* on which I was working at the time, to four men—Anwar Sadat, Menaḥem Begin,

Jimmy Carter, and Nahum Goldmann—who, I felt, have, each in his own way, brought us a step nearer to the Messianic era of peace between Israel and other nations, and I asked for his consent. In the concluding paragraph of my letter, I mentioned my wish to write a study of his role as the foremost statesman and spokesman of the Jewish people vis-à-vis the Gentiles in the twentieth century. On April 20, 1979, Goldmann replied. About the question of the dedication he wrote that he agreed to my dedicating *The Messiah Texts* to Sadat, Begin, Carter, and himself, despite the fact that he did not believe in the effectiveness of the agreement. In the short term, he felt, it would polarize the Arab world and create crises. However, from a long-term point of view he assumed that the beginning of the recognition of Israel by an Arab leader would have a positive effect, and for this reason he agreed to my dedication.

As for my idea of what we later came to refer to briefly as "the Goldmann book," he wrote:

> Your proposal to study my role in the history of our generation is most flattering, and only because I know what a serious, responsible and good writer you are, I agree to it and shall be ready to give you the information you may require. You may be interested to learn, in this context, that I am re-writing my autobiography in German, doubling the present content; the first volume, of some 400 pages, should be ready for September, the second to be published in the first months of 1980. We may discuss details of your using this material when I see you.

This was the beginning of a lively correspondence and a series of meetings between Goldmann and me, which continued until his death, on August 29, 1982. The meetings took place mostly in Paris, where he maintained his home; a few in New York; and one in the home of his son Guido in Concord, near Boston. All the interviews were taped. Inevitably, when I subsequently listened to the tapes and had them transcribed, questions arose, and much of the correspondence between Goldmann and me contained my questions and his answers. I also asked him for written sources, such as articles he wrote, speeches he made, interviews he gave, and he always supplied these willingly and promptly, aided by his efficient secretary Miss Hella Moritz. In view of his active help with the book, I became at one point somewhat apprehensive lest he should feel that he could control what I wrote. Hence, in one of my letters to him (dated November 30, 1979), I stated:

I must be assured of complete independence as author. I can undertake the writing of the book I have in mind only if I have the certainty that I shall be free to write it as I best see fit, to include or exclude data and all other kinds of material, to present, judge, emphasize, analyze, evaluate, interpret, etc., all statements made by you or others either orally or in writing, as well as all events, acts, situations, plans, sequences, results, etc. which I shall discuss in the book. I shall, of course, always welcome suggestions; in fact, I shall solicit your suggestions, opinions, interpretations, etc., but the final determination of what will be in the book and in what form must be mine.

Goldmann replied by return mail (letter dated December 6, 1979) that he naturally did not have the slightest intention to influence the way I shall write the book. If I wished to consult him, he would be at my disposal, but I did not even have to show him the manuscript before it was published. I was free, he stated, to judge what he had said and done, and to criticize it. And he added that he had always preferred to be criticized by competent people rather than being complimented by incompetent ones, and concluded, "I have full confidence in your judgment of Jewish developments in our time."

Thus assured of my independence as author, I nevertheless felt that the best way of making sure that no factual errors crept into my manuscript and that I was not guilty of omitting important details was to send each chapter, upon its completion in first draft, to Goldmann for review and comments. This procedure proved to be of considerable advantage for the book because it enabled Goldmann to suggest changes, deletions, or additions, though I remained free to use my own judgment in accepting or rejecting them. In any event, Goldmann suggested only a few corrections in my manuscript. In most cases, he found the draft I sent him "very good," and "very well written," without suggesting any changes.

He was especially pleased with the method I adopted in writing the chapter on Adenauer and the German reparations, which used only sources other than Goldmann's own writings. On January 4, 1981, he wrote to me: "I fully approve your method to use other sources than my autobiography for the chapter on 'Adenauer and the German Reparation.' . . . The manner you prefer in presenting the matter is very valid." Two days later, he again wrote: "I received your chapter on 'Adenauer and the German Reparation.' I read it and found it very good, and am returning it to you under separate cover. Your method to use other sources than my own—as I wrote you before—was a very good idea and its implementation resulted in an excellent article."

At the same time, Goldmann was somewhat piqued by my reference in that chapter to the accusation leveled against him in some quarters that he was a "bluffer." This was the only occasion he took exception to material I presented in the book. In his January 6, 1981, letter to me, he wrote that my argument that many regarded his reports as exaggerated or as bluff was not very well founded, in his opinion, if I gave no other source for it than the letter from Kurt Blumenfeld, whom he, Goldmann, could accuse of a similar tendency for which he could adduce much better illustrations. However, he allowed that I may have other sources which I did not want to quote. There may have been many people, he added, who could not believe the truthfulness of his reports on talks with important statesmen, and he quoted one unnamed person who once told him that he could not imagine anyone having the presence of mind to respond in an important talk with so much wit as Goldmann reported to have done. He, Goldmann, may have overestimated the impact of his replies, but that was only natural for a man who believed in himself and could point to significant results in his negotiations which confirmed his self-appreciation and the importance of his role in such talks. The same, he wrote, was probably true of many other people; he added that he could level this accusation against some of the more popular leaders of Israel.

During the course of my work on the book, Goldmann sent me a considerable amount of printed material that he thought I could utilize with advantage. The most valuable was doubtless his German autobiograhy, whose first volume I received on June 4, 1980. A few days later, I wrote to him (on June 13, 1980):

> Since I received your book (on June 4), I spent much time with it and have just finished reading it. It is a great human document. I am greatly impressed by many things in it, but mostly by your love of the Jews which comes through from all its pages. You say somewhere in the book that you admire the Jews but do not love them. I think you are too harsh in the self-judgment contained in this sentence. Your whole life's work proves the opposite. Only somebody who loves the Jews deeply and totally could do all you have done for them, could consider the problems of every Jewish group and of every Jewish individual everywhere in the world as a matter which concerns him directly, could devote his entire life to the service of the Jewish people as a whole. Ultimately it was your love of the

Jews which was your charter for your unique role as spokesman of world Jewry. No man in our days deserves more than you the designation *Ohev Yisrael* [Lover of Israel] which is the highest traditional accolade Jews could give to a Jew.

Our letters dealt repeatedly with the question of the title of the book. Goldmann vetoed several of my suggestions, and in a letter dated January 31, 1982, he suggested the title "Nahum Goldmann: A Jewish Life in Our Times." I felt that this title was not suitable for the volume because it was not a biography. We bandied the idea back and forth in several letters, and on July 26, 1982, I summed up the reasons for my objection:

> My book is not a biography of Nahum Goldmann as this title would make the reader believe. It is, essentially, a discussion of three major undertakings of Nahum Goldmann as a representative of the Jewish people vis-à-vis the Gentiles: the partition of Palestine; the German reparations; and the (unsuccessful) attempt to establish contact with Nasser. While I believe that these three undertakings were perhaps the most important ones in your long public career, a biography, such as indicated by the title "A Jewish Life in Our Times," would have to include infinitely more than this. Hence I believe this title is not suitable.

However, Goldmann was still not convinced, and on July 31, 1982, just four weeks before his death, he wrote to me: "As for the title, we may still think of another one. Personally I find 'A Jewish Life in Our Times' quite good, even if the book is not really a biography in the usual sense. Maybe the publisher will have some other suggestion." This was the last communication I received from Goldmann, and one of the last letters he wrote. Shortly thereafter he fell ill and was taken to a hospital in Bad Reichenhall, where he died on August 29, 1982, at the age of eighty-seven.

During the course of his long life, Goldmann achieved much of what he set out to do for the *Yishuv,* for Israel, and for the Jewish people. Some of his major goals remained beyond his reach. On balance, he was one of the most remarkable sons of Jewry, not only in the twentieth century, but in all ages. His vision of his people and their destiny was global. As he said in the last paragraph of his article on the neutralization of Israel that was published in the July 11, 1980, issue of the German newspaper *Die Zeit:*

Looking at it from the point-of-view of world history, a neutralized Jewish state would give the Jewish people the concrete possibility, instead of wasting its strength on military and political successes, which it can surely not continue for long, and by foregoing to play a role in the so-called world politics, to stand again in the center of intellectual history *(Geistesgeschichte)*. This would again enable it to continue its contributions of many centuries to human culture, and thereby to secure for itself a future which would correspond in significance and contents to the unique character of its past.

Part One

Preparation

1. Childhood Memories and Influences

Two books, written by Goldmann approximately ten years apart (the first about 1965, when he was seventy, and the second around 1975, at the age of eighty), contain, in their first pages, his memories of childhood and youth. Neither of them is strictly speaking an autobiography or a personal life history because, interspersed with actual reminiscences, are philosophical observations on Jewish history; political views; conceptual discussions of Zionism, the State of Israel, and Judaism; the relationship between Jews and Gentiles; and numerous pen pictures of leading Jewish and Gentile personalities. This nonbiographical material consumes more than half of each of the two books. Because of these frequent excursions into the extrapersonal, both volumes, as Goldmann himself states in his preface to the first, "are both more and less than an autobiography."[1]

As far as biographical data are concerned, Goldmann is highly selective in both books, leaving untouched many questions that a biographer, even if he does not belong to the psycho-historical school, would like to see discussed. The more significant are those remarks that do occur, mostly with slight variations, in both volumes. A careful perusal of them shows quite clearly that, when writing the second one, Goldmann did not consult the first, nor did he compare, once the text of the second book was finished, the new manuscript with the printed version of the first. This is shown, for example, by minor contradictions and variations of fact, which would undoubtedly have been eliminated had such a comparison been carried out. Independent double references to the same circumstances, or comments on the same events or situations made ten years apart, can therefore be taken as an indication of the indelible impression they left in the memory of the autobiographer, and of his attribution of considerable importance to them for his life, work, and achievement.

The first indication of Goldmann's full consciousness of the formative and lasting effect on his personality of his first five years of life in the Lithuanian *shtetl* Visznevo (or Wischniew) is given clearly and emphatically on the very first page of his *Autobiography*. There he describes how, shortly after his birth, on July 10, 1895, his parents left for Germany, where his father studied in Königsberg and Heidelberg before moving to Frankfurt am Main, and left him in the care of his paternal grandparents. "I vividly remember," he writes, "those early experiences, and have always been aware that the most important influences on the development of my mind and character came from Eastern European Judaism."[2]

When Goldmann wrote this sentence, those early experiences were sixty-five or more years back in the past. Another ten years later, writing at a distance of more than seventy-five years from the events recalled, he comes back with stronger emphasis to the lasting effect on him of his childhood years: ". . . all the peace, kindness and attention that surrounded me [in the grandparents' home] gave me the feeling of great inner security which I still have today. In the course of my public life I have dealt with plenty of eminent people, but at no time have I ever felt any inferiority or weakness by comparison. There can be no doubt that I owe it to this exceptional upbringing."[3]

The upbringing Goldmann received in his grandparents' home was, in fact, not exceptional at all so far as the loving atmosphere that surrounded him was concerned. That was quite typical of Jewish family life everywhere, as is well known today from a number of reliable studies. What was exceptional was the manner in which he reacted to being the only child in a family that consisted of an elderly father-substitute, his grandfather (one wonders at what age Goldmann found out that the master of the house was not his father but his grandfather), and a triad of mother figures: his grandmother, and her two daughters, who at the time were still unmarried and lived at home. His reaction, to put it succinctly, was to bask happily in the warmth of love that radiated to him from all the members of the household. He describes the loving attention lavished on him by his grandmother and the two aunts who cared for him[4]—and again one wonders when he grasped that none of these three mother-figures was his actual mother.

One wonders even more about the lasting effect of this pampering feminine multiplicity on Goldmann's relations with his mother. When he was in his sixth year, she arrived in Visznevo and took him home to

Frankfurt. Although Goldmann is silent on the subject, no special powers of empathy are needed to surmise that the effect of being suddenly torn from the bosom of his loving family by a "strange" woman must have been traumatic for the five-year-old child. The shock never quite wore off, and it is known from what he wrote about his mother some sixty-five or more years after the event that his relationship with her was never warm; that he considered her an ambitious, domineering, intellectually frustrated woman; and that, in reversal of the usual Jewish child-parent relationship pattern, he respected her, stood in awe of her, and even feared her, while it was his father whom he loved. But more of this in the next chapter.

It is also tempting to speculate on the effect the three loving, coddling, omnipresent females during the first five years of his life had on Gold-mann's later relationship to women. Both his books are totally silent on this subject, though, according to both the gossip that never ceased to circulate about him and his own frank admission in my interviews with him in 1980, he always was, and remained well into his old age, a great ladies' man. As one of his friends once explained to me, "Nahum was the closest the Jews ever came since King David to having a Don Juan of their own."

In his three autobiographical books, Goldmann gives not even a hint as to whether or not he was aware during his later years that first his childhood experiences and conditioning, and then the relationship between him and his mother, contained the key not only to his achievements in his unique public career but also to his attitude to, and long series of successes with, women. Whenever he speaks of those earliest formative influences, which he does repeatedly in his three autobiographical books, he always refers only to his public, never to his private, life. Thus, he writes, "As the only grandchild in the home I was spoiled accordingly. My memories of those early years are unclouded by a single unhappy incident, and I attribute much of my self-confidence as an adult, a quality that proved more valuable than any other in my later political work, to the harmony and serenity of early childhood."[5] And again: "I have always remained aware that the serenity born of the security I enjoyed in those early years has been a blessing through all my later life."[6]

In the retrospect of seventy and eighty years, Goldmann generalizes his own feelings of security and happiness during the first five years of his life and attributes the same sense of well-being to all the Jews in the *shtetl.* Visznevo of the late 1890s, as he sees it from the perspective of the

15

1960s and 1970s, was emphatically not a ghetto in which the Jews lived and felt like pariahs.[7] "The *shtetl* of Visznevo did not live a life of sadness or despair."[8] It was one of the many *shtetls* in which

> the Jew inhabited his own kingdom. He constituted the majority. All around were peasant villages, and the *shtetl* Jew quite justifiably felt superior to their inhabitants. While he was not well-off economically, he was better off than the peasants of Czarist Russia. As a buyer of the peasants' produce, he was in a stronger position than they were, both psychologically and economically (except when there was a pogrom in the making). In his *shtetl* he lived in splendid isolation, and the great non-Jewish world hardly existed for him. He did not enjoy full civil rights, but civil rights meant nothing to him. . . . He was immersed in his own world, endowed with all the strength and dignity of a great past and a tradition dating back thousands of years. The only problems that had any meaning were the problems of Jewish life, and these absorbed him totally.[9]

Ten years later, when Goldmann returns to the subject, he writes: ". . . it is not the objective facts that determine a life, but the psychological reaction to those facts. And from that angle the Jews [in the *shtetl*] were generally a fairly happy people."[10] This is how Goldmann's memory registered "the spiritual climate of Visznevo," which "played no small part in the serenity I knew as a child."[11] In retrospect, he felt that in all this

> one thing is paramount: the warmth and security of my family relationship extended to the life of the *shtetl* where I grew up. I am sure that if my parents had taken me with them to Germany in my first year, I would never have acquired the self-confidence that I never lost again. In Visznevo I took it for granted that I was a Jewish child. No other possibility existed. To be sure, there were the peasant children, but no Jewish child would have wanted in his wildest dreams to be a peasant child. Being Jewish was something one took for granted, like breathing, eating, or saying your prayers. . . . The primary formative factor in my life was the absence of a Jewish inferiority complex. My parents' decision to leave me with my grandparents in Visznevo was one of the most important things they did for me.[12]

A few paragraphs later, he comes back to this central theme of his childhood memories and the influence of his early years on his later life:

I have never been subject to the Jewish fear of the dominance of the non-Jewish world. In later years I had dealings with.eminent leaders of non-Jewish peoples and countries. Often I confronted these men, who represented great powers, as the spokesman of a powerless people. Although I was always conscious of the power discrepancy, I cannot remember any encounter, whether with Mussolini or Prince Regent Paul, with General Gamelin, the French Chief of Staff, or with American presidents or British foreign ministers, when I had the least feeling of inferiority. I recognized that they were different, and in most cases more powerful, but never that they were superior.[13]

Thus, as Goldmann sees it in retrospect, the most valuable features of his personality—his self-assurance, his serenity, his solidly secure Jewish self-image, his confidence in his ability to measure up to the world's leading statesmen—all came from his first five years of life in the house of his grandparents and in the *shtetl* of Visznevo. And the same love and affection that surrounded him in his grandfather's house he remembers as having encountered in the *shtetl* as a whole.

Whatever reality lies behind these memories must have been partly shaped by the fact that little Nahum's grandfather enjoyed a privileged position in Visznevo, as the only medical man in the *shtetl*. Although in his autobiographical books Goldmann refers to him as "a country doctor,"[14] in one of my interviews with Goldmann in 1980 he explained that his grandfather was not a real doctor; he was a *Feldscher*, that is, a kind of medic. Among his patients were not only people of the *shtetl*, but also many peasants from the surrounding villages. He was also, for many years, the *Gabbai*, or head, of the synagogue. Thus, he was revered by the Jews and was the last person to whom the peasants would have given utterance to any of the anti-Semitic sentiments that they unquestionably harbored. He was an active, energetic man, a good, observant Jew, but not what could be called a great *Talmid ḥakham* (scholar). He loved animals and always had many dogs.[15]

As the only grandchild of the "doctor" and the apple of the eye of the whole family, young Nahum had the run of the *shtetl*, of which he took full advantage. He would ride about on the back of his huge St. Bernard dog, a present from his doting grandfather. On one occasion, on a Sabbath, he rode on it straight into the synagogue, which caused panic, especially among the women.[16]

Another thing that remained preserved in Goldmann's memory from the years of his infancy in Visznevo and that was indicative of his later personality was his role as the leader of a children's gang. Although because of ill health he attended the *ḥeder*, the traditional Jewish elementary school, rather irregularly, he was well and strong enough to organize a gang of children and to lead them in various escapades which, in the retrospect of sixty-five years, seemed to him to have been "not entirely innocuous." But he not only led his peers in pranks; he was also ready to assume responsibility for them.[17]

As he was later to remember, he "felt nothing but goodness in his environment" and built a trust in other people as well as a corresponding readiness to help them.[18]

It was undoubtedly the Visznevo experience that created in Goldmann an understanding for, and identification with, the typical Jewish world view that has always viewed the Gentile persecutors of the Jews as an inferior race. "Every Jew felt ten or a hundred times superior to these lowly tillers of the soil: he was cultured, learned Hebrew, knew the Bible, studied the Talmud—in other words he knew that he stood head and shoulders above these illiterates."[19] It is no longer possible to establish how much of this Jewish elitistic attitude toward the illiterate Gentile Lithuanian peasants Goldmann actually imbibed during the first five years of his life in Visznevo and how much of it he acquired in later years when he had become an assiduous student of the Jewish condition in the Diaspora. Nor is it easy to gauge how much of his later knowledge of Jewish life he projected back into his childhood years when he was writing his memoirs and casting his mind back into his earliest years, which he came to regard as the formative period of his life. Whatever the answer, the fact remains that, so far as his recollections are concerned, his self-assurance and the high valuation he put on Jews and Judaism were his major early childhood acquisitions.

One more Visznevo impression must be referred to here. In my book *The Jewish Mind,* I discussed in some detail the high intellectual aspirations Jewish parents have for their child, the parental reinforcements of different types of intellectual performance by the child, the opportunities for learning provided both inside and outside the home, and the value parents place on the child's intellectual achievements. I summed up the difference between the Gentile and Jewish home in this respect in one brief statement: "The Jewish home, more than the Gentile home, is a place in which learning is highly valued," and proceeded to draw far-reaching conclusions from this fact for the development of the Jewish psyche.[20]

Goldmann's recollections of his Visznevo childhood are a perfect illustration of this general thesis and of the results such a home environment produces in the mind of the Jewish child. The fact that in his case the home was grandparental rather than parental makes no difference. What is remarkable is that in Goldmann's memory the intellectual expectations directed toward him turned into yet another source of his lifelong self-confidence. He writes in the late 1960s: "My later self-confidence may also have something to do with the fact that my grandparents, encouraged by the rabbi of the *shtetl,* expected great things of me, and devoted themselves to my development."[21]

At the end of the chapter in his *Autobiography* depicting his childhood in Visznevo, Goldmann gives a kind of summary of his recollections of the effects the Visznevo experience left on him for the rest of his life. He took along from Visznevo "the decisive consciousness of a complete Jewish reality such as only the *shtetl,* never Jewish life in the big cities, could bestow." But it bestowed upon him much more than that. The first glimpse of a train at night, at the Smorgon railway station, "the locomotive, with its great lights, rolling to a stop," did not frighten him as it does many children. "I was glad to see it coming and felt that it was going to take me into the world . . . it was for me a good, almost blissful experience." He explained this unusual reaction as follows: "Since I have been able to shape my own life, the one thing I have striven for above all has been to seek out the positive element in every experience. The effect an event or a fact produces on us is at least partly determined by our own reaction. The capacity to react positively is one of the decisive prerequisites for a happy, constructive life."[22]

One wonders why this emphatic assertion of his power of positive thinking is inserted into the midst of his otherwise extremely sparse description of his removal by his mother from his grandparents' home. Can it be that, even at a distance of sixty-five years, he felt that this was the first truly painful experience in his life and that he felt impelled to put forward his positive philosophy instead of allowing his true feelings to surface? The very fact that his reaction to this first major upheaval in his life is couched primarily in terms of denial of any negative reaction seems to point to the suppressed existence of precisely the negative reaction he is at pains to deny. A certain note of regret, one feels, has nevertheless crept into the bland statement with which the chapter of his Visznevo childhood closes: "I had been happy there, but from the very first I felt quite at home in Frankfurt, the city where I spent my first school years."[23] Note the contrast between happiness in Visznevo and the "quite at home" feeling in Frankfurt.

2. Frankfurt
Boyhood

Although the emotional bases of Goldmann's personality were laid down during the first five years of his life in Visznevo, he acquired his intellectual foundations during the twelve years from the age of six to eighteen that he spent in his parents' home in Frankfurt am Main.

To obtain a feel of the potential of manifold cultural influences to which an intelligent, middle-class Jewish boy would be exposed in a city like Frankfurt requires some knowledge of its Gentile and Jewish population from the turn of the century, when little Nahum was brought there by his mother, until 1912, when he left the city to take up university studies in Heidelberg, a mere fifty miles away.

Located near the western border of Germany, Frankfurt had been an important Jewish city since the eleventh century, and by 1900 some 22,000, or 7.5 percent, of its 300,000 inhabitants were Jews. Although their number increased in subsequent years—many from the rural environment were attracted to the city, which experienced an economic boom in the nineteenth century—they could not keep pace with the more rapid growth of the general population. Although in German history Frankfurt was most famous as the city of Goethe, for the Jews it had two other claims on fame: it was the city in which the House of Rothschild was founded; and in which, in 1876, the neo-Orthodox movement, known as *Trennungsorthodoxie,* or "Secession Orthodoxy," was born.

By the turn of the century, Frankfurt was well on the way to becoming a major commercial center not only in Germany but in west-central Europe as well. As early as in the seventeenth and eighteenth centuries, the city had established a world-famous banking system, in which the House of Rothschild played a leading role. The German Imperial Diet selected Frankfurt as its seat from 1815 to 1866, thereby recognizing the significance of the city as a symbol of German unity, and the German National Assembly met in Frankfurt in 1848–49. In 1866 the Jewish newspaper publisher Leopold Sonnemann (1831–1909) founded the *Frankfurter Zeitung*, which he built into one of the foremost dailies in the German language and a staunch mouthpiece of liberalism and freedom of political thought.

The most prominent Jewish figures in nineteenth-century Frankfurt were Ludwig Boerne (1786–1837), the political essayist and champion of Jewish emancipation, who in 1818 converted to Lutheranism in order to widen the scope of his public activity; Isaac Marcus Jost (1793–1860), a founder of the *Wissenschaft des Judentums* as well as the first modern Jewish historian; and Moritz Oppenheim (1799–1872), the painter of contemporary Jewish life. During the late nineteenth and early twentieth century, Frankfurt Jewry could boast of such names as Paul Ehrlich (1854–1915), the pioneer of modern histology, immunology, and chemotherapy who was awarded the Nobel Prize for Medicine in 1908; the sociologist and economist Franz Oppenheimer (1864–1943), who initiated cooperative agriculture in Jewish Palestine; the sculptor Benno Elkan (1877–1960); Franz Rosenzweig (1866–1929), the Jewish theologian and religious philosopher, close friend and collaborator of Martin Buber (1878–1965), who himself became a professor at the Frankfurt university, founded in 1912 by Jewish donors.

Although the foundation of the *Freies jüdisches Lehrhaus* (Free Jewish House of Study) by Franz Rosenzweig with the help of a group of outstanding Jewish scholars (including Buber, Rabbi N. Nobel, Eduard Strauss, Richard Koch, Erich Fromm, Ernst Simon, Gershon Scholem, and Nahum Glatzer) in 1920 came after Goldmann's Frankfurt years, the fact that such an institution was set up in Frankfurt in preference to other cities where the Jewish communities were much larger is an eloquent testimony to Frankfurt's growth into a foremost Jewish intellectual center during the preceding decades.

The economic basis for this development was provided by the generosity of the rich Frankfurt Jews and by their interest in Jewish matters. Although the Frankfurt branch of the House of Rothschild was discontinued after the death of Wilhelm Karl Rothschild (1828–1901), the city remained a center of Jewish banking and finance, as represented by the Schwarzschilds, the Kanns, and the Schiffs. In general, the Frankfurt Jews constituted a wealthy layer in the city, as indicated by their tax records. In 1900, the year little Nahum arrived in Frankfurt, its 35,000 non-Jewish taxpayers paid 3,600,000 marks in taxes, or a little more than 100 marks each; the 6,000 Jewish taxpayers paid 2,500,000 marks, or some 417 marks each.

Although these figures indicate that the Jews, on the average, were four times as wealthy as the Gentiles, they do not mean, of course, that no poor Jews resided in Frankfurt. Their presence reminded the rich that one of the primary Jewish religious duties was to support the poor, which did occur in the form of both institutional charities and private, personal donations. Nahum's father, Solomon Zevi Goldmann, a teacher, writer, editor, and Zionist activist, was one of the men through whom some of these charities were channeled to the poor. This circumstance early implanted into young Nahum's mind the imperative of helping other Jews, which was to remain a guiding principle of his lifework.

During Nahum's childhood years, "Secession Orthodoxy" was a long-established fact in the life of Jewish Frankfurt. It had been in the making since the middle of the nineteenth century in reaction to the rapidly spreading Jewish religious Reform movement, advocated by a group of rabbis who had held their conference at Frankfurt in 1845. At that time, the number of Orthodox Jews in the city was estimated at not more than 10 percent of the total Jewish community. Members of this group took the initiative in 1851 to found *Adass Jeschurun,* known in German as *Israelitische Religionsgemeinschaft,* or Israelite Religious Community. Elected as rabbi was Samson Raphael Hirsch (1808–1888), who was to leave his mark in Jewish history as the leader, as well as foremost exponent and moving spirit of modern, German-based, uncompromising Ortho-doxy. During the thirty-seven years of his ministry as the rabbi of the *Adass Jeschurun* congregation, he determined once and for all the devel-opment of German Jewish Orthodoxy in general and built his commu-nity in Frankfurt into a veritable fortress that was hermetically sealed off from all cooperation with non-Orthodox Judaism. During Nahum's Frankfurt years, the *Adass Jeschurun* was headed by Solomon Breuer (1850–1926), Hirsch's son-in-law, a product of the famed Pressburg Yeshiva of Moses Sofer. Breuer succeeded his father-in-law upon the latter's death in 1888, and his main achievement lay in consolidating Hirsch's work, but he also introduced some of the Hungarian Orthodox rigidity into Frankfurt by founding a Yeshiva that he headed for thirty-six years, until his death.

Arrayed against the Hirschian Orthodoxy was Abraham Geiger (1810–74), leader of the Jewish Reform and an outstanding scholar in the young Science of Judaism. A native of Frankfurt, he served as rabbi in various communities in Germany, including his hometown from 1863 to 1870. But his fame and influence reached far beyond the congregations in which he officiated, and in 1845 and 1846 he was the leading spirit in the Reform synods that were held in Frankfurt and Breslau, respectively. In Nahum's days, the violent struggles between the Secession Orthodoxy and the other Jews had simmered down, but the antagonism persisted. The main community comprised both Reform and Orthodox synagogues, while the *Adass Jeschurun* maintained its splendid isolation, operating a separate synagogue, schools, Yeshiva, cemetery, and other institutions.

Echoes of the intercommunity tension inevitably found their way into the Goldmann home. Solomon Goldmann was a teacher at the training college for Hebrew teachers that was maintained at Frankfurt by the Jewish Colonization Association, a philanthropic association dedicated to the assistance of Jews in depressed economic conditions or in countries where they were persecuted by helping them to emigrate to Argentina, and, later, to Palestine. Because the ICA, as it was usually referred to, was financed by Baron Maurice de Hirsch and other French and British Jews, Solomon Goldmann's position in an ICA institution gave him a certain independence from the local congregation. In addition, being a man of strong Jewish heart, he devoted much of his time to voluntary welfare work, and especially to helping Jewish students who would apply to one or the other of the well-known Jewish philanthropists in Frankfurt for assistance while studying in Germany or Switzerland. Several of these philanthropists let Solomon Goldmann handle the distribution of their donations. As a result, the Goldmann home was constantly besieged by aspiring young Jewish students and would-be students—especially newcomers from Russia—who were frequently served meals by Mrs. Goldmann, and occasionally given lodging as well.

This traffic strongly affected young Nahum's intellectual growth. Several of the students befriended the precocious boy, let him listen to their spirited debates, and encouraged him to offer his own opinions. Thus, as a child in his father's house, he enjoyed the opportunity to become acquainted with some of the youths who were later to be outstanding Jewish writers and thinkers. Among them were Moshe Glickson (Gluecksohn) (1878–1939), under whose editorship the Tel Aviv daily *HaAretz* was to become one of the most important papers of the *Yishuv;* the journalist and author Samuel Max Melamed; and Jacob Klatzkin (1882–1948), one of the foremost modern Jewish writers on philosophical subjects. Although these men were much older than Nahum, who was a child when they were young adults, over the years the palpable age difference diminished, and their initial interest in the son of their patron grew into a lifelong friendship. The tributes Goldmann pays in his *Autobiography*[1] to Klatzkin and Melamed are among the most incisive pages in that book.

A study of Goldmann's personality reveals that he was endowed, from his early youth, with a highly developed critical streak. During his life, he admired quite a few people, but even the strongest admiration could not blunt the edge of his critical acumen. Like many people with a superior intellect, he could not overlook even slight failings in people, however much he admired them. The only person about whom he has nothing critical to say is his father. This absence of criticism, more than the positive adjectives that spring from his pen when writing of his father, eloquently bespeaks his deep filial love and reverence.

In his autobiography, Goldmann describes his father as "a yielding, kindhearted, idealistic man," "imposing in appearance," "always dedicated to a cause, to an ideal, to any opportunity of helping," "a gifted stylist and a competent writer, as much at home in Hebrew as in German, and combining a great wealth of Jewish knowledge with a great familiarity with Western European, especially German, philosophy." His father, he writes, "was greatly beloved and radiated generosity, always helping other people, raising money for them, securing fair treatment from the police, and so on. He played a respected role in the Jewish life of Frankfurt, and although he was not cut out to be a leader, and disliked being involved in conflict, he was unshakable in his convictions, which often forced him to take a journalistic stand against ideas and trends he thought harmful and dangerous."[2] No warmer tribute could be paid by a son to a father, who possessed all the human qualities young Nahum admired, except the one he admired most: leadership.

It is characteristic of Goldmann's love for his father that in his recollections, written decades after his father's death, he endowed him with a position of more importance than he actually filled during his early years in Frankfurt. He writes that his father "was also a writer and editor of the (Frankfurter) *Israelitisches Familienblatt*,"[3] and repeats in his later book that his father "edited a Jewish weekly paper in Frankfurt."[4] In fact, the owner-editor of the paper was Saly Geis, and Solomon worked under him in an editorial capacity. As Goldmann recalled in 1980, his father was a Russian Jew whom the Germans refused to naturalize, and Geis did not want a foreigner to figure on the masthead as editor of his paper.[5]

Of his own relationship to his father, Goldmann said in 1980: "I was closest, emotionally, to my father. I have learned from him to be good-hearted, to help people."[6] Goldmann is equally unstinting in his recollections of other things he learned from his father. Although Solomon Goldmann was religious, he considered Jewish observances to be not an end in itself but rather a means for the preservation of "Jewishness as something distinct," as a "guard against the danger of assimilation. But on this and many other questions he was tolerant and never tried to force me to observe rites I rejected." His influence, as Goldmann clearly sees it, though strong, was due not to "what he said," that is, not to his teachings and admonitions, but rather to his personality, which was for Nahum an exemplar to follow. A most revealing statement in this connection is, "His example taught me that however indispensable ideas and convictions may be, human relationships are just as important; that the elementary virtues of kindness and helpfulness are more creative than fanaticism and ideological aggressiveness. To him more than anybody else I owe my introduction to the world of Judaism." Moreover, it was to his father that Nahum owed his Zionism: it was "a sort of inborn inheritance: I did not become a Zionist—I always was one."[7]

Goldmann's first Hebrew teacher was his father. Then, somewhat later, one of the students who was a protégé of his father became his tutor. Subsequently, he became a pupil of Jakob Posen, a broker in the employ of the Rothschild family, a rich man, who considered it a great *Mitzva* to give Talmud lessons to young students. Thus Nahum was initiated into the mysteries of the Talmud and was able to understand and explain *a blatt Gemore* ("a page of the Gemara").[8] However, his main source of Jewish knowledge was Jacob Klatzkin, to whom he became close after World War I.

Goldmann's relations with his mother were cool. One does not have to read between the lines of the reticent and meager paragraphs he devotes to her in his *Autobiography*—not a word is contained about her in his *Paradox*—to learn of the awe and fear this formidable woman inspired in her sensitive son, who until her sudden appearance in the *shtetl* when he was five years old knew nothing but love and doting on the part of his grandfather and the three mother-substitutes in his house. The word "love" is conspicuously absent in what he remembers and recounts about his mother. "While love bound me to my father," he writes, "my relationship to my mother was based chiefly on respect and admiration. Although she rarely punished me"—punishment does not at all enter the horizon of his relationship with his father—"I was always in awe of her, an awe that sometimes became fear. There were a lot of things I could have confessed to my father but never to my mother."[9] These few sparse words are all he has to say about his relationship with his mother.

Evidently, what is involved is a reversal of the usual relationship between a child (and especially a boy) and his parents. Instead of fearing his father, as is or was generally the case in traditional Jewish families, Nahum loved him and enjoyed his permissive support in whatever he did or planned. And, instead of loving his mother, again as is or was usually true in traditional families, he respected and feared her, an attitude engendered in him by the demands she made on him. Although this inverse son-father and son-mother relationship was unquestionably unusual, it was not as exceptional or out-of-the-ordinary in a family steeped in Jewish lore as it would have been in one where the literary, religious, and traditional heritage was not an integral part.

From a few random remarks scattered in various contexts in his recollections, it is clear that Goldmann was deeply interested all his life in mysticism.[10] This inclination must have originated in childhood and boyhood impressions. Although Lithuania was the stronghold of the *Mitnagdim,* the opponents of Hasidism, the study of the pre-Hasidic sources and trends of Jewish mysticism was as much a part of traditional Jewish learning in Lithuania as in the more southern areas of Eastern Europe that became the Hasidic centers in the late eighteenth century. Even the renowned Elijah ben Solomon, the Gaon of Vilna (eighteenth century), who was a bitter enemy of Hasidism and in whom hardheaded Lithuanian Jewry came as close as it could to having a patron saint, studied the Kabbala and even tried his hand at its practical, that is, magical, application. It therefore stands to reason that it was in his childhood and youth that Goldmann first became acquainted with Jewish mysticism, though no traces of such early influences seem to have remained in his memory.

Now it so happens that in Kabbalistic teachings as embedded in the Zohar and in the writings of the sixteenth-century Safed Kabbalists, in which a male and a female aspect of God is daringly discerned, the male aspect of the deity, designated "the King," is characterized by love, mercy, and wisdom; while his female aspect, termed *Shekhina* or *Matronit* ("Matron"), and conceived, even more daringly, as the King's spouse, stands for power, is warlike, is said to have been entrusted by the King with all his weapons, and is described in many myth-like passages as attacking with determination, even cruelty, the enemies of Israel. (This reversal of the customary roles of the father and the mother in the male and female aspects of the deity goes back to Philo of Alexandria, the first-century C.E. Hellenistic-Jewish philosopher. He explains that the divine name *Elohim* ["God"] symbolizes the male, fatherly, aspect of God, whose attributes are goodness, peaceableness, gentleness, and beneficence; to the female aspect of the deity, expressed by the name *Yahweh* ["Lord"], Philo ascribes the attributes of sovereignty or kingly power as well as the legislative, chastising, and correcting virtues.)[11]

In making reference to these old Jewish archetypal concepts of the triangular relationship between God the King, the *Matronit,* and Israel I do not intend to suggest that young Nahum was, or even could have been, familiar with them. His perception of the relationship between his father and mother and between them and himself was certainly based on the real differences between his parents in character and in their attitudes to the world and to him. And yet, the resemblance between the picture he paints of the relationships in his parental home and the grandiose metaphysical concept presented by the Kabbala is intriguing. Could it be that the child's perception was colored by that unconscious psychic factor that is the reflection in the individual of the cosmic archetype encountered in the great myths of mankind?[12] In any case, the images of father and mother as they registered in young Nahum's mind, evoked his response, and remained embedded in his memory duplicate most remarkably, albeit reduced from the divine to the human level, the two "reversed" sets of traits attributed to the male and the female aspects of the deity by Jewish mystical thought in both antiquity and medieval times.

The few things Goldmann tells about his mother, in addition to their relationship, flesh out her portrait as the strong partner in the couple. In her childhood, Rebecca Goldmann used to stay awake most of the night in her room reading German and Russian literature, something strictly forbidden in the Vilna home of her Orthodox father, who was a *dayyan,* a rabbinical judge, of the community. She also managed to learn Hebrew, something quite unusual for religiously brought-up girls at that time. Throughout her life "she was in love with learning," and was "crazy for learning."[13] "Knowledge and ideas were more important to her than people,"[14] in contrast to the attitude of her husband, who emphasized human relationships and "the elementary virtues of kindness and helpfulness."

Across a distance of sixty or more years, Goldmann remembers his mother as an "extremely puritanical" person who "set up very rigorous standards in everything, and insisted that they be maintained."[15] More-over, her childhood thirst for learning grew during her youth and later life into an unquenchable intellectual ambition for herself and for her son. Reminiscing about her in 1980, Goldmann recalled that she used to attend, three or four times a week, lectures on German literature and other subjects given at the *Hochstift*, a Frankfurt institution for popular culture, even though this meant that she often needed to leave the boy alone in the evening as well as to neglect her household duties.[16]

However, Rebecca Goldmann would not have been a Jewish mother had her intellectual ambitions not included, and even focused on, her son. She supervised his education carefully, in fact, with such insistence that young Nahum felt obliged to attain the honor roll at school.[17] It is no longer clear whose decision it was, his father's or his mother's, that he was, at the age of twelve, transferred from the *Realschule*, the Orthodox Jewish school, to Frankfurt's finest high school, the *Musterschule* ("Model School"), a modern experimental school in which administration, su-pervision, and disciplinary matters were all in the hands of student committees.[18]

Equally strict was his mother's control over Nahum's awakening in-terest in the other sex. At the age of eighty-five, he still remembered how his mother, with resolute firmness, prevented him from becoming pre-maturely involved with girls. "At the age of fifteen-sixteen I was a well-known speaker. This impressed women. They often wanted to seduce me. And my mother was very puritanical. She was very much afraid that, God forbid. . . . I remember that several times when I began to chat with a woman, she would cut me off, because she was afraid I would get to like her."[19]

Once he had to write an essay in school comparing Joan of Arc with a famous modern woman author (whose name escaped Goldmann in 1980 when he told me of this event).[20] He wrote that Joan of Arc was not a normal person because she did not want to have love and sex. His teacher read this with consternation, viewed it as an immoral attitude on the part of a young man, and called in his mother. Sharing the teacher's view of the matter, she became very angry with Nahum and gave him a scolding that left him devastated. She never hit him, but a tongue-lashing was worse, he felt, than a beating would have been.

Goldmann's mother was clearly a powerful, intimidating, and inhib-iting archetypal figure to the youth. Even sixty or seventy years later, when writing or talking about her, the adjectives that crop up most frequently are "puritanical," "powerful," "strict," "very strong," and the like. Her "outstanding characteristic," he writes, "was tremendous will-power; she was one of the strongest-willed people I have ever encountered."[21] He also recalls that "she hardly ever relaxed. Everything had to serve a purpose; life consisted exclusively of responsibilities and challenges."[22] She was physically frail, in poor health, and her life-forces were constantly taxed by the tensions she carried within her all the time. She died at the age of fifty-five.

Inevitably, as soon as young Nahum could escape his mother's control, he rebelled against her. It was equally inevitable that his rebellion should take the form of engaging in precisely that type of behavior which his mother had insisted on preventing. He had to become a ladies' man, a conqueror or seducer of women to whom, in retrospect, he humorously but characteristically refers to as "my victims." Apparently each conquest represented a posthumous victory over his strong-willed, inhibitive mother.

The differences, even contrasts, in the personalities of Solomon and Rebecca Goldmann were bound to lead to clashes at times, but, as Goldmann remarks in an understatement that leaves much unsaid, "She was a very strong nature, a much stronger character than my father. And she was the dominating figure in the family."[23] He continues, "Conflicts were rare, since my mother's stronger will always enabled her to get her way." Then, as if he felt that even this revealed too much, he goes on to reassure himself: "I owe much to *both* my parents [emphasis mine], and even after I left home I kept close ties with *both* of them [emphasis mine], never marred by misunderstandings."[24]

No external corroboration is available concerning her son's memories of the personality of Rebecca Goldmann. A few photographs show her as a young woman, dating from the years Nahum spent in his parents' home in Frankfurt. One is a group picture taken in 1908, when he was thirteen. It shows Solomon Goldmann, his brother Szalkowitz, the Bar-Mitzvah boy, and Rebecca. The two men, bearing a definite family resemblance, evince a soft, kindly expression. The boy, standing next to his uncle and sporting a large Eton collar as well as an oversize tie, looks uncomfortable, an admixture of worry and irritation crossing his face. His mother stands with her left arm leaning upon the right shoulder of her seated husband, dressed in what undoubtedly was the Frankfurt fashion of the period; a huge hat is perched on top of her Gibson-girl hairdo. She towers over the other three and dominates the picture. Her expression is severe, her lips are puckered and compressed, her eyes look down and out from above. In front of her right breast dangles a pince-nez. In another picture, which must have been taken about the same time, Mrs. Goldmann wears an even larger and more impressive hat, decorated with flowing plume at the front; what appears to be a monocle is in her right eye (though it could be but the same pince-nez). Her expression is, possibly, even more severe than in the other picture.[25]

Whatever the divergences in personality between Solomon and Rebecca Goldmann, however different their relationship to their son, in one thing they were in wholehearted agreement: the boy Nahum was destined to be a leader in Israel. That his mother "pushed" him in this direction was stated, as indicated earlier in this volume, by Goldmann himself. He says nowhere that his father, too, pressured, or even as much as influenced, him to embark on a Jewish public career, but the circumstantial evidence is sufficient to prove it. At the age of twelve or so, he was caught selling *shekalim* (membership certificates in the Zionist Organization) at school, thereby scandalizing the teachers of the strictly Orthodox *Israelitsche Realschule,* which, like the entire Orthodox community, was vehemently anti-Zionist. The only source from which he could have obtained the *shekalim* was, of course, his father, who was intensively active in the small but energetic Zionist movement in Frankfurt.

At the age of thirteen, Nahum delivered his first speech for the local Zionist Organization, which, again, he could only do with the help of his father, and probably upon the latter's initiative. The occasion was the Hanukkah celebration of 1908. The subject Nahum chose was "Judaism and Hellenism." He spoke extemporaneously, and the audience, several hundred strong, which filled the rented auditorium, gave him an ovation. It is interesting and characteristic of his lifelong attitude to speech-making that he considered the speech primarily a matter of a bravura performance.

As Goldmann recalls in his *Autobiography,* in order to impress a girl of his own age with whom he was friendly (this is the only reference in the book to any girl),[26] he told her he would perform a trick: the fifth time he would use the word "Hellas" he would take out his handkerchief to demonstrate his self-assurance. He pulled off the trick without a hitch, but the look of intense admiration the girl gave him so confused him that, for a moment, he lost the thread of his thought, an experience that thereafter often haunted him in his dreams: he would be struggling in vain against the waves of a raging ocean. Only his mother, who watched him with an eagle's eye, noticed the momentary confusion and pointed it out to him when they reached home.[27]

All these early extracurricular activities of speech-making and writing, as well as budding interest in the other sex, constituted a strain on the adolescent. As he recalled in 1980, "As a young boy I was very nervous. There was a great neurologist in Frankfurt, a Professor Edinger, a very famous man at that time in all Germany. He was a friend of our family. One day Edinger called my father and said to him, 'Look here, you must take care of Nahum. He can easily end up in a mental institution. He is too nervous, too precocious. He gives speeches, he reads too much, writes a lot, this is quite abnormal, very dangerous. *Wunderkinder* [child prodigies] are always in danger.' "[28] No trace of all this is found in Goldmann's 1969 and 1978 autobiographies, and even in the expanded German version published in 1980 he indicates only briefly that as a youth he had a tendency to neurosis which he later totally overcame.[29]

But, to return to the father's invisible, or rather, unmentioned, directing hand, when Nahum was fourteen he arranged for him to begin writing book reviews and a column for the *Israelitisches Familienblatt.* Because, however, the strict rules of the school the youth attended did not allow pupils to publish articles, he was forced to write under a pseudonym. The *nom de plume* he chose again expresses his love of, and emotional dependence on, his father. Inasmuch as his father's name was Solomon, and, according to Jewish tradition, Koheleth, the author of the Book of Ecclesiastes, was none other than King Solomon, he chose the pseudonym Ben-Koheleth, or "Son of Koheleth." Thereby he not only identified himself, unbeknownst to the public, as the son of his father, but symbolically raised his father to royal status.

Everything Goldmann published from 1910 (when he was in his fifteenth year) to the end of 1912 (his seventeenth year) he published under the *nom de plume* Ben-Koheleth. Then he began to use his own name, but, interestingly, as late as in July to November 1914, when he was nineteen years old, he still published several articles signed "—n — th," that is, "(Be)n (Kohele)th." Evidently, it was not easy for him to give up his identification as the son of his father.

In one more way, Solomon Goldmann facilitated his son's extracurricular Zionist and writing activities. During his last few years in the experimental *Realgymnasium,* Nahum found that he could easily keep up with his studies even if he played the truant two or three days a week. At his request, his father wrote out three separate undated excuses for him—one for toothache, one for stomachache, and one for headache—

which he would present alternatingly to his teachers and then get them back and submit them again. Before long, "my teacher told me not to bother anymore, thus sanctioning my frequent absences, at least unofficially."[30] From the age of fifteen, Nahum was part-time student and part-time Zionist lecturer and writer. In addition, he fostered a voracious reading habit, devouring hundreds of books on German and French literature, Jewish history, German philosophy, and mysticism.[31]

Thus, by the age of fourteen, Nahum Goldmann had been gently but firmly placed by his father on the road he was to follow all his life. He became a Zionist speaker in Frankfurt and in places outside the city that he could visit without interfering with his school schedule, and acquired the habit of writing critical and analytical articles. Throughout his life, these two modes of literary expression were the only ones he pursued: speech-making and article writing. Although highly gifted in both areas, he never went beyond the limitations inherent in them. He was never to write a book-length study, except for his several autobiographies, on which he embarked when he was more than seventy. What he had to say—and it was a lot—he always condensed into the compass of a public address or an article in a newspaper or a journal.

But the form in which Goldmann expressed what he had to say is of minor significance. What is important is *what* he had to say. And that can be described in one brief sentence: all his speeches and published writings deal with the Jewish people, their problems, their achievements, their goals, their demands, their past, their present, and their future. His aim in everything he said and wrote was to improve the Jewish condition. He became what his father, with oracular clarity, foresaw and stated when asked what he thought his Bar-Mitzvah son would become: "Advocate of the Jewish people."[32]

Although Zionism was a heritage Goldmann received from both his father and mother and it was his father who facilitated his early entry into the field of Zionist activities, he remembers with particular clarity the intense, emotional Zionist devotion of his mother. At the age of eighty-five, he recalled her reaction to Herzl's death, which took place in 1904, seventy-six years earlier: "I remember the day when Herzl died. She began to cry. . . . She was supposed to leave with me on that day to go to a summer camp. But she gave it up, and all day long she was sitting in her room, crying." A few years later, she said to him: "You will one day be a successor to Herzl. . . . This is what she dreamt of. . . . She had great dreams for me. . . . Had she lived to see me president of the Zionist Organization she would have been the happiest woman alive."[33]

3. Student Years and First Visit to Palestine

Although the basic features that contribute to the emotional make-up of a person's individuality are etched in his psyche during the years of infancy and childhood, his intellectual proclivities receive their most decisive impetus during and after adolescence, and especially in those years that for many middle-class Jewish youths in the early twentieth century were a time of university studies. However, intellectual impetus does not necessarily mean that the environment in which it takes place leaves an indelible impression on the individual's memory. Still, it is remarkable how little Goldmann retained in his memory from his first two years as a student in Heidelberg and how meager the information about that period he included in his three autobiographical works.

In Goldmann's book *The Jewish Paradox* (published in English in 1978 but written several years earlier), no mention is made of his student years. The *Autobiography* (1969) and the most recent *Mein Leben als deutscher Jude* (1980) each contain a brief chapter, entitled "Student Days and a First Visit to Palestine" (1969:35–44) and "Universitäts-studien und erste Palästinareise" (1980:71–93). Both chapters cover essentially the same material and dwell mostly on Goldmann's 1913 visit to Palestine, which lasted five months and caused him to miss a whole semester in Heidelberg. Because a person retains in his memory things, events, and experiences that are important for him and tends to forget incidents or even entire periods that do not impress him in particular, or are of only minor import, it can be concluded that the one significant event of Goldmann's student years was his trip to Palestine, but that Heidelberg made no lasting impression on him.

Goldmann passed his *Abitur*, the final high-school examination, in June 1912, when he was a month short of his seventeenth birthday.

Upon applying for admission to the University of Heidelberg, he found he was too young to be admitted: eighteen was the minimum age. However, a Jewish lawyer and city councillor of Karlsruhe, Ludwig Haas (1875–1930), who had just become a deputy in the *Reichstag* as a member of the Progressive People's (later Democratic) party, intervened with the university authorities on Goldmann's behalf, and he was admitted.[1]

Although studying at the University of Heidelberg, which enjoyed in Germany a reputation similar to that of Oxford in England, was the foremost desire of young Goldmann during the last two or three of his high-school years, once admitted to the old and venerable seat of learning he took little interest in the law curriculum for which he had registered. As he explains in his memoirs, "academic freedom" at the German universities in the pre-World War I years meant that students of humanities, history, literature, law, and philosophy did not need to attend classes, but were only required to pass the final examination. This system enabled him to be a rather irregular visitor in the law classes, which evoked only mild annoyance in his teachers. Despite his cavalier attitude toward his studies, he did finally—after a lengthy interruption by the four war years, most of which he spent in the employ of the German Foreign Office (see next chapter)—pass his exams and receive a Doctor of Law degree. "If anyone," he remarks caustically, "holds an unearned Doctor of Law [degree], it is I."[2]

Goldmann took more interest in philosophy and attended lectures by Heinrich Rickert and Karl Jaspers, as well as the classes of the famous sociologist Max Weber and the literary historian Friedrich Gundolf. However, he obtained most of his university education not from lectures, but from his own reading. Sixty years later he remembered, "The most I achieved was through self-education."[3]

At the same time, the youth acquired a keen interest in mysticism. As he remembered in 1980, during his Heidelberg years he had a strong mystical proclivity:

> You know, Goethe once said, *Ich hätte ebenso ein Verbrecher werden können wie ein Dichter* (I could just as well have become a criminal as a poet). I, too, had many choices. I could have become a mystic, living in isolation and burdened by the problems of the world. When I was seventeen or eighteen I was much older than I am today. When I was in Heidelberg I experienced something like a great breakthrough in my life. I used to go for the weekends to one of the beautiful little towns on the Neckar— Neckar Steinach, Neckar Gemünd—and lie for hours in a field, contemplating problems of the world. The philosophers who impressed me most

were Schopenhauer, Nietzsche, and, above all, with regard to the life to be followed, Goethe: to stand above the things and to be involved in the things. . . .

I was, all my life, a great Goethe fanatic. One of my favorite poems was his *Wanderers Nachtlied* (The Wanderer's Night Song). You know, *Über allen Gipfeln ist Ruh* (Over all summits is stillness). . . . One day, I must have been sixteen or seventeen, I read in a biography of Goethe that he had written and rewritten this short poem ten to twelve times. I was heartbroken. I couldn't sleep all night. I had thought the writing of such a great poem was a matter of a moment's inspiration. But then I recognized what was the true greatness of Goethe: to be inspired and to be a great technician. To be in the things and above the things.

I call this the aesthetic relation to the world. Morally the world is terrible. Lack of justice, brutality, wars, suffering. . . . The world can be accepted only on an aesthetic basis, only if you see it as a work of art, if you, so to speak, don't take it too seriously, as the religious and morally puritanical people do. . . . This, really, is my *Weltanschauung* (world view).[4]

Heidelberg boasted a chapter of the Zionist Jewish student union, the *Kartell Jüdischer Verbindungen,* in which Goldmann was a member, but again he did not demonstrate much interest. The only thing he remembers of this union is that he was the sole opponent of the near-unanimous majority decision that required all members to react with a challenge to duel to anti-Semitic abuse by non-Jewish students. What preoccupied him during these years was neither the university nor the Jewish student union but his reading and his frequent speaking engagements, which took him to many Zionist and non-Zionist groups. On the occasion of one of these lectures in Heilbronn, he met Theodore Heuss (1884–1963), editor of the *Heilbronner Neckarzeitung* and later (1949–59) the first president of West Germany, and as such one of the German leaders with whom Goldmann negotiated concerning the German reparations agreement.

The vivid impression Palestine made on the eighteen-year-old Goldmann strongly contrasts with his lack of interest during his first Heidelberg years. The opportunity to visit Palestine presented itself when Dr. Theodor Zlocisti (1874–1943)—a Berlin physician, litterateur, early Zionist leader, founder of the Berlin Jewish Students Association, and delegate to the First (1897) and subsequent Zionist Congresses, who a few years later (in 1921) was to settle in Tel Aviv—organized a group visit for students to Palestine. "A wealthy friend of the family"[5] offered to defray the expenses of Goldmann's participation. He "jumped at the chance," and, though as a minor born in Russia who had been living since his early childhood in Germany he had no passport, he joined the group after Dr. Zlocisti assured him that he would see to it that this would cause no problem. (Within a year after he met Zlocisti, Goldmann wrote a study of Zlocisti's literary work, which was published in two installments in the May 22 and 29, 1914, issues of the *Frankfurter Israelitisches Familienblatt.*) Upon their arrival at Jaffa in the spring of 1913, a friend of Dr. Zlocisti, Zalman David Levontin (1856–1940), met the group at the port. Levontin, a member of the Hoveve Zion, was a longtime resident of Palestine, who since 1903 had been the director of the Anglo-Palestine Company (which later became the Anglo-Palestine Bank and then the Bank Leumi) and as such was an influential person with the Turkish authorities. At Zlocisti's request, Levontin took Goldmann through the passport control as his guest.[6]

Goldmann's accounts of his experiences in Palestine, written more than sixty years later, are sketchy and anecdotal, but the impression the country made on him comes through as vividly in them as in the series of articles he wrote during his visit, which were published from May 1913 to March 1914 in the *Frankfurter Israelitisches Familienblatt,* and subsequently in a book entitled *Erez Israel: Reisebriefe aus Palästina* (Frankfurt a.M.: J. Kauffmann, 1914). After all those decades he still remembered the deep impression Palestine made on him as a youth, an impression never again matched during his many later visits. This, as he recalled, was owing not just to the fact that he was young and impressionable and less distracted by things he had to deal with in subsequent visits, such as meetings and conferences. It was the quality of the land itself which was unique, and which, as young Nahum sensed it, could not be explained by its landscape and nature. It had a mystical meaning which revealed itself to him at that time, and only at that time, and which he could not recapture later. In 1913 Palestine still had a pristine character; its nature, mountains, and fields could be enjoyed and experienced without one's being concerned with such practical matters as roads and settlements. One could ride across the plains and see them unmarred by buildings and highways and sense the "millennial enchantment" of the land. In those early days Palestine was a tranquil land (Goldmann uses the adjective "idealistic" to describe it), still dominated by its great past, with the spirit of the biblical prophets, the Talmudic sages, Jesus of Nazareth and the apostles, and the Safed Kabbalists still lingering in the atmosphere.

Looking back across half a century and more at Palestine as it was then, Goldmann feels that the Zionist settlement work, which transformed that somnolent country into a dynamic industrial state, did the land a wrong, that the "original sin inherent in all cultural development" was palpable in Israel more than in any other country that underwent industrial development.

As for the early Jewish "colonies," as the first Zionist agricultural settlements were called, they did not make a lasting impression on young Nahum. In fact, as he recalled in 1980, some of his most gripping experiences had no connection at all with Jewish Zionist work in the country. The most memorable impressions of Palestine as it was in 1913 were conveyed to him in the garden of the Benedictine monastery at Tabgha on the shore of the Sea of Galilee, in the cloisters of the Italian monastery at Kubeiba on the road between Jaffa and Jerusalem, and among the hills of Ein Karem, which today is a suburb of Jerusalem but where at that time there was as yet no Jewish settlement.[7] In 1969 he wrote,

> Today Palestine means something quite different to me from what it did in those days, but the essentials of my present feeling for it, which are closely bound up with my memories, date back to those months. In this sense my first encounter was a decisive event for me, an event that linked my future with that country. Since then I have established many other ties of a political, organizational and personal nature with individuals, collaborators, and colleagues in Palestine, but my decisive, mystical experience of the country dates back to that first visit. . . .
>
> When I left Palestine my Zionism had been enriched by a momentous factor. Until then Zionism had been an abstract idea to me, and I had no real conception of what the return of the Jews meant in any concrete sense. My visit gave me that feeling for the soil without which Zionism is bound to remain quite unsubstantial. From then on I began to understand what it means, not merely negatively in terms of leaving the Diaspora behind, but also positively, as a new beginning in a Jewish homeland.[8]

In his 1969 *Autobiography* Goldmann's reminiscences from his first visit to Palestine are brought to a close on this strongly positive note. Ten years later, while reproducing all the above, he added a few comments that reflect the doubts he had about the direction taken by the economic, social, and cultural developments in modern Israel. In the course of those ten years his heart grew fonder of the natural features of the land than of what her returning sons had built on her bosom. He quotes the words he uttered on the occasion of the celebration on the fiftieth anniversary of his first visit: "If the Land of Palestine had a soul and a will, it would probably spit out all of us Jews into the Mediterranean because we have completely ruined this unique landscape."[9]

Then he goes on to bemoan the reality that fell far short of the ideal as envisaged in the pre-World War I days. He repeats that at that time Palestine was pure, untouched, idealistic, suffused with the pioneering spirit. At its inception, Zionism intended to create not just a Jewish state, but an exemplary new society based on the ethical teachings of the biblical prophets and of Jewish tradition. Jewish Palestine was to become a spiritual center as envisaged by Aḥad Haᶜam, and it was to attract the majority of the Jews from all over the world. This has not come to pass. Although the Law of Return, enacted upon the achievement of independence, entitles every Jew to settle in Israel and to receive automatically Israeli citizenship, only a very small part of the Jewish people has come. The ideal of pioneering has been replaced by an ideal of business acumen, and the new Israeli scene is characterized by all the unwelcome phenomena of crime, tax evasion, and corruption, all too familiar from many countries in the rest of the world.[10]

Contemplating the change that has taken place in the course of half a century in the Jewish population of Palestine-Israel, Goldmann felt in 1980 impelled to seek a psychological explanation for it. Can it be, he muses, that the traditional love of Zion, which was part of Jewish life throughout the long exile, was but an example of that love relationship in which the essential is not the fulfillment but the yearning, because the lovers are afraid of disappointment? And he concludes sadly that "the Jewish people yearns for Zion, but does not want to go there, in order not to be disappointed in its yearning."[11]

This insight came as a great shock to the octogenarian Goldmann, for, if it were true, it meant that a great part of his life, devoted to the service of Zionism, was wasted. But, turning away from these dark thoughts, he hastens to assert that they in no way lessened his admiration for the positive achievements of Israel. After two thousand years of statelessness, the Jews have built in Israel a state that compares favorably with many other, older states; after having lacked for two millennia armed forces of their own, the Jews have created in Israel an outstanding army and have won four wars against overwhelming odds; and, above all, Israel has given a homeland, dignity, and self-assurance to three million Jews.[12]

Although these utterances do not reveal much about the sentiments his visit to the Land of Israel evoked in the eighteen-year-old Nahum, they do provide insight into the ambivalent attitude of the eighty-year-old Goldmann to Israel. Clearly, he both feels disappointment at the reality of the Jewish State and deeply admires its achievements. Israel does not live up to the ideal that, in retrospect, he remembers was the promise of the small pre-World War I *Yishuv*. Part of his disappointment, however, though he does not say so explicitly but only implies, is with the reaction of the Diaspora to Israel and the possibilities it offers.

The simile of the love relationship is especially enlightening in this connection. The Diaspora's love for Israel, Goldmann in effect says, proved after the establishment of the Jewish State to be the kind of love that refuses fulfillment or consummation: most of the Jews preferred to continue to yearn for Israel—manifested in their unstinting political and material support of the Jewish State—rather than settle in Israel and become part of the polity they so wholeheartedly support and of which they are so proud. In making this observation, he comes quite near the position taken by his old friend and lifelong adversary, David Ben-Gurion, who stated to the consternation of Zionist and Jewish leaders in the Diaspora, among them Goldmann himself, that only he who settled in Israel was a true Zionist. And this issue touches, of course, closely upon the complex problem of the future of the Diaspora, on which, within five or six years after his visit to Palestine, Goldmann formulated his own definitive position, from which he was never to deviate thereafter.

However, in 1913 all these doubts and misgivings about the direction Zionism and the *Yishuv* took lay far in the future. In 1913, as indicated by his published on-the-spot reports, young Goldmann was, to use another simile from human love relations, smitten by what he saw of the new *Yishuv*, which was at the time only thirty years old, and of the work of the Second Aliya, which brought the ideal of *Halutziut*, pioneering, into the country barely a decade before Goldmann's visit.

His first reaction to the new Jewish Palestine is one of utter enchantment. As soon as he emerges from the narrow, noisy, and dirty streets of Jaffa and enters the new Jewish quarter of Tel Aviv—only four years old in 1913—he feels transported into a new world, a Zionist Utopia realized. Generalizing with the rashness and impetuosity of youth, he extrapolates after a brief walk along the main street of Tel Aviv and concludes that the new Jewish life in Palestine "still has that cooling, refreshing breath which only a primitive, naive culture can possess. . . . Palestine still has the purity and natural morality of a child as yet at the beginning of its development."[13]

At first sight, he falls in love with Tel Aviv. "I can barely believe my eyes. Before me is a magnificent street, as clean as the most beautiful avenue in Europe, with stylish houses on both sides, surrounded by gardens." When he approaches the *"gimnasiya* (high school) Herzliya," and hears its pupils talk, flirt, and argue in Hebrew, "tears flood my eyes, tears of joy and happiness. Here, for the first time, I am in Eretz Israel, in the Old-New land,"—the name Herzl gave to his utopian novel about the rebuilt Jewish Palestine—and "it appears to me as a little paradise. Wherever I look, only joy, jubilant voices of children, only joyous faces, only happy moods, and, above everything, the wonderful sun pouring down its rays. Everywhere only light, air, verdant trees and laughing people—there seems to be an eternal holiday and eternal joy." Contrasting the beauty that was Tel Aviv with Whitechapel, the miserable Jewish slum of London, which he had seen two years earlier while on a visit to London with his parents, he writes: "From now on no more words are needed in order to prove the negation of the Galut; this one Tel Aviv means a hundred times more than all the theories."[14]

The first euphoria is soon followed by the inevitable sobering-up. He describes the disadvantages under which the Yemenite Jews suffered in Rishon l'Tziyon,[15] and laments the miserable condition of actual Jerusalem, a far cry from the ideal city of millennial Jewish dreams: "This city lifts you up with the splendor of its past, and beats you down with the cruelty of its present. You tremble with pride when you remember what it was, and are swallowed up in shame when you see what it is."[16] Yet all that he has learned and heard about Jerusalem from his ardently Zionist parents now overwhelms him. When he arrives by train in Jerusalem, he writes, "From all the confusion which fills me, one single feeling detaches itself as the victor: it is like the sensation I have when, after a long absence, I return to the parental home. And as I leave the railroad station, I feel only one thing: a son is returning to his mother. 'Where to?' asks my young friend who has come to meet me. 'To the Wailing Wall!' I cry impetuously. When going to see a mother there can be no formalities and no waiting. The first steps must lead directly to her heart."[17] And when, after wading through the filthy and malodorous alleys of the Old City he arrives at the wall, he can scarcely control his emotions: "Were it not for the strangers who stood about me, I would have kissed these stones, as one kisses a mother into whose arms one throws oneself, seeking consolation after years of nameless sufferings."[18]

But the ugliness and squalor of the present intrude even at the Wailing Wall. An Arab leads his donkey through the narrow passageway in front of the Wall, the donkey brays, and Goldmann is seized with a deep feeling of shame at the condition in which Jews worship at the holiest relic of their great past.[19]

Several of his subsequent letters are sharply critical of the things he finds in Palestine. He pours his wrath on "Halukka-Jewry," the ultra-Orthodox and Hasidic Jews who live on charity and do nothing all day but study the Talmud.[20] He is keenly disappointed by the Sephardi Jews, who lack even the saving grace of being sustained by a devotion to ceaseless religious study.[21] He flees from the ugliness of the present into the beauty of the future, and waxes enthusiastic over the imaginary day

> in which all these disparate quarters [of Jerusalem] will become one single united great city, where there will no longer be Bukharans and Yemenites, Persians and Caucasians, Sephardim and Ashkenazim, but only Jews. And I believe that the future type of Jew will be much richer and more talented than that of today's West European Jew. Resulting from the fusion of such different types, it will unite in itself the best of the heritages of all. And Jerusalem, the city where all these Jewish types first encountered one another, will also be the center of that culture which will be the creation of the Jews, and which will be able to draw its best powers from the union of all these varieties of Jews.[22]

In one of his last letters from Palestine, Goldmann discusses the problem of Diaspora Judaism and the role the small and young *Yishuv* was already playing in its solution in 1913 and was to play in the future. At that early stage, his Jewish and Zionist ideology was still concentrated in its entirety on the *Yishuv,* and the future of Diaspora Jewry—a major concern of his from 1919 on and throughout his life—still lay outside his ken. There are, he writes, two basic aspects of the Jewish problem in modern times: "One is the spiritual Jewish question, the moral Jewish plight, the tragic quality of the modern Jewish soul, or however else it has been termed." It is a consequence of life in the Diaspora, he says, that a duality exists in the intellectual and emotional life of every Jew, because he can live neither wholly as a Jew nor wholly as a European.[23]

And Goldmann goes on to adumbrate the image of the Jew as the prototypical marginal man, thus anticipating by six years the premise of Thorstein Veblen's famous hypothesis about the marginal position of the Jewish intellectual in relation to both the Jewish and the Gentile cultures that enables him to achieve preeminence.[24] This duality, says Goldmann (or, as modern psychologists would say, marginality), of the Jew in the Diaspora has two consequences: on the individual level it results in an inner rupture *(Zerrissenheit)* which he sharply criticizes as "that unprincipled spinelessness, that moral decadence, which are well enough known from everyday life to every Jew who does not choose to be blind, which has been so often and so amply demonstrated and described that

I can surely forego a more detailed presentation of these phenomena. On the collective, national level, the abnormal mental life *(Seelenleben)* of the Jews causes a decadence in their culture, renders them incapable of great national-cultural products, and makes a strong, original Jewish culture impossible."[25]

Following this harshly negative appraisal of Jewish cultural life in the Diaspora—subsequently Goldmann radically reversed himself on this issue—he goes on to present the achievements of the *Yishuv:*

> What have we achieved in Palestine for the solution of the Jewish spiritual problem? Much, unexpectedly much. Above all on the individual level. One can assert today [this was written in 1913!] without exaggeration that already the possibility exists in Palestine for the individual to solve the Jewish moral problem for himself. The European or American Jew who wants to escape the torture of the Jewish moral plight, who wants to remove his children from the schism in their education, is today already in a position to live in Palestine in a purely Jewish milieu, and to give his children, on the basis of Hebrew, a harmonious education which is the equivalent of the European schooling. . . . So that one can state already today as a fact: *the individual Jewish moral problem is already solved in Palestine* [italics in the original].

As for the national-cultural level of the Jewish problem, Goldmann states that, though much less has been achieved, "it is remarkable how Palestine develops more and more into a spiritual center."[26] His impression of what has been attained materially is less positive, especially because most of the "colonies," the agricultural settlements established by members of the First Aliya (1882–1904), are based on Arab labor and because a sizable emigration of Jews from Palestine is occurring.[27]

Goldmann concludes his letters from Palestine on a moderately hopeful note: "In the first month of my sojourn in Palestine I was enthused; in the second—desperate; in the third—resigned and satisfied. And I left the country a hundred times stronger in my convictions about the realization of the Zionist ideals than I had been prior to my visit. . . . An objective grasp of the real bases" of the possibilities offered by Palestine, "coupled with energetic work and self-sacrificing perseverance will undoubtedly be able to overcome the difficulties, and achieve the great world-historical aim: the solution of the Jewish question in the Jewish land."[28]

Within a few years of his visit to Palestine, Goldmann's views were to change radically. He came to recognize the crucial role the Diaspora fulfilled in the history of the Jewish people and became convinced that the "Jewish land" alone could not be a complete solution to the Jewish question, that the Diaspora was here to stay, and that the future of the Jewish people lay in the continued duality of its existence: in its center, the historic Land of Israel, and in the peripheries, the Diaspora, with Israel and the Diaspora as partners, tied to each other in an unbreakable community of fate.

After his return from Palestine, Goldmann spent another year in university studies until they were again interrupted by the outbreak of World War I for a period of four years, three of which he spent as an official in the propaganda department of the German Foreign Office (see next chapter). When he returned to Heidelberg to finish his studies and earn his Doctor of Law degree, he was twenty-three years old, a man experienced in the ways of German bureaucracy, used to social intercourse with members of the officialdom and the aristocracy, and equally at home in German and Zionist politics. The memories he retained from his second Heidelberg period are more detailed than those of the first, but are also more critical of the university atmosphere, of the students, and of the foibles of the professors.

As Goldmann views it from a distance of sixty years, his contact with his teachers was a kind of contest of wits. He passed his orals because, he says, "I had the presence of mind, in case of difficult questions, to get out of the quandary with a joke or a rhetorical counter-question," and then proceeds to describe how, with a combination of keen wit, psychological insight into the mentality of his examiners, and sheer "cheek"— the famous Jewish *ḥutzpa*—he managed to pass the doctoral exam, though he lacked much knowledge about the actual questions put to him by his professors. One of the ruses he reports having used reminded me of an anecdote that was current in my own student days in Budapest: The candidate is asked about King Solomon, of whom he knows nothing; but he knows about King David, so he answers: "Solomon was a great king, but did not approach the stature of his father, David, who . . ." and therewith he embarks on a presentation of all he knows about the great warrior king of Israel. Similarly, Goldmann relates that, when one of his examiners asked him to describe the philosophy of law of Stammler, he answered that "in order to understand Stammler properly, one must begin with his philosophical 'ancestor,' Hermann Cohen," about whom he knew quite a bit, and went on to speak for several minutes about Cohen, until the time allotted to this part of the examination ran out.[29]

His continuing interest in philosophy prompted Goldmann to transfer, early in 1914, from Heidelberg to the University of Marburg, which at the time was a major center of the neo-Kantian school, founded by Hermann Cohen (1842–1918). Although Cohen had retired from Marburg two years previously, his school continued to flourish and constituted a strong attraction for Goldmann, who continued to be preoccupied with the problems of Kantian philosophy.[30]

Within half a year, Goldmann's studies at Marburg were interrupted by the war. Following its end, he returned to Heidelberg and, after having obtained his Doctor of Law degree, he also passed his Doctor of Philosophy orals. Rickert gave him a subject for a doctoral thesis, but Goldmann was too impatient to get away from the university and felt unable to stay for another half year in Heidelberg working on it. So he gave up and remained the possessor of a Doctor of Law and half of a Ph.D. degree.

In any case, it is clear that Goldmann considered even the acquisition of his Doctor of Law degree a mere formality, more a matter of obligation to bring to a conclusion the university studies he had started almost ten years earlier than an achievement of real interest. He was determined not to become a practicing attorney, nor to embark on a university teaching career, for which possession of a doctoral degree was a prerequisite. Even before he could call himself Dr. Goldmann, he had decided to devote himself to the service of Zionism and of the Jewish cause in general.

4. *In the German Foreign Office*

Goldmann's first close contact with Gentile officialdom and diplomacy took place within the framework of the German Foreign Ministry. Although he was not a German citizen—the authorities were reluctant to grant citizenship to East European Jews—the outbreak of World War I evoked in him, as in all Jews within Germany and many without, strong pro-German sentiments. Among the German Jews, a major factor in their wholehearted support of the German war effort was their hatred of Russia, the classical land of anti-Semitism, Jew-baiting, and pogroms. Because Russia was the archenemy of the Jews, any country fighting it almost automatically gained the sympathy of Jews everywhere. But the anti-Russian feeling was especially strong among the Russian Jewish emigrants in Germany, who knew from personal experience the harsh conditions under which their people were forced to live in Russia and were beholden to Germany for having given them an opportunity to live in peace and in incomparably better circumstances. Similar feelings among Russian and German Jews in America placed them in quite a difficult situation, first in view of the general American sympathy with England, an ally of Russia, and later the entry of the United States into the war against Germany.

It was inevitable that Goldmann, growing up in a Russian-Jewish home in Germany, attending German schools, imbued with German culture, and enamored of the German landscape, should build a strong attachment to the country. He volunteered for military service, but was not accepted because—as he later interpreted it—foreigners who served in the German Army earned the right to German citizenship, and the authorities, convinced that victory would be theirs in a few weeks, felt that the coveted citizenship would be too large a reward for a short stretch of service in the ranks of the army.[1]

The only unpleasant consequence of the war for young Goldmann was that, as an enemy alien, he was ousted from the university. He was "exiled" from Frankfurt to nearby Bad Nauheim, a fashionable resort, where hundreds of East European Jews who became stranded in Germany when the war broke out were concentrated. However, he soon discovered several fields of Jewish activity that interested him. He organized a Zionist club, wrote articles for the *Frankfurter Zeitung,* and also found time to take Russian lessons from the wife of a prominent Warsaw Jewish attorney, who had joined her husband among the foreigners who were forced to stay in the city. In fact, the atmosphere was so congenial that he remained at the spa for several months after he received official permission to return to Frankfurt.

The tenor of Goldmann's articles was emphatically patriotic. He marshaled philosophical-historical arguments to justify the position of Germany toward her enemies. He proceeded to show that her system of government, whose authoritarianism and advanced social legislation had made giant strides in imperial Germany, was superior to the individualistic liberalism of the Western powers and of the United States. "Partly out of intellectual playfulness, and partly because of the journalistic need to be timely," Goldmann titled this series of articles "The Spirit of Militarism," in reference to and refutation of the great slogan of the Allied powers, which was "Fight against German militarism." Sixty years later, when the octogenarian Goldmann penned his memoirs, he was quite embarrassed by these articles, which he judged to be "contrived and immature," but, he added, "as everybody else, I too committed my intellectual sins, and as for the emotional ties I had to the country and the culture in which I grew up, I am even today not ashamed of them."[2]

Because these articles—which were within a year (in 1915) published in pamphlet form in a series in which the foremost German intellectual leaders participated (see below)—are among the earliest serious pieces of writing produced by Goldmann as well as the only ones dealing with a non-Jewish subject, they deserve a closer look. They are a curious mixture of bold, original, and immature generalizations that are reminiscent of the sweeping assertions of another Jewish juvenile genius, Otto Weininger, and provide keen insights into the German spirit which, as a horrified world was to learn two decades after World War I, could apply itself with equal thoroughness, method, and precision to good and evil. What Goldmann says about the German instinct to obey and the

German idealization of discipline goes a long way to explain the horrors of Auschwitz and the silence with which one of the most civilized peoples in Europe reacted to first the dehumanization and then the extermination of the Jews. At the same time, one is surprised at the familiarity of the young man of nineteen with the work of not only the German writers and philosophers, but equally with that of the leading French and English authors and thinkers.

What Goldmann did in this series of articles was nothing short of an intellectual sleight of hand. Although ostensibly speaking of German militarism, he tacitly reinterpreted the term and treated it as if it were synonymous with such patently democratic concepts as equal rights and equal duties, the orderly management of society, cooperative organization, and the like. He begins by stating that the leading French and English men of letters, such as Bernard Shaw, G. K. Chesterton, Henri Bergson, Émile Boutroux, and Anatole France, argue that the military spirit dominates not only the German Army, which, of course, is inevitable, but also German culture as a whole, the German spirit, and the life of the German people in general.[3] Then he proceeds to investigate the actual meaning of militarism. It consists, he says, of uniformization and subordination. The first is but an expression of the democratic idea because the uniform itself eliminates all differences of class, economic status, and thought. Subordination, on the other hand, is an outcome of the aristocratic idea. It is necessary for the prevention of anarchy. Nowhere is the separation between those who command and those who obey carried out so completely as in the army. However, modern militarism goes back to an even deeper, more elemental, principle of existence: it derives equality not from equal rights, but equal duties. "As a human being," Goldmann writes, "one has rights; as a soldier, one has, in the first place, duties. The free-born man of Rousseau's *contract social* demands, the soldier obeys. Therewith the democratic idea, as one encounters it in the army, acquires, instead of a utilitarian character, an ethical one, instead of a revolutionary character, a conservative one, instead of a plebeian character, an aristocratic one: the fulfilling of his duties lends man a sense of dignity, a proud self-consciousness. . . . The Prussian sergeant-major can be designated the personification of Kant's categorical imperative."[4]

The idea of human equality, Goldmann continues to expound, based on duties that are common to all men, is a specifically German idea. It finds its highest expression in the concept of society as an organism. And no other social grouping can transform a random mass of individuals into a uniform organism as can the army. The democratic principle fused with the aristocratic produces the idea of the organism. Theoretically, as well as practically, the organism is the guiding idea of militarism. "This idea is one of the most significant and most consequential ideas of the whole German philosophy, of the entire German spirit. Whether one names Kant or Goethe, Fichte or Schiller, Schelling or Lessing, Hegel or Herder, Novalis or Marx—to mention two men of the greatest polarity of existence and thinking—in all of them it is the idea of the organism which guides and dominates their whole thinking."[5]

Then, in an aside, Goldmann refers to an article of his, published in the *Frankfurter Zeitung* (first morning edition of September 18, 1914), in which he "attempted to define the German spirit as the spirit of order." If this is so, then the specific German spirit can be termed the spirit of militarism. However, the West European industrial complex is also a militaristic phenomenon. The spirit of modern industry, characterized by its regimentation, order, subordination, and chain of command, is a militaristic spirit. Therewith Goldmann has accomplished a veritable tour de force: he has equated militarism with orderly, organized society, which only anarchists can oppose. Henceforth, he is free to use the word militarism when actually speaking of orderliness.

Goldmann elaborates on the need of tempering the democratic principle of equality, which is the controlling idea of modern Western spiritual and intellectual life, with the aristocratic principles of subordination. There is no such thing as complete equality. The very idea is absurd: there are men and women, old and young, strong and weak, beautiful and ugly, clever and stupid. The necessary correction demanded by the democratic principle of uniformity is furnished by the principle of aristocratic subordination, which teaches that there must always be rulers and ruled: "The true, pure aristocratic principle has been made dominant only in our time. Only today is the statement valid that only he should rule who wants and is able to rule." Today, the man who possesses the proper abilities can achieve everything: "All are soldiers in the great army which calls itself modern civilization. Everyone can become everything: officer, colonel, general."[6]

This is followed by another bold generalization. Because the spirit he thus described is the spirit of Germany and is found also in the rest of the modern world, "therefore let us say it in opposition to all those who want to annihilate Germany: The German spirit rules the world."[7]

After two sections in which he subjects the spirit and motivations of

England and France to a critical analysis—interesting more for what it shows of Goldmann's familiarity with the cultures of those countries than for the validity of his criticism—he comes back to Germany and the tasks he envisages for her:

> Only the victory of militarism will enable our times to solve the problems posed by world history. The meaning of the historical mission of our times can be summarized briefly: its task is the ordering anew of the civilized world, the replacing of the social system which has been dominant until now by a new one. First, all the social layers and formations of society created by the old system must be annihilated; the individual must be torn out of his inherited milieu; no tradition must count as sacred any longer; age, from now on must be regarded only as a sign of sickness; the slogan is: whatever was must be swept away![8]
>
> Then follows the second, more difficult task: the building of the new order. New formations and categories must be created. A new pyramidal, hierarchical system must be erected. This can be achieved only by the spirit of militarism with the great guiding principle of subordination. Neither descent nor name, neither property nor power will be decisive, but the talent to rule. In a society built upon the principles of an army advancement will depend only on one factor: the ability to command and to lead.[9]
>
> Then follows a third phase: it will be necessary to shape the new society into a united, closed organism. This is the greatest and most important task. But we are familiar with it under another name: the solution of the social problem. For what else is the social problem than the state of an inner social anarchy? That the few have too much and always more, but the majority have too little and always less, that production and consumption are not harmoniously balanced, that agriculture and industry do not complement each other . . . all these are but forms of expression of inner anarchy and disorganization. What force can overcome this anarchy? Only one: the idea of the organization, of the organism; precisely the idea which we have recognized as the highest, the supreme idea of the militaristic spirit. Hence only the militaristic spirit can achieve this last and greatest task of our time, the solution of the social problem, or, what amounts to the same thing, the organization of the new social system. It is today already generally recognized, or at least felt, that the militaristic spirit alone is called upon to do this. All the proposals and directives which aim at the solution of the social problem move in this single direction. The co-operative movement, socialism, Communism—they all aim at the same thing: only the idea of the organism can bring about the solution of the social problem. This, however, means: only the spirit of militarism will give it to us. . . .[10]

With the solution of this greatest central task of our time the militaristic spirit will also realize yet another ideal which actually has developed only in the present century: the ideal of peace. It certainly seems to be paradoxical still to believe in the realization of the peace concept, and even more paradoxical to hope that it will be realized by the spirit of militarism. One must, however, understand this idea properly and it must not be distorted. To consider the possibility of an eternal, absolute peace for the whole of mankind is meaningless. For the whole of mankind does not belong to our circle of culture *(Kulturkreis),* and the day will come in which our culture will have to wage its war against other, younger cultures. But one is surely justified in hoping for the attainment of a situation of lasting, inviolable peace within our circle of culture, and in considering it possible. And, again, however paradoxical it sounds—this can be expected precisely from a victory of the militaristic spirit. It is not too difficult to recognize that in a social system which is constructed by the militaristic spirit and is ruled by it, there is no place any longer for war, because war is a contradiction to all the guiding principles and ideas of the militaristic spirit. That the democratic principle of uniformization rejects war needs no proof; democracy has always been peace-loving in principle, because all wars stem from the principle of inequality, whether one people wants to subject the other, or within one people one class wants to dominate the other. The idea of equality rejects war as the negation of all equality. But also the aristocratic principle of subordination, if consistently realized, leads to a setting aside of war. In a society, in which the criteria for the differentiation between the rulers and the ruled have been firmly established, there can be no war any more; for war is nothing but the anarchical attempt of one group to seize the rule over other groups. Where the distribution of power is regulated according to firm principles and criteria, every war appears to be a rebellion, just as every attempt by a number of officers to seize the supreme command of an army is considered a rebellion. However, most decisively the militaristic spirit must reject war on the basis of its highest idea of the organism. The idea of the organism and war stand opposed to one another as irreconcilable contrasts; every war means anarchy; every organism, however, rejects all anarchy from the very ground, and thus also everything warlike.[11]

And on this note of universal peace imposed by a victorious Germany on the world Goldmann concludes his spirited defense of the German spirit of militarism.

This series of articles made Goldmann's name known and led to a job offer from the propaganda department of the German Foreign Office. The way this came about was that Dr. Heinrich Simon, the publisher of the *Frankfurter Zeitung,* was so impressed by Goldmann's feuilletons that he sent them to Dr. Ernst Jäckh, who edited a pamphlet series entitled *Der deutsche Krieg* (The German War), which was devoted to high-level political propaganda. Jäckh (who subsequently became professor of political science at Columbia University) reprinted Goldmann's articles as one of the brochures in his series with a prefatory remark to the effect that "This treatise gains in significance due to the person of its author: Nahum Goldmann is by birth a Russian Jew; he was born in 1894 in Wischnevo as the son of a writer. Having come to Germany in his early youth, he became such a good German in thinking and feeling that he could write this fine treatise for Germany."

When Goldmann subsequently wrote to Dr. Jäckh to ask his help in obtaining permission to move to Berlin, he received an offer of employment from the propaganda division of the Foreign Office. Goldmann accepted. But, because it occurred to nobody in the section which had to pass on new employees that a candidate for office in the Foreign Ministry might not be a German citizen, he found himself for several years in a peculiar situation: on the one hand he was required to report to the police twice a week as an enemy alien; on the other, he worked in the German Foreign Office and traveled on a German diplomatic passport.[12]

In the beginning, Goldmann was detailed to the press department. There his work consisted of glancing through forty to fifty newspapers every day and summarizing the articles that were of interest to the propaganda department of the Foreign Office. This task, in which he was engaged for six months, taught him how to read and absorb statements rapidly as well as how to compress their gist into a few clearly formulated sentences.[13]

Goldmann's colleagues and superiors in the Foreign Office took it for granted that a Russian-born Jew should work for and be a wholehearted supporter of the German war effort. But some assimilated Berlin Jews, who looked down with contempt upon their East European co-religionists and considered the Yiddish language an inferior tongue, and for whom the concept of Jewish nationhood was anathema, could not reconcile themselves to the fact that a young *Ostjude* should be employed in the most prestigious ministry of the Reich. One day, three well-known Jewish leaders of this ilk, as Goldmann's superior, Baron Buri, subsequently told him with considerable glee, called on the baron to express their surprise that Goldmann had been invited to work for the Foreign Office and asked him whether he was aware that Goldmann was not a German but an *Ostjude*. Baron Buri's answer was that, if Goldmann's patriotism was good enough for the Kaiser's government, it should satisfy his interlocutors as well. The latter then switched to another line of attack and asked whether the Herr Baron knew that Goldmann was a sworn Zionist, a movement that most German Jews opposed. The baron dealt with this line of inquiry by coolly stating that, though he knew little about internal Jewish affairs and differences of opinion, he had known ever since his youth that the German Jews were constantly complaining that each applicant for a government position was asked whether he was Jewish or Christian. Now, said the baron, you gentlemen wish that, if the government employs a Jew, it should inquire about the *kind* of Jew he is, which would really seem to go too far.[14]

His work opened a whole new world to young Goldmann. Only those familiar with German officialdom can form any idea about the atmosphere that permeated and surrounded the German civil service and the respect bordering on fear that government offices and officials instilled into the German public. The very term designating official authorities, *Obrigkeit,* which lacks a precise equivalent in English, carries the connotation of something superior and awe-inspiring. *Ich habe die Obrigkeit nicht zu befürchten* asserts the respectable and staid protagonist of Heinrich Mann's classic *Professor Unrat* (1905), which became world-famous as the film *The Blue Angel.* The *Obrigkeit* is the realistic background of Franz Kafka's nightmarish description of the amorphous authority in *Der Prozess* (1925; translated into English as *The Trial,* 1937). Neither work could have been written in any other environment but a German one.

One can imagine what it must have meant to a twenty-year-old Russian-Jewish youngster to become, quite unexpectedly, a member, albeit a modest one, of the German *Obrigkeit,* and, to boot, to achieve such a position in wartime when the power of any office connected with the war effort was strongly intensified. It is a pity that no notes on the impressions and reactions of Goldmann are available from those years, when he was a cog in one wheel of the massive German propaganda machine. In his memoirs of that early period in his life, written more than half a century later, he could look back upon himself as a young recruit in a huge and awesome German office, and upon that office as a whole, with a certain humor, detachment, irony, and even disparagement. Nothing is left in these memoirs of the awe he must have felt, of the intimidating airs of the German aristocrats who were his colleagues and superiors in the office, of the unease he must have experienced knowing that any moment somebody might discover that he was a Russian enemy alien, which could even have resulted in the suspicion that he was a spy. (In fact, on one occasion, he was taken to a police station and accused of being a spy, but, upon the intervention of his superior in the Foreign Office, was released with an apology.)

Instead, the memoirs provide humorous pen pictures of his colleagues and superiors, their antics and foibles, their proclivities and shortcomings, their pomposity and clumsiness, and their utter inability to deviate in the slightest from established routine. Although it cannot be known to what extent these late observations reflect the actual reactions young Goldmann had to the people in the German propaganda department during World War I, one suspects that, given his critical vein, his skepticism, and his sense of humor—all of which he had acquired at an early age—he actually did, after an initial period of groping about to find his way, develop enough of a detached attitude to be able to see clearly what lay behind the awe-inspiring facade of the office and its personnel.

However, Goldmann learned two significant things from his work in the German propaganda department. One was self-assurance in dealing with and relating to Gentile—in this case German—officialdom, in putting across his ideas, in making suggestions, and convincing others of their rightness. By the time he left his position, he had acquired an ease, perhaps not yet in negotiating with persons in power, but certainly in talking to them, in appraising them, and in finding ways to influence them. It was on this ability, as Goldmann further fostered it subsequently, that his entire career as a Jewish political negotiator with world leaders was built.

The other thing Goldmann learned was how to shape propositions he wished to put forward for the betterment of the Jewish condition in a form acceptable to those in a position to approve or reject them. After working in the news division of the propaganda office for about a year, he was transferred to Jewish affairs. Of all the powers fighting in World War I, Germany was the most closely involved with the Jewish problem. Soon after the beginning of the war the German Army occupied the western parts of Russia, including Poland and Lithuania, which were the home of millions of Jews, who had no love for the oppressive government under which they had lived, and whose sympathy Germany—for political reasons of its own—was determined to win. The Austro-Hungarian empire, an ally of Germany, also had a huge Jewish population, many of whom, especially in Galicia, were Yiddish-speaking and of an ethnic character similar to that of the Jews of Poland and Lithuania. Turkey, another ally of Germany, had a large Sephardi Jewish population, and, in addition, controlled Palestine, the Holy Land of all Jews, which was considered by most East European Jews to be the future homeland of the Jewish people. All in all, during much of the war period, Germany had under its rule or influence the great majority of world Jewry.

Young Goldmann, because of his Russian background and Zionist upbringing, was fully aware of this situation. Soon after having found his footing in the bureaucratic maze of his department in the German Foreign Office, he suggested to his superiors that a section for Jewish problems be set up within the department. His proposal was accepted, but, because of the bureaucratic ponderousness that characterized all German government offices, the Jewish section was actually established only close to the end of the war, by which time Goldmann had left the department, and Germany had been forced to give up all the eastern territories she had conquered during the war. Still, the section continued to function until the Nazis came to power in Germany.

Despite this delay in the formal establishment of the Jewish section, Goldmann's own work in the propaganda department of the German Foreign Ministry was concentrated more and more on Jewish affairs. He took special interest in the legal status of Polish and Lithuanian Jewry, at the time under German military rule. The German plan was to detach all western territories from Russia and to establish a Polish grand duchy, headed by a Prince Radziwil, as well as separate Lithuanian and other Baltic provinces. Because these were precisely the areas of heaviest Jewish concentration, the so-called "Pale of Settlement," where under czarist Russia the Jews were allowed to live, the fate of this part of the world was of great interest to the Jews. German Jewish leaders set up a "Committee for the East," headed by Franz Oppenheimer, Adolf Friedemann, Moritz Sobernheim, and others, and Goldmann found in it concerned collaborators with his efforts to obtain national minority status for the Jews who in Russia had been deprived of all rights. He traveled several times to Warsaw, where he became acquainted with Polish Jewry and its conditions under German occupation, and wrote memoranda for the Foreign Ministry in which he recommended that the *Ostjuden* be given cultural autonomy so as to preserve and promote a distinctive Jewish way of life in the areas of strong Jewish concentration. Although Germany soon thereafter lost the war and thus was in no position to do anything about Jewish life in Eastern Europe, the idea of Jewish cultural autonomy and national minority rights was taken up by the victorious Allies and imposed upon Rumania, Poland, Lithuania, and the successor states carved out of Austria, Hungary, and Germany.

5. Klatzkin and the
Diaspora Issue

It occasionally happens that a devoted disciple, despite the strong influence exerted upon him by his teacher, whom he reveres as his mentor, yet finds himself unable to go along with the master on a fundamental issue. Then, debating it with him, he formulates and hardens his own diametrically opposed views, which in turn determine his entire outlook and even his whole life's work. The classical example of such a relationship, which, however, did not lead to a rift between master and disciple but to a divergence of positions, is that of Aristotle, who, as his own thought evolved, became more and more critical of the basic tenets of his master Plato. In Jewish intellectual history, one example is that of Elisha ben Abuya and his disciple Rabbi Meir, though the meager allusions contained in the Talmud—the only source covering the event—allow only a guess as to the point where Rabbi Meir refused to follow the unorthodox conclusions of his master.

Something similar happened between the young Nahum Goldmann and Jacob Klatzkin (1882–1948), who was thirteen years his senior and who decisively affected his intellectual and ideological growth—except for the one crucial issue of the Diaspora.

The reverence Goldmann as a youth conceived for Klatzkin never diminished while Klatzkin was alive and remained with Goldmann throughout the three decades that have elapsed since Klatzkin's death. In 1980, in his eighty-fifth year, looking back upon a long life extraordinarily rich in human contacts and friendships, Goldmann still felt that of all the friends in his life Klatzkin had probably exerted the deepest influence upon him.[1]

The story of Goldmann's discipleship under Klatzkin in all things Jewish, and of his defiance of the master on the Diaspora issue, is not only fascinating psychologically; it is significant because in that one experience lie the roots of Goldmann's specific view of the Jews as a global people, of the Diaspora as a condition that satisfies a deep-seated need in the Jewish psyche, and of the inevitability of the Jewish ethnic dichotomy into Israel and the Diaspora. That view, in turn, determined once and for all the direction of Goldmann's public activity.

Jacob Klatzkin's father, Elijah Klatzkin (1852–1932), was a prominent Russian-Jewish author, rabbi, and rabbinical scholar, who gave his son a thorough education in all branches of traditional Jewish learning. At the age of eighteen, Jacob went to Frankfurt am Main, where he became a frequent guest in the house of Nahum's parents. Before long, the child became impressed by and attracted to Klatzkin, and, as he grew older, conceived an admiration for the brilliant and charming young man, who was thirteen years his senior and who seemed to possess a rich storehouse of all those intellectual treasures the precocious boy hoped to acquire. Whenever the group of students who frequented the Goldmann house and who unquestioningly recognized Klatzkin as their leader gathered, Nahum would eagerly listen to their debates and as time went on found the courage to participate in them. By the age of ten, he had ideas of his own, to which the much older youths listened, at first with amused tolerance, and later with growing respect.

Klatzkin went on to the University of Marburg, where he became a student, but not a disciple, of Hermann Cohen. Klatzkin received his doctorate from the University of Berne relatively late, in 1912, when he was close to thirty. Throughout his student years, he continued to visit the Goldmann home, and by the time Nahum reached adolescence the two had become close friends.

From 1909 to 1911 Klatzkin was editor of *Die Welt,* the journal of the Zionist Organization that had been founded by Theodor Herzl in 1897, and in 1921 he and Goldmann founded and edited in Heidelberg an independent Zionist paper that they named *Freie Zionistische Blätter,* and which, although short-lived, exerted considerable influence on Zionist thinking in Germany. Lacking organizational support, the journal folded in 1922, but the experience in journalistic writing it afforded young Goldmann proved to be invaluable and enabled him to obtain, aided by his uncle Szalkowitz, a commission from the New York Yiddish daily *Der Tog (The Day)* to write for it two or three articles monthly. This income enabled Goldmann to rent a house in Murnau, a small town on the Staffelsee near Garmisch-Partenkirchen in Bavaria, about an hour's distance from Munich. A neighboring cottage was occupied by Klatzkin, who at the time was working on the revision of his important book of Zionist theory, *Probleme des modernen Judentums* (Problems of Modern Judaism), whose title subsequently was changed at Goldmann's suggestion to *Krisis und Entscheidung* (Crisis and Decision).

Later, Goldmann was to recall that the two years he spent at Murnau "were among the most enjoyable and fruitful" of his life.[2] They also were the most crucial years of his intellectual growth and of the broadening of his Jewish horizon, under the guidance of Klatzkin, with whom he carried on hours of conversation day after day. As he later recalled, it was Klatzkin who introduced him to medieval religious philosophy, Kabbala, and Hasidism, and guided him in his reading on these subjects. At the same time, Goldmann branched out into other fields and engaged in what he later termed "a more searching investigation of mysticism." He read the prominent mystics of antiquity and spent a period in the monastery at Beuren, where several eminent experts on medieval Christian mysticism were assigned. His fascination with mystical apperception remained with him all his life, and as late as in 1969 he wondered whether his "propensity for mysticism may not camouflage some religious need."[3]

In 1980, returning to the subject of his lifelong interest in mysticism, Goldmann discussed the matter in more detail. He recalled that, throughout his life, he was rather skeptical of the possibility of reaching absolute truth by way of pure logic and through what he terms "the critique of apperception [*erkenntniskritisch*]," and was always "fascinated by other sources of experience and apperception, and, in the first place, by the mystical experience." If it was at all possible, he felt, to experience the absolute anywhere, it was in mysticism. On the other hand, he recalls that precisely in those years it became clear to him that there was a paradox in the mystical apperception, which was mirrored in the words of Meister Eckhardt who said that the true mystic must remain silent. Rational speech was incapable of reproducing adequately the experience of a great mystic, and "hence all mystical writings were basically nothing but stammering." The mystics spoke in similes and symbols, wherein lay both their fascination and difficulty.[4]

In addition to reading the works of the great mystics of antiquity and the Middle Ages, Goldmann embarked in Murnau on writing a treatise on the antinomy of the mystical experience. Although this undertaking never came to fruition, mysticism retained for him throughout his life the fascination of the unattainable.

As for the impression Klatzkin made on Goldmann, the most eloquent testimony is provided in Goldmann's own words, written almost half a century after the friendship between him and Klatzkin ripened in Murnau:

> He was a fascinating man, a most unusual mixture of Eastern European Jewish intellect and Western European thought. Except for one or two great Jewish scholars, I have never known anyone with such an extraordinary memory yet this faculty . . . was combined with an analytical sharpness that was the product of centuries of intellectual breeding and undoubtedly would have made him a foremost rabbinical authority had he stayed in Eastern Europe and remained an Orthodox Jew. (His father had been a great Talmudic scholar in Poland.) These brilliant qualities were complemented, as very rarely happens, by great artistic sensitivity, and Klatzkin was undoubtedly the greatest enricher of the Hebrew language in the field of philosophy in the past hundred years. . . . [5]

However, the remarkable thing about the relationship between Goldmann and Klatzkin is not the friendship itself between the youth and the man; nor the fact that Goldmann became Klatzkin's disciple in Judaism, Jewish history, philosophy, and Zionism; nor even the profound admiration of the younger man for Klatzkin's scholarship, personality, and brilliant mind. All this was almost inevitable, given the age difference between the two, the sensitivity and intellectual insatiability of Goldmann, the brilliance of Klatzkin's way of expounding his views, and his inexhaustible storehouse of knowledge in all fields of Jewish learning. What is truly unusual, and an eloquent testimony to Goldmann's mental maturity at an early age, as well as to the independence and steadfastness of his thinking, is the fact that, when it came to the cardinal point in Klatzkin's Zionist ideology that Goldmann could not accept, he remained opposed to him, refused to let himself be swayed by the views of his admired mentor, and continued to oppose him as long as Klatzkin lived.

The issue on which Klatzkin and Goldmann remained lifelong opponents was the future of the Diaspora. Klatzkin, generally recognized as one of the foremost Zionist ideologists, was the leading theoretical exponent of the school known as the "Negation of the Diaspora" (Hebrew: *Sh'lilat haGalut*). This school held that the Jewish people could not maintain a national existence in the Galut, exile, because the persistence of anti-Semitism and other external circumstances, as well as inner conditions, such as the decline of Jewish tradition and the spread of assimilation, have brought about an inevitable erosion of the substance of the Jewish community. Hence, the only way the Jewish people could be saved from disappearance was by gathering those who saw themselves as members of the Jewish nation in a country of their own.

To an extent, the Negation of the Diaspora was implicit in the thinking of the founding fathers of Zionism, beginning with those who led the *Hoveve Zion* (Lovers of Zion) movement in 1881–97. Herzl himself envisaged the Jewish State as a factor that would make assimilation easier for those Jews who wished to opt for it. The Second ʿAliya (wave of Jewish immigration to Palestine, 1904–14), which represented a major milestone in the development of post-Herzlian Zionism, was a practical expression of the Negation of the Diaspora in that its members sought to realize in their own lives the Zionist ideal of establishing a Jewish national existence in Palestine and negated the Diaspora by leaving it.

Klatzkin, like other Jewish thinkers, viewed the Jewish religion as the crucial factor in the survival of the Jews as a people in the Diaspora. He held that, so long as the Jewish religious framework was maintained, a full national and social life would be possible for those in the Diaspora because their Judaism itself served them as a substitute for state and country. Once the religious framework disintegrated, as it began to do with the onset of Emancipation and Enlightenment, Jewish life was bound to experience a national "degeneration," which would inevitably lead to the disappearance of the Jewish people. Cognizant of the major Jewish migration from Eastern Europe to the West—of which, incidentally, both Klatzkin and Goldmann's parents were part—Klatzkin held that whatever Jewish life still existed in Central and Western Europe and in America was due solely to the reinforcements the Jewish contingents in these parts of the world received from the East in the form of a steady stream of newcomers who replenished the waning numbers of Western Jewries and infused a Jewish religious-national consciousness into their thinning ranks. Although Klatzkin could not, of course, foresee the destruction of East European Jewry by the Nazi holocaust, he did envisage that ultimately the inexorable processes of assimilation would reach East European Jewry as well with fatal results.

In contrast to Aḥad Haʿam, who held that the creation of a Jewish spiritual center in Palestine would enable the Diaspora to survive because it would be nourished by cultural forces emanating from the *Yishuv*, Klatzkin maintained that the magnetism of the Jewish center in Palestine would attract all the dynamic Jewish national forces and thereby drain the Diaspora, weaken it, and hasten its demise. Anticipating by several decades Ben-Gurion's argument that the Zionist movement in the Diaspora was but a scaffolding destined to be dismantled once the edifice, the Jewish State, was completed, Klatzkin viewed the entire Diaspora as the temporary reservoir in whose existence the Zionist movement was interested only inasmuch as it needed to draw from it manpower and means for the upbuilding of the Jewish homeland in Palestine. He advocated the fostering of Jewish education and culture in the Diaspora, but saw in such efforts nothing more than temporary measures that would not prevent the ultimate disintegration of Diaspora Jewry. Consistent with these views, Klatzkin believed that the fight for Jewish minority rights in Eastern Europe, which was waged by Yitzḥaq Grünbaum, Leo Motzkin, and other Zionist leaders, was a futile and wasted effort.

One can imagine that Klatzkin, in his numerous and lengthy conversations with Goldmann, repeatedly and eloquently expounded these views to the young man whom he felt was a rising star on the horizon of the Zionist movement and whom he hoped to make into his disciple, not only in his concepts of Jewish history, culture, and values, but also in his political views of contemporary Jewish issues. And one can also envisage how difficult it was for young Goldmann, who had acknowledged Klatzkin as his master and mentor in all fields of Jewish culture, to resist succumbing to his influence precisely when it came to what for Klatzkin was the most crucial issue, his negative view of the Diaspora. Yet, difficult or not, Goldmann managed to do it.

However, in contrast to Klatzkin, who presented his doctrine of the Negation of the Diaspora in a detailed as well as logically and brilliantly argued discourse in book form, Goldmann's original counterarguments in defense of the future of Diaspora have not been preserved. What we do have are his memories of that "endless dialogue,"[6] as he called it in the late 1960s, and his reconstruction of his own thinking as he recalled it in 1980, some sixty years after the event.

Goldmann's recapitulation of Klatzkin's views furnishes a sense of the reverence he as a young man in his twenties had for Klatzkin. He terms Klatzkin "the most Zionist of all the thinkers in the movement, the only really hundred percent Zionist, who uncompromisingly pursued the basic concept to its conclusion as nobody else did."[7] After presenting Klatzkin's thesis, which, he says, was supported by "an extraordinary wealth of arguments from philosophy, psychology, and the history of ideas,"[8] he contraposits to it his own convictions, not based on anything resembling Klatzkin's polyhistoric erudition, but simply on his reading of Jewish history. The fact that the Jewish people survived not one, but several, dispersions, that they had lived for nineteen centuries in Diasporas without a country of their own, led him to the conclusion that their history was unique and was characterized by a distinctive rhythm of its own, alternating between concentration and dispersal.[9] This historic oscillation between a preponderance of centripetal and centrifugal forces is brought about by the existence in the Jewish national character of two opposing psychological trends: the "instinct for dispersal," which has been "at least as strong as [the other instinct, that] for the Land of Israel and territorial concentration."[10]

Therefore, Goldmann was convinced that it was naive, and, worse than that, erroneous, to believe that the various dispersals were simply imposed upon the Jews through coercion and the superior power of the Gentiles. His credo was that "in the long run a people cannot be coerced, and despotism is never more than an episode."[11] Although historians may take exception to this bold generalization they probably would go along with the thought that immediately follows it, namely that "ultimately a people lives as it wants to live, and in some way [it] deserves its fate. . . . If a nation's impotence causes it to despair so that it can no longer muster the revolutionary spirit it needs to resist the enemy's apparently invincible superiority, it perishes, but this is a case of suicide, not murder."[12]

Goldmann was, and throughout his life remained, convinced that "the Diaspora fulfills some deep need of the Jewish spirit or of the collective Jewish soul." Although conceding that there was always present in the Jewish people "a yearning for the homeland, a longing to be left alone with God and [its] culture," at the same time the Jews were possessed of the "roving, adventurous spirit of a world people." This is why Jewish history has always shifted back and forth "between the two poles of the Land of Israel and the Diaspora."[13]

Thus Goldmann was led to the conclusion that was to dominate his thinking and his work throughout his life: "Our situation cannot really be normalized by assembling a small portion of the people in Palestine and writing off the rest. I cannot accept the desirability of our becoming just a nation like all the rest, relinquishing the openness of the world and the global breadth of our outlook that characterize us today. If the Diaspora could survive along with the Jewish center, this would make our little country, which is destined to remain forever small, distinctive, and unique."[14]

Goldmann considered his concept of the mutuality between Israel and the Diaspora so basic in his philosophy of Jewish history that in his 1980 German autobiography he repeated almost verbatim the entire argument he had marshaled against Klatzkin's thesis in the early 1920s, which he had already presented in detail in 1969. In both versions he, seemingly inadvertently, switches from the past to the present and back again, so that in fact he seems to expound not so much the original views of the youthful disciple in his twenties he was in Murnau, but a reformulation of the same views sifted through the experience of a man who had fought for Jewish rights and existence in the arena of international politics for more than half a century.

He states that since he does not believe (present tense) that there are laws in historical events, he rejected (past tense) Klatzkin's thesis that the Jewish communities in the Diaspora had no future, because peoples without a homeland could not endure. He reminded Klatzkin that the history of the Jewish people was unique, and that, in contrast to other peoples, they had survived not one but several Diasporas. He argued that Jewish history consisted of a back and forth, of alternate shifts, between territorial concentration and dispersion. There was in the Jewish national character an instinct, or impulse, for dispersion, which was just as strong as the Jewish yearning for Eretz Israel and territorial concentration. Hence he believed in the 1920s, and still believed fifty and sixty years later, that the Diaspora corresponded to a deep yearning of the Jewish spirit, of the "collective Jewish soul." The Jews went into the Diaspora of their own free will, just as they created for themselves the ghetto voluntarily in order to survive in the Diaspora. They have the impulse to go out into the world; they are a "global people," finding pleasure in adventure. At the same time, they are possessed by a yearning for the homeland, for being alone with their God and culture.

Goldmann therefore came to the conclusion that the normalization of the Jewish condition could not consist of the ingathering of part of the Jewish people in Palestine accompanied by a renunciation to the other parts. This would mean that the Jews would become like all other peoples, without the world-wide openness and the global horizon which have characterized them until today, and this was a prospect which did not appear desirable to him. Only if both the Diaspora and the Jewish center continue to exist will the Jewish community in Palestine—inevitably destined to remain small—be endowed with a uniqueness and singularity.

As against this argument Klatzkin asked how could the Diaspora communities, after emancipation and the opening up of the ghettos, preserve their intellectual specificity and maintain their connection with the Jewish state? In reply Goldmann pointed to the historical reality of the Jewish condition and the uniqueness of Jewish autonomy in the Diaspora, which he considered a magnificent expression of the Jewish national genius.

In both of his books Goldmann gives an identical account of an argument he remembered having often used in his discussions with Klatzkin. "Suppose," he said, "a Jacob Klatzkin had been living after the destruction of the Second Temple and the so-called expulsion of the Jews from Palestine. He would have proved with all your logical brilliance that there was no hope of their surviving as a people after the loss of their national and religious center." Perhaps there was indeed such a Klatzkin who wrote a book as splendid as Klatzkin's own *Crisis and Decision*. But if he did exist, no trace of him has survived. For whatever is detrimental to its existence, the people often erases from its memory, just as the individual does with hurtful things. Memory is an instrument for self-preservation. The fact remains that the Jewish people survived, because despite all the so-called historical laws it had an indomitable will to survive, and it brought forth life forms which made its continued existence possible.

From this Goldmann concluded that something similar would again happen once the Jewish state existed. The Jewish people would find some new form for the continuation of the intimate, fateful relationship between the state and the people, between the center and the periphery, and therewith would acquire the spiritual strength needed to safeguard the continued existence of the Diaspora. His final conclusion was that what he termed the normalization of the Jewish condition required the creation of, not only a state, but of a center in Palestine, with the preservation of the Diaspora which will be tied to the state in an enduring, fruitful, reciprocal relationship. This, he believed even in 1980, was one of the most important problems of Jewish existence, for without mutual solidarity between Israel and the Diaspora neither of them could survive.[15]

Whether or not this thesis was fully expounded by Goldmann in his Murnau dialogues with Klatzkin, it is evident that throughout his life he not only subscribed to it, but attributed it to his early efforts to oppose Klatzkin and to formulate his own pro-Diaspora philosophy.

One more point must be made in connection with Goldmann's stand on the "Affirmation of the Diaspora." One cannot help gaining the impression that, underlying his global concept of the Jewish people, his emotional, though not political, identification with the Diaspora is somewhat stronger than his solidarity with Israel. This is suggested by his statement in the 1969 formulation, repeated almost verbatim in 1980, that "the Jews' survival throughout the Diaspora represents a unique achievement of national instinct for self-preservation and the national genius—perhaps its most impressive achievement of all time."[16] This statement seems to underlie the concluding paragraph in his first reconstruction from memory of his pro-Diaspora argument in his discussions with Klatzkin which, too, is repeated very closely in 1980. In 1969 he wrote:

> We shall find some new way of continuing the intimate, fatal relationship between the state and the people, the center and the periphery, and thus acquire the spiritual strength necessary to guarantee the survival of the Jewish communities in the Diaspora. The situation of the Jews will never be normalized through a state alone, but only by creating a center in Palestine while at the same time retaining the great Diaspora, linked with the state in an enduring and mutually enriching relationship.[17]

What one misses in this credo is a reference to the survival of the Jewish population in Israel. To be precisely balanced, the reference to the "spiritual strength" that will be derived from "continuing the intimate, fateful relationship" between the state and the people should have read: "and thus acquire the spiritual strength necessary to guarantee the survival *of the State of Israel and* of the Jewish community in the Diaspora." The omission of the words I added in italics cannot be due to a belief that the State of Israel would survive even without "the intimate, fateful relationship" between it and the Diaspora. Goldmann is well known for believing that, without the continued existence of the Diaspora and the "intimate, fateful relationship" between it and Israel, the existence of the latter would be in jeopardy. Hence, the only explanation of the omission is that, when presenting his argument for the imperative of the "intimate, fateful relationship" between Israel and the Diaspora, his primary, but of course not his sole, concern was about the Diaspora. Subsequently, in the 1969 autobiography, as if to rectify the omission, he writes that the creation of the State of Israel has "by no means solved" the question of Jewish survival, and that "there still lies ahead the great task of forging between Israel and the Jewish people outside it a bond that will guarantee the survival of both, in keeping with the unique character of their past."[18]

On a factual rather than theoretical level, Goldmann's closer affinity with the Diaspora becomes evident from having elected, throughout his long career in the service of the Jewish people, never to become a permanent resident of Israel (though he acquired a spacious apartment in Jerusalem that was at his disposal on his frequent visits to the country), as well as from his refusal to accept a position, even a very high one, in the Israeli government.

It is difficult to establish from the present time-distance how precisely Goldmann formulated his pro-Diaspora argument in his Murnau debates with Klatzkin in the 1920s. However, one indication shows that at the time those discussions took place Goldmann's thinking on the relationship between the Jewish population of Palestine and the Jews of the Diaspora had become crystallized more or less in the form in which it was to remain the central tenet in his thought and work throughout his life. In 1919, or three or four years before the Murnau interlude, he had published a thirty-two page pamphlet entitled *Die drei Forderrungen des jüdischen Volkes* (The Three Demands of the Jewish People).[19] This political treatise was his exposition of, and commentary on, the so-called Copenhagen Manifesto, the appeal issued by the Copenhagen Bureau of the World Zionist Organization on October 28, 1918, setting forth the demands of the Jewish people to be addressed to the Paris Peace Conference, which was to convene on January 18, 1919. The manifesto stressed the fact that lasting peace could be achieved only when the just demands of all peoples, whether great or small, were fulfilled, and when every nation was given the opportunity to develop its potential in the service of mankind. Specifically, the manifesto enumerated three demands of the Jewish people:

1. The confirmation of Palestine in its historical boundaries as the National Home of the Jewish people, and the creation of conditions necessary for its unhindered development.

2. The granting of full equality to Jews in all countries.

3. The granting of national autonomy, culturally, socially, and politically, to the Jewish population in countries of Jewish mass settlement (that is, in Eastern Europe) and in all other countries where the Jewish population might demand it.

In the pamphlet, Goldmann fully expounded the rationale of the three demands. He begins with the statement that, in the war which had just ended, the Jewish people had been recognized as a people, and that all peoples had acknowledged that the Jewish people had the right to come to them with demands and to decide their own future. Until the war, the characteristic feature of the Diaspora was that Jewry was merely the *object* of the historical process. The recognition of the rights of the Jewish people has changed their status from being an object to being a *subject* of history. Therewith, internally and ideologically, the Galut-status has been overcome even before the rebuilding of a new Jewish Palestine.[20]

Then Goldmann goes on to assert that the transformation which has taken place in Jewry during the preceding several decades, and especially during the war, can be termed the *nationalization of the Jewish people.* Among the factors that had brought about this transformation were the American Jewish Congress movement in the United States, whose Jewry has become a leader of the Jewish people everywhere; and the trauma and politicization of Russian Jewry in the wake of its terrible sufferings during the first years of the war.[21] These events and factors have prepared the ground for the three demands that are common to all Jewry.

The first demand, that of a Jewish Palestine, is based on the fact that the Jews are the Palestinian people of history. Palestine must become the center of the Jewish people. It will not bring about the disappearance of the Diaspora because that constitutes an essential part of the Jewish mode of existence in history, but it will result in a change in its character: it will no longer be Galut (exile) because it will have its historical center in an independent Jewish country. Moreover, the problem of the Jewish cultural situation can only be solved in Palestine.[22]

The second demand is that of Jewish national autonomy in the Diaspora, which means an affirmation of the Diaspora. The Jews are a nation wherever they live and therefore can claim national rights wherever they reside. "Palestine and the Diaspora are the two forms of existence of the Jewish people. Palestine is the higher, purer, more harmonious form; the Diaspora the more problematic, more difficult, more specific. But the Jewish people constitute one unit *(Einheit)* in its two spheres of existence." It is a people *sui generis.*[23]

The third demand is that of emancipation. In the past, when emancipation was granted the Jews, it was granted them as human beings, as citizens, and the Jews were asked in exchange to give up everything specifically Jewish. The formula that governed the entire process of Jewish emancipation was: to the Jews as individuals—everything; to the Jews as a nation—nothing. But "now that we have become politicized, we demand a revision of emancipation, and we, as Jews, ask that we, recognized as the Jewish people, with the right of remaining Jewish, be emancipated."[24]

Going a significant step further, Goldmann writes: "We consider this issue an international one. Therefore we do not recognize that any state has the right to declare that its treatment of its Jewish population is an internal matter. The emancipation of each and every individual Jewish community of any country will, therefore, from now on be a concern of Jewry as a whole." This means that "the Jews will no longer live in the Diaspora as strangers, and that they say 'yes' to their form of existence in the Diaspora."

Goldmann concludes his argument by affirming that "we are always and everywhere parts of the Jewish people, carriers of its culture, members of its country, Palestine; and nevertheless everywhere also parts of the polity of the state in whose midst we live, members of our individual native lands with equal duties and equal rights."[25]

Goldmann was twenty-three-years old when he wrote this pamphlet. The tenets contained in it withstood the formidable onslaught of Klatzkin a few years later and were to remain Goldmann's credo throughout his life. For not only did he not succumb to Klatzkin's powerful, erudite, and logical Negation of the Diaspora, but he devoted throughout his life at least as much of his attention and energies to fighting for the survival of the Diaspora as he did to his Zionist and pro-Israel work. That is to say, it was on his ability to resist Klatzkin on this pivotal point that his entire Jewish orientation hinged, as well as the scope of his lifework. And it is perhaps equally as important that, in retrospect from a distance of more than half a century, it appeared to him that this crucial and enduring commitment of his life was finalized at that time, partly at least in response to Klatzkin's intellectual challenge.

One can envisage how Goldmann's career would have shaped up had he succumbed to Klatzkin's views about the demise of the Diaspora. He still would have achieved a position of leadership in the Zionist movement and would have become a leading statesman of Israel, but he certainly would not have become the unique representative and spokesman of world Jewry vis-à-vis the Gentiles that he was and that he took pride in being.

That all this did not happen was attributable not only to a maturity of thought quite unusual in such a young man, but also to a combination of traits that have remained characteristic of Goldmann throughout his life: a boundless self-assurance, an independence of will, and an unshakable belief in the rightness of his own views even if opposed by men of the keenest intellect, highest position, greatest influence, and most widely recognized leadership.

Goldmann's defiance of Klatzkin on this most crucial issue of the value, significance, and future of the Diaspora was a supreme test of will. That the friendship between the two men survived this contest not only shows the depth of their mutual attachment, but also proves the sterling quality of their character.

The Diaspora issue is of such importance that, leaving aside for a moment the personalities involved, it warrants, in conclusion, a few words on its own merits. The Negation of the Diaspora is the expression of a pessimistic and defeatist view of the Jewish future. If the Diaspora is doomed to extinction—whether due to the irresistible processes of assimilation as Klatzkin envisaged it, or to the recurrence of a Nazi-type holocaust as our generation has learned to fear—the entire future of the Jewish people will hinge on the continued existence of the State of Israel alone. Although all Jews, whether Zionist or not, fervently hope for the future security of Israel, the fact is that, during the course of the three millennia of Jewish history, the Jewish State was destroyed twice by the overwhelming power of its enemies, and it was only thanks to the unstinting and devoted support of the Diaspora that the small remnant which was left in the country managed to survive.

Had there been no Diaspora, there would have been no return to Zion under Cyrus; there would have been no rebuilding of the Temple of Jerusalem and no second Jewish commonwealth on the ancestral soil; and, after the Roman Exile of 70 C. E., there would have been no faithful communities, first in Babylonia and around the Mediterranean, and later, in other, more remote, parts of the world, to preserve the loyalty to the land of Zion and Jerusalem, to remember it and pray for its restoration in the daily prayers, and to be ready to return when the opportunity at last presented itself. And, quite apart from this hypothetically incontestable negative outcome, there would have been none of the rich cultural developments that were experienced by the Jews in the various countries of their dispersion. There would have been no Jewish flowering in Hellenistic Alexandria, no Jewish Golden Age in Spain, no Kabbala, no halakhic codes, no Jewish religious philosophy, no Hasidism, no Jewish enlightenment, no Zionism, and no rebuilt Israel. The destruction of Jerusalem by the Romans would have been the end of the Jewish people.

By the same token, the disappearance, for whatever reason, of the Diaspora in our days or in the near future would mean that, should Israel go under, as it did twice in its history, the millennial existence of the Jews would come to an end. Despite all our love for Israel and our prayerful hope that it will thrive and enjoy a secure and glorious future, the possibility that Jewish survival as a whole should depend on Israel alone is frightening. If one were religious, one would argue that the very survival of the Jewish people in the past, despite two destructions of their homeland, is a manifestation of the divine will that the Jews should survive even if their country falls. Hence, however total one's commitment to Israel, one must hope and work for the survival of the Jewish people in the Diaspora. Viewed in this light, the Affirmation of the Diaspora, in contrast to its Negation, is a powerful positive doctrine, the position that, above everything else, the survival of the Jewish people, irrespective of their places of residence, must be the primary and overriding concern for every Jewish leader, movement, and endeavor.

I cannot know how many of these thoughts were entertained or formulated by young Nahum Goldmann when he established his own pro-Diaspora position in opposition to Klatzkin's Negation of the Galut. But all of them are at least implied in the Affirmation of the Diaspora, of which Goldmann was destined to become the foremost and most eloquent expositor. And it was due to this one central concept that he became the modern Jewish political apostle to the Gentiles.

Part Two

Three Missions

6. Partition and Statehood

I Goldmann's role in the partition of Palestine, which made the establishment of Israel possible, comprised two phases: his advocacy of partition, and his winning for it the support of Under Secretary of State Dean Acheson, and through him, of President Truman. The first phase stretched out over many years; the second required intensive concentration in the course of a few tense and fateful days.

The idea of the partition of Palestine into a Jewish and an Arab sector is almost as old as political Zionism itself, and it split the Zionist movement into two opposing camps for almost half a century like no other issue did. Herzl himself first broached the idea in his negotiations with Sultan Abdul Hamid II when, faced with objections on the part of the Sublime Porte to awarding the Zionist Organization a charter for a colonization company in the whole of Palestine, he asked for a concession for such settlement work "in Mesopotamia and in a small part of Palestine."[1] Subsequently, Jewish "colonization" in part of Palestine was on the Zionist agenda on and off for many years.

The Balfour Declaration of November 2, 1917, speaking of "the establishment in Palestine of a national home for the Jewish people" seemed to have left open the question of whether all, or merely part, of Palestine was envisaged as the planned Jewish national home. However, Balfour's own interpretation was clearly that his declaration covered the territory on both banks of the Jordan. On June 26, and again on August 11, 1919, he wrote to Prime Minister David Lloyd George: "In determining the Palestine frontiers the main thing to keep in mind is to make a Zionist policy possible by giving the fullest scope to economic development in Palestine. . . . Palestine should extend into the lands lying east of the Jordan." As late as February 1921, T. E. Lawrence, who had played a leading role in shaping British Middle East policy, told Professor (later Sir) Lewis B. Namier, the historian and Zionist leader, that the intention had been "to include Transjordan in Palestine, to make it indistinguishable from Palestine, and to open it to Jewish Immigration." This was confirmed in 1937 by the Royal (Peel) Commission (see below), which, on the basis of official documentation and testimony, stated authoritatively that "the field in which the Jewish National Home was to be established was understood, at the time of the Balfour Declaration, to be the whole of historic Palestine," that is, including Transjordan.[2]

On April 25, 1920, the Supreme Council of the Allied Powers awarded the Mandate over Palestine on both banks of the Jordan River to Great Britain. The Churchill White Paper of June 1922, again vague in its wording, insisted that the intention of the Balfour Declaration was not "the imposition of a Jewish nationality upon the inhabitants of Palestine as a whole." Although the Zionist leaders regarded this as a whittling down of the declaration, they had no choice but to acquiesce in it. A month later came the publication of a revised draft of the Palestine Mandate that included Article 25, entitling the Mandatory "to postpone or withhold application of such provisions of the Mandate as he may consider inapplicable to the existing local conditions. . . . in the territories lying between Jordan [river] and the Eastern boundary of Palestine." In April 1923 Britain recognized the existence of an independent government in Transjordan. Thus, the original Palestine of the Mandate was partitioned into the Emirate of Transjordan (containing 34,140 square miles) and (Western) Palestine (10,152 square miles). Again, the Zionist Executive reluctantly acquiesced, but the Revisionists, led by Vladimir Jabotinsky (1880–1940), refused to recognize the separation of Transjordan and, from 1925 on, made the demand for an "undivided Palestine" the cornerstone of their program.

The Seventeenth Zionist Congress, meeting in Basle from June 30 to July 17, 1931, passed a resolution about the "ultimate aims" *(Endziele)* of the Zionist movement. The resolution was submitted to the plenum of the congress by the Political Committee, in which Goldmann, for the first time in his Zionist political career, played an active part. It was he who presented to the congress the resolution whose crucial paragraph read (my translation from the German): "The 17th Zionist Congress declares . . . that the homeless, landless [Jewish] people, eager for emigration, wants to overcome its economic, spiritual, and political distress by striking roots again in its historical homeland through uninterrupted immigration and settlement, and to renew in the Land of Israel its national existence equipped with all the characteristics of a normal national life."[3]

The resolution suggests, in an indirect way, the Zionist goal of a Jewish State in the Land of Israel, but it does not touch upon the question of whether it claims the whole or part of the Land of Israel (that is, Palestine) for the Jewish national home.

However, beginning in 1932, proposals, first of a division of the remaining, western, part of Palestine into Jewish and Arab administrative units, and then of its political partition, were made by both the British and the Jews. Although the Arabs, with the sole exception of Emir Abdullah of Transjordan, were adamantly opposed to any partition of Palestine, the British vacillated on the issue. The Palestine Royal Commission, headed by Lord Peel, advocated it in 1937. The Woodhead Commission of 1938 advised against it and suggested two alternative plans, which envisioned a minuscule area for a Jewish province. The 1943 ministerial committee appointed by the Churchill government suggested the establishment of federated Jewish and Arab states. Three years later, the Anglo-American Committee of Inquiry of 1945 recommended the continuation of the British Mandate pending its replacement by a trusteeship under the United Nations. Later in the same year, the Morrison-Grady plan proposed the cantonization and federalization of Palestine under British trusteeship. And, finally, the United Nations Special Committee on Palestine (UNSCOP), after conducting inquiries in June–July 1947, issued a majority report recommending partition; a minority proposed a federated Jewish-Arab state. The Arabs rejected all these proposals and threatened armed resistance.

II   Although these various approaches to a solution of the Palestine problem were mooted by successive commissions, Goldmann, whose star was rapidly rising in the hierarchy of the World Zionist Organization, consistently advocated partition. In 1933, at the Eighteenth Zionist Congress, he was elected as a member of the Zionist Actions Committee and of the Jewish Agency Administrative Committee.[4] In 1935, at the Nineteenth Congress, he served as one of its vice-presidents and chaired several sessions. Most importantly, he was also elected as delegate of the Executive to the League of Nations, won a seat on the Executive itself, and gained the right to vote in matters pertaining to his office.[5] He was to remain as political representative of the World Zionist Organization at the League of Nations in Geneva until 1939.

The extent to which the Executive relied on Goldmann as its spokesman at the League of Nations is illustrated by a letter David Ben-Gurion, chairman of the Executive, sent to him from London on July 22, 1937. Ben-Gurion paints in this letter (see full text in appendix A) a detailed picture of the political situation in government circles in London, where wide opposition existed to the Peel partition plan, and details "the line the Executive decided to take before the [Permanent] Mandates Commission of the League": to warn it against adopting such "palliatives" as reduced immigration, which it may do in the hope of making partition more palatable to the Arabs; to demand that it protest against the small number of immigration certificates—8,000 for eight months—proposed by the British; and to insist that the commission must not reject the partition proposal.

Ben-Gurion's letter is interesting on several counts. It shows, first of all, his readiness to accept the Peel partition plan and to fight for modifications in it to make the proposed Jewish State better able to fill the needs of the Jewish people—in which position Goldmann was in full agreement with him. It shows his bitter opposition to those Jewish leaders—he calls them by the contemptuous term "Yahudim"—who from a misguided sense of either loyalty to England (Herbert Samuel and others) or a noble but irrealistic idealism (Judah L. Magnes, Moshe Smilansky, and their friends), were willing to sacrifice the chance of obtaining a Jewish State in Palestine. As for the relationship between Ben-Gurion as chairman of the Executive, and Goldmann, who was at the time only a junior member of it, the letter contains not a single word of instruction as to what the Executive wanted Goldmann to do in Geneva. It merely presents the "line" the Executive decided to take in response to the Peel plan. It leaves it entirely up to Goldmann how to proceed, whom to approach, and what arguments to use. It is the broadest possible guideline, within which Goldmann was free to do as he saw fit. All in all, the letter is an illustration of the high degree of independence he possessed in acting for the Executive already at the early stage of his career. Later, as he rose in the ranks, his mode of action was to become even more independent.

As the representative of the World Zionist Organization, Goldmann occupied a key position in the Zionist political arena. The League of Nations was the international body that in 1922 had approved the award of the Mandate for Palestine to Great Britain. It was the League's Permanent Mandates Commission that exercised supervisory power over Britain's compliance with the provisions of the Mandate and that was the responsible forum to which Great Britain had to submit its plan to terminate the Mandate by partitioning Palestine between Arabs and Jews. Incidentally, the Peel Commission's partition proposal (see below) was criticized by the League's Permanent Mandates Commission, but was reluctantly admitted as a possible solution of the Palestine problem. The task entrusted to Goldmann as the Geneva representative of the Zionists was therefore of crucial importance: to exert all possible influence on the League of Nations in general and its Permanent Mandates Commission in particular to accept and vote for the solution of the Palestine problem favored by the Zionist movement as organized into the World Zionist Organization and the Jewish Agency for Palestine.

Early in 1937, after Dr. Chaim Weizmann (1874–1952) had testified before the Peel Commission, on his return from Palestine he invited Goldmann to his hotel in Paris and told him in strictest confidence of a significant development that had taken place behind the scenes: Professor Reginald Coupland, a member of the commission, had asked him unofficially what he would think of solving the Palestine problem by partitioning the country into a Jewish and an Arab state. Weizmann had given no immediate answer to Coupland and sought Goldmann's opinion before going on to London to sound out his friends there.

Goldmann's reaction was unhesitating and total support of the partition idea. The only condition he advised Weizmann to attach to his consent was that the area to be allotted to the future Jewish State be adequate to permit large-scale immigration.[6]

Whether or not Goldmann's endorsement influenced Weizmann, at the next Zionist Congress, the Twentieth, held in Zurich from August 3 to 16, 1937, he did advocate the acceptance of partition.

The Jewish State, proposed in the July 7, 1937, report of the Peel Commission, was to comprise all of Galilee, the Jezreel Valley, and the coastal plains from the Lebanese frontier to the south of Ashdod, except for a sector around Jaffa that was to be included into a Jerusalem-Jaffa corridor and remain under British Mandate. The total land area the plan allocated to the Jewish State was about 2,600 square miles, or about 26 percent of western Palestine. However, the Palestine Arab leaders were unwilling to cede even this small part of Palestine to the Jews—though the latter constituted at the time about 28 percent of the total population of the country—and rejected it outright.

When the issue came up at the Twentieth Congress, the reaction was mixed. Menaḥem M. Ussishkin (1863–1941), head of the Jewish National Fund since 1923 and a powerful, uncompromising personality, was vehemently opposed to the partition plan, which he considered a "betrayal of historic Zionism." Also opposed to partition, but on entirely different grounds, was the B'rit Shalom ("Covenant of Peace") group, a small organization founded in 1925 and headed by (or, more precisely, consisting of) a small number of leading Jewish intellectuals, such as Samuel Hugo Bergmann, Rabbi Binyamin, Arthur Ruppin, Ḥayim Kalvariski-Margolis, and Gershom Scholem, and supported by Judah L. Magnes and Martin Buber. The B'rit Shalom, which had no Arab counterpart, advocated a binational Jewish-Arab state.[7] Another opponent of partition was Berl Katzenelson (1887–1944), respected founder and editor of *Davar*, the influential daily of the Palestinian Jewish workers' movement.

Among the American Zionists, the most eloquent opponent of partition was Rabbi Stephen S. Wise (1874–1949), a towering figure, strong personality, and masterful orator, who served as one of the vice-presidents of the congress. Also Louis Brandeis (1856–1941), the revered dean and mentor of American Zionists, was against partition, as were others who reiterated, in varying formulations, the basic argument that the Jewish people could not renounce their historic right to any part of their homeland.

The propartition forces were led by Chaim Weizmann, president of the World Zionist Organization and the Jewish Agency, and by far the most respected and influential of all Zionist leaders. However, he himself had so many serious reservations about the partition scheme of the Peel Commission that, though his final conclusion was that the plan should be accepted by the congress, he was unable to formulate his arguments forcefully enough to win for them a majority in the deeply troubled and divided congress. Also David Ben-Gurion (1886–1973)—labor leader and chairman of the Executive of the Jewish Agency in Palestine from 1935 to 1948, when he became the first prime minister of Israel—argued for the partition plan on the ground that an independent Jewish State, even in a greatly reduced area, would afford a refuge to European Jewry, whose very existence was then menaced by Nazi Germany.

The most outspoken advocate of partition at the Twentieth Congress was Nahum Goldmann. In an impassioned midnight speech, he contended that it was the only way to bring a large number of immigrants to Palestine and to achieve the age-old dream of a Jewish State of which Herzl had said 35 years earlier, "If you will it, it is not a dream." At one point in his address, Goldmann resorted, as was his wont, to telling a story, or, rather, a conversation he had some months earlier with the unnamed foreign minister of a likewise unnamed country, who, he said, was no particular friend of the Jews. The minister asked him how many immigrants the Jews intended to bring into Palestine during the next two decades. Goldmann answered, "About a million-and-a-half to two million." The minister gave a start and said, "If there will be two million Jews in Palestine, you will be the strongest factor in the Near East."[8] An immigration of this order of magnitude, Goldmann was convinced, could be brought about only if the Jews had a country of their own in Palestine, and, if the price of it was partition, the movement must pay it.

However, even the combined persuasive powers of Goldmann, Weizmann, Ben-Gurion, and the others who favored acceptance of partition were of no avail against the formidable forces of opposition. The vote, albeit a close one, went against them and the congress went on record against the partition of Palestine. The advocates of partition could obtain only one concession from their opponents: the Executive was empowered to negotiate with the British government to clarify the specific terms of the British proposal to establish a Jewish state in Palestine.[9]

III Looking back on this Congress resolution three decades later, Goldmann recalled that he was in favor of the partition idea "provided the area allotted to us would permit large-scale immigration. I have held to this opinion ever since, and when the war ended, I was the first to revive the partition plan and get it accepted by the Zionist movement and the American government. If there has been a tragedy in the history of Zionism, it is the fact that largely through our fault partition was not put into effect the first time it was suggested, in 1937."[10]

Goldmann saw a tragic connection between the rejection of partition in 1937 and the annihilation of a major part of Jewry by Hitler: "If the Zionist movement had accepted the proposal then, spontaneously and without delay, it is quite conceivable that it might have been implemented. We would then have had two years' time before war broke out, and a country to which hundreds of thousands, possibly millions, of European Jews might have escaped."[11]

And Goldmann went on to explain that "the Zionist movement's attitude toward this first partition plan was a major sin of our generation, second only to world Jewry's inadequate reaction to the Nazi peril and its irresponsible belief that Hitler would never carry out his threats. One of the motives that later led me to revive the idea of partition was the awareness that we ourselves bear some of the guilt for the annihilation of one third of our people."[12]

The point only alluded to in this last sentence was made clear by

Goldmann in one of my interviews with him at Paris in the summer of 1980. As he explained it, he had felt that, if a Jewish State had existed at the time World War II broke out, it would have been able to absorb many Jews who perished under the Nazi onslaught only because no country was ready to admit them. But, of course, in the summer of 1937 few Jewish leaders could envisage the holocaust, and thus people of such disparate views and orientations as Menaḥem Ussishkin, Berl Katzenelson, Louis Brandeis, and Stephen Wise were united in their opposition to partition.

As for the motives behind the opposition to partition, they were the same in 1937 as in 1945 and 1946: an "inability to compromise, determination to hold on to every inch of Palestine as something historically sacred, the obstinacy and fanaticism of a persecuted people that for two thousand years had set beliefs and ideals above reality and practical necessity, an unwillingness to recognize that a people not content with waiting, hoping, and having faith must reckon with realities, even if this means sacrificing some cherished historic ideas as a means towards shaping its own destiny."[13]

What Goldmann does not say in this context, but what emerges with unmistakable clarity from his entire lifework, is that he valued the Jewish *people* infinitely higher than the preconceived image of a Jewish *state*, and that he believed the state was merely a means for securing the survival of the people. This is why he considered it a tragedy and a sin not to have accepted the British offer of a Jewish state even in a part of Palestine, when even a small Jewish state could have saved many Jews from perdition.

Although Goldmann was strongly in favor of partition as early as 1937, during the early war years he went along with Weizmann in opposing any official demand for a Jewish State. This stand on his part was merely tactical. He "had always been convinced that a sovereign state in Palestine was the only possible solution, and that it was just a matter of waiting for the right moment to make the demand." The holocaust, in Europe, convinced him that the time had come to prepare public opinion for the idea of a Jewish State, or, in the more flexible phrase the Zionist leadership used in America, a "Jewish commonwealth."[14]

In the spring of 1940, Goldmann left Geneva and moved with his wife and two sons, aged three and five, to America. After an exciting and perilous Atlantic crossing on the USS *Washington,* they arrived in New York on June 21, 1940. In the United States, Goldmann threw himself into the two interconnected tasks that were to remain his paramount concern for many years: to save European Jewry from destruction, and to solve "the Palestine problem." Tragically, he could do very little to achieve the first, but his role in obtaining partition and the establishment of a Jewish State was considerable. Considering that he was an outsider, and, in fact, a war refugee from Europe, Goldmann's rise to top rank of leadership in American Zionism was phenomenal in its rapidity.

During the first three war years, the issue of the partition of Palestine and the establishment of a Jewish State lay dormant. All Jewish efforts were, of necessity, concentrated on saving the Jews of the Continent, whose doom became increasingly clear as the war progressed. The saddest pages in Goldmann's 1969 *Autobiography* are those in which he describes his futile efforts in conjunction with other Jewish leaders to rescue Jews from the Nazi clutches. He writes, "Despite our efforts, only an infinitesimal number of Jews could be saved." And again, "However, I failed in these efforts." The stories he tells about his attempts to make a dent in the rigidity of Cordell Hull, Sumner Welles, and other high American officials are often heartbreaking. These experiences hardened in him the resolve to fight with all his ability for the establishment of the Jewish State as soon as the war came to an end.[15]

A major step in this direction was taken at the Extraordinary Conference of American Zionists, held in New York on May 9–11, 1942. It was convened by the American Emergency Committee for Zionist Affairs, consisting of a group of prominent leaders of the major American Zionist bodies—the Zionist Organization of America, Hadassah, the Labor Zionists, and Mizrahi—for the purpose of promulgating a definitive plan for the postwar solution of the Palestine problem. The work of the conference, in which Goldmann took an active part, culminated in the Biltmore Program (so called after the hotel in New York in which the conference took place), whose most important point was "that Palestine be established as a Jewish Commonwealth integrated in the structure of the new democratic world."[16]

In retrospect, it would seem that even a motion to accept the more modest aim of partition and a Jewish State in part of Palestine would have been carried. In 1937 Hitler was merely a serious menace to German Jewry; in 1942 the Nazi holocaust was in full swing over most of Europe. The time to hold out for bigger and better things in the future had definitely passed, and the burning issue was how to save those Jews who were being crushed by the German juggernaut. Under these conditions, partition would probably have been accepted, and the adoption of a resolution calling for a Jewish State in all of Palestine was a foregone conclusion.

With the Biltmore Program, the Zionist movement officially went on record as demanding the establishment of a Jewish State in the whole of Palestine. This program was quickly ratified by all branches of the Zionist movement, thus, in effect, acquiring the validity of a resolution of a Zionist Congress.

IV The next logical step was to obtain the support of the non-Zionist Jews for the Biltmore Program. When the American Jewish Committee, at the time the most influential Jewish organization in America, refused to subscribe to the Biltmore Program, Chaim Weizmann, Stephen Wise, Louis Lipsky, and Goldmann conceived the idea of organizing an overall Jewish representative body on a democratic basis for the purpose of formulating and carrying out an action program to meet the problems that would confront the Jewish people during the postwar era in Europe and Palestine. At their initiative, Henry Monsky (1890–1947), president of B'nai B'rith, invited thirty-two national Jewish organizations to send their representatives to a preparatory meeting that was held in Pittsburgh, on January 23–24, 1943. This was followed on August 29 by the conference at New York, in which delegates representing sixty-four national Jewish organizations, whose members numbered some 2,250,000, participated. Goldmann "reported on the Palestine problem, and voiced the demand for a Jewish commonwealth."[17] An emotional debate ensued, but, after an impassioned plea on behalf of the commonwealth, the conference adopted a pro-commonwealth resolution, whereupon the American Jewish Committee, led by Judge Proskauer, withdrew from the conference (see below). This, incidentally, was one of the few instances of forceful and effective cooperation between Goldmann and Abba Hillel Silver.

On May 15, 1943, Goldmann was appointed as head of the political office established by the Jewish Agency in Washington.[18] The mandate given him was spelled out in a detailed letter (see Appendix B) Chaim Weizmann wrote to him on June 23, 1943. Although the letter states that Goldmann and Louis Lipsky (1876–1963), the longtime American Zionist leader, were to be in charge of the Washington office, Lipsky's duties kept him mostly in New York, so that, in effect, Goldmann alone was in charge of the agency's political work in Washington.

To this work in Washington (and subsequently in San Francisco, see below) Goldmann brought his experience of many years in Geneva, and the friendly relations he had established there with the representatives of many countries at the League of Nations. In America he was greatly helped by Stephen Wise, who had been his close friend ever since their joint efforts in 1935 to establish the World Jewish Congress.

On the other hand, the relationship between Goldmann and Silver deteriorated after the establishment of the Jewish Agency's political office in Washington. When the agency decided on setting up this office, there had been in that city (since January 1942) an office of the American Zionist Emergency Council (AZEC). It was the coordinating body of the American Zionist organizations established in 1939, and its Washington office, like that of the Jewish Agency, was initiated by Weizmann, who felt that the Zionist political and public relations work in Washington should be broadened and contact with State Department circles intensified. During his visit to America in 1943, Weizmann explained to the American Zionist leadership that the Executive of the Jewish Agency felt the need for an official representation in the capital, whose role in world affairs and in the Middle East was rapidly on the increase.

Wise and most members of the AZEC supported this decision, but Silver opposed it energetically, arguing that the setting up of the agency's political office contravened the decision of the AZEC to the effect that there should be only one Zionist political representation in Washington. Weizmann did not succeed in swaying Silver, whose antagonism increased when Goldmann was appointed as head of the agency's office in Washington. Silver saw in this a slight of both his authority and his person.

The inner Zionist difficulties in connection with the establishment of the agency's Washington office were paralleled by the initially negative reaction on the part of the State Department. Wallace Murray, former head of the department's Office for Near Eastern and African Affairs and at the time political adviser to the department, sent a memorandum to the secretary of state in which he suggested that no official recognition be given to the new office of the Jewish Agency; and that Dr. Goldmann, Mr. Louis Lipsky, or any other representative of the Jewish Agency, be received as usual, but that, if they came to submit a statement to the State Department in the name of the Jewish Agency, they should be asked to do so through the British embassy.

The differences between the Silver faction and the Jewish Agency, as represented by Goldmann, smoldered for several months until, on September 12, 1944, they came to a head in an executive meeting of the

Zionist Organization of America, to which Goldmann was invited. Emanuel Neumann, who took an active part in the work of the AZEC political office and was the first lieutenant of Silver in the movement, argued that the interests of Zionism were damaged by the existence of two offices in Washington, and demanded that the agency's office (that is, Goldmann) should restrict its activities to contact with foreign embassies and economic affairs. Goldmann, in his response, emphasized that the Jewish Agency had never recognized the right of any local Zionist organization to conduct political work that was of concern for the whole movement. The AZEC should, he said, deal with Zionist public relations in non-Jewish Washington, obtain the support of senators and congressmen, maintain contact with the press, and distribute material on Zionist subjects. But, as for the political negotiations with governments, including that of the United States, these must be conducted only by the Jewish Agency. No understanding was reached in this meeting, and the lack of unity in the American Zionist ranks continued to trouble the movement for the next two years.[19]

In the meantime, Goldmann continued his independent political work in American government circles. On June 20, 1945, he met with Loy W. Henderson, director of the Office of Near Eastern and African Affairs of the State Department, and two of his aides. Goldmann explained that now that the war, in which millions of Jews were slaughtered, was over, the survivors were near desperation, and, unless an early solution was found for the Palestine problem, the Jewish youth in Palestine was ready to take up arms in defense of their rights. On the American Zionist front, too, the danger existed that the politics of extremists, such as Silver, could win approval. The only way to avoid these trends was to adopt a favorable solution in Palestine (see Appendix C). Two days later, Henderson, in a memorandum (Appendix D) informed Acting Secretary of State Joseph C. Grew of Goldmann's presentation, and on June 27, 1945, according to yet another State Department memorandum, "Dr. Goldmann brought Mr. Ben-Gurion and Mr. [Eliezer] Kaplan to meet Mr. Henderson and to discuss the Palestine question" (see Appendix E). Next day, Grew himself met with Goldmann, Wise, Greenberg, and Shulman.[20]

In August 1945, at the meeting of the Executive in London, Silver again demanded that all political work in Washington be concentrated in one single office, that of the AZEC. Weizmann, Ben-Gurion, and several American Zionist leaders objected to this suggestion, and a lengthy and tense discussion ensued. At the end, Silver, Wise, and Lipsky were made members of the Executive, so that, together with Goldmann, the number of the American members of the Executive was increased to four. It was also decided that these four, together with four other Americans—Israel Goldstein, Leon Gellman, Chaim Greenberg, and Rose Halprin—should constitute a "Committee of Eight," entrusted with the conduct of the agency's political activities in the United States, subject to the control of the entire Executive. Silver was elected as chairman of the committee, but because Goldmann was left in charge of the agency's Washington office, Silver remained dissatisfied with this arrangement.[21]

The appointment by the Executive of Eliahu Epstein (Elath), an expert on Arab affairs, in May 1945, as adviser to the representatives of the agency at the San Francisco meetings of the United Nations (see below), and his arrival in America had strengthened the agency's position in its differences with Silver. Goldmann not only welcomed Epstein, but suggested that he remain in America for six months or longer. This suggestion was supported by Wise, Lipsky, and Greenberg, as well as by Eliezer Kaplan (who was in America at the time). On July 2, 1945, at a meeting of the Jewish Agency in New York, at which Ben-Gurion, Goldmann, Kaplan and Lipsky were present, it was decided to appoint Epstein for one year as director of the agency's Washington office, to serve under Goldmann, and to strengthen the political work of the agency in Washington. As Epstein wrote: "My friendly relations with Dr. Nahum Goldmann and the nearness of our ideas on the basic issues of Zionist politics served as a good foundation for our joint activities throughout the period in which Goldmann was in charge, in behalf of the Agency Executive of our political work in Washington."[22]

V Once the war was over, Goldmann felt that the time was ripe to embark on an energetic action program for achieving the ultimate aim of the partition of Palestine and the establishment of the Jewish State in part of it. On and off, he had advocated this program for many years. Now, however, the time had come to tackle and eliminate the numerous obstacles that blocked the way. This meant (not necessarily in this chronological order): to convince the Jewish Agency Executive that the Biltmore Program, by which it still felt bound, was unworkable, and that the agency must opt for partition instead; to convince the Zionist Congress, whenever it would be convened, of the same; to persuade the American government and the president to support the partition plan; to persuade the British government to accept it; and to obtain the support of Russia and of the United Nations for the partition of Palestine. A Jewish State could be established only if Goldmann was successful in *all* these tasks, each one of which was a formidable undertaking. Taken together, and carried out as they were within the relatively short time of two years, they required a stupendous expenditure of energy; constant air travel from continent to continent and from country to country; innumerable, long, tense, and difficult meetings with Jewish and world leaders who not only all had strong minds and preconceived notions of their own but also were not easy to influence; and a supreme confidence in his own judgment that enabled him to pit his will and convictions against those of dozens of men who held opposing positions.

Although on February 27, 1945, Prime Minister Winston Churchill announced in Parliament that the Palestine question would not be on the agenda of the Conference on International Organizations to be convened in San Francisco (April 25–June 26, 1945), whose sole task would be to prepare the United Nations Charter, it was evident that the trusteeship clauses of the projected charter would have a bearing on the Palestine problem. The Jewish Agency submitted a memorandum to the conference calling, in accordance with the Biltmore Program, for the reconstitution of "Palestine as a free and democratic Jewish Commonwealth." All the American Zionist and pro-Zionist organizations engaged in intense deliberations on how to utilize the international gathering for the purpose of furthering their cause.

Because the Jewish Agency was a nongovernmental organization, its representatives could act only unofficially, outside the conference itself.[23] The chief representative of the Jewish Agency at the conference was Nahum Goldmann, ably assisted by Eliahu Epstein (Elath). During the two months in which the conference was in session, Goldmann was practically a commuter between San Francisco and New York (and Washington). From a detailed diary Epstein kept of the events of those two months, a picture can be formed of Goldmann's activities in connection with the conference. He met almost daily with many of the representatives of the fifty nations participating, and because the agency was accorded no official status, his credentials were not as important in these meetings as was his personal ability to win the confidence of his interlocutors and to convince them of the justness of the Jewish cause.

Among the delegates with whom Goldmann conferred was Charles Malik, the Lebanese representative, to whom Goldmann explained the Zionists' "desire to establish friendly relations with the Palestinian Arabs and the rest of the Arab world, most especially with our neighboring countries, on the basis of mutual trust, understanding, and cooperation." Because Malik, a Christian Arab, was a philosopher, the conversation moved to philosophical topics, including Bergson's concept of the ethics and the modern school of theology in Europe and America.[24]

Among the other delegates with whom Goldmann conducted negotiations in San Francisco were Ambassador Paul-Emile Naggiar, the French representative on the Trusteeship Committee; Sinasi Hisar, legal counselor to the Turkish delegation; Mostafa Adle, chairman of the Iranian delegation; Jan Masaryk, of Czechoslovakia; and Stojan Gavrilovic, of Yugoslavia. Mindful of the German reparations issue, to which he was to turn his full attention in 1952, Goldmann suggested to Masaryk and Gavrilovic that the Czechoslovak and Yugoslav delegations issue a statement confirming their readiness to participate in an international agreement that would transfer to the Jewish people all, or certainly most, of the property belonging to heirless Jews murdered by the Nazis, to be used for the resettlement of holocaust survivors in Palestine. "Goldmann pointed out the public importance of such an announcement, as it would encourage other states where Jews suffered under the Nazi occupation to follow the lead of Czechoslovakia and Yugoslavia. Masaryk at once agreed to issue such a statement during the Conference, and Gavrilovic promised to cable to Belgrade seeking permission to do so. Masaryk was greatly moved throughout our talk."[25]

With Viscount Cranborne, the British representative on the Trusteeship Committee, who was viewed as a friend of Zionism, Goldmann took a firm line. He told Cranborne, "We have waited five years [during the war]. We had to wait, we had no choice. . . . But now the war is over. We have lost six million Jews. We have no more to lose. If Great Britain will not reach an acceptable solution . . . in the next six months . . . five million Jews in the United States will become the Irishmen of America, and 600,000 Jews in Palestine will begin to shoot."[26]

In one of his periodic reports to the AZEC, which he had to fly back to New York to deliver, Goldmann stressed that, though the aim of the Zionists was to establish a Jewish State, which implied the liquidation of the British Mandate over Palestine, they must, at the same time, defend the Jewish rights under the Mandate: "We were in a very paradoxical situation in San Francisco. We spent three hard weeks, investing tremendous energy, in defending something we do not want—the Mandate. I had to come to delegates and say: 'I am coming to you to defend our position under the Mandate, but we do not want the Mandate.' But it was the only thing we could do. As nobody knows whether we will get a Jewish State, we have to say that we must retain the rights we have under the Mandate, which was our position for 25 years."[27]

Suffering as he did from the drawback of not being a representative of a sovereign state, Goldmann felt like an outsider in San Francisco, and was confirmed in his determination that the Jews must have a state of their own: "As long as we do not have a recognized Jewish Commonwealth, we remain on the outside. As one who worked for eight years in Geneva on the outside, I say that to remain outside now will be much more difficult. First, because five Arab States are now inside. The position will go on deteriorating if we do not get in as a State."[28]

VI After the end of the war, President Truman sent Earl G. Harrison, the American representative on the intergovernmental committee on refugees, to Germany to investigate the condition of the Jewish displaced persons and report back to him. Shaken by Harrison's report, Truman wrote on August 31, 1945, to the British government suggesting that all the Jewish refugees who wished to go to Palestine be enabled to do so and giving his support to the demand of the Jewish Agency that 100,000 immigration certificates be put immediately at the disposal of those who were in displaced persons camps in Germany, Austria, and Italy. This was the first Zionist achievement in the struggle against the 1939 White Paper, and for American participation in the search for a solution to the Palestine problem.

Even before this step of President Truman was officially announced (on September 29, 1945), Goldmann wrote from Washington (on September 18, 1945) to Ben-Gurion, who at the time was in London, alerting him to the fact that the American government, though supporting the Jewish demand for immigration to Palestine, kept aloof of the basic issue of the establishment of a Jewish State: "It is a hard and difficult task," he wrote, "to make the public, and even many of our friends in Washington, aware that without having a State of our own it will be impossible to organize large scale immigration and absorb it."

Goldmann was seriously concerned about the British government's intention to establish an international trusteeship over Palestine, which would be the easy way out for both London and Washington, but which would indefinitely postpone the realization of the hope for a Jewish State. "I am deeply worried," he wrote, "over this inclination. You know my unshakable view that without a State we, I will not say are lost, but shall certainly be in a very difficult position. . . . Without governmental authority I cannot see how we can bring in and settle even the first 100,000 immigrants, let alone the half a million we need in order to attain majority."

Therefore, Goldmann went on to urge Ben-Gurion that "we must be ready to act in Palestine. The only arguments which can impress upon public opinion here [in Washington] and in London that immigration alone cannot solve the problem is if the Jews of Palestine declare in words, and, if need be, even in acts, that they are not prepared to continue to live under a foreign rule, in a status lower than that of the neighboring Arab states. And, when I say 'foreign rule' I mean also a new trusteeship administration in Palestine (I myself am not at all sure that a joint administration or joint trusteeship of America and Britain will be better from a practical point-of-view than was the British administration.)"[29]

At this time, the importance of the role of the permanent representative of the Jewish Agency in Washington became suddenly and strongly enhanced by the step British Foreign Secretary Ernest Bevin took after Prime Minister Clement Attlee received President Truman's suggestion that 100,000 Jewish refugees be admitted to Palestine immediately. Upon the initiative of Bevin, who was unwilling either to comply with this suggestion or to reject it out of hand and thereby offend the American president, Attlee proposed that a joint Anglo-American Committee of Inquiry be appointed to look into the whole question of Palestine. Truman consented, and, on November 13, 1945, the establishment of the committee was announced simultaneously in London and Washington. Bevin promised that he would carry out the committee's recommendations. In this way, the American government became, for the first time, an official participant in the search for a solution to the "Palestine problem," and the significance of Washington as a focal point for Zionist activity increased tremendously.

The Zionist leadership was now faced with the question of what position to take in the testimonies it was about to give to the Anglo-American Committee. A week before the committee was to begin hearings in Palestine, Goldmann wrote to Moshe Shertok (Sharett) (on February 20, 1946) analyzing the situation and presenting his views. First of all, he stated that there were five possible solutions to the Palestine problem: "1) Giving independence to Palestine as she is today. 2) The adoption of the Biltmore Program, which would mean immediate large scale immigration, and the proclamation that Palestine would become independent the moment a Jewish majority was attained. 3) Continuation of the Mandatory regime. 4) Palestine as an independent state on the basis of federal legislation with autonomous Jewish and Arab cantons, with large scale or free Jewish immigration to the Jewish canton. 5) Partition."

Then Goldmann proceeded to dissect with keen political insight the possibilities and consequences of each of the five solutions. Solution 1, he wrote, would mean acquiescence in the White Paper policies, which, as he was informed by members of the Anglo-American Committee, was unacceptable to the committee. Solution 2 would be rejected because it contained no concessions whatsoever to the Arabs of Palestine. Solution 3 was not realistic because of a general tendency at the United Nations to give independence to all Mandated territories, and because Russia would oppose both a British and a joint Anglo-American trusteeship over Palestine. This left a choice between solutions 4 and 5, and Goldmann expressed his concern about a tendency toward 4: a federal state, which would contain Jewish and Arab cantons:

> This solution is much worse than partition which would give us decent boundaries. Even if the Jewish canton would be given autonomy together with the right to free immigration, the Arab majority in the federal state would find ways and means to obstruct it. In addition, in all matters of foreign policy, such as representation at the United Nations, etc., the Arab majority would have the upper hand. Can you imagine Jamal Husayni [a radical Palestinian Arab leader] and one of us, who would represent Palestine, defending "common" interests? Today we are in need of sovereign status more than ever in the past, and the more I consider the situation the more I am convinced that not only must we prefer a good partition over a federal state but we must fight for it.
>
> I think there is a good chance to get partition both as the recommendation [of the Committee] and as the ultimate solution, but we must press to attain it. I am sure that the Committee will ask questions about it in the public hearings or in the private meetings which I have recommended to its members to have with you and with other members of the Executive. I know that it is very difficult to raise this issue now, but if we persist in a passive approach, if we continue storming and demanding only the Biltmore Program, we may lose the battle and get only a federal Palestine.
>
> The plan which our friends in the Committee are considering is to detach the Nablus-Jenin triangle from Palestine and to tie it to Transjordan. In this manner 300,000 to 400,000 Arabs will be taken out of the country, which will enable us to reach a majority within two or three years with an immigration of 100,000 to 200,000, and to establish our State. The Jewish State in Palestine will then have to come to an agreement with Transjordan on the joint utilization of the Jordan and other development

plans for the benefit of both states. Ultimately the Jewish State will join the other states of the Near East in a Middle Eastern federation—but of course, not the Arab League—in order to remove the fear of the Arabs that the Jewish State in Palestine would become a spearhead of European imperialism against the Arab states, and in order to ensure a common foreign policy for the whole region. I think that we must press for such a solution in unofficial talks with our friends in the Committee, and, should there be need for it, with the whole Committee. What I am afraid of is that, because of internal political considerations, and the fear of the reaction of the opponents of partition, we shall maintain silence and remain passive, and thus shall miss an opportunity which undoubtedly exists.

I also want to warn against all public statements such as that of Prof. Brodetzky in London in which he declared that we would welcome being incorporated into the framework of the British Commonwealth of Nations. Such a policy would inevitably make Russia inimical, and would increase the suspicions of the Arabs that we may become a tool of British policy against them. . . . I hope to meet with Gromyko next week and to clarify the possibility of sending somebody to Moscow. Despite all the news in the papers, I myself do not consider it a proven fact that Russia will be against us, but we must prevent suspicions that at the end we shall side with Britain against Russia.[30]

From January 1946 on, the committee held exhaustive hearings in Washington and London; in displaced persons camps in the British, American, and French zones of Germany; and then in Poland, Cairo, Palestine, Damascus, Beirut, Baghdad, Riyadh, and Amman. In April the committee retired to Lausanne, Switzerland, to prepare its final report. At this point, Goldmann felt that a last-ditch effort was called for to ensure that the American chairman, Judge Joseph C. Hutcheson, should take the minimum Zionist demands into consideration. The only person who could exert influence on Hutcheson was President Truman. On April 5 Goldmann telephoned from Geneva to Meyer Weisgal of the Jewish Agency's New York office and requested him to transmit an urgent message to David Niles, Truman's adviser on minority affairs, to the effect that it was "extremely essential that the boss in Washington should cable [Hutcheson] encouraging him in his stand, and expressing confidence in his efforts to bring about a quick solution to the whole problem."[31] On the same day, Goldmann also phoned Eliahu Epstein asking him to forward the same request to Niles and to Samuel Rosenman.[32] Niles received the messages, but for some reason he did not act upon them until April 16, when he prepared a draft of a cable that

Truman sent to Hutcheson on the same day. The message expressed the president's hope that "the American delegation shall stand firm for a program that is in accord with the highest American tradition of generosity and justice."[33]

Four days later, the committee completed its report. It contained ten recommendations, including the immediate admission of 100,000 Jewish refugees to Palestine and the creation of a trusteeship over Palestine under the auspices of the United Nations.

Despite Bevin's explicit undertaking, the British government was not willing to accept the committee's recommendations and indicated a desire to see the United States assume a share in the responsibility for furthering President Truman's suggestion about admitting the 100,000 to Palestine. Truman thereupon appointed a special Cabinet Committee, consisting of Under Secretary of State Dean Acheson, Secretary of the Treasury John W. Snyder, and Secretary of War Robert P. Patterson, to advise him on the Palestine problem. The three secretaries, in turn, appointed a working body of three representatives, headed by Henry F. Grady, who began consultations with their British opposite numbers, led by Deputy Prime Minister Herbert Morrison.

Grady was an economic and legal expert who lacked any knowledge or experience in the Middle East. When Goldmann met him the first time, he was shocked by his ignorance. Grady asked him what was the name of the Palestinian port "on the shores of the Black Sea"! Grady was thus totally dependent on the State Department experts,[34] whose well-known pro-Arab point of view could be expected to influence him against the Zionist position.

VII   On June 11, 1946, Goldmann reported to Shertok (Sharett) on his contacts with the Russian statesman Andrei Gromyko and Dr. Oskar Lange, the Polish representative at the United Nations, and made use of the occasion to press for the adoption of a clear propartition position by the Executive:

> Furthermore, I discussed fully with Mr. Gromyko the question of sending somebody to Moscow in order to discuss the Palestine problem with his Government. He promised to consult his Government in the matter. He took the position that the issuance of an invitation to a Zionist deputation to go to Moscow would be considered a pro-Zionist position on the part of his Government, and that therefore it was perhaps still too early to do

so. He said that as far as information was concerned he did not think that a man going to Moscow could give the Russians more information than they already possessed.

He pressed me to indicate what we wanted, and in my talks with all the other members of the Security Council I had to face the same question. As I told several times to Ben-Gurion, this was now the main weak point in our position in reference to our long-range policy: they all ask whether we want a trusteeship administration? If we say, "No," they ask, What do we want? If we answer, "The Biltmore Program," they reply that that is not an immediate policy since we have no majority in Palestine, and then we are left without an answer. I think that prior to the September meeting of the General Assembly of the U.N. the Executive will have to take a position on this matter, otherwise we shall be hanging in the air without a clear policy with which we could come to the U.N. . . .

I had a long talk with Dr. Lange, the Polish representative in the U.N., who can serve as a good intermediary between us and the Russians whose full confidence he enjoys. It is possible that soon he will be in Moscow, and he asked me for a memorandum which outlines our concrete suggestions in case he should have an opportunity to discuss the matter with the Soviets. Here again I could not give him such a memorandum, unless we went back to the Biltmore Program to realize which no immediate step could be taken.[35]

In the meantime, the situation in Palestine had rapidly deteriorated. Embittered by Britain's refusal to soften its stand on the burning issue of Jewish immigration, the *Yishuv* evinced more and more sympathy with the violent tactics of Menaḥem Begin's *Irgun Tz'vai L'umi* (Etzel), the Stern Group, and other organizations that considered acts of terror the only language the British would understand. The railroads were sabotaged; bridges destroyed; and coastal patrol stations, radio and radar installations crippled. Large-scale demonstrations were staged, and *'Aliya Bet*—unauthorized immigration—organized on a large scale. On June 29, 1949 ("Black Sabbath"), the British detained several members of the Executive and interned them in 'Atlit, and the countrywide searches and arrests carried out by the British Army reminded the *Yishuv* of the Jews' European experiences.

While these painful events were taking place in Palestine, the Anglo-American working committee (as it was referred to) completed its deliberations and, in July, presented its findings in the form of a new plan. This provided for the division of Palestine into four provinces: two British, comprising 43 percent of the land area; an Arab, comprising 40 percent; and a Jewish, comprising 15 percent (or about 1,500 square miles). Apart from other unacceptable features, from a purely territorial aspect, this was a serious whittling-down even in comparison with the Peel Commission's scheme that had allotted 2,600 square miles to the Jewish State.

During June and July 1946, several meetings took place between Truman and Jewish leaders, and many more of the latter sought to see the president. Late in May, Silver had asked Niles to set up a meeting with Truman for a Jewish delegation to consist of Stephen Wise, Henry Monsky, and Silver himself. Because Truman was too busy in June, the meeting was scheduled for July 2, after the White House informed Silver that, inasmuch as the Jewish Agency had submitted to the president a memorandum on the immigration of the 100,000, he wished that Goldmann and Lipsky, as representatives of the agency, should participate in the meeting. This suggestion aroused Silver's wrath because he felt that the White House was interfering in the composition of the delegation, which was for the AZEC to decide. He suspected that Goldmann, aided by Niles, tried in this manner to obtain recognition from the White House of his special status as the one in charge of the agency's political office in Washington. But, lacking any choice, Silver was forced to acquiesce.

In the meeting, which took place on July 2, and was announced on the same day in a White House press release, four members of the agency's Executive participated: Wise, Goldmann, Lipsky, and Silver. The concrete results were few. Truman stated that he was adamant in his demand for the immigration of the 100,000 and informed the delegation that he was ready to take care of the technical arrangements as well as the expenses of their transportation to Palestine.[36]

After this meeting with Truman, Goldmann felt that the time had come to launch an energetic public opinion campaign for the partition plan and the immigration of the 100,000. In an interview with *The New York Times*, he described partition as "the only practical solution of the Palestine problem." The article based on this interview was published in the July 11, 1946, issue of the *Times*. Although Goldmann's name was not mentioned and the opinions expressed were attributed to "Zionist leaders" in America, Silver unhesitatingly identified the unnamed leaders with Goldmann; and, at the July 15 meeting of the AZEC, unleashed a strong attack against the Jewish Agency's political office in Washington—that is, Goldmann, whom he did not name—and accused it of a breach of the Zionist discipline and lack of coordination. Because the Committee of Eight proved incapable of settling the conflict between the AZEC and the agency's Washington office—that is, between Silver and

Goldmann—Silver demanded that the Executive reconfirm the authority of the Committee of Eight as the only Zionist body charged with control over all the political work of the agency in America until the forthcoming Zionist Congress. Because Silver was the chairman of both the Committee of Eight and the AZEC, his intention clearly was to make Goldmann cease and desist from his independent political activities.[37]

Undaunted by these efforts, Goldmann in the meantime continued to proselytize for the partition idea. He used every possible opportunity to convince Jewish public opinion and the Zionist leadership in America that partition and the establishment of a viable Jewish State were the only solutions not only of the Palestine problem but of the problem of the Jewish refugees who were languishing in displaced persons camps in Europe. One of the forums to which he presented his views was the meeting of the executives of Hadassah, the Women's Zionist Organization of America, on July 17, 1946. In what a historian of the Zionist political work in America in the years 1945–48 termed "a brilliant and persuasive speech,"[38] he presented the thesis that the only way out of the extremely precarious situation in which the Zionist movement found itself was to opt for partition, and to do it now lest the opportunity be missed. Many of the arguments he marshaled in this speech he was to use again and again in addressing the most diverse audiences, including, in the first place, the Executive of the Jewish Agency (on August 5), whose authorization he needed before he could officially approach the American government. These will be presented in detail below, in the discussion of what transpired at the special August meeting of the Executive in Paris.

Two weeks after Goldmann's address, the leadership of Hadassah gave the other side an opportunity to present its arguments. This was done by Emanuel Neumann, who accused Goldmann of presenting the partition plan as if it represented the consensus of the American Zionist leadership, and of initiating talks with American government officials on the subject. Neumann reproached the agency's political office in Washington, and its director, Eliahu Epstein, with engaging in political work that was the preserve of the AZEC.[39]

VIII On July 25 the British government announced in London that it would convene a Round Table Conference of Jews and Arabs (including representatives of the Arab League), in which American observers would participate. On the 31st Herbert Morrison presented in Parliament the new plan of the Morrison-Grady committee on cantonization (or federalization, as it was also called).

Faced with these events, the Jewish Agency Executive finally agreed, at the urging of Goldmann, to convene in order to consider the steps to be taken to prevent the adoption of the cantonization plan by the British and American governments. The Executive was unanimously opposed to this plan because it meant an indefinite postponement of the realization of the Jewish State. The historic meeting opened in Paris on Friday, August 2, at 10:30 A.M. By a sheer coincidence, a day earlier Winston Churchill advised the British government to surrender the Palestine Mandate to the United Nations, unless the United States "come in and share the burden of the Zionist cause."[40]

Inasmuch as several members of the Executive residing in Palestine were still in detention, the Paris meeting was attended by only part of the Zionist leadership. Because of ill health, Weizmann could not participate, and Silver refused to attend.[41]

On the day the meeting opened, Goldmann phoned Epstein in Washington and asked him to immediately contact David Niles to obtain from him a general appraisal of the situation and a clarification of Truman's position. Niles told Epstein that he thought the first thing Goldmann ought to do was to impress his colleagues on the Executive with the seriousness of the situation. Even if the president were to cancel the Morrison-Grady cantonization plan, the dangers of that plan would not be eliminated. Niles asked Epstein to inform Goldmann that, based on his conversations with Truman during the preceding several days, interspersed with exasperated rhetorical questions from the president such as, "What is it that the Jews want?" he, Niles, clearly understood that the president "had become convinced that the Jews objected to what was offered to them without having a proposal of their own which would have chances to fulfill at least part of the demands and requirements of all the interested parties, which would make it possible to advance the Palestine problem toward a peaceful solution." For a number of political considerations, Niles explained, a danger existed that the Morrison-Grady plan could reemerge. The president also seemed to have reached the conclusion that he could no longer confine his efforts to the admission of the 100,000 to Palestine, but needed to come to a decision on the Palestine problem in general. Hence, Niles was convinced, it was imperative to present Truman with a clearcut Zionist initiative.[42]

Epstein immediately informed Goldmann over the phone of everything Niles had told him. In view of this latest report on the Washington situation, the task facing Goldmann at the meeting of the Executive was, first of all, to convince his colleagues to accept the idea of partition without delay. Secondly, he had to convince them to undertake the necessary steps to persuade the American government—closely involved with the Palestine problem since the appointment of the Anglo-American Committee—of the impracticability and unacceptability of the Morrison-Grady cantonization scheme, and to persuade them at the same time to support the partition of Palestine.

At the opening of the meeting, a cable from Silver (transmitted by Leo Kohn) was read. He requested that no contacts be made with American government officials, and that no expressions of reactions to the plan of the solution of the Palestine problem should be made without prior consultation with him because "independent approaches by Agency representatives and the [American Zionist] Emergency Council were distinctly harmful at this time." At Ben-Gurion's suggestion, the Executive decided to cable Silver that "for the time being the status quo could not be changed."[43] Thus, the first attempt by Silver to gain control of the negotiations with the American government was rejected by the Executive.

At this first session, Goldmann reported on the political situation in America. He felt that "the Zionists were beginning to become a nuisance" and that a general tiredness of Palestine prevailed, especially in Congress and the administration. Nevertheless, until the November elections, the Zionists were in a relatively favorable position. The growing anti-Russian feeling in America meant that the government would want to maintain its alliance with Britain, in which the Zionists were a disturbing element. The State Department was pro-Arab, and the Office of Near Eastern and African Affairs deemed the Arabs to be a stronger force than the Jews. President Truman's demand for 100,000 immigration certificates was viewed by the State Department as a cardinal mistake because it aroused the resentment of the British.

Goldmann then spoke of the efforts made to prevent the acceptance of the trusteeship proposal. The work done by Eliahu Epstein, Stephen Wise, and some others was exemplary. But Secretary of State James F. Byrnes, with whom Goldmann had argued about the smallness of the area allotted to the Jewish province, showed no sympathy for the complaint.[44]

After an address by Ben-Gurion, Goldmann again took the floor on Saturday, August 3. He began by explaining that he asked for a meeting on the Sabbath, the traditional day of rest, because the day before he had received word from Washington that President Truman had set up a meeting for Wednesday, August 7, of the three members of his Cabinet Committee, the three American members of the Morrison-Grady Committee, and the six American members of the Anglo-American Committee of Inquiry. Friends close to the administration had indicated to him that it would be highly desirable that one of the members of the Executive, authorized to speak in its name, should come to Washington for a few days to present to the government the minimum demands of the agency in connection with the new British proposals. Therefore, the Executive had to decide, the next day at the latest, whether or not it wanted to send somebody and what directives it wished to give to him. The designated member would need to leave for America on Monday, August 5, in the evening at the latest.

Then Goldmann went on to present his position. He agreed with most of the principles enunciated by Ben-Gurion the day before, but he differed with him as to the tactical conclusions he drew from them. He agreed with Ben-Gurion on the demand that the unity of the movement and the *Yishuv* must be preserved at all costs. He agreed with him that the first and foremost aim of the Zionist movement was a Jewish State. "I speak of the political aim of Zionism today, in 1946, and of what I am convinced we must achieve within the next year or two. . . . Our aim is the Jewish State now, this year or the next. The reformulation of the Zionist aim in the Biltmore Program was absolutely correct. We can no longer continue in Palestine under foreign rule."

Goldmann explained that he was not optimistic as to the future available manpower in the Jewish world. The great Jewish reservoir had been emptied by the Nazi genocide of six million Jews. As for America, unless it was swept by Fascism and pogroms, no Jewish mass emigration would be made from there to Palestine. Of the one-and-a-half million Jews left in Europe, at least half a million would be able to settle in their old countries. If the one-half or three-quarters of a million European Jews who could not maintain themselves in Europe and who urgently desired to emigrate to Palestine would need to wait for years, they would find other places to go to and would be lost to Palestine. If Palestine remained closed, the Zionist morale of the displaced persons would inevitably deteriorate, and, one way or the other, arrangements would be found for them outside Palestine. Hence, immediate large-scale immigration was imperative, and this could be achieved only if a Jewish State was established. "Any other solution will mean political defeat at this crucial moment of Jewish history. Therefore the conclusion on which I agree with Ben-Gurion is that we cannot accept any continuation of British rule in Palestine."

Goldmann then stated that he also opposed any Anglo-American or Anglo-American-Russian trusteeship over Palestine. In agreement with Ben-Gurion, he was convinced that the Jewish Agency "cannot conduct a policy of Russian orientation" because Russia was unwilling "to commit itself fully in favor of Palestine as a Jewish State," and because "generally the time has come for us to give up a specific orientation on one great power. . . . We must return to the classical position of Zionism as an international movement. The Jewish problem is international, and ultimately it must be solved by the community of nations. As a people we are neutral by definition, because we are dispersed all over the world."

Goldmann then emphasized that he was in total agreement with Ben-Gurion on the need for friendly relations with the Arab world:

Our future depends on this. Long before the war I took the position that if we must choose between being part of the British Empire or part of a Middle Eastern federation with the Arab states, we must choose the latter. Our history does not lead us into a permanent association with the British Empire. For our people the return to Palestine means to try to become again one of the peoples of the Near East, and to make our contribution to its development. This can be done only in friendship and good neighborly relations with the Arab world. But we cannot achieve this until we have the same status as they, and until we are recognized by them as equals in Palestine. Once we have a Jewish State, our main task will be to establish close relations with the Arab world.

Having thus sketched the common ground between Ben-Gurion and himself, Goldmann then presented his differences. He said they were merely tactical. Ben-Gurion had completely given up all hope that Britain would make a positive contribution to the solution of the Palestine problem. Therefore, he concluded that "we must orientate ourselves towards the small nations of the world, appeal to the oppressed minorities, and align ourselves with all those in the Middle East and in the world who are interested in ousting Britain from the Middle East." On the contrary, Goldmann felt that a last attempt should be made to reach a compromise with Great Britain. Unless this were done, the establishment of the Jewish State would be postponed for a long time, and the gates of Palestine would, in the meantime, remain closed. Zionism would become a militant policy, possessing a negative orientation, confined to protest meetings in America and an "activist" policy in Palestine, where violence would spread with open rebellion, and many more incidents like that of the King David Hotel would take place.

Ben-Gurion's suggestion of a revolutionary Zionism would inevitably reduce the number of the Jews who were Zionists today and who could be estimated to comprise 80 percent of the Jewish people. "The Jews of America are prepared to talk big, but I am not at all sure that they are prepared to fight their government over the Palestine problem not only in Madison Square Garden rallies but also by voting against the administration, by losing the sympathy of the government, encouraging anti-Semitism in America, and accepting all the consequences of a policy conducted along these lines. I believe we shall lose the support of many of our friends. We shall become an illegal underground movement."

Goldmann's own conviction was that so long as the least possibility of conducting a legal struggle existed the movement must pursue that course. "We should turn to the policy suggested by Ben Gurion only if all other means fail. I believe there is still such a possibility with the help of America. England is desperately anxious to have America enter the Palestine picture. The refusal of the President [Truman] to endorse the Grady report was a great and unexpected shock for Britain. It demonstrated our strength in America."

Next, Goldmann presented his suggestions as to what he felt had to be done in the present situation:

> We can advise the President to take one of two lines of action:
> One is to wash his hands of the entire Palestine problem. For him this might be the easy way out. He then could say to the Jews: "I tried my best. I failed. What else can I do?" The State Department would be glad not to have to share with the British in the responsibility vis-à-vis the Arabs. Had it not been for the enormous pressure on our part, America would never have entered the Palestine picture. We pressed the President to obtain something for us, and the British said that they could not do it without the participation of America. We could simply advise him to withdraw from the whole affair, and possibly he would welcome it. But in that case he would have no influence at all on the Palestine problem, and we would be left facing Great Britain alone. Then the British would have the alternative of either saying that they could do nothing for the Jews and leave the situation as it is; or turning the issue over to the United Nations, which would mean endless delay, the intervention of Russia . . . the Arabs officially in, and Britain in a position to prevent an anti-British decision in the UN by using its power of veto and thus legally maintaining her present position in Palestine with the White Paper regulations.

The second thing, Goldmann went on, that the Jews could suggest to President Truman was not to withdraw but to demand improvements in the British plan. Goldmann envisaged the following four improvements:

1. The immediate issuance of 100,000 immigration certificates.
2. The granting of the right to supervise immigration to the Jewish province.
3. Territorial improvements: concretely, the inclusion of the boundaries of the Peel partition plan plus the Negev.
4. A clear declaration that this cantonization was but the first step toward a Jewish State, with a time limit of one to two years until the establishment of the State.

And Goldmann added, "I think there is a chance that the President will accept this advice, and an additional chance that, if he insists, he will get it from the British. We can accept this as the basis for negotiations. As for the Arabs, I think they will be more willing to accept us when they see that the British accepted these improvements."

Then, at the end of his long presentation, Goldmann came to the crucial issue:

All this presupposes one decision: that we are ready to accept partition. For years we have postponed the discussion of this issue. We were afraid of internal differences of opinion. We are afraid to play out the cards and take positions. I have always warned that the time would come when we shall have to decide, without advance notice, and this is the moment. Unless we are ready to tell the President that we are willing to accept the Jewish State in an adequate part of Palestine, it is no use going to Washington and trying to obtain these improvements. I have felt for years that the partition of Palestine was the only way out. The Biltmore Program is not a realistic policy at present, because we have no Jewish majority, and because we cannot wait until we attain the majority in order to get the State.

I know this is a tragic decision. But we have only the choice between two things: British rule with the White Paper policy, or a Jewish State in part of Palestine. For the reasons I have given, I choose the Jewish State in a part of Palestine today. If the Executive agrees and assumes the responsibility, since we cannot wait for the [Zionist] Congress, we must send a representative to Washington to advise the President along these lines.[45]

Thus, Goldmann concluded his presentation, and the deliberations on his proposal began. The debate was more than heated; it was passionate, though essentially no new arguments against partition were put forward compared to what had been said at the Biltmore Conference four years earlier.

At the Sunday (August 4, 1946) session of the Executive, Stephen Wise suggested that "Dr. Goldmann should go at once to Washington. . . . [He] should be accompanied by Mr. Ben-Gurion. It is a tremendous responsibility for one person to go on this mission, and therefore he should go together with the Chairman of the Jewish Agency Executive, and I believe that Dr. Goldmann would welcome that."[46]

At a later session on the same day, Ben-Gurion said, "I believe that we must demand one thing only, and that is a Jewish State in Palestine or in a part of Palestine." Later in his address, he added: "Goldmann should say in Washington that if we are given a Jewish State, he will accept it in the name of his colleagues, and then we will bring it before the Congress. If that is his instruction, then I am in favor of Goldmann going to Washington. It means that he would say 'yes' to a Jewish State, and 'no' to any other proposal. . . . I am in favor of an emissary going to Washington if he will demand a Jewish State, otherwise I am opposed to it."

In reply to a question by Goldmann, Ben-Gurion stated that he himself was not prepared to go to Washington and repeated, "There was only one thing to ask for, and that was a Jewish State, if necessary in part of Palestine."[47] These statements by the chairman of the Executive constituted unequivocal instruction to Goldmann to *ask for*—even *demand*—a Jewish State in Palestine.

In the midst of these discussions, several dramatic developments took place. First, on August 4 a cable was received by Goldmann from Harry L. Shapira, Silver's right-hand man in the AZEC, informing him that Dr. Silver urgently advised Goldmann to refrain from all contact with U.S. government offices or spokesmen unless it was first cleared with Silver. The AZEC, the cable stated, had an action plan that was well underway, and all separate steps would be harmful. At the same time, Emanuel Neumann cabled Dr. Israel Goldstein saying that Goldmann should not come to Washington because Silver was leading the action there and that, in view of the tense relations between the two men, somebody else should come.[48]

Silver himself cabled Ben-Gurion informing him that Bartley C. Crum and James G. McDonald—two American members of the Anglo-American Committee of Inquiry—supported the long-range political proposals of the Anglo-American Committee if reasonable chances existed for the establishment of a viable Jewish State in part of Palestine. Ben-Gurion interpreted this cable as signaling that Silver would not stand in the way if the Executive decided it was ready to negotiate about the partition plan.[49] Goldmann received a phone call also from Niles who informed him that, disheartened by the British government's rejection of the proposals of the Anglo-American Committee, as well as by the attacks on him by American Zionists—probably a reference to Silver, who, as a Republican, did not hesitate to assail the Democratic president for any act or statement that did not satisfy the Zionist position—"the President was threatening to wash his hands of the whole matter unless the Jewish Agency Executive came up with a reasonable realistic plan."[50]

These urgent transatlantic messages, added to Goldmann's forceful and logically incontrovertible presentation, tipped the balance. Israel Goldstein could not vote for partition because he represented the Zionist Organization of America, which, led by Abba Hillel Silver and Emanuel Neumann, was against partition, but he stated that personally he was in favor of Goldmann's resolution.

Louis Lipsky, in what turned out to be prophetic words, described what he foresaw would happen in the wake of Goldmann's mission between him and the AZEC: "I do not envy Dr. Goldmann. He will be in a very difficult position. The general atmosphere in the U.S. has been whipped into a direction just contrary to what we propose to do. Goldmann cannot be expected to go there and expound our view in Washington, and as soon as he emerges from his meeting, he will be condemned by the Jewish press and others, including the Zionist Organization [of America]. As soon as the [American Zionist] Emergency Council knows what he is going to say in Washington, they will start a press campaign against it."[51]

The next day (Monday, August 5, 1946), at 10:45 in the morning, another session took place. All the participants, Golda Meyersohn (Meir), Chaim Greenberg, Berl Locker, Stephen Wise, Dr. Emil Schmorak, Dr. Israel Goldstein, Mrs. Rose Halprin, Prof. Zelig Brodetsky, and Louis Lipsky, gave detailed explanations of their positions. This was followed by a reading of several motions. After that of Ben-Gurion was rejected, Goldmann's proposals were adopted by an overwhelming majority; only one member of the Executive voted against one paragraph.

As formulated, paragraph 1 of the resolution rejected the Morrison-Grady plan of cantonization, which had been presented to the House of Commons only five days earlier. The crucial paragraph 2 read: "The Executive is prepared to discuss a proposal for the establishment of a viable Jewish state in an adequate area of Palestine." Paragraph 3 contained demands connected with the implementation of paragraph 2.

Goldmann's management of the Paris meeting of the Jewish Agency Executive was, first of all, remarkable as a strategic achievement. As the supreme governing body of the Zionist movement between one Zionist Congress and the next, the Executive was the only Jewish authority that could make a decision with reference to the partition of Palestine. At that juncture, partition was not even an actively envisaged or pursued possibility in Washington, London, or elsewhere. The endorsement of the plan for a Jewish State in part of Palestine by the Executive was therefore an indispensable prerequisite of any further step that could be undertaken for the purpose of presenting it to, and obtaining the support of, the United States and other nations. Before the Paris meeting, most members of the Executive, whatever their personal preference, felt officially bound by the Biltmore Program, which called for a Jewish commonwealth in all of Palestine. To come out openly for partition was judged by them to be the political equivalent of heresy, the wanton abandonment of the principle that the Jews had a historical right to every inch of their Holy Land. Internal Zionist party jealousies and rivalries also played their role in the reluctance of the representatives of any parties on the Executive to expose themselves to the charge that they were the ones who initiated or supported such a fateful step.

Goldmann's presentation in the August 5 meeting of the propartition position, his irrefutable arguments showing that the establishment of a Jewish State in part of Palestine was the only realistic choice that had a chance of being accepted by America and the United Nations, broke through the Executive's resistance, which had been its traditional and official stance ever since the Biltmore Conference of 1942. Under the influence of his irresistible plea, the Executive adopted his motion almost unanimously; only one vote opposed one part of it. Thus, for the first time in the ten or more years ever since Goldmann had begun to advocate and, more than that, to fight for partition, this solution of the Palestine problem became the official policy of the Zionist movement as a whole as represented by the Executive. As Goldmann remarked in his *Autobiography*, "Without doubt the resolution was of historic importance and paved the way for the ultimate acceptance of partition by the United Nations, and for the proclamation of the Jewish state."[52] The road was now open to embark on the fight for the Jewish State in the councils and chanceries of the major powers and in the United Nations.

First, however, one urgent issue needed to be settled. It was imperative to bring the resolution immediately to the attention of those in the

American government who were in a position to decide whether it should support or oppose the plan to partition Palestine and to establish a Jewish State in part of it. Efforts had to be started without delay to persuade them to support the plan. The question of who should be entrusted with this vital and delicate task was debated at some length. Several motions were made. Ben-Gurion asked Goldmann what he thought about the possibility of entrusting Silver with the task. Goldmann opposed it because of the tension between Silver and the White House. As Niles subsequently indicated to Epstein, before the congressional elections the White House, controlled by Democrats, would not be eager to hand a plum to a Republican Zionist leader. The motion of Ben-Gurion and Moshe Kleinbaum (Sneh) that Goldmann alone be entrusted with the mission was carried with nobody voting against it. "When Dr. Goldstein said he would vote only on condition that whoever went to Washington would work together with, and through, the [American Zionist] Emergency Council, Mr. Ben Gurion said this condition was unconstitutional. The Jewish Agency was not dependent upon the Emergency Council."[53] For this reason, Goldmann had a clearly stated mandate to work in Washington on his own, as the emissary of the Jewish Agency, without being dependent on the wishes of the AZEC. Nevertheless, at the end of the meeting (at 1:30 P.M.) Ben-Gurion expressed the hope that Goldmann and Silver would fully cooperate, and Goldmann asked Epstein over the phone to arrange an early meeting with Silver upon his arrival in America.[54]

After the conclusion of the meeting, Ben-Gurion cabled Silver, telling him that the Executive had rejected the Morrison-Grady plan and that Goldmann was about to fly to Washington carrying precise directives. "I hope that the two of you," he said in the cable, "will work in full cooperation and in harmony, and that you will be able to participate in our discussions [in Paris]." At the same time, Goldmann, too, cabled Silver and asked him to meet him upon his arrival in New York. He also cabled Niles in the White House and asked him to set up for him a meeting with Dean Acheson, the acting secretary of state, as well as an unpublicized meeting with the president. Goldmann also wrote a short letter to his good friend Stephen Wise, in which he said: "I tried to reach you but did not succeed. I fly at 3 p. m. I wanted to get your blessings both as a rabbi and as a friend. You know better than anybody else how much I need them. . . . I hope, if all goes well, to be back on Sunday. If things go very badly, and the President decides to accept Grady's report . . . I may be back earlier, not with flying colors, but with a feeling of having done my duty."[55]

IX Even before Goldmann's arrival in America, the Morrison-Grady cantonization plan had been leaked to *The New York Times.* The Jewish reaction was a bitter public outcry against the plan. Had this not been the case, Washington may well have adopted the Morrison-Grady plan, and Goldmann, upon his arrival, would have been faced with a *fait accompli.* Also, influential friends of Zionism, among them the Senators Robert F. Wagner and Robert A. Taft, made no secret of their categorical opposition to the Morrison-Grady plan, which seriously weakened Truman's resolve to approve it.

On August 1, 1946, *The New York Times* carried a story to the effect that the day before President Truman had recalled from Paris the three alternates of the Cabinet Committee, consisting of Ambassador Henry F. Grady, chairman, and members Goldthwaite H. Dorr and Herbert Gaston, for the purpose of further discussion. Zionist spokesmen gave credit for this move, which was judged to be an initial victory for the opponents of the Morrison-Grady scheme, to the sharp bipartisan reaction to it in the Senate. In addition, Judge Proskauer (see below) asked the president to press for an early immigration of 100,000 Jewish displaced persons to Palestine; and James G. McDonald, one of the American members of the Anglo-American Committee of Inquiry, called on Truman to protest personally.

As a result of these moves, and of the strong plea of David K. Niles, Truman informed the British government on August 5 that his first impression of the Morrison-Grady proposal was unfavorable[56] and that he had directed the State Department to invite the six American members of the Anglo-American Committee of Inquiry to meet with the three American members of the Morrison-Grady committee, which had produced the cantonization plan, under the chairmanship of Acting Secretary of State Dean Acheson (see above). Grady and his two colleagues left Paris posthaste and arrived in Washington on August 2.[57] The group of nine met on August 7–9 and recommended that the U.S. government reject the whole of the Morrison-Grady plan, which Judge Joseph C. Hutcheson, the American chairman of the Anglo-American Committee of Inquiry termed a "complete sell-out" that provided for a "ghetto in an attenuated form."[58]

These developments coincided with Goldmann's mission to Washington. He arrived in New York on Tuesday, August 6, in the afternoon. Before he could begin his talks with officials in Washington, he first needed to clear one more Jewish hurdle. Rabbi Abba Hillel Silver was still as adamantly opposed to partition as ever, and, if he voiced his objections in Washington, this could have easily frustrated Goldmann's efforts. Silver was at the time the most influential American Zionist leader, president of the Zionist Organization of America and chairman of the American Section of the Jewish Agency. Although as a rabbi (he was rabbi of the Temple in Cleveland, Ohio, from 1917 until his death in 1963), Silver had to be professionally a man of peace, in fact he was a born fighter, whose pugnaciousness could not be totally sublimated in his personal dynamism and brilliant, often overwhelming, oratory. Although he was a leader of the General Zionists, serving as president of the Zionist Organization of America from 1945 to 1947 and as honorary president thereafter until his death, his predilections and the methods he advocated were close to those of the right-wing Zionist Revisionist party. In 1943, as chairman of the American Zionist Emergency Council, he had delivered an impassioned plea to the American Jewish Conference on behalf of the Jewish commonwealth that changed the climate of the conference and led to its adoption of a procommonwealth resolution, that is, its endorsement of the Biltmore Program.[59]

However, impressive and powerful as Silver was in supporting a cause, his fighting nature found its full expression when opposing an issue. In connection with the Palestine problem, he found himself repeatedly in opposition to Weizmann, Ben-Gurion, and other top leaders of the movement. As a Republican, Silver opposed the Democratic administration and was the first responsible Zionist leader to attack publicly (in 1943) President Franklin D. Roosevelt and the State Department for their handling of the Palestine issue. In 1945 he was against cooperation with the Anglo-American Committee of Inquiry. Although he was all for a Jewish commonwealth, he opposed partition, or, at least, any Zionist initiative in connection with it. In his opposition to the British Mandatory government of Palestine, he sympathized with the drastic methods resorted to by extremist Jewish groups.

On July 31, 1946, Silver wired the American office of the Jewish Agency and requested that "no contact be made with American Government officials, and no expression of reaction to a plan [relating to the solution of the Palestine problem] be given without prior consultation with him." The next day, he convened a meeting of the executive committee of the AZEC, of which he was chairman, and convinced it to adopt a resolution to the effect that a new supreme command, to be called the Central Council for Zionist Affairs, be set up, and that this body alone should carry on all Zionist political activity in America. This body would be dominated by Silver.[60]

This was the man whom Goldmann had to "neutralize" before he could embark on his Washington mission. As spokesman of American Zionists, Silver was in a position to present his own views in Washington with the full weight of both his offices and his personality. Even though he bowed to the will of the Executive, as expressed in the August 5 resolution, which was conveyed to him by Goldmann, if he insisted on participating in Goldmann's meetings with American statesmen, he could seriously damage the chances of convincing them that the entire Zionist movement believed partition to be the only acceptable solution to the Palestine problem. At the request of Goldmann, Silver met him immediately upon his arrival in New York, but unfortunately Goldmann left no record of their meeting. In his report to the Executive on August 13, after his return from Washington, he only stated briefly that "Dr. Silver met me, and the two of us set out together for Washington, and had a friendly, informative talk. He said nothing against the decision of Ben-Gurion that the Executive had the right to negotiate about partition, and was even ready, albeit against his will, to accept it."[61]

This account is at variance with Goldmann's even briefer statement about the same meeting made some twenty years later on one minor point: the trip from New York to Washington. According to the *Autobiography*, he and Silver did not travel to Washington together, but he talked with Silver in New York "and asked him, in spite of his opposition, to go along with the majority resolution and refrain from interfering with my negotiations in Washington. To this he agreed. Then I flew to the capital."[62] In any case, just as Silver did not participate in the Paris meeting of the Executive, so he was not present at Goldmann's Washington talks.

Upon his arrival in Washington on August 6, after a full night's flight from Paris and a tense discussion with Silver in New York, the indefatigable Goldmann met, on the same day, with David Niles, through whose offices the sense and fervor of American Zionists were transmitted to the president; and with Bartley S. Crum, the San Francisco lawyer who was one of the six American members of the Anglo-American Committee of Inquiry earlier that year and was a sincere friend of Zionism. Their consultations were in preparation for his meeting next day with Dean Acheson, who, as the representative of the State Department on the three-man Cabinet Committee, appointed by Truman to advise him on the Palestine problem, carried the most weight in the issue. Moreover, because Acheson was chairman of the August 7–9 meetings of the nine Americans who were members of the Anglo-American Committee of Inquiry and of the Morrison-Grady working committee, he was undoubtedly the key person in the Cabinet Committee, though the final decision of Truman on the partition of Palestine would be made on the basis of the recommendation of all three of its members. Thus, Goldmann knew he had to focus his attention on Acheson.

As for the Zionist Executive, when they dispatched Goldmann to Washington, instead of entrusting Silver with the task, they clearly felt that what was called for was strong diplomatic skill and friendly persuasion, which were Goldmann's forte, rather than the battering-ram technique that Silver would have employed. In addition, the Executive was fully aware of the lack of sympathy between Silver and Truman, who had repeatedly expressed to his confidants his irritation with the forceful Republican Zionist leader.[63]

That same evening (Tuesday, August 6), an informal meeting took place between Goldmann, Silver, Emanuel Neumann, and members of the executive staffs of the AZEC and the Jewish Agency's Washington office, at the Statler Hotel in Washington. At this meeting, as reported in detail by Rabbi Feuer, Goldmann presented the background of the Jewish Agency's decision of the previous day in Paris, and then a discussion of tactics took place:

> Dr. Silver expressed the view that the proper approach in the circumstance would not be to go to American officials and try to "sell" them partition; but instead to press for the immediate immigration of the 100,000 and for the implementation of the other short-range recommendations of the Anglo-American Committee report. But, if in the discussions between the six members of the Committee of Inquiry and the three members of the Cabinet Committee the subject of partition would come up, as it was bound to arise in any deliberations regarding cantonization, and if someone of that group were then to ask about the attitude of the Jewish Agency towards such a proposal—the representative of the Jewish Agency would then be in a position to indicate that under the pressure of present conditions it would be prepared to consider partition as a possible compromise solution. Dr. Silver emphasized—as he had stressed at earlier meetings of the Council—that Zionists must not place themselves in the position of pressing for a policy which whittles down the full Zionist program; because once that is done—and official Zionist spokesmen advocate partition— that becomes the new "maximalist" Zionist position, beyond which it becomes impossible to go and from which the British can always proceed to do *their* whittling down.
>
> It was, therefore, agreed at this informal meeting that these were the proper tactics to follow. *These tactics were agreed to by Dr. Goldmann.*[64]

The last sentence, emphasized in the original of Rabbi Feuer's memorandum, from which it is quoted, is contradicated by the account given by Eliahu Epstein of the same meeting. According to the latter, Goldmann "did not express his explicit consent" to Silver's views.[65] This indicates that Goldmann remained determined to act, not in accordance with the consensus of the AZEC, which was dominated by Silver, but in compliance with the explicit resolutions of the Jewish Agency Executive, the only ones truly binding for him, which contradicted, and thus canceled out, the wishes of the American Zionists. Having lined up his meetings with Acheson and others in the American government, beginning the very next day, it would have been a practical impossibility for Goldmann to convince, at the last minute, the American Zionist leaders that there was simply no time to wait for members of the Anglo-American or the Cabinet committees to bring up the partition issue if and when they felt inclined to do so. Once the agency resolved that it "was prepared to discuss a proposal for the establishment of a viable Jewish State in an adequate area of Palestine," it was his duty to discuss partition, from which no desires expressed by American Zionist leaders must deter him. An attempt to bring them around to the Executive's—and his own— view would have been hopeless. And, had he insisted that discipline demanded that they accept the Executive's decision, the danger always existed that one or more of those present would leak to the press something of what went on at the August 6 meeting and thereby make the American government aware of a disunity in the Zionist ranks which, at that critical stage of the negotiations, may have been sufficient for the government to wash its hands of the whole issue.

Incidentally, the question of whether or not Goldmann should contact the U.S. Government, and of whether or not Silver or somebody else should accompany him, was not touched upon. The deliberations that took place at this August 6 meeting go a long way to explain why the next afternoon, when he was invited to a meeting of the executive committee of the AZEC, Goldmann felt it advisable to say nothing of his talk with Dean Acheson.

In 1981 Goldmann still clearly recalled the considerations that had motivated him thirty-five years earlier to keep silent about his talk with Acheson at that meeting of the AZEC executive. His recollections agreed, not with Rabbi Feuer's, but with Eliahu Epstein's account of what had transpired. In a letter dated February 22, 1981, Goldmann wrote me:

> I can only confirm what Eliahu Elath [wrote], that I never agreed to Rabbi Silver's demand. Had I done so, it would have jeopardized my whole

mission to Washington. To keep silent about my first talk with Acheson was the only way to achieve a result. Had I told Silver about it, I doubt whether there would have been a decision in favour of the Jewish state at the U.N. later on.

It is almost a necessity in diplomacy not always to inform those who want to know or who think they have a right to know about what is going on, and I could quote many examples when Ben-Gurion kept silent vis-à-vis his own cabinet on actions he intended to undertake.

X   For the next day, Wednesday, August 7, Goldmann's appointment-book entries read: "Edward Farley, Treasury. Acheson (won him over for partition). David Niles. Proskauer. Emergency Committee conflict with Silver."

Goldmann's talk with Acheson took place in the early afternoon. Acheson had chaired that day the meeting of the nine and was steeped in the Palestine problem. The Goldmann-Acheson meeting lasted for two hours. As Goldmann reported six days later to the Executive in Paris, he told Acheson that he had come in the name of the Executive and that he had to inform the secretary that the Executive would not enter into negotiations on the basis of the Morrison-Grady plan. Acheson replied that he understood that the Executive could not accept that scheme, but asked why the Executive could not participate in a conference to change the plan. Goldmann explained that the Executive could participate in the planned London Round Table Conference and discuss the renuncia-tion of part of Palestine only if the Jews obtained a state in the other part. "If the ghetto is turned into a State, it is no longer a ghetto," he said, in reference to Judge Hutcheson's remark. The Morrison-Grady plan could not be improved much unless the principle of a Jewish State was adopted. Acheson understood this and pointed out that the situation was desperate from all points of view. The president was very nervous and upset over the entire issue. If the Morrison-Grady plan was not accepted, America was liable to withdraw entirely from the Palestine problem. In that case, the Jews would be left alone facing the British, which would be good neither for them nor America because America promised its help to them. Also, the situation in Palestine would dete-riorate. The Jewish lobby angered the president, and the American Jews could become embittered to the point of angry outbreaks.

The situation in Palestine to which Acheson alluded was serious. During the summer of 1946, contacts between the Jewish Agency and Britain had practically been broken off. Weizmann and British Foreign Secretary Bevin had not seen each other for months. After the arrest of members of the Jewish Agency Executive who were at the time in Palestine on the "Black Sabbath" of June 29, the following two weeks saw the most thorough cordon and search operation in the entire history of the Mandate.[66] On July 22 Etzel blew up a wing of the King David Hotel that housed the British Criminal Investigation Division (CID). The British had ignored a telephone warning to evacuate the building, and consequently ninety-one Britishers, Arabs, and Jews were killed in the explosion, and forty-five injured. Thereupon the British clamped a curfew on the entire *Yishuv*. Ben-Gurion, who at the time was out of the country, furiously denounced the Etzel, and urged the *Yishuv* to turn in its members. On July 24 the British government published a White Paper on the ties between the Jewish Agency and terrorists. The Hagana, on its part, with the blessing of the Jewish Agency, intensified its efforts to bring Jewish immigrants illegally into the country. In 1946 the Mosad l'Aliya Bet (Institution for Immigration B), headquartered in Paris, brought on its boats 22,365 illegal immigrants to Palestine. (In 1947 more than 41,000 were to come on Mosad boats.)[67]

After discussing the manifestations of the tension between the Jews and the British, Goldmann presented to Acheson the minimum demands of the Jewish Agency concerning the borders of the future Jewish State. They must include the Peel partition plan plus the Negev. Then Goldmann went on to explain that he had come to Acheson not merely as a Zionist, but with a full awareness of the American interests. Should the president suffer a loss of prestige, the Jews too would suffer because America and the president were the last friends left to them. He knew, he said, that considerable pressure was being exerted on the president to throw all his weight behind the demand for the 100,000 immigration certificates and leave the rest for the future. He, Goldmann, would advise the president not to do this inasmuch as the matter could place the president in a ridiculous situation: he had already personally requested the 100,000 certificates no less than four times, and did not receive them; he certainly could not obtain them in the future either. The British believed they could not reach a solution of the Palestine problem without the support of America, and wanted America to be involved in the issue until the final decision. The British were apprehensive that, if they gave in to the president's demand for the 100,000 certificates, this would assure the president the Jewish vote, and thereafter, if the British encountered troubles with the Arabs about the final decision, the president would no longer involve himself in the problem. Therefore, he must come out in support of the Jewish State plan in the fullest sense of the word, which would help both him and the Jews.

The argument seemed to have impressed Acheson. He said that Gold-mann was the first Zionist who spoke to him not only about the Jewish interests, but also about the American point of view.

This positive reaction of Acheson to Goldmann's proposal was sub-sequently confirmed by Acheson in his meeting with Abraham Tulin and Professor Milton Handler, two members of the AZEC executive staff, on August 20. Tulin reported that Acheson had told him and Handler that "Dr. Goldmann had brought the first sign of reasonableness in an im-possibly difficult position." Acheson further said that "the Government had decided to wash its hands of the whole business," but that Gold-mann's proposal "was something that the Government could back." In fact, said Acheson, after his talk with Goldmann, "the American Gov-ernment decided to transmit it [the Goldmann plan] to the British Gov-ernment as a proposal of the [Jewish] Agency, however, with a statement that the American Government gave its approval to the proposal."[68]

At the conclusion of his talk with Goldmann, Acheson said that he was willing to accept "the Goldmann plan," and even fight for it, pro-vided Goldmann could convince David Niles, whose opinion was highly valued by the president, as well as Snyder and Patterson, Acheson's colleagues in the Cabinet Committee.

During the course of Goldmann's talk with Acheson, the latter inquired as to the reaction to the partition plan that could be expected from American Jewish leaders. He said he could not fight for partition if a major sector of American Jews came out against it because it implied the relinquishment of part of Palestine. Goldmann's reply was that he felt that the majority of American Jews were behind the plan and that all the Zionists would support it. Acheson then asked, "What about Silver?" Goldmann assured him that Silver did not oppose partition and that only tactical differences prevailed between him and the position of the Executive. Goldmann added that the Revisionists and the Bergson group would attack the plan, but Acheson, surprisingly well informed of internal Zionist politics, deemed this to be of no significance. When Goldmann mentioned the American Council for Judaism, which main-tained a strongly anti-Zionist position, Acheson dismissed it as repre-senting only an insignificant minority. Then, he asked, what would be the position of Judge Proskauer, who carried much weight in the eyes of the government. Goldmann replied that he planned to meet with Proskauer, who he was certain would not interfere.

To Acheson's question about the position of the non-Jewish friends of Zionism in the Senate, Goldmann answered that he believed that most senators would support the agency's position and that "we will ask them not to be more Zionist than the Executive." He added that he could not guarantee where Senator Robert A. Taft, of Ohio, and former Senator Guy M. Gillette, of Iowa, would stand, but Acheson did not attribute much significance to their position. On the other hand, he stressed the importance of the support of the senators friendly to the Zionist cause, such as Alben W. Barkley, of Kentucky, Claude D. Pepper, of Florida, and James M. Mead, of New York, and Goldmann assured him it would be forthcoming.

The foregoing summation of what transpired between Goldmann and Acheson is based on the report Goldmann gave to the Executive in Paris six days after the meeting (for Acheson's description of the meeting, see Appendix F). When, more than twenty years later, he retold the story of his talks with Acheson in his 1969 *Autobiography*, he saw them from a different perspective, omitted much of what he had included in his August 13, 1946, report, and recalled a line of argument he had not mentioned at all in 1946. The relevant 1969 passage reads as follows:

> Although Dean Acheson was never strongly pro-Zionist, he was a statesman of stature and an unusually candid man. In presenting my case I found him responsive to the argument that if the present state of affairs continued, the terrorists would gain the upper hand in Palestine and an actual war between the Jewish population and the British administration would become inevitable. A development of this sort would place not only American Jewry but also the American government in an extremely difficult situation, quite apart from the disastrous consequences for England if it had to appear in the eyes of the world as the enemy of the Jews so soon after the war and the Jewish tragedy.[69]

Goldmann took along a lasting impression of Acheson from his meetings with him. Although in his 1969 *Autobiography* he confines himself to referring to Acheson as "a statesman of stature and an unusually candid man," his *Jewish Paradox*, written three decades after the event, contains a vignette of the man that is worth repeating. Acheson, Goldmann remembered,

> was a very cultured, aristocratic-looking man, not at all popular with the members of the Congress, who sensed his superiority. They used to say that there was nothing American about him, and he ought to be at Westminster. In fact he came over a lot more British than Yankee. He had no trace of the provincial politician, and as a student of world history he always put problems in a universal framework. He was a friend of the Jews, but not of Zionism, and I am quite proud of having persuaded him to help us.[70]

This was evidently a man after Goldmann's own taste with whom he could be at his best and most persuasive self. Acheson was initially opposed to a Jewish State. Such a state, he felt, established over the opposition of the Arabs, would enjoy no peace for decades and would be risking catastrophe because America would not be able to go on supporting it indefinitely. Goldmann countered this objection by arguing that a failure to let the Jews have their own state would unleash Jewish terrorism against the British, which would lead to a bloody struggle between the Jewish population of Palestine and the British forces in the country. This would be inevitable because the Jews simply could no longer acquiesce in the exclusion from Palestine of the half-million Jewish refugees who had survived the Nazi genocide. These refugees had only one desire: to leave the countries that had become huge cemeteries for six million Jews. "Are you willing," Goldmann asked Acheson, "to receive them in America? No. In other countries? No. Then Menahem Begin, the extreme rightist leader, will take power. . . . The extremists will be dominant. . . . What will be your attitude then? When the Jewish terrorists are killing the British, will you take a stand against the British? And when the British are killing Jews, where will you be?"[71]

Despite Acheson's serious initial misgivings, at the end Goldmann did succeed in having him accept the partition plan and become its supporter. This was undoubtedly the key link in the chain of events that culminated in the American endorsement and advocacy of the partition resolution in the United Nations.

XI From his talk with Acheson, Goldmann went directly to a meeting of the executives of the American Zionist Emergency Council, which had been in session since 4:00 P.M., and to which he had been invited by Silver. He arrived two hours late. Silver, who did not know of Goldmann's meeting with Acheson, opened the proceedings by presenting a report on the meeting that had taken place the previous evening at the Statler Hotel.

Silver's position, as we noted earlier, differed from that of Goldmann and the agency Executive in tactics. Silver felt it would be a grave tactical error to propose partition as a Jewish demand because, by doing so, the agency would reduce its "maximalist" position to part of Palestine, and the British then could proceed to whittle it down further. He reiterated that he interpreted the agency's August 5 resolution to mean that the idea of partition was not excluded from consideration, as a possible

solution of the problem, and that, if in the course of the ongoing negotiations, such a proposal was presented to the Zionist leadership, the
latter would not out-of-hand reject it. If the proposal was satisfactory,
"we will take it back to the Executive or to another competent body for
action. This was not a mandate to Dr. Goldmann or to Dr. Silver or to
the [American Zionist Emergency] Council to go to the President of the
U.S., or to Mr. Acheson or to anybody else and say that the Jewish
Agency is in favor of partition and that we want to press for it."[72]

When Goldmann arrived at the meeting and his turn came to speak,
he did not inform his colleagues that he had just succeeded in convincing
Acheson to support the partition plan. Instead, he explained why and
how the Executive of the Jewish Agency had resolved two days earlier
to adopt the partition plan: it "was a tragic decision taken in what was
regarded a desperate situation." He reiterated the arguments for the
partition plan and, when asked whether the agency's resolution would
be submitted to the administration in Washington, he replied that it
certainly would, for this was the purpose of his mission. He added that
he had received directives from the Executive to inform the American
government that the Jewish Agency rejected the Morrison-Grady plan.
When asked, "What is your proposal?" he replied, "Partition."

Silver then reemphasized that his understanding of the Executive's
resolution was that the partition proposal must first emanate from the
American government before the Jewish Agency's representative would
say that the agency was prepared to consider it. Goldmann in turn stated,
"We shall have to await and examine the decision of the Committee of
Nine," that is, the American members of the Anglo-American and Morrison-Grady Committees, but cautioned that the situation might change
rapidly and stressed that "the Agency Executive reserves the right to
negotiate with all governments," including the government of the United
States, though, of course, it will conduct negotiations in cooperation
with the members of the Zionist Emergency Council. This had to satisfy
Silver, who, not having been present at the Paris meeting of the Executive, was not in a position to insist on his interpretation of its crucial
resolution. At the end, he said that he and Goldmann "were both in
agreement."[73]

Although it is evident that Goldmann was less than candid in his
August 7 report to his Zionist colleagues—especially blatant is his omission to mention that he had just come from a long talk with Acheson,
whom he had succeeded in winning for the partition plan—he had good
reasons to do so. The American Zionist leadership, headed by Silver and
Emanuel Neumann, was still far from reconciled with Goldmann's taking

over the management of the Zionist contacts with Washington. This factor exacerbated the serious tactical differences between them and Goldmann, who was convinced that the time had come to put all the cards on the table if a further and deeper involvement of the American government with the Palestine problem was to be attained. Finding himself called upon to report to his colleagues while in the very midst of his negotiations with the Cabinet Committee—his talk with Acheson was to be followed next day by no less than seven more meetings, ranging from important to crucial—it is totally understandable that he felt constrained to withhold from them a piece of information that some of those present may have leaked or even used to create opposition and take steps against the partition plan.

A glance at the text of the Executive's August 5 resolution suffices to show that Silver's interpretation of the resolution was, in fact, an attempt to read into it a meaning it did not have and did not intend to have. Paragraph 2, when taken alone, is perhaps somewhat ambiguous: it states that the Executive "is prepared to discuss a proposal for the establishment of a viable Jewish State in an adequate area of Palestine." This could mean that the Executive was willing to entertain such a proposal put to it by others, that is, the British government; or, it could mean that the Executive was ready to go ahead and initiate such a discussion, that is, make the proposal. That it was unquestionably the latter meaning the Executive had in mind becomes clear from paragraph 3, which specifies that "as *immediate* steps for the implementation of paragraph 2, the Executive puts forward the following demands: (a) the *immediate* grant of 100,000 certificates and the *immediate* beginning of the transportation of the 100,000 people to Palestine; (b) the grant of *immediate* full autonomy (in appointing its administration and in the economic field) to that area of Palestine to be designated to become the Jewish State; and (c) the grant of the right to control immigration to the administration of that area of Palestine designated to be a Jewish State [emphasis added]."[74] The fourfold repetition of the adjective "immediate" leaves no room for doubt that the meaning of paragraph 2 was to propose the establishment of a Jewish State in partitioned Palestine and to insist on the *immediate* initiation of steps that the Executive considered the first moves toward a full implementation of the establishment of the state. It is hard to understand how, in view of the language of paragraphs 2 and 3 together, their meaning could be construed as anything else than a clear-cut decision to press *immediately* "for the establishment of a viable Jewish State in an adequate area of Palestine."

In fact, independent testimony shows that the members of the Executive understood the decision they took on August 5 precisely as interpreted by Goldmann. One of those present, Judith (Mrs. Moses P.) Epstein, president of Hadassah, on August 21 presented to a meeting of the Hadassah executives a detailed report on what transpired at the Paris meeting. She reported that the Jewish Agency Executive had decided to send Goldmann to America "to speak to our friends on the [Anglo-American] Committee [of Inquiry] (Crum, McDonald, and Burton), and to present the substitute plan. But we were to go beyond that. Government people were to be urged to sponsor the plan." She also reported that Goldmann explicitly stated that he would see Acheson "since he was the strategic person in this picture. Snyder and Patterson were mentioned."[75]

Knowing precisely what the Executive had entrusted him with, and faced with Silver's arbitrary reinterpretation of the Executive's August 5 resolution, Goldmann was confirmed in the conviction he had formed at the informal meeting the previous evening: that he must prevent interference in his negotiations by Silver and his followers until such time that adoption of the partition plan by the Cabinet Committee and approval by the President were *faits accomplis*. The only way to make sure that no such interference would take place was to keep from the Silver-dominated AZEC the knowledge that he already had begun to carry out the mission entrusted to him by the Executive, had spoken to Acheson, and was about to speak the next day to the other two members of the Cabinet Committee.

XII The next day, Thursday, August 8, was one of the rare days for which Goldmann's appointment-book entries carry not only the names of the people he met but also the hours of the meetings. They read as follows:

> 8. August   Washington
> 8:30 Proskauer
> 10:30 Lord Inverchapel
> 11:30 Snyder, Secr. of Treasury
> 2:00 Crum
> 3:30 With Proskauer to Patterson
> 6:00 Niles
> 9:00 Proskauer

(According to Elath, the meeting between Goldmann and Niles at which he, Elath, was present, took place on August 8 at breakfast, during which Goldmann convinced Niles that partition was the only solution and won his support for it. Niles expressed the hope that the proposal, when brought before the president, would prove that the Zionists are moving ahead, and that hope prevailed for a solution of the Palestine problem. He also promised to get in touch with Acheson and to work out a common plan of action with him on the manner in which the "Goldmann plan," as he put it, should be presented to Truman.)[76]

Before discussing Goldmann's meetings with Proskauer, what is known of his talks with the British Ambassador Lord Inverchapel will be presented. As Goldmann reported to the Executive on August 13, at first they talked about the ships carrying illegal Jewish immigrants that were being detained by the British in Haifa harbor, which was the burning issue of the moment. Inverchapel said he wanted to be totally frank: he was not inclined to intervene in favor of the continuation of illegal immigration. The British government would not tolerate it. He understood the motivations of the Jews, but could not approve it. However, he was willing to accept the Executive's argument that at that moment the immigrants needed to be taken off the ships and would immediately contact the British Foreign Office, to do the best he could.

Then Goldmann said he had larger issues to discuss with him. He had come on behalf of the Executive of the Jewish Agency. He did not want him to feel that the Executive was acting behind his back, or that a Jewish-American plot was in the making. "We would not mind plotting if through plots we could achieve a Jewish State, but America cannot give it to us." He reported to Inverchapel what Acheson had said, which made a strong impression on him. "Will you go to the London conference?" asked Inverchapel. "Not on the basis of the British plan," answered Goldmann. "We cannot do it while our people are detained in Latrun." Inverchapel exclaimed, "Are you saying that Moshe [Shertok] has been arrested? Oh, God! How they spoil everything!" He asked Goldmann to show him the Executive's resolution, but Goldmann refused. Then he asked Goldmann to submit a memorandum, but again the answer was negative. That would mean a first step, and he, Goldmann, was not authorized to do so. Inverchapel then asked Goldmann to specify in writing under what conditions the Jewish Agency would be willing to attend the conference. Goldmann thereupon stated in writing that under no conditions was the Executive prepared to participate in the negotiations on the basis of the Morrison-Grady plan, but only on the basis of the principle of a Jewish State in an adequate area of Palestine. Inverchapel said he would immediately notify the Foreign Office by phone.[77]

This account is augmented in Goldmann's 1969 *Autobiography* by a résumé of what had happened at the meeting with Inverchapel. The British ambassador expressed his personal approval of the partition scheme and asked Goldmann to keep him informed of developments during Goldmann's Washington visit. "In our final talk [Inverchapel] said that I ought now to go to see Bevin and submit the proposal to him, but to this I replied that without being authorized by the Executive I could not enter into such communication with the British government, and in any case, the more than strained relations between the Executive and Bevin made it doubtful that he would even receive me. Lord Inverchapel then offered to cable the gist of my proposals to Bevin and to recommend that he invite me for a series of talks."[78]

Still the same day (Thursday, August 8), following up on Acheson's suggestion that he meet with the other two members of the Cabinet Committee, Goldmann saw Secretary of the Treasury John W. Snyder, who "quickly gave his approval."[79] No additional details of what transpired at this meeting are available.

Secretary of War Robert P. Patterson presented more of a problem. Trained as a lawyer (LL.B. Harvard, 1915), he had served in the American army in France in World War I, won the Distinguished Service Cross, and, after two decades of practice as an attorney and judge, became, in 1940, under secretary of war, and in 1945 was nominated by President Truman to succeed Henry L. Stimson as the secretary of war. Like most officials in the Pentagon, Secretary Patterson was opposed to the partition of Palestine, which, he feared, might lead to fighting between the Jews and the Arabs as well as militarily and politically costly entanglements for America. Thus, the approach to Patterson required circumspection and preparation.

It so happened that upon his arrival in Washington Goldmann received a phone call from his close friend and coworker Rabbi Stephen Wise, who informed him that Judge Proskauer was on his way to Washington to meet Secretary Patterson. Joseph M. Proskauer (1877–1971), president of the American Jewish Committee and an outspoken opponent of partition, had close connections with Patterson. It was evident, Wise told Goldmann, that the purpose of Proskauer's meeting with Patterson was to strengthen the secretary of war in his resolve to oppose partition. Wise and Proskauer, though adversaries in Jewish politics, were personal friends. Both had summer homes on the same island, where they would frequently meet, and it was during the course of such a meeting that Wise learned of Proskauer's planned visit to Patterson.[80]

Goldmann knew that the American Jewish Committee, as the oldest and most respected American organization dedicated to the defense of the interests of the Jews all over the world, had in the past repeatedly influenced American policy; and that the word of its president would therefore carry considerable weight in Washington when it came to a decision on a Jewish issue. As far as Proskauer himself was concerned, he had become president of the American Jewish Committee in 1943 on a platform that he himself had prepared and which supported free Jewish immigration into Palestine and international trusteeship, but opposed a Jewish State. Thus, both personally and in his capacity as president of the American Jewish Committee, Proskauer was committed to an antipartition stand.

Goldmann had an appointment with Proskauer later in the week as part of a series of meetings he had scheduled with non-Zionist leaders for the purpose of winning their support for the partition plan. Now, however, it had become imperative to meet Proskauer before the latter would see Patterson. So, demonstrating the self-confidence that had been one of his major strengths since early childhood, immediately after seeing Acheson, Goldmann "took the very dangerous chance of picking up the phone and calling Proskauer."[81] Proskauer agreed to see Goldmann that same evening (August 7).

The meeting lasted late into the night. Basically, Goldmann's main argument was identical with the one he used in his meetings with Acheson. As he reported to the Executive on August 13, he said to Proskauer: "You have come here in order to help us. This is the Jewish position," and went on to explain that, failing partition, the situation would remain frozen, America would drop the whole issue, and immigration to Palestine would stop altogether. In that case, the Jews of Palestine would be unable to remain quiet. "Our youth, if it will not be given the means to carry on its efforts to build, will feel compelled to destroy as a reaction. There will be unpleasant incidents. You will wash your hands of the whole affair, but it won't help you, and the Gentiles will say that you are responsible for the explosion in the King David Hotel and other such occurrences."

Having had his say (Goldmann reported to the Executive), he and Proskauer went to see Patterson.[82] In his 1978 memoirs, Goldmann recalled a few additional points he used in his talk with Proskauer. He appealed to Proskauer's Jewish conscience:

> You are a good Jew, and you've done a lot for Jewry. So you ought to understand what convinced Dean Acheson. I told him what a dilemma he would face if terrorism took hold in Israel. But it would be worse for you.

If Begin and his Irgun friends take power, Moshe Sharett, Weizmann and I will resign, but there will be terror just the same: Jews will kill British and British will kill Jews. So where will you stand as an American Jew? With the Jews who kill the British, and consequently against your own government, or with the British who will be killing Jews two years after Auschwitz?[83]

The effectiveness of this argument, whether it was presented to Acheson or to Proskauer, hinged on the credibility of the threat of violence. Goldmann undoubtedly firmly believed that, if partition were not approved, the extremist element in the *Yishuv* could gain the upper hand, and bloodshed would ensue. Goldmann was always at his most effective when he tried to convince others of what he himself firmly believed in. He convinced Acheson, who would look at a British-Jewish conflict in Palestine from the outside, from the perspective of an American statesman, and elicited a much stronger emotional response from Proskauer, who throughout his life had identified strongly with the Jewish plight.

Proskauer stood up with tears in his eyes and said: "I am with you one hundred per cent. I'll take you with me to see Patterson, but before that I must resign the presidency of the American Jewish Committee, which is against the Jewish state." Although it was by then past midnight, Proskauer said he would immediately call the chairman of the executive committee of the American Jewish Committee, Jacob Blaustein, to inform him of his resignation. "Go to the next room and listen on the other phone," he told Goldmann.

Jacob Blaustein (1892–1970), cofounder with his father of the American Oil Company in 1910 and reputedly one of the richest men in America, was a prominent philanthropist and a sworn anti-Zionist. When he, awakened by Proskauer's call, heard what his friend Joe intended to do, he was indignant and upset.

"Joe, you've fallen into a trap," he cried into the phone. "Do you know who you're dealing with? Nahum Goldmann is the shrewdest operator in the world, let alone the shrewdest Jew. He's making a fool of you. You're ruining your career!"

But Proskauer stuck to his resolve. "I'm older than you," he said, "and not more of a fool than you, if I may say so. It's an insult to tell me that Nahum has trapped me. He has convinced me, and that's different. I won't pursue this discussion. Call an emergency meeting for tomorrow morning and announce my resignation. If not, I shall announce it to the newspaper myself."

On August 8, 1946, at 3:30 P.M., Proskauer took Goldmann along with him to his appointment with Patterson. The secretary of war was surprised to see the two men come together because he, of course, knew that they had been on opposite sides on the question of partition and the Jewish State. Proskauer stated briefly that Goldmann had convinced him that he had been wrong and that everything Goldmann would say to Patterson had his approval. Thereupon, Goldmann again launched into a presentation of his argument, which did not fail to impress the secretary of war. The conversation ended with Patterson saying that, inasmuch as Joe Proskauer and Nahum Goldmann, who had been lifelong adversaries, had agreed that partition was the solution of the Palestine problem, he had no right to oppose it.[84]

The Goldmann-Proskauer-Patterson meeting is described in more detail in Goldmann's report to the Executive on August 13, 1946. When Patterson expressed his surprise to see Proskauer and Goldmann together, Goldmann said, "Palestine makes for strange partnerships." Proskauer then said, "Bob, you know that the American Jewish Committee was always opposed to a Jewish State, or at least did not support it. I have always seen in the Hutcheson report a great political document. But Dr. Goldmann has convinced me that the best way to a solution of the Palestine problem was to establish two states." Therefore, he was willing to support the plan, but without thereby committing the American Jewish Committee.

Following this introduction, Goldmann made a forty-minute presentation of the Executive's plan, explaining its main features and advantages. Patterson replied that he was convinced and that the fact that Proskauer agreed was a boon. The administration did not want to see much controversy among the Jews. Patterson asked for a memorandum on the partition plan because, he said, he needed a written document. He also said that he had already spoken to Acheson, who supported the Jewish plan.[85]

The foregoing accounts of the Goldmann-Proskauer-Patterson meetings are based on Goldmann's August 13, 1946, report to the Executive; on his *Autobiography*, written some 20 years later; on his *The Jewish Paradox*, written after another ten years had elapsed; and on his recollections during my interview with him in 1980. It so happens that the second participant in the meetings, Judge Proskauer, also recorded them in two documents: one is a memorandum he sent on August 16, 1946, to John Slawson, executive vice-president of the American Jewish Committee (see Appendix I); the other, an account in Proskauer's autobiography, written three or four years after the event.[86]

From Proskauer's memorandum to Slawson, it becomes evident to what extent he was influenced by Goldmann's arguments. He came to believe, as argued by Goldmann, that only the establishment of a Jewish State could make it possible to rescue the Jews suffering in the displaced persons camps in Europe. He found "undisputable evidence" that Lord Inverchapel approved the partition plan, and that the State Department backed it, in fact, was "absolutely sold on it" and hopeful of "being able to put it across." He deemed the acceptance of the partition plan by the Jewish Agency as "enormous concessions from the former demands," and stated that "no Jews should block this earnest attempt based on mutual concessions."

As for the account contained in Proskauer's autobiography, as would be expected when two people describe events in which they were principals, his recollections do not coincide on every point with those of Goldmann. Apart from such minor discrepancies as the exact time of the Goldmann-Proskauer meeting (according to Goldmann it took place in the late evening; according to Proskauer, in the morning), the two accounts contain only a few major points of difference.

According to Goldmann, the original purpose of Proskauer's meeting with Patterson was "to tell him that American Jews were against the [establishment of a] State of Israel." According to Proskauer, he was told by Patterson, and subsequently by Acheson (whom Proskauer met after seeing Patterson), that they were for partition. Acheson, Proskauer reports, told him that "he had decided that partition was the only feasible course, and suggested that as the representative of a great Jewish organization which had not committed itself to the ideology of statehood [Proskauer] could render a great service by supporting the partition plan. With the authority of my governing board, I thereupon gave the endorsement of the American Jewish Committee to that plan."

Proskauer tries to play down the change in his and the committee's position on partition. He writes: "For me [the support of partition] represented no reversal of attitude, for it had become apparent that partition was the most promising, if not the only means of throwing open the gates of Palestine. From that time on, therefore, I gave my wholehearted support to the accomplishment of the plan." Yet it is clear that, before his meeting with Goldmann, Proskauer was against partition. In fact, in recording his meeting with Goldmann in which the latter solicited his aid for the partition plan, he states that he remained noncommittal: "I told him that my attitude would be determined largely by the attitude of the American government." That is, according to Proskauer, it was only during his meetings with Patterson and Acheson, whom Goldmann had won over for partition, that "it had become apparent" to him that partition was the right solution to the Palestine and Jewish refugee problems.

Proskauer says nothing about the arguments put forward by Goldmann in soliciting his support for partition. Nor does he state that he changed his mind as a result of Goldmann's pleading. What he says, is that, after Goldmann had "explained his plan to the Secretary," he, Proskauer, "asked Goldmann to leave the room" and "asked the Secretary to give to me, as the head of the American Jewish Committee, his frank reaction. He answered in substance that his immediate reaction was that partition was the only way to quick [Jewish] immigration into Palestine, that he deemed it vital because of the frightful situation in the DP [displaced persons] camps; but he added the caution that this was merely his tentative personal view and that, of course, it would have to be subject to the decision of the Department of State."[87]

The difference in the two men's accounts of their meeting with Patterson boils down to Proskauer's role in the decision of Patterson to support the partition scheme. According to Goldmann, Proskauer, whom he had converted to a propartition stand a day earlier, informed Patterson that he endorsed whatever Goldmann was about to tell him, and this surprising harmony between the two old antagonists was partly responsible for Patterson's positive reaction to Goldmann's presentation of the case for partition. According to Proskauer, on the other hand, he himself played an entirely passive role in the meeting. Goldmann explained the partition plan to Patterson without any support or participation by Proskauer, and yet Goldmann's presentation was sufficient to produce an immediate positive reaction and a "tentative personal view" on the part of Patterson to the effect that partition was the only way to a quick solution of the displaced persons problem.

Whatever the actual course of events, the two accounts agree on the crucial point: it was Goldmann's argument that persuaded Patterson to support the partition scheme.

After the meeting, Proskauer went to see Dean Acheson, who told him "in substance that he had canvassed the situation, had decided that partition was the only feasible course, and suggested that as the representative of a great Jewish organization which had not committed itself to the ideology of statehood [for the Jews in Palestine], I could render a great service by supporting the partition plan." Seeing that "partition was now the project of both the Jewish Agency for Palestine and of the government of the United States," Proskauer, bolstered by the authority of the governing board of the American Jewish Committee, gave its endorsement to the partition plan.[88]

As for whether or not this position represented a "reversal of attitude" on the part of Proskauer, the following facts must be considered. Before his meeting with Goldmann, Proskauer had been in the forefront of those who opposed the idea of a Jewish State. In an essay of appraisal of Proskauer (who died in 1971), published in the 1972 *American Jewish Year Book*, the official publication of the American Jewish Committee, David Scher describes the "climactic final session of the American Jewish Conference," held in May 1942, at which "several thousand delegates gathered from all over the land to demand the creation of a Jewish state in Palestine. It was in a critical period of World War II, and the Judge [Proskauer] was convinced that such a demand at that time was unwise and unrealistic, especially with Palestine then two-thirds Arab and one-third Jewish. The huge auditorium was charged with emotion. The crowd, overwhelmingly Zionist, was fired by the oratory of Abba Hillel Silver, Nahum Goldmann, and Stephen Wise, all at the pinnacle of their powers and their power. Each could manipulate a crowd as though it were a huge baby."

When the chair recognized Proskauer, he "walked resolutely to the center of the platform, and, looking out over the audience, purred, 'I now know how Daniel felt when he entered the lions' den,' " and proceeded to state his reasons for opposing the Jewish State.[89] When the Conference, by an overwhelming majority, endorsed the Biltmore Program, calling for a Jewish commonwealth in the whole of Palestine, Proskauer, as president of the American Jewish Committee, led his organization out of the conference.

However, after Proskauer was brought around by Goldmann (or, according to Proskauer's own account, by the U.S. secretaries of state and war) to the partition plan, the Executive Committee of the American Jewish Committee at its meeting on September 15, 1946, resolved to support the partition of Palestine along the lines suggested by the Jewish Agency a month earlier.[90] It must be noted, however, that the support the committee gave to the partition plan was neither wholehearted nor definitive. After the United Nations Special Committee on Palestine (UNSCOP) was set up (on May 15, 1947), Proskauer as president and Jacob Blaustein as chairman of the Executive of the American Jewish Committee submitted (on June 1) a brief to UNSCOP in which, in the first place, they urged the establishment of a UN trusteeship over Palestine, which harked back to the committee's 1943 platform, prepared by

Proskauer himself, and only "in the event, however, that an immediate political solution would be considered preferable by the Assembly [of the United Nations] to a United Nations trusteeship" did they urge that Palestine be partitioned.[91]

As for Proskauer's resignation from the presidency of the American Jewish Committee, the fact is that, even if he did announce his intention to resign, he did not carry it out and remained its president until 1949. Here, Goldmann's description of the events in *The Jewish Paradox* is incomplete. In fact, in his *Autobiography* he merely says, "I managed to change Judge Proskauer's mind and he declared himself ready to shift his position, even at the risk of having to resign the presidency of the American Jewish Committee, which was committed to opposing a Jewish state.[92]

It would seem that what happened was that the matter did not rest with Proskauer's demand that Blaustein call an emergency meeting of the board and announce his resignation, as described by Goldmann in his *Jewish Paradox,* but that subsequently, after Proskauer informed the board of the committee of the propartition stand of the American government, the committee followed his lead and endorsed partition, which made it unnecessary for Proskauer to resign.

XIII   Once all three members of the Cabinet Committee were won over to the partition plan, President Truman had to be informed of the committee's unanimous support of it. David Niles advised that Goldmann himself should convey the sense of the committee to the president, but Goldmann felt that the matter would require a detailed discussion of all the implications a propartition stand would involve for American internal and foreign politics, and that therefore Truman's own men should present the matter to him.[93] It was agreed that Niles and Acheson would put the recommendation before the president, which they did the next day. He accepted the plan without reservation and instructed Acheson to inform the British government accordingly.[94]

According to Elath's account of those events, Goldmann's work day on August 8 ended when he held a second meeting with Acheson. Goldmann reported to Acheson that he had obtained the support of Niles for the partition scheme as well as the consent of Snyder and Patterson. Acheson told Goldmann that he had already heard about it from Niles and Patterson and added that the way was now open to bringing the proposal to the knowledge of the president for a decision. It was decided that Niles and Acheson, and not Goldmann, should do so.

The meeting between Truman and Niles and Acheson was scheduled for the next morning (Friday, August 9, 1946). Goldmann and Epstein went to the office of Niles in the White House and waited there for Niles to return from the Oval Office. Suddenly, the door opened, Niles burst into the room, all excited, and cried, "It's settled!" Tears flowed from his eyes, and he said, in Yiddish, "If only my mother of blessed memory could have heard that there will be Jewish State!" It took a long time until Niles, although he was as a rule a calm and controlled man, could get hold of himself. He reported about his and Acheson's meeting with the president. He said that the fact that a possibility could be envisaged for a solution of the Palestine problem which took into account the interests of all the three sides involved in the Palestine conflict was the decisive factor in Truman's decision to accept the partition plan and to inform London via the regular diplomatic channels. When Acheson was asked by the president about the chances that the Arabs would accept the plan, the acting secretary of state cautiously replied that the matter depended to a large extent on the British. The problems with partition would become evident in London, rather than in Cairo or any other Arab capital. Also, Niles himself doubted whether the partition plan would be well received in England because Bevin was committed to his own cantonization plan. Nevertheless, inasmuch as the partition plan involved considerable concessions on the part of the Jews, who wanted a Jewish State in all of Palestine, and because, moreover, the Jews were ready to promise to safeguard British interests in their future state, the chances to come to an agreement with London might be better now than they were in the past. The very fact that the partition proposal came from the Jewish Agency testified to a more practical approach to the Palestine problem than was the Biltmore program's "all or nothing."[95]

At noon on the same day, Goldmann met again with Acheson. This time, Loy W. Henderson, assistant secretary of state for the Near East, was also present. Acheson said: "Now that we have a joint approach, and we are allies, we have decided that we must discuss with you our announcement to the British government. Henderson will read out the general lines of our announcement, and we want to know whether you agree with it. We want to be completely frank and to supply you with information." Then Acheson asked what the Zionist position would be on the loan of $300 million to the Arabs America was considering. Goldmann's answer was that "if we get the State we shall have no objection to loans given by America to the Arabs. We shall not interfere in this issue with the act of the American Congress. But why should not the bulk of this money go to encouraging the Arabs to leave Palestine and settle elsewhere?" Acheson said that this was a constructive suggestion that would be included in the draft of the announcement to the British government.

Goldmann suggested several changes, and then Acheson asked Henderson to show Goldmann the text of the cable Acheson intended to send to the British government, which stated that the State Department was unable to recommend to the president approval of the Grady report. This was not possible because of the leak and the Zionist propaganda. The American Congress would never approve the loan of $300 million, which was a vital part of the report. Also, the cable continued, Dr. Goldmann had informed them that the Jewish Agency would not negotiate on the basis of that report. Acheson asked on what basis the Jewish Agency would be prepared to negotiate, and Dr. Goldmann thereupon presented the plan for the establishment of two states. He also added that the Jewish State meant a majority of Jewish citizens and that a transition period of two years would be in effect. The boundaries of the Jewish State would include those of the Peel partition plan plus the addition of the Negev. The Jewish administration would have the immediate right of supervising immigration, which would solve the problem of the 100,000 certificates because then the matter would be in the hands of the Jews. They would also possess economic rights and would be able to elect their own administrative institutions with the approval of the High Commissioner. The cable also added that the American government was prepared, as approved by the president, to support this plan, and was interested to know the position of the British government. The American government was willing to take upon itself certain financial obligations in connection with the realization of this plan.[96]

Goldmann found the contents of the cable to be satisfactory. Henderson said he could not put it in final form before the next day (Saturday, August 10). Goldmann stressed that every day was precious. Acheson said, "What a criminal stupidity it is for the British to hold a discussion on this in Parliament before they have heard from us." Goldmann agreed, and pointed out that Grady had misled the British into believing that the Morrison-Grady plan would gain the support of the American government. Acheson suggested that Henderson could perhaps cancel his lunch appointment and work instead on the cable. Henderson agreed, and Acheson told him right there, in Goldmann's presence, that the president had approved the partition plan.[97]

At the conclusion of the meeting between Goldmann and Acheson, the latter asked Henderson to show Goldmann the memorandum of their first talk, which he wanted Goldmann to approve. Goldmann read and initialed it.[98]

Although for the Zionist cause the meetings that took place in the four days from August 6 to 9 in Washington were events of crucial political importance because President Truman's support for the partition plan could be obtained only through Acheson and his two colleagues in the Cabinet Committee, it is characteristic for the entirely different perspective from which the American statesmen viewed the Palestine issue that Acheson in his 1969 book, *Present at the Creation,* does not even mention his talks with Goldmann and with Proskauer, nor the unanimous advice he, Snyder, and Patterson gave to the president to lend America's support to the partition of Palestine. Although Acheson devotes a brief chapter to "The Puzzle of Palestine," he does not say a word in it on this particular phase of the political process that some fifteen months later resulted in America's propartition vote at the United Nations.[99]

His mission in Washington accomplished, Goldmann flew back to Paris on Sunday, August 11, and reported to the Executive two days later. His report is the only more or less detailed account of what happened during those hectic five days, when he had lengthy talks with Dean Acheson, John Snyder, Robert Patterson, David Niles, Loy Henderson, and last but not least, Joseph Proskauer—converting all of them to a propartition position—not to mention the efforts that went into "neutralizing" Abba Hillel Silver and other meetings with colleagues in the Zionist leadership. Rarely has one man in such a short time converted so many people of such different outlooks to his own point of view, and rarely has a complex political action been accomplished with such complete success. Although the partition plan came up for a vote in the United Nations only fifteen months later and its support by the United States could not always be counted upon with absolute certainty, ultimately America not only voted for it but actively helped the representatives of the Jewish Agency in lobbying for the votes of several other nations. That this had come to pass and that the Jewish State was given a solid international basis on which to set itself up, was to a large measure due to the work of Goldmann.

However, Goldmann's task in connection with the establishment of Israel was not completed with his accomplishments in Washington. As he stated on August 13 to the Executive, "the American government has submitted the partition plan, as we wanted it, but it is the British government which has to decide what to do. It has to clarify its position. We can either wait until they reply to the American government, or we can contact them ourselves and try to influence them for our benefit." He went on to report that, at one point during the course of his talks with Acheson, the secretary had asked him how this resolution could be given a legally valid form. The British Mandate, of course, must come to an end, but what about the United Nations? Goldmann replied that it could be done in the form in which it was done in Transjordan and with the same speed. His reference was to what had happened only a few months earlier: after having been the Mandatory power over Transjordan since 1922, on March 22, 1946, Britain terminated the Mandate and recognized Transjordan as an independent kingdom. Acheson thought that this was a splendid idea, and if so, what was the point in bothering about legalities?

But Goldmann said that he wanted an immediate discussion and decision about the position of the Executive vis-à-vis Britain and about the major lines of its policy. He felt that the Executive must make official contact with the British government to negotiate on matters of policy. As recently as last Monday (August 5), he reminded his colleagues on the Executive, he had opposed a meeting between Weizmann and British Colonial Secretary George Hall because it would have been premature before the clarification of the American position. But now, after the Americans had given their support to the partition plan, it was no longer possible to continue without contact with the Mandatory power, whose position was the decisive factor in the whole issue. Should the British government ask Jewish representatives to come, he said, he saw no reason to refuse. Hall had phoned Weizmann several times and asked him to meet with him. As Goldmann said, "We must go to the British government and declare that we will not go to the conference on the basis of the Morrison plan, but we are willing to negotiate on the basis of a Jewish State, and let us hear their reaction. If we refuse to do so, we shall be in an intolerable situation vis-à-vis the American government and in relation to the issue itself. There is now a chance of a constructive outcome, and we cannot permit ourselves to refuse to talk to the British government."[100]

After listening to Goldmann's detailed report, the Executive authorized him to contact British Foreign Secretary Bevin.

On the same day (August 13) on which Goldmann reported to the Executive in Paris about his five-day mission in Washington, *The New York Times* published a detailed account of Goldmann's meetings with Acheson, Snyder, Patterson, and Lord Inverchapel, all of whom, according to the author of the report, Felix Blaire, saw in the partition plan as proposed by Goldmann a reasonable solution to the Palestine problem.

Blaire also reported that Goldmann's proposal was included in President Truman's reply to the British government.[101]

The next day (August 14, 1946), Silver cabled Ben-Gurion his resignation from the Executive of the Jewish Agency. In his long cable, he stated that it was he who was "fortunately able, in cooperation with many friends, to avert disastrous decisions favoring Grady committee proposal" and "that we stand to suffer major political setbacks as well as protracted delay in transference of 100,000 can be ascribed to a very large degree to inept and willful procedure followed here by your emissary [i.e., Goldmann]." Silver stated that Goldmann disregarded the understanding reached by the AZEC not to broach the subject of partition with governmental officials; did not inform the AZEC that he had met with them; did not discuss the planned talks with him, Silver; and did not ask him to accompany him on any of his official calls.

Ben-Gurion refused to accept Silver's resignation and in his reply pointed out that the representatives of the three major Zionist parties that were members in the AZEC supported the decision of the Jewish Agency and that none of the participants in its August 5 meeting objected to it. He did not say a word about the complaints of Silver against Goldmann and the manner in which Goldmann carried out his mission in Washington.[102] Ben-Gurion showed himself in this issue, as in many others, to be a hardheaded political realist. Although he, too, felt that it would have been more desirable to wait for the proposal for partition to be made by British or American statesmen, he recognized that time was running out and that circumstances compelled the Jewish Agency to take the initiative.

As for Goldmann, a generation later, Eliahu Epstein (Elath), who worked closely with him during that crucial period, characterized his work and its results as follows:

> Dr. Nahum Goldmann was qualified to carry out this mission not only by his good relations in the White House and with David Niles, who fulfilled a key role in this affair, but also by his personal traits and his ability to resort to unusual measures at times of crisis. Ben Gurion therefore actually gave free hand to Goldmann, who acted at his own discretion, not in accordance with the decisions of the Jewish Agency Executive, and even in disregard of his agreement with Silver.
>
> It should be noted that even if Dr. Goldmann's mission did not have the immediate concrete results which we expected at that time, it served as the laying of the foundations for the continuation of the activity in that direction, and contributed its share afterwards when the partition plan was on the agenda.[103]

XIV It was characteristic of Goldmann's position in the Executive and of its reliance on him that, despite his exhausting week in Washington, it was he, and not any other member of the Executive (which included British Jews), who was entrusted with the mission of contacting Bevin. The next morning, Goldmann called Bevin, who happened to be in Paris in connection with the Peace Conference of the Allies. Bevin told him that he had been expecting Goldmann's call and that he had been informed by Lord Inverchapel of the Washington developments. The meeting, the first of several between Goldmann and Bevin, took place the same day, August 14, and still on the same day Goldmann reported on it to the Executive.

"I told Bevin," Goldmann informed his colleagues,

that the very fact that I had come to him indicated that there was an inclination among us to do everything possible, as Sir Stafford Cripps formulated it, to turn over a new page in our relations. The situation is very difficult. You will tell us that we violated the laws of the country; we shall tell you that you sinned against us, moral sins, and violated international law. Only history will settle the final account. We must find a reasonable basis for solving the Palestine problem, acceptable to you and to the Arabs. For us this is a question of life and death. For you too, this is an important question. You staked your career on it.

At this point, Goldmann reported, Bevin interrupted him and said, "I did stake my career on the solution of the problem, and shall surely solve it." Goldmann then said that he would present to him the minimum Jewish demands. The Jews were in a very excited mood. Had they had an empire of two hundred years, they too would be calm and collected. But, instead, they had experienced two thousand years of persecutions, and then came Hitler. When the Jews will have lived for two generations in their state, they too will be calmer. "You must know," he said, "whether you agree or not, that the Jews cannot sit quietly in Palestine and do nothing. They must build, and if the possibility to build is denied to them, they will turn to destruction, to war. They cannot sit calmly and wait while Jews are being murdered in Europe." As for America, Goldmann said, when he arrived there it was almost out of the whole issue. The president was under tremendous pressure. In America, five million Jews can be decisive in the presidential elections. The president knows this, though he becomes irate when it is pointed out to him.

When Goldmann mentioned the Morrison plan, Bevin asked him not to be hard on Morrison, who merely read the statement in Parliament,[104] but apart from that had no connection with the report. "Accuse Brooke, or Grady, or Attlee, or me, but not Morrison," he said. Goldmann told him that the president could not support the Grady report. He had requested the 100,000 immigration certificates again and again, but had not received them. The easiest way out for him was to say that he had tried and failed. This would satisfy the Jews and win him their votes, and the matter would be finished. But this would not be good for the Jews.

Goldmann told Bevin that the only constructive contribution Bevin had so far made to the problem was his demand that America should participate in the search for a solution. It would not be good for Britain if America withdrew. A freeze would be created, all of whose consequences were liable to be catastrophic for the Jews, but that would also cause much unpleasantness for Britain. The Jews had asked the president not to wash his hands of the problem, but rather continue his participation to the very end, and the president was willing to do so politically, though he would not give any military aid. He accepted the Jewish plan, which now was no longer the Jewish plan alone, but also the plan of America.

Bevin again interrupted and said that he was familiar with the plan, had studied it, and that he had received long cables from America. Goldmann said, "Fine, I shall tell you what are our conditions, and which are the subjects open for discussion. There is one condition: the basis for all negotiations must be the partition plan and the establishment of two states. Once this principle is accepted, we can begin negotiations. The negotiations could still fail if you offer us impossible boundaries, such as, for instance, little more than Tel Aviv and Petah Tikva, in which case we shall leave the negotiating table. But we can negotiate over all the details."

Bevin complained that the Jewish Agency rode two horses. Goldmann replied that this was no crime; at times it was definitely a good thing, and everybody did it. Bevin repeated, "I staked my career on the solution of this problem, and I mean it seriously. I am, after all, an old friend of Zionism. Had it not been for me, the 1930 White Paper of Passfield would still be in force." He mentioned that he had met Dov Hos, the Palestinian Jewish labor leader, who died in 1940, and who was a wonderful fellow. After speaking with Hos, he went to Prime Minister Ramsay MacDonald and tried to convince him not to put the White Paper into effect. Bevin emphasized that "we must find a solution which will be acceptable to all. And there is also Russia."

Goldmann said that all this was well known to him. Bevin remarked that, if the Jews established themselves in Palestine, they would hold in their hands the key to the Middle East—the most strategic region of the world. Goldmann replied, "It was good that this key should be in our hands, for I understood that many interests were involved apart from our own." Then Bevin suddenly asked, "Who organizes the pogroms in Poland? The Communists?" Goldmann replied in the negative, whereupon Bevin asked, "Who organizes the illegal immigration to Palestine?" Goldmann replied that, first of all, if he did know, he would not tell, and that the Jews were clever enough to make sure that the Jewish Agency should not be involved. Of course, the agency knew about it and looked at it with sympathy. If some Jews want to flee from murder, other Jews will try to help them. The American Jews give money, and many Jewish organizations can give support. The agency itself does not need to do anything.

Bevin said that he had always seen a possible solution in partition, but entertained doubts about "a racial state." Angered by this statement, Goldmann said that Bevin was surely too intelligent to use such an expression. In the Jewish State, there will be 300,000 Arabs possessing equal rights, and the 15 million Jews in the world will not want to risk their rights by arousing the wrath of the Arabs. What kind of a racist state will be one consisting of 65 percent Jews and 35 percent Arabs, and especially because the Arab state to be set up in Palestine will also have Jews? Bevin said, "If you want to say that this is utterly stupid, say so. I'll understand it." And he went on to say that, of course, the rights of Jews who remain in Europe must be assured and that he would not sign a peace treaty without such guarantees. Then he asked why America did not admit Jews. Goldmann told him that he had nothing against the absorption of Jews by America, but that some of the Jews prefer to wait in Europe another year and then go to Palestine rather than to America. The Congress of the United States does not want more Jews. England does not want them either, nor does any other country.

Bevin said, "It would be very difficult to persuade the Dominions to accept Jews. You have a stubborn religion which does not make assimilation possible." Goldmann replied that, were it not so, no Jews would be left today. Bevin said that the Australians had promised him at first to admit ten thousand Jews, but then they explained to him that the Jews did not assimilate and therefore they refused to accept them.

Then Bevin tried to talk about the Jewish religion, but Goldmann interrupted him by saying he would send a rabbi to him to discuss these matters.

Bevin said that he had never excluded the possibility of partition. Had the Jews accepted the Grady report, it would have led to partition. This being the case, why should we not negotiate on that basis? He said, "If only you had accepted the Peel report!" He was surprised when Goldmann pointed out that, in fact, the Jews did accept the Peel report.[105] However, Goldmann continued, today the situation is different. Many of the Jews who at that time had opposed partition now supported it. But they could not renounce most of Palestine in the mere hope that in a few years they would gain partition. In that case, the Jews preferred to wait in order to obtain all of Palestine. Hence, the principle of the state must be laid down before negotiations could begin.

Bevin reiterated that he did not reject the possibility of partition *a priori*. But he could not give Goldmann an answer right away. He said, "I understand your impatience, but this is a two thousand year old question. You waited two days before you came to see me.[106] I must weigh the Arab problem. The Palestinian Arabs are not ready for a compromise. But that is not the decisive factor. The Arab League, which is the decisive factor, is not so uncompromising. It will come to a conference with the Jews. The newspaper reports on this issue are mistaken. We can talk to the Arab League, but so far we have not spoken to them about the question of partition."

Goldmann said that he could tell Bevin what the Arabs would say to him. "They will not agree to a cantonization or partition. They think they can continue to hold on to the White Paper, for at the end they will get an Arab state in Palestine. But if you would tell them once and for all, together with Truman, that part of Palestine shall be given to the Jews, that the Jews are a *fait accompli* in Palestine, it is possible that they then would prefer full partition to cantonization, since they too want to be independent."

Bevin said that he did not want a colonial regime in the Middle East. The British were leaving Egypt; they forced the French to leave Syria. Goldmann asked him, "If so, why do you remain as an occupying power in Palestine? You will, after all, get military bases from the Jews, just as you got them from the Arab states. America is not interested in military bases." Bevin replied that he was not so sure that the British were interested in military bases, and asked whether according to the Jewish plan the Arab part of Palestine would be tied to Transjordan. Goldmann's reply was that, if the Arabs want a small state of their own, that is their business. It was not part of the Jewish plan to demand that they should tie up with Transjordan. The Jews will not interfere in Arab affairs. They will, of course, need a treaty with the Arabs about economic development, such as the Jordan Valley plan.[107] "This would be simpler if Transjordan would be a real state and not a joke as it is today."

Bevin said that he had read the Jewish version of the borders. He agreed to the proposal concerning the Negev, but the Jews must not hold him responsible later for having given them a desert. Goldmann replied that the Jews had a long list of complaints against the British government, but they would not include the Negev. He said that the Jews were referring to the entire Negev, which meant not only the desert part. It seemed that the British definition was that only what was desert was the Negev. This was mistaken.

Bevin answered, "The Negev must be given to you." And he added, "And what about Jaffa with its 200,000 Arabs?" Goldmann explained that only 40,000 Arabs were in Jaffa, and that the American loan, which was being offered in the amount of $300 million, could be used to transfer part of these Arabs to an Arab state. He stated that he agreed with Bevin on his negative view on corridors,[108] but told him that he was not qualified to discuss details, but only the principle. Bevin said, "Once we accept this, it would mean that if we go to the conference we have already accepted the Jewish demands." Goldmann reiterated that this was the minimum Jewish demand. Partition for the Jews was a compromise because their real aim was, of course, all of Palestine. For the time being, the borders did not need to be considered, but only a declaration of the principle of the establishment of two states. The Arabs, too, would prefer to obtain a state of their own.

Then Goldmann explained why the Jews were opposed to a trusteeship. If the matter should come before the United Nations, they would declare that they could not negotiate on the basis of a trusteeship. This did not mean that the Jews were anti-British. They wanted no American trusteeship either. And certainly not an international one that would be a variant of the administration of Berlin. If Transjordan is sovereign, the Jews too can have sovereignty.

Bevin said he could not give a commitment that day. Goldmann replied that he was not expecting any. Bevin said that he would need to talk to Attlee. He had spoken over the phone with George Hall, who had learned that Weizmann was willing to meet him with several of his colleagues. Hall knew of the American proposals. Bevin repeated that he must first talk to Attlee, and said that he had asked Hall to come to Paris on Friday because the whole matter was actually Hall's business.

During the course of the discussion, Bevin said repeatedly that he was thinking aloud, without committing his government. He said that, after the King David incident, the cabinet was strongly inclined to break off all relations with the Jews, to cancel the conference, and to give a free hand to the army to do as it saw fit in Palestine. But he had prevented the adoption of that course and had asked his colleagues to keep calm. He was proud of what was done after the King David incident. Goldmann said he was prepared to admit this, but what of General Barker?[109] Bevin's reply was, "His feelings are certainly known to you, but this matter is now in the hands of Montgomery.[110] The fact is that he did not allow the army to react as it wanted to."

Then Bevin asked, "What do you demand before you go to the conference?" Goldmann replied that the British government must declare publicly that the basis of the negotiations was the establishment of two states. This did not mean that it must immediately accept all the particulars, but that it would negotiate along this line. Bevin remarked that the word "basis" had hidden pitfalls. He regarded it as a starting point, but the Russians explained it as if the British had undertaken to accept it. Goldmann interjected that, in his interpretation, the Jews were inclined to agree with the Russians and emphasized that the British government must proclaim that the Jewish State was one of the aims within the competence of the conference. Thereafter, the particulars of the borders, the transition period, and the like could be negotiated.

Bevin said that now he understood the situation completely. He would phone Attlee and have a long talk with him. On Friday (August 16) Hall would come to Paris. Goldmann should phone his private secretary on Friday, and then they would see what the situation was. Either Goldmann would see him then, or would see him together with Hall, or would have to wait until next week.

Then Bevin said, "In the meantime you must discontinue the illegal immigration." Goldmann replied, "You cannot tell us to discontinue it, since it is not we who are organizing it." Bevin said, "You must exert influence on the people who are organizing it. Tell them, why should you not wait for a period of two months while the conference is in session?" Goldmann argued that the British-Jewish negotiations had not yet begun and that he was talking with Bevin only about the conditions under which the conference could be convened. Once the negotiations started, on the basis of the Jewish conditions, Bevin could make his proposals.

Bevin said, "Don't you understand, you are making us ridiculous with this illegal immigration. No government could tolerate such a thing." Goldmann replied, "Perhaps you are right. But as for us, you do not make us ridiculous, you create tragedies, and tragedies are much worse than ridicule." Bevin reiterated the demand that for the duration of the conference the Jews should make a gesture and discontinue the illegal immigration. Goldmann said that, if an agreement was reached to the effect that the establishment of the state was the basis of the negotiations, "we would then see."

The question of the composition of the Jewish delegation to the conference was not touched upon in this discussion with Bevin.

At the conclusion of the meeting, Bevin said that he was very glad to have had this talk. It clarified many things for him. Goldmann said, "You behaved toward us in a disgusting fashion." Bevin replied that he always wanted to be decent toward the Jews. He knew their tragedy and sufferings. Goldmann said that, ever since Labor came into power in England they had never invited the Jews for discussions. Attlee twice refused to meet with Weizmann, while throughout they were meeting with the Arabs. Bevin complained that he was overburdened with work beyond his strength; he was suffering from heart disease; he could not carry the burden. Goldmann replied with a stinging remark: "But you have always found time to see the Arabs. Had you been in touch with us all the time, not even part of the bitterness against you would exist." Bevin repeated that the problem must be settled within the next few weeks. He was serious in saying that he staked his career on its solution. The Jews were too impatient; they did not want to give him even six months. Goldmann replied, "We had already been forced to wait almost a year."[111]

XV   After the conclusion of his talk with Bevin, Goldmann flew from Paris to London to inform the ailing Weizmann of the latest developments. The next day, August 15, at 11 A.M., he went with Weizmann, Stephen Wise, and Joseph A. Linton to see Colonial Secretary George Hall, who was assisted by Sir Arthur Daw, Sir Douglas Harris, and Trafford Smith. Then, at 4 P.M., Goldmann flew back to Paris,[112] where the same evening he reported to the Executive.

Hall, he informed his colleagues, had solemnly declared that the British government was not committed to anything, neither with regard to the Jews nor with regard to the Arabs. The government was not committed even to its own plan. It would see how the conference went, and it would also consider other plans submitted. It may decide to enforce a plan without the consent of the Arabs or the Jews. At this point, Dr.

Weizmann asked Goldmann to speak. He began by asking Hall how much time he could give them, and Hall replied, "The whole day if necessary. We must settle it. We are very keen on having this conference, and a lot of time has already been lost. Dr. Weizmann could not see me, and you were in Paris. We want a conference as soon as possible."

Goldmann said that he wanted to inform Hall about the position in America and about his talk with Bevin. When he went to America, Goldmann said, the possibility existed that America would withdraw altogether. This would have been the easy way out for the president, but it would have been useful neither to the Jews nor to the British. Hall said, "I agree with you there. It would be more useful for us if America were to assist in the matter. I see that the American Government has agreed to your proposals for a solution."

Goldmann pointed out that the program accepted by America was not the Zionist program. "Our program is a Jewish state in the whole of Palestine. The proposals accepted by the American government represent a tremendous sacrifice on our part. They are the maximum concession we might be prepared to make in order to break out of the present stalemate and enter a new constructive period. But since it is such a great compromise for us, we must be very categorical about certain conditions. We have decided, and so informed you officially, that we will not go to a conference on the basis of the Morrison plan, but only on the basis of a Jewish state in a part of Palestine. This must be absolutely clear."

Then Goldmann asked Hall whether or not Bevin had informed him of Goldmann's talk with him. Hall said he had not, but Bevin did have a long talk with Attlee last night. Thereupon Goldmann gave him the gist of his interview with Bevin.

Hall then said, "Why do you insist on your conditions for this conference? I told you already that we are not committed to our plan." At this point, Sir Douglas Harris suggested that the Jewish Agency should submit its plan in detail. Perhaps, in the course of the conference it might lead to partition or to federalization.

Hall said, "If you come to the conference, we will discuss it and see what can be done. We said the same to the Arabs." Goldmann replied that this was not good enough. Hall's suggestion was logical, but if the Jewish Agency accepted it, it meant, by implication, that the negotiations would be based on the Grady report. He reiterated that for the Jews their proposals meant a major compromise. Many important sectors of Jewry, especially in America, could be persuaded only with great difficulty to accept them. If the Jewish people were to agree to negotiations, they must know that the basis is a Jewish State and that this was clearly recognized by all. Otherwise, they cannot participate.

Hall said, "This will make it much more difficult to get the Arabs to come." Goldmann said, "That is not our business. Of course it would be better to come to an agreement with the Arabs, but they are not only against partition, they are also against cantonization. They may even prefer partition, since they too are not enamored of the Mandatory regime in Palestine." Harris repeated, "Why not come to the conference and submit your plan, and the Arabs will come with their plan, and we will discuss them all." But Goldmann was adamant. "Sorry, but we cannot do it. Our public opinion would not stand for it."

Hall insisted that he could see little difference between the British and the Jewish points of view and asked how the Jewish Agency proposed to proceed. Goldmann replied that the British might send the Jews an official invitation because the letter addressed to Weizmann was not one. Then the Jewish Agency would reply that they could not go to the conference on the basis of the Morrison proposals.

At that point, Hall said, "I should have made that speech in the House of Commons and not Morrison. It was neither Bevin's nor Morrison's business, but they asked Morrison to do it." Goldmann continued, "We shall answer that we cannot go on the basis of your proposals, and suggest that the basis of discussion should be a viable Jewish state in an adequate part of Palestine. Then we will state our other conditions. You will answer us that you have received our letter and accept it as a basis for the discussions."

Hall said, "All right, let us come together this afternoon, two of you and two of us, and we will draft the two letters and try to reach an agreement." Goldmann remarked that there were also other conditions and that the issues had to be discussed with the members of the Executive who were in Paris. "I cannot take upon myself," he said, "the drafting of the two letters without authorization from the Executive." Hall said, "We must somehow shorten the procedure. Let me now solemnly invite you, on behalf of His Majesty's Government, to participate in the conference on Palestine, representing the Executive of the Jewish Agency. Now you can go to your colleagues and draft your reply." Goldmann said he accepted this oral declaration as an official invitation, and the Jewish Agency would send him its reply.

During the course of the discussion, Dr. Weizmann made a strong plea against trusteeship, stressing that the Jews could no longer live under a foreign regime. However, they would, of course, give the British military bases and conclude treaties with them. Hall said, "We do not want to have any bases. We want to get out." Dr. Weizmann said that after the latest events in Palestine the Jews could no longer tolerate a colonial regime. "We must have freedom. There will, of course, be an interim period, but, believe me, we cannot continue under a foreign regime."

Stephen Wise then spoke about the position of the Jewish people, the losses it suffered, and the tragic situation of the survivors. He also mentioned the American loan to Britain, saying, "In return for you giving us a state, I asked America, and the Jews there, to give you a loan." Hall said, "I appreciate that, but the loan is not only good for England, it is also good for America." Dr. Wise stated "Of course, that's why I was for it."

The next point of discussion was the Jewish Agency's condition that the delegation must include all those leaders who were being kept in detention by the British. Goldmann made an appeal to Hall: "If you have criminal charges against our people, go to court, and we will know how to defend ourselves. The detention of our people is a political act. It is impossible for us to present our proposals, which entail great sacrifices, without all our leaders. Otherwise we cannot bear the responsibility. If the greater part of the Jewish leadership is not with us, we cannot go to the discussions. If you are keen on having the conference, make a gesture and set our people free."

Hall replied that he, too, would like to have Shertok, whose presence would be very useful, but he alone could not decide it; the decision must be made by those who arrested him. Goldmann suggested that the British cabinet would also have a say in the matter. Then he informed Hall of the third condition of the Jewish Agency: that the composition of the Jewish representation must be decided only by the agency. He told Hall that it was interested in a broad representation. It would invite all significant organizations except those unfriendly or hostile to a Jewish State. This condition caused the most serious fight with the British representatives and the lengthiest discussion.

Hall said, "You are asking for a privilege which the Jewish Agency has never enjoyed." Goldmann, in reply, referred to the St. James conference of 1939, to which Jewish delegates were invited after consultation with the Jewish Agency. He also pointed to the Jewish position under the Mandate and read its Article 4, which states that "an appropriate Jewish agency shall be recognised as a public body for the purpose of advising and co-operating with the Administration of Palestine in such economic, social and other matters as may affect the establishment of the Jewish national home and the interests of the Jewish population in Palestine. . . . The Zionist organization, so long as its organization and constitution are in the opinion of the Mandatory appropriate, shall be recognised as such agency. It shall take steps in consultation with His Britannic Majesty's Government to secure the co-operation of all Jews who are willing to assist in the establishment of the Jewish national home."

Hall said, "This does not mean that we have no right to talk to other organizations." Goldmann replied, "You can, of course, talk to anybody you like. This is a free country. But this would be an official conference on Palestine, and under the Mandate the Jewish Agency is recognized as the official Jewish body in all questions relating to Palestine." Hall said, "We did not want to withdraw that recognition, but wish to invite others too."

Goldmann replied that Hall could not expect the Executive to agree to the undermining of the agency's authority. There could be a broad Jewish front at the conference, but the agency must issue the invitation to the various bodies. Hall said, "If we accept that, the Palestinian Arabs will say, 'Why do you invite other Arab states?'" Goldmann pointed out that the independent Arab states could not be compared to Jewish organizations. Also, the Jewish Agency did not ask the British to invite the Arab states. Harris remarked that this was a major point that the cabinet must consider. Goldmann made it clear that the Jewish Agency would not attend the conference if it was merely one of several Jewish bodies invited by the government.

During the discussion of the proposed basis for the conference, Hall suggested that the simplest thing to do would be to convene the conference, perhaps separate conferences, and then all would try to sit together. "Whatever happens, we will propose our plan, and then we will discuss it." Goldmann replied, "You are very keen on calling this conference. We, too, desire to have talks if there is any chance of solving the problem. We must make it clear that when we ask for a Jewish state, that is not a mere tactical maneuver. If we come to a conference based on your plan and not on a Jewish state, we will reject your plan, and the conference will break down on the second day, which would not be helpful. Therefore, we must have this point clarified in advance."

At the end of the deliberations, Hall said in an unofficial manner, "Can't you help us and stop this illegal immigration for the next few weeks? It creates a terrible situation. Why don't you put a stop to it while the conference is on?" Goldmann replied that he had told Bevin that the Jewish Agency was not the right authority to address in this matter. The agency had nothing to do officially with the illegal immigration. Moreover, there was as yet no conference and no discussion. The agency does not yet know whether its three conditions will be accepted. There are no immigration certificates, and the Jews cannot wait. The conference may last a month, and long delays may occur before any further legal immigration became possible. Goldmann also mentioned that the agency had received information to the effect that the British military might occupy the Jewish Agency building in Jerusalem. Hall said that he had not heard of it, but would look into the matter. Smith said such a step would not be taken. There was no reason to worry about it, but he would keep the matter in mind.

After concluding his report on this meeting to the Executive, Goldmann read a draft, prepared by Berl Locker, Harry Sacher, and himself, in reply to the British government's invitation. He suggested that the letter, to be signed by Dr. Weizmann, should be sent to Hall the next day and that the matter should be discussed without delay.[113]

At the same meeting, the Executive discussed also the cable of resignation of Abba Hillel Silver. Both Ben-Gurion and Goldmann suggested that a reply be sent to him not accepting it and asking him to cooperate loyally with the Executive's decision. This was adopted and Silver was requested to come to Paris immediately. Goldmann also stated that, if Silver published in America the cable he sent to the Executive, and the Executive did not, in turn, publish a statement supporting his, Goldmann's, activities in America, he would not participate in further meetings of the Executive. Ben-Gurion's response was that Goldmann's bitterness was understandable, but "let us not discuss the matter now; let us wait and see what happens."[114]

On August 16 Weizmann summarized in a draft letter to Winston Churchill what Goldmann had accomplished within the preceding ten days. He wrote:

> A member of the Executive, Dr. Nahum Goldmann, visited Washington and had conversations with Mr. Acheson, the Acting Secretary of State, to whom he outlined a scheme for the division of Palestine into two States, a Jewish and an Arab. The Jewish State to comprise the Peel Scheme area plus the Negev. Special arrangements were to be made for Jerusalem, Bethlehem, and other Holy Places; and in the brief interim period before the two States become fully independent, the control of immigration into

the area destined to become the Jewish State, and the election of its administration, would be in Jewish hands. I understand that Mr. Acheson and subsequently President Truman accepted this scheme, and have transmitted it to H.M.G. [His Majesty's Government] with their recommendation. On his return to Paris, Dr. Goldmann saw Mr. Bevin and reported to him on his Washington visit.[115]

XVI On August 17 Weizmann, Goldmann, Stephen Wise, Eliezer Kaplan, and Berl Locker met with Bevin and George Hall. At the meeting, which lasted two hours, Hall was assisted by two of his top aides. The British officials tried to convince the Jewish delegation that the Jews should participate in the London conference, where they could argue anything they chose. The Jewish position was that they would attend the conference only if three conditions were met: 1) that the basis of the conference was the creation of a viable Jewish State in an adequate area of Palestine; 2) that the Jews would choose their own representatives, including those who were detained or were subject to detention, that is, Shertok and Ben-Gurion; and 3) that the Jewish Agency, as recognized under the terms of the Mandate, would, after consultations with the British government, name the persons or groups to be invited.

Stephen Wise reported on this meeting to his daughter from London. He wrote, "they argued about all three points. Weizmann exceedingly well, at moments with a suavity of manner which almost hides the firmness of his purpose; Goldmann astutely and strongly and almost with too much prolixity. I got in a few decent shots."[116]

In the afternoon of the same day, Goldmann met with Jan Masaryk, the foreign minister of Czechoslovakia, and in the evening he reported to the Executive concerning the latest developments.[117] At that meeting, Ben-Gurion said, "I was in favor of Dr. Goldmann's mission to America, and I repudiate the accusations which are now being made against this mission, even though the result was negative."[118]

The next day (Sunday, August 18) at 10:00 A.M. another meeting took place with Bevin and Hall. On the Jewish side, Ben-Gurion, Goldmann, Wise, Locker, and Rabbi Fischman (Maimon) participated. That same evening, reporting on the meeting to the Jewish Agency Executive, Goldmann stated that he had begun by saying that the Executive had studied the matter until one o'clock in the morning and then asked to be permitted to outline the background of its discussions and the subsequent decision. He said, "It was impossible for us to accept the invitation to attend the conference. We had adopted this decision unanimously. Our letter was not meant to be an ultimatum; but we wanted to make our position quite clear."

Bevin seemed to accept this, saying, "Let's forget about the letter."

Goldmann then explained that the Executive had come to Paris to find a way out, and if at all possible, to start a new chapter in its relations with Britain. "The present stalemate," he said, "is very bad for you; but it is worse for us, since to us Palestine is vital, while for you it is just one among many other troubles. It was in this spirit of compromise that we decided to accept partition, which is the absolute limit to which a Jew and a Zionist can go. Partition is not the Zionist program; the Zionist program is a Jewish State in the whole of Palestine. If nothing comes out of these discussions, we shall revert to, and stand by, our old program. This compromise is our last effort to come to an agreement."

"In America," Goldmann pointed out, "the President was ready to withdraw from the whole affair, which would have been bad for you as well as for us. Through our decision, which we submitted to him, we saved the situation in that respect also for you. The President sent you a cable saying that if you accept the compromise suggested by us, he will support it. If we go to the conference, it will be only for the purpose of finding out how to realize our compromise plan. We cannot discuss any other plan, and certainly not the Morrison plan. Jewish public opinion will not stand for it. But it is not only a question of public opinion. It is a question of finding a solution. The conference, after all, is only a method, it is not a solution in itself, and it is not really necessary at all."

"You know," Goldmann went on, "what the Arabs want."

If the Arabs are intransigent and won't sit with Jews, insisting on an Arab state in the whole of Palestine, then the conference will break down. We say partition is our absolute minimum, and unless that is accepted, the conference will collapse. There will be great agitation in America. So perhaps it might be better not to have a conference at all, but to start informal talks with us so that we may make our position clear. You know our program in general terms, but there are other things to discuss. You may also have informal talks with the Arabs; if not, there may be an unpleasant repetition of the St. James conference. Perhaps in the course of the informal talks the Arabs themselves may decide that partition was better than cantonization, and then you can call a conference. You told us that even if we did not go, you would have a conference. What is the great hurry? Why not first prepare the ground through informal talks which could start immediately, without preparation?

Bevin listened quietly, carefully, and, it seemed to Goldmann, in a friendly manner. At any rate, he appeared friendlier than Hall, who regarded the conference as his own special concern. Bevin said he was ready to conduct informal talks, insisted that he must find a solution, and thought the suggestion had some merit. He said, "If we have such talks, we must clear the deck first, and improve the atmosphere. You are in a state of war against us; you are sending ships with illegal immigrants."

Locker interjected that no people in the world were less desirous of war against Britain than the Jews, who had always found sympathy and interest for their problems in Britain. He referred to the Balfour Declaration and the support by the Labor party for the Jewish and Zionist aspirations during many years. Certainly no war existed as far as the Jews were concerned. "If we have discussions, that alone will improve the atmosphere, but there must be no conditions. As for illegal immigration, Morrison himself said that the White Paper was an illegal document."

Bevin said that he was not putting any conditions, or making any demands, on the Jewish Agency; he only said that the decks must be cleared for discussions.

Locker then said that the Jewish Agency did not organize the illegal immigration. Bevin said, "But somebody organizes it." Locker replied that, of course, it is organized, but it is done by others, not by the agency. Of the twenty-two members of his own family, only four were left, and he would not refuse them any help he could give them if they tried to get to Palestine illegally in order to flee from the pogroms in Germany.

To demonstrate that the Jewish Agency did not organize illegal immigration, Goldmann mentioned that Acheson and Patterson had called a meeting with Dr. Stephen Wise some months previously, at which the American statesmen expressed the view that too many refugees were entering the American zone in Germany, that the position was becoming difficult, and they asked the Jewish leadership to see to it that not more than eight to ten thousand people should enter monthly. "Our reply was," Goldmann said, "that we could not promise anything, since the matter was not in our hands. However, we did send emissaries to Poland urging the people there to reduce the influx of refugees into the American zone. Then the Kielce pogrom took place, whereupon three to four thousand people crossed the border every day."

Bevin said that he understood the position, and that many Jews must leave Europe. "But, couldn't you put a stop to it while a solution was being worked out?" He said angrily that, if President Truman had not asked for the admission of the 100,000 without assuming any responsibility and without consulting the British, 50,000 refugees might already be in Palestine by now. But Truman had made it impossible.

Goldmann then told him that, when he went to America, the president again wanted to ask for the 100,000 and leave it at that, but he, Goldmann, did everything to prevent him from doing so because it was clear that the British consent was not forthcoming, and it would have been damaging from the point of view of prestige. If Truman wanted to help, he should remain involved in the Palestine problem until the end. Ultimately, Goldmann said, he succeeded in convincing him to accept the Jewish Agency's plan for the solution of the problem. Many people, including some Jewish leaders, had wanted Truman to ask again for the 100,000, and Goldmann was severely criticized for the line he had taken. Turning to Bevin, Goldmann said, "We are on common ground in this matter. We all wish to be constructive."

Bevin said, "This means that you want to start informal talks with us. Should we call the Arabs too?" Goldmann answered, "Yes, of course. As long as the Arabs are not clearly told that there must be a compromise, the conference is absolutely useless. But once they know that there must be a compromise—and you will have a certain influence over the Arab League—I am sure they also will prefer partition to cantonization." Hall said, "Why not propose all this at the conference? Why have informal talks? We know your demands. We have your plan from America."

At that point, Bevin said that two years were too short a time for the transition period.

Hall continued, "We will discuss all the details at the conference. Perhaps by the second day we shall have finished with the Grady plan."

Goldmann explained that a conference, because of all the publicity involved, would be a much more difficult proposition, whereas informal talks could be confidential, without letters, memorandums, and the like. Once a basis has been found, the parties could proceed to the conference, which, however, would be quite useless without adequate preparation.

Bevin said, "What about other Jewish organizations at the informal talks?" Locker replied that only the Jewish Agency would be represented. Bevin asked, "Who of your people will lead the informal talks?" Goldmann replied, "We would put no conditions. We would see. But, frankly, as I had already told Mr. Hall, it would be best from the political point-of-view if Ben-Gurion would be in on the talks."

Bevin said that this was a difficult matter for them. There would be trouble because the Arabs would want the Mufti, and "We cannot have the Mufti." Locker contended this was an unfair comparison. How could Bevin compare the Mufti with Ben-Gurion, who, together with Shertok, had done everything possible to help Britain in the war? Bevin replied that he had not meant it that way, but all the same it was very difficult for them. Goldmann said, "I am telling you that it would be better for you to negotiate with Ben Gurion, but we are not making this a condition for the talks."

Hall again complained, rather unhelpfully, that two weeks had been lost because he could not see Dr. Weizmann, and now, if informal talks were held first, more time would be lost before the conference could be held. Goldmann said that it was better to lose two or three weeks than have the conference without any chance of success.

In the end, Bevin, who seemed to have been influenced by Hall in the matter, said he would summarize what Goldmann had said. He said, "We must commit ourselves to accept partition and get the agreement of the Arabs, otherwise there will be no conference because you will not attend. This is what you mean." Goldmann replied that this was putting the matter in a rather exaggerated form. The conference could, of course, fail, but if the Arabs would accept partition it could be a success.

Bevin said he would propose it to the cabinet. He then got up, saying, "I am disappointed with you." Goldmann replied that he appreciated the fact that Bevin accepted the disappointment graciously.

Goldmann concluded his report to the Executive by informing his colleagues that the next talk with Bevin was scheduled for Tuesday or Wednesday. His impression was that Bevin was not against the procedure suggested by the agency. Hall, however, was definitely opposed. Goldmann suggested that efforts should be made to influence members of the cabinet in favor of the agency's proposal, and also try to persuade Acheson to press Attlee to accept the procedure suggested.[119]

In a 1978 interview, Goldmann recalled two incidents from the August 18 meeting. One was humorous, the other inspiring:

> First of all, Rabbi Fischman insisted that he should be the first speaker.
> He would speak in Hebrew and I should translate it literally into English.

He began by saying, "Mr. Secretary, I must tell you that ever since Titus overrran Palestine there was no man as wicked as you." Then he turned to me and said, "Translate." I said, "I shall translate when you finish your speech." He spoke for about ten minutes, and Bevin, who was a very nervous man, scribbled and doodled all the time. When Fischman finished, I said, "Mr. Secretary, the rabbi criticizes sharply your policy in Palestine, and adduces several examples of it." Rabbi Fischman asked, "Did you translate everything?" "Yes," I said, "English is shorter than Hebrew."

Then Ben-Gurion spoke. I am not easily impressed by speeches, but that time I was overwhelmed. He spoke of the Jewish people, of the sufferings, of the holocaust, and of socialism. It was the speech of a prophet. It was truly a wonderful speech.

But Bevin was an extremely cynical man. Had Ben-Gurion asked me, I would have told him that it was a waste of time. While he listened, Bevin showed signs of nervousness. At the end he said, "Mr. Ben-Gurion, you are telling me about prophets and socialism. As for the prophets, it is not my duty to fulfill their prophecies; nor can I realize the socialism of Marx. What you ask of me is against the interests of England." Bevin spoke sharply and with cynicism. Ben-Gurion sat there like a man crushed.[120]

XVII Next morning at 9:00 Goldmann met again with Jan Masaryk, and at 10:30 he reported to the Executive that no appreciable progress had been achieved in the British-Jewish talks. The British demand remained that the Zionist representatives attend the London Round Table Conference without any precondition, but the Executive stuck to its guns and refused to attend unless the partition of Palestine was to be the basis of the discussions.

On August 20, 1946, Goldmann had a transatlantic phone conference with Loy Henderson, and the next day he was received by Jan Christian Smuts, prime minister of South Africa and a major figure in United Nations circles. Smuts said he wanted to see Goldmann alone, so as to have an off-the-record talk with him. Goldmann gave him a detailed report of his talks with the American cabinet officials, and Smuts said that what Goldmann achieved in America was truly remarkable. He, himself, had always believed that partition was the only way out. When Goldmann told him about the difficulties with Hall, he became angry and said, "These bureaucrats of the Colonial Office will ruin the situation."

Goldmann told him that Bevin might have agreed to some of the Jewish Agency's proposals, but that Hall seemed to be adopting a very stiff attitude. Smuts said that he had seen Bevin the previous day and that he was sorry he had not spoken to Goldmann earlier. He had said to Bevin that he was very worried about the Palestine situation. No people had suffered so much in the war as the Jews. "We must treat them generously, and this, what we are doing now, is not the way to treat them." Bevin had said that for the first time he was beginning to see a ray of hope. They were making progress. "Now," said Smuts, "I understand what he meant. I may see him again."

That same afternoon (August 21, 1946) at 3:30, Goldmann reported this conversation to the Political Commission of the Jewish Agency Executive. He also informed the commission that he, Stephen Wise, and Jacob Blaustein, as well as Phillip Forman, of the American Jewish Committee, were invited by General Joseph T. McNarney, commander of the American zone in Germany, to discuss the large-scale influx of Jewish refugees into that zone. Goldmann asked his colleagues whether or not they thought he should go to Frankfurt to meet the general, and, because their reaction was affirmative, he left the next day on a five-day visit.[121]

After leading a delegation to consult with Gheorghe Tatarescu, the Rumanian vice-premier, Goldmann met once again with Bevin in Paris, on August 29, at 2:30 P.M., which he reported in detail to the Executive. His talk with Bevin began by Goldmann stating that he was carrying in his pocket the draft of the Jewish Agency's answer to the invitation to participate in the London conference, and that the answer was negative. Bevin wanted to say something, but Goldmann asked him not to respond right away but to let him explain first why the agency could not accept the invitation. He told Bevin, "We cannot accept the invitation as it stands now, for two reasons. First—an internal reason. I agree with your view that foreign policy decisions should not be allowed to be influenced by internal political considerations. This was a very wise rule, but, like every rule, it too had exceptions. If those who elected you or those who elected me are in disagreement with a foreign policy decision, neither you nor I can carry it out. Zionism is not a totalitarian movement, and none of us is the Führer of the movement. We must act in accordance with public opinion."

"We made an enormous concession," Goldmann continued, "by agreeing to partition."

This was the limit of our concessions, and now we must make sure that a great majority of our people and our movement should support us, because otherwise we would be unable to carry out the agreement and we would have no value at all as a negotiating partner. We have succeeded until now to preserve the unity of our movement, but only because the movement is convinced that we shall not accept the Morrison plan even in an improved version, and that we shall negotiate only on the basis of a real partition and the establishment of a Jewish State. Should the slightest impression be created that we cut ourselves off from this basis, and were willing to discuss the Morrison plan, we should be assailed by great parts of the movement, and justly so, and this would have dire consequences, since it could cause the American President to wash his hands of the matter and to get out of the picture. The support of partition on the part of large sectors in Jewish public opinion was one of the conditions of the American support of this plan, and we would jeopardize this condition if we should accept the invitation to the London conference on the given basis.

Secondly, there is the external policy consideration, which compels us not to accept the invitation. There is no other way of compromise in the solution of the Palestine problem in a manner acceptable to all sides. I have been convinced of this, I said, for more than ten years. If we had had a million or a million-and-a-half Jews in Palestine before Hitler appeared, we would have obtained all of Western Palestine as the Jewish State. But we didn't have a million-and-a-half Jews there, and since an arrangement must be found today and immediately so as to prevent tension and chaos, we must accept partition. If, I said, His Majesty's Government intended really to reach a compromise acceptable to all, they must seek a solution within the framework of partition. If, on the other hand, His Majesty's Government wished to liquidate Zionism, as several advisors suggested, why should we participate in a conference which had this as its aim?

At this point, Bevin interrupted Goldmann with considerable heat and said: "I do not dream of a liquidation of Zionism. Don't use this expression!" Goldmann said he was glad to hear this, but if so, then partition was the only way out. There had never been as good a chance as now. "I have brought you," he said, "the support of the Jewish Agency for this plan, and the support of the American government. It is known to you that the Conservative Party in England supports the plan, that large parts of the Labor Party look at it with sympathy, and, as you know, important leaders of the Arab League are willing to accept it. If you present such a plan you can get consent for it, and the conference would only be hurt if confusion were to be introduced into it by other proposals which neither we nor the Arabs could accept. Therefore we must insist that we shall go to the conference only on the basis of the partition plan."

These arguments made a deep impression on Bevin. He said, "Why could you not come to the conference with the declaration that you are willing to negotiate only on the basis of the partition plan, and say so at the conference itself? After all you know that we shall not insist on keeping the Morrison plan, and that we are willing to discuss your plan."

Goldmann replied that, as he had said in previous talks, this argument would have weight "if we were sitting in a seminar on logic; but we are dealing with politics, and, for the reasons I had stated, we cannot accept the invitation. Moreover, I told you that the conference was not well prepared, and I asked you to conduct unofficial talks with us and with the Arabs prior to its opening. For reasons unknown to us His Majesty's Government did not accept this suggestion. Why then should you not talk with the Arabs in the conference, if you have not done it so far, try to obtain their consent to the partition plan, and then invite us?"

"In our letter," Goldmann added,

it will be stated that while we reject the invitation in its present form, we shall always be willing to come to either unofficial or official talks after it will be agreed that partition is the basis for the discussions. The Arabs anyway do not want to sit down with us around a table, and therefore there would be in effect two parallel conferences. Why do they have to start at the same time? Start with the Arabs. They will come, to begin with, with the demand to set up an Arab State in all of Palestine, which, we hope, you will reject, since we shall never agree to live as a minority under Arab rule, and the outcome would be civil war. After you have rejected the Arab demand for the whole of Palestine the moment will come for you to propose your federalization plan. I am sure that the Arabs will reject it. Then you will have to obtain their consent to the partition. Once you got it, you can invite us.

Bevin said, "There is much sense in what you say. This could prevent a rift. I attach the greatest importance to this conference. I stake my career on finding an agreed-upon solution. I shall leave the Peace Conference in Paris and shall go back to London for the conference on the Palestine issue. I told Hall that the problem of Palestine was too great to be left in the hands of the Colonial Office. You know that the Colonial Office is very touchy."

Goldmann said, "With all due respect to Mr. George Hall, I dare say that if we had conducted the early talks with you, Mr. Bevin, alone, we would have advanced much more." "You must understand," Bevin replied, "that the problem of Palestine is something like a pet child of the Colonial Office, and they are very sensitive on this point. But let us go back to your idea. It makes sense. Let me discuss it with the cabinet and with Mr. Attlee, and perhaps we shall reach an agreement about it. In the meantime don't write us any letter. Let us forget letters, yours and ours, and let us continue to talk. That is the better way to get results."

Goldmann said that, should such a procedure be adopted, namely that the official participation of the Jewish Agency would be postponed for a short time until after the British government would have found a common ground with the Arabs or with the Jewish Agency in relation to the partition plan, it would be necessary to say something to the press and to inform the public. In such a case, some kind of a statement would need to be issued by the British government or by the Jewish Agency, with a text mutually agreed upon, in order to indicate why the agency will enter into negotiations at a later date and in order to forestall the need for the agency to reject the British invitation.

"Let us wait a day or two," said Bevin. "Don't send us any letter. Perhaps on Sunday or Monday I shall call you, and then we shall agree on some statement. But if I accept a procedure of this kind, I shall want you to be in London from September 8 on when I shall return there. I want you to remain in touch with us."

Goldmann said that he would have no problem being in London. Dr. Weizmann, too, will be on hand. Bevin asked about Weizmann, and Goldmann told him that for the next two weeks Weizmann would be on the country estate of Lord Rothschild, a member of the House of Lords, who belonged to the Labor party. "One comes and goes in high society," remarked Bevin. Goldmann told him that the second and third paragraphs of the invitation to the conference, to the Agency's delegation and the Jewish delegations, remained to be discussed. "We shall come to an agreement about that," said Bevin; "there won't be many difficulties in connection with it. We better don't discuss it today."

This first part of the talk lasted about twenty minutes. Then Bevin broached another issue which, he said, had great importance in his own eyes and the eyes of the Arabs. "If you will have a Jewish State," he said, "you cannot continue to maintain the Jewish Agency. You will not be able to hold on to both ends of the rope, both a state of your own and an organization of world Jewry which is tied to the state politically. This is a very important problem and it must be fully cleared up."

Goldmann replied, "I can only repeat what I told you in our first talk. Once the Jewish State is established, the Jewish Agency will not continue to exist in its present structure. The Jewish Agency is a unique instrument constructed for the period in which the Jewish people is building its state, before the state is established. Once the state is recognized officially and is independent, it is self-evident that no Jew or Jewish organization of any other country can speak politically in the name of the State or decide its policies. That would mean double loyalty and double citizenship, which would not be agreed to either by the Jewish State or by the other countries."

"If an American Jew," Goldmann continued, "will want to be tied politically and legally to the Jewish State, or to represent it as an envoy, for instance, he will have to give up his American citizenship and become a citizen of the Jewish State. The same thing holds good for the Irish. The mayor of New York, O'Dwyer, who is a good Irishman, cannot speak to President Truman officially as a representative of the Irish Republic. He can be concerned about Ireland, and give it moral, financial, and spiritual aid, but not political or legal aid. The Jews all over the world will be concerned, quite naturally, about the Jewish State, will give it financial aid, and will maintain cultural and religious relations with it, but all the political and legal authority will pass into the hands of the citizens of the Jewish State. Neither the Jews, nor the Arabs, nor world Jewry will be able to identify themselves with it politically."

"This," said Bevin, "is a very important point. Could you give me this statement in writing, if it should become necessary?" Goldmann said: "You can get it in writing, in return for an absolute decision to establish a Jewish State."

"Fine," said Bevin. "You clarified these problems and I shall use it in my talks with the Arabs. But are you aware that the transition period could last more than two years?"

"Mr. Bevin," Goldmann said, "this is a debatable point. Our negotiations will not fail because of this issue. Some of us think that it is possible to establish the state within one year. I think we shall need two years, but a year more or less is not a vital issue, if one condition is met: that we get free immigration and full autonomy immediately."

"This means," said Bevin, "that the promise must be given immediately, and the consent to the establishment of the state after a transition period."

"It is clear," said Goldmann, "that this is the central point of the whole plan. We shall not enter into such a plan with the probability that after the transition period we shall have to discuss it again. The consent to the establishment of the state is the vital part of the whole plan."[122]

That same evening, after the meeting with Bevin, Goldmann and Wise flew over to London to apprise Weizmann of what had occurred. They returned to Paris on August 30, and on September 2 at 6:00 P.M. Goldmann met once again with Bevin, concerning which he reported to Ben-Gurion two hours later.[123]

XVIII Despite these seemingly forthcoming overtures and his apparent reasonableness, Bevin did not budge from his position. During the very days of Goldmann's next visit to London (September 3–5), the British government sent invitations (on September 4, 1946) to Jewish leaders in America, Britain, and Palestine to the Round Table Conference on the basis of the Morrison plan. None of the invitees accepted. Nevertheless, the conference opened on September 9 in Lancaster House, London, though only British and Arab states representatives were in attendance.

While Goldmann was busy on the British front, his implacable opponent Rabbi Silver continued his efforts to remove him from the American Zionist scene. On September 2, Louis Segal, the representative of the Poale Zion in the AZEC, informed Epstein that Silver had suggested to him, Segal, that a close alliance be formed between Silver and Ben-Gurion against Weizmann. An essential part of Silver's plan was to enter into a gentlemen's agreement according to which, until the next Zionist Congress, Goldmann's activities would be confined to Europe, and all political work in the United States would be accomplished by the AZEC. Silver asked Segal to discuss this plan with several of his friends and to make sure that a reply was received from Ben-Gurion by September 7. Epstein informed Ben-Gurion in a cable of these developments, and in response Ben-Gurion sent Silver a handwritten letter in Hebrew, dated Paris, October 1, 1946, which was a political masterpiece of dealing with a highly sensitive issue, without committing himself in any way. Concerning Silver's arguments against Goldmann, Ben-Gurion wrote:

> In paragraph 2 [of the August 5 decisions of the Jewish Agency] we did not intend to put forward on our part an alternative proposal, but to inform the American Government that if such a plan will be proposed to us we shall discuss it with good will. Directives were given [to Dr. Goldmann] to make efforts in Washington and in talks with our friends that they should bring it about that the American Government should propose an alternative plan; that is, that we should not be passive and wait until Plan B will be proposed to us, but also that we on our part shall not officially propose such a plan to the Government, but take the initiative in our

hands, and thereby, through our friends, induce the Government to accept Plan B.

In fact, it did not come about precisely as we wanted it, and I do not blame anybody for it. It can be that our fine distinction was impossible to begin with, and I see no great misfortune in it, for nevertheless something has been achieved: a) a negative achievement: the president will withhold his support from the Grady plan; b) a positive achievement: the President and the S.D. [State Department] supported the principle of the Jewish State.

I don't know—and I don't think it is so decisive—all the particulars of the talks and meetings of Goldmann in New York and Washington, and I don't want to make myself a judge. It is possible that your criticism is justified, but even then we all thought that there is no basis for your resignation, and that you must not resign in this hour, and we did not accept your resignation and I am glad that you are continuing your work.[124]

Conspicuous is the absence from Ben-Gurion's letter of any reference to Silver's demand that Goldmann be removed from activities in America. In the remainder of the letter, Ben-Gurion deals in a similar evasive vein with Silver's demands for organizational changes.[125]

On August 30, 1946, Goldmann wrote to Acheson reporting to him on his talks with members of the British government, and requesting Acheson, too, to try to persuade Bevin to be more forthcoming. Goldmann explained that, if the Jewish Agency were willing to negotiate on the basis of the Morrison-Grady plan, this would be interpreted as being ready ultimately to accept an improved version of the cantonization plan and would lead to violent attacks by those in the movement (Silver and others) who are opposed to the very plan of partition. During the course of his talks with Bevin, Goldmann wrote, he gained the impression that the foreign secretary was willing to hold advance informal talks with the Jewish Agency, but the colonial secretary insisted that they must be held within the framework of the conference. Goldmann then suggested to Acheson that the State Department refrain from sending observers to the London Conference until the Jewish Agency came to an agreement with the British government concerning its participation. If the agency will take part, it will be most desirable that the State Department, too, should do so, at least in the capacity of observer.

Goldmann referred to the renewal of Silver's opposition to the partition plan and added that most Zionists in the United States will not go along with Silver. The Executive would soon send a delegation to the United

States to regulate matters in the Zionist movement. Goldmann concluded by emphasizing that partition had not yet received public support on the part of the American government and asked Acheson that either the president, or Acheson himself, should issue a statement in support of the partition plan. Such a statement would make the extremists' propaganda difficult as well as limit their influence in the Jewish arena and would even make an impression on the leaders of the Arab League.[126]

Goldmann sent a copy of this letter to Epstein and asked him over the phone to take steps to persuade the White House, too, to act in the spirit of his request. Because both Acheson and Secretary of State James Byrnes were absent from Washington at the time, William L. Clayton, who was unfamiliar with the Palestine issue and hence dependent on Loy Henderson's advice, was in charge of the State Department. Knowing Henderson's negative attitude toward the Jewish cause, Epstein felt there would be no point in talking to Clayton and instead spoke to Niles. Niles, however, explained to Epstein that he felt that the objections of the State Department and of the Pentagon to "the Goldmann plan" and such foreign policy considerations as the relations between the United States on the one hand and Great Britain and the Arab countries on the other would render the president hesitant to issue the statement proposed by Goldmann.[127]

In fact, the State Department did object to the issuance of a statement, and Truman himself was not eager to do it. However, Epstein, under instructions from Goldmann and working with and through Niles, was able to make the president change his mind. Niles informed Truman that Thomas E. Dewey, the Republican standard bearer, was about to make a strong statement in favor of Jewish immigration to Palestine in his address to the United Jewish Appeal on October 6, 1946, and urged the president to beat Dewey to the punch by issuing a statement on October 4, on the eve of Yom Kippur.

The long-fought-over statement, when it was finally issued, fell short of what the Zionists hoped for. Truman actually suggested a compromise between the Morrison-Grady scheme of cantonization and the partition plan. Instead of endorsing the plan of a viable Jewish State in Palestine, he stated that "this proposal received widespread attention in the United States, both in the press and in public forums" and went on to say that "from the discussion which has ensued, it is my belief that a solution along these lines would command the support of public opinion in the United States." Then came the suggestion of a compromise: "I cannot believe that the gap between the proposals which have been put forward is too great to be bridged by men of reason and good will. To such a solution, our Government could give its support."[128]

Although the Truman statement was a disappointment to Goldmann and Epstein,[129] it was sufficiently out of line with British policy to arouse the dismay of Attlee, who was informed by Truman a day ahead and who tried to persuade Truman not to issue it or, at least, to postpone it.[130]

It is difficult to judge whether this fruitless exchange between Truman and Attlee made Goldmann's continued efforts with Bevin easier or more difficult. In any case, he continued his talks with members of the British government. On the very day on which Truman's Yom Kippur statement was published and on which Attlee received a cabled copy of it from Truman (October 4), Goldmann proposed to the British government that it enter into a temporary agreement with the Jewish Agency to embrace the following three points:

1. Immigration into Palestine to be resumed immediately on the basis of a total of 15,000 people for the next three months, including the approximately 4,000 who were being detained in Cyprus.
2. Immediate release of the Jewish Agency leaders detained in 'Atlit.
3. Cessation of the general searches for arms.

As an additional point Goldmann suggested that General Barker, who had become an intolerable irritant to British-Jewish relations in Palestine (see above), be immediately removed. Goldmann reported this discussion to the United States chargé in the United Kingdom who, in turn, cabled it to the secretary of state on October 5, 1946.[131]

Until October 17 Goldmann commuted between Paris and London and met repeatedly, either alone or in the company of Weizmann and other Zionist leaders, with Bevin, George Hall, British Minister of Health Aneurin Bevan, and new Colonial Secretary Arthur Creech-Jones. But all these efforts in London to create conditions that would enable the Zionist leadership to participate in the conference remained unsuccessful.

Goldmann returned to America on October 18 and stayed until December 4. In news conferences on October 2–3 in Washington, he explained the reasons for the lack of progress in the talks between the Jewish Agency and the British government. He put the failure squarely at the door of the latter and accused the British Mandatory Government of Palestine of arbitrary acts. The conditions in Palestine, he said, would continue to deteriorate unless urgent measures were taken to find a constructive solution to the problem. He explained that the Jewish Agency refused to attend the Round Table Conference, in London, because it was opposed to participation in negotiations on the basis of the Morrison-Grady plan and insisted instead that the partition plan be taken as the basis. The British government refused to accept this condition. Also, the unofficial negotiations between the British and the Jewish Agency bore no fruit. Goldmann warned of the tragic consequences of the British refusal to discuss the rights of the Jews to a state of their own in Palestine and to allow the rescue of the survivors of the holocaust.[132]

This was the situation on the British front, so Goldmann fell back on the American connection. He was now more than ever convinced that the realization of the partition plan depended primarily on the American government. Both he and Epstein agreed that an extreme effort was called for to obtain the support of the State Department for the plan. Consequently, Goldmann embarked on a series of intensive talks and consultations with David Niles, Dean Acheson, Loy Henderson, and Secretary of State James F. Byrnes; with Richard Crossman, Sumner Welles, Lord Inverchapel, General Jan Christïan Smuts, General John H. Hilldring, General Lucius D. Clay, Senator Arthur H. Vandenberg; and with such American Jewish leaders as Felix Frankfurter, Joseph Proskauer, Jacob Blaustein, and Emanuel Neumann. In some of these meetings, Goldmann was accompanied by David Ben-Gurion, Berl Locker, Moshe Kleinbaum (Sneh), Louis Lipsky, Stephen Wise, or Abba Hillel Silver.[133]

On November 6, Goldmann met with Loy W. Henderson and William J. Porter, of the Office of Near Eastern and African Affairs of the State Department, and stated that the return of Secretary of State Byrnes was "a heaven-sent opportunity to get something done before the World Zionist Congress convened at Basle on December 9." Goldmann said that, as the matter now stood, the congress would convene in a vacuum unless Byrnes and Bevin could come to some agreement. He added that all the essential people were in New York: the Arab delegations, key members of the Jewish Agency Executive, and top-ranking British and American officials.

If the World Zionist Congress convened with matters standing as they were now, it would give the extremists, led by Dr. Silver, a prime opportunity to embarrass Dr. Wise and other moderates by questioning what the latter had gained by their policy of moderation and their partition proposal. Goldmann said that the extremists could do much damage in certain circumstances. On the other hand, if an agreement could be reached informally in New York, the Zionist leadership could easily keep matters in line at the Basle Zionist Congress, even though a formal settlement might have to await the reconvening of the Round Table Conference, in London, later in December. Then Goldmann gave an account of factionalism in the Zionist movement and an intended organization of the main branches of the Jewish Agency outside of Palestine.[134]

On December 3, 1946, Goldmann met with James Byrnes, at which time he reported about his contacts with Bevin on the Palestine issue. The progress in these exchanges toward the removal of the impasse had been minimal. At the end, Byrnes warned Goldmann that, if the Jewish Agency refused the British invitation to the conference, Britain would have no choice but to hand the Palestine problem over to the United Nations.[135]

Silver, meantime, had continued his two-pronged attacks on partition and Goldmann. True, at the September 10, 1946, meeting of the executive committee of the American Zionist Emergency Council, at which he presided, he seemed to have made a major concession when he stated that, though he was of the opinion that the agency had made a mistake in urging partition, "Still, we must get our Government to throw its resources behind it since it had approved of it. We are going to make the major effort of our career to see that the Government is prepared to back the Agency's proposal by action."[136]

But, six weeks later, at the opening session of the annual conference of the Zionist Organization of America, in Atlantic City (October 27, 1946), Silver rejected the partition plan, characterized the August 5 decision of the Jewish Agency Executive as "a hasty act," and accused the Executive of having reached that decision without prior consultation with the supreme organs of the Zionist movement. He announced that at the next congress he would demand the rescinding of the Paris decision on partition. He attacked Stephen Wise and his friends for supporting the American loan to Britain and Goldmann for his "irresponsible announcements" and his "harmful" political activities. These activities, he said, were carried out by Goldmann "on his own responsibility," in defiance of the agreement reached between him and the AZEC. Most of the delegates expressed support for Silver's views.[137]

XIX On the Jewish side, one more step remained to be taken before the partition plan became the officially endorsed policy of the Zionist movement as a whole: the Zionist Congress, the parliament of the Zionist movement, had to adopt it. The Twenty-second Congress, the first since World War II, met in Basle from December 9 to 24, 1946. It was full of bitterness against Britain because of her enforcement of the provisions of the 1939 White Paper, especially because she was keeping the gates of the Jewish national home closed to the survivors of the holocaust.

On December 12 Goldmann gave his propartition speech (in Yiddish), in which he reviewed the background of the Executive's decision to accept partition, and placed the whole issue in a historical and political perspective. In conclusion, he said:

> We are faced with a pressing problem. The status quo will not stand forever—neither in Eretz Israel nor in Europe. Inevitably, the situation will either improve or deteriorate. Inevitably, there will come in Eretz Israel an explosion, an internal collapse, an outbreak, if the present situation continues. We must know this, and try everything in our power, even at the price of great concessions, and do even things which are difficult for each one of us—if the situation demands it. We must find the courage in our hearts to build ourselves a basis from which we can break out of the impasse, and to go out and open the gates of Eretz Israel, if not of all of it, at least of most of it, to open them to large Jewish immigration immediately, and to lay the foundations for the liberation from foreign rule—so that we can dwell in most of the land and shall not be dependent on a colonial rule; so that we shall be a people of status, of honor, and a real political factor in the world.[138]

After this speech, which was greeted with "stormy applause," it was a foregone conclusion that the congress would go along with the recommendations of the Executive. Accordingly, the congress rejected participation in the second stage of the London Round Table Conference, expressed its conviction that the Mandate was dead, and contended that only the establishment of a Jewish commonwealth in Palestine could rescue the Jewish survivors in Europe and ensure the furtherance of the aspirations of the *Yishuv*, the Zionist movement, and its non-Zionist supporters. Weizmann tried to keep the lines of communication with Britain open, but the congress felt that he had lost touch with the realities of the Palestine problem and did not reelect him to the presidency of the World Zionist Organization. Goldmann was elected as a full member of the Executive, after having been, since 1939, a member with restricted rights.

The congress also introduced far-reaching changes in the American Zionist leadership. Stephen Wise was eliminated from official leadership, and his longtime antagonist Abba Hillel Silver was made chairman of the American Section of the Jewish Agency. Zvi Ganin, the historian of this phase of American Zionism, states that Goldmann became "the first casualty of Silver's ascendency; his bête noire, so Silver thought, was banished to London never to meddle again in American affairs. Silver, however, underestimated Goldmann's resiliency, his ability to bounce back after each punch. Only a short time later, the Zionist diplomat was back in America, involved in U.N. activities." Shertok replaced Goldmann as the chief diplomatic official of the Jewish Agency in America and the head of the Washington political office of the Jewish Agency.[139]

As for the first, British-Arab, stage of the London Round Table Conference, it had ended in failure. The Palestinian Arabs refused to attend, as long as Ḥajj Amin al-Ḥusayni, the exiled Mufti of Jerusalem who lived in Cairo, was not allowed to lead their delegation. Representatives of the Arab states who attended demanded arrangements that, in effect, would lead, after a relatively short period of transition, to an independent Arab state in Palestine, in which the Jews would be condemned to remain a perpetual, and ever decreasing, minority. Two days after the Arabs delivered their plan, the British suspended the conference.[140]

Faced with this impasse on the Arab front, the British went through a number of conciliatory motions vis-à-vis the Jews. They fulfilled two of the demands presented to them by Goldmann on October 4th: on October 22 they replaced General Barker; and early in November they set free the leaders of the Jewish Agency and a hundred other Jews who had been interned since June. The agency still refused to attend the second stage of the London Conference, but Ben-Gurion and Shertok held informal talks with Arthur Creech-Jones, who was friendly to Zionist aspirations.

During this period, Bevin attempted to suggest certain modifications in the Morrison-Grady scheme, which, however, both the Arabs and the Jews rejected. Finally, despairing of finding a solution, on February 14, 1947, Bevin announced in the House of Commons that the government saw no prospects for a settlement of the Palestine problem and had no choice but to submit it to the United Nations. On April 2, 1947, the British delegation to the U.N. asked the secretary-general to summon a special session of the General Assembly for the purpose of constituting a special committee to prepare recommendations. After a lengthy debate, the special session resolved to permit representatives of the Jewish Agency to present their views.

Now that the Palestine question was in the hands of the United Nations, Goldmann felt that it was imperative to close the Jewish ranks. Early in 1947 he had requested Proskauer that the American Jewish Committee take no stand on partition until Proskauer had a chance to consult with Acheson. Proskauer complied and so advised the Steering Committee of his organization. Now, in April, during the course of steps that were taken to achieve cooperation with non-Zionist bodies, Goldmann sounded out Proskauer on two major issues: the joining of the Jewish Agency by the American Jewish Committee; and mutual consultations between the two organizations about the Jewish appearance before the United Nations. On the first question, Proskauer was reluctant because the committee would be a minority in such an enlarged Jewish Agency. But, as to the second, he also felt the need for a "united front" and coordination. The agency thereupon invited the American Jewish Committee, the American Jewish Conference, and the Agudat Israel. A problem arose with reference to the invitation of the World Jewish Congress, which Silver opposed, but, at the insistence of Goldmann, he had to give in. All the organizations accepted and when the United Nations General Assembly, early in May 1947, decided to admit no other Jewish organization but the Jewish Agency to present the Jewish views, the status of the agency as the spokesman of the Jewish people on the question of Palestine was confirmed.[141]

On May 13, 1947, the United Nations Special Committee on Palestine (UNSCOP) was set up. It consisted of eleven members, of whom three were from Latin America, two from the Communist world, two from Western Europe, and one each from Australia, Canada, India, and Iran. No Arab country and no major power was represented. UNSCOP held hearings in Palestine, Lebanon, and Geneva for several months; met with representatives of the Jewish Agency, Egypt, Iraq, Lebanon, Saudi Arabia, and Yemen; and visited displaced persons camps in Germany and Austria.

While this work was going on in Asia and Europe, hearings were being conducted at the United Nations headquarters, in New York. It was somewhat ironic that the man who had been the most vociferous opponent of Goldmann's procedures in putting the partition plan before the United States government and who had felt slighted and misled by

Goldmann less than a year before should have been the chief spokesman of the Zionist propartition position at the United Nations First (Political and Security) Committee, to which the hearings on Palestine were referred by the General Assembly. It was Abba Hillel Silver who, on May 8, 1947, made the first presentation of the Jewish case. It was a historic occasion: never before had representatives of the Jewish people enjoyed the opportunity to address directly the community of nations. Silver's forceful, convincing, and impassioned presentation made a deep impression on the committee. He was followed by Moshe Shertok (May 10), and David Ben-Gurion (May 22). Later, Shertok and Emanuel Neumann participated on a regular basis in the work of both the UN Ad Hoc Committee on Palestine and its Subcommittee One, which was entrusted with the task of preparing a detailed plan for the partition. Other members of the Jewish Agency delegation were Rabbi Zeev Gold, Chaim Greenberg, Rose Halprin, and Nahum Goldmann.[142]

However, Goldmann's main task during those crucial months of 1947 was "behind the scenes in Washington and in the UN Secretariat."[143] His aim was to win over the Western European and Latin American countries to the Zionist cause. As far as Russia was concerned, during his years in Geneva he had conducted talks with Russian Foreign Minister Maxim Litvinov and the Russian Ambassador in Paris, Vladimir Petrovic Potemkin, and subsequently, while in Washington, he had contact with Russia's representatives Konstantin Oumansky and later Andrei Gromyko. Indirectly, Weizmann and Goldmann received word, in March 1945, from Stalin through President Edward Beneš of Czechoslovakia to the effect that Stalin wanted to redress the wrongs done to the Jewish people in recent years and that the Jews "need not worry about the position of the Soviet Union."[144] In 1947, in addition to working with his colleagues at the United Nations, Goldmann traveled frequently to Paris and to South America and established friendly relations with Latin American statesmen, among them Oswaldo Aranha, the Brazilian foreign minister who served as president of the UN General Assembly when the partition issue came up for the final vote.[145]

The final report of UNSCOP was prepared on August 31, 1947. The majority—seven of the eleven members—proposed the establishment of a Jewish and an Arab state in partitioned Palestine; the Jewish State was to comprise 5,579 square miles, or roughly 56 percent of Western Palestine, including Eastern Galilee, and most of the coastal area and of the Negev. Jerusalem and its environs were to be internationalized—a severe blow to Zionist hopes and aspirations.

The UNSCOP report was discussed for several weeks by the UN Special (Ad Hoc) Committee on the Question of Palestine, during which numerous territorial adjustments were made. On November 25 the Ad Hoc Committee approved the report and passed it on to the General Assembly, where its adoption required a two-thirds majority.

The fateful day of voting at the General Assembly was November 29. During the last few days before the meeting, Goldmann and his colleagues "campaigned frantically." On the morning of the 29th, he and Shertok went to see Alexandre Parodi, the French delegate. Goldmann took away the impression that France would vote "yes."[146]

The scene at the General Assembly hall on the afternoon of that day was described by Goldmann:

> . . . the Assembly hall was packed. Hundreds of Jews filled the spectators' gallery and even the delegates' lounge was crowded. The suspense was unbearable, particularly when the roll-call began, and hundreds of delegates and guests sat there with crumpled lists of members, checking off the results. Since members vote in alphabetical order, France was called fairly early. Parodi's *Oui* produced an ovation lasting several minutes. When the result was announced the Arab delegates began to make angry protests, but the vote was final. The delight of our delegation can hardly be described. Scenes of jubilation and tears were still going on in the U.N. corridors several hours after the session had been adjourned. In New York the Jews celebrated the decision with spontaneous dancing in the streets. The Jewish Agency delegation, led by Dr. Weizmann, celebrated in my home, and although I had invited only my closest colleagues, hundreds of friends and journalists, including many non-Jews, joined us.[147]

To recapitulate: 33 votes were in favor of the partition plan, 13 opposed, 10 abstentions, and one nation was absent. The Arab and Muslim nations of Afghanistan, Egypt, Iran, Iraq, Lebanon, Pakistan, Saudi Arabia, Syria, Turkey and Yemen, as well as Greece and Cuba voted against the partition plan. Several Latin American nations (Argentina, Chile, Colombia, El Salvador, Honduras, and Mexico) as well as China, Ethiopia, the United Kingdom, and Yugoslavia abstained. The pro votes included those of the East European nations of Byelorussia, Czechoslovakia, Poland, Ukraine, USSR; of the Latin American states of Bolivia, Brazil, Costa Rica, Dominican Republic, Ecuador, Guatemala, Nicaragua, Panama, Paraguay, Peru, Uruguay, and Venezuela; and Australia, Belgium, Canada, Denmark, France, Haiti, Iceland, Liberia, Luxembourg, the Netherlands, New Zealand, Norway, the Philippines, Union of South Africa, and the United States. The nation absent was Siam.

Thus the struggle for statehood was concluded, and the struggle for securing the existence of the State of Israel began.

*   *   *

Goldmann's achievements in connection with the birth of Israel can be summarized briefly: For more than ten years, he was the most indefatigable advocate of the establishment of a viable Jewish State in an adequate area of Palestine. In innumerable speeches and personal talks, he obtained more and more sympathy for this idea among Zionist and non-Zionist Jewish leaders and among Gentile statesmen in the international forums of the League of Nations and the United Nations as well as in many capitals of the world. He was the peripatetic salesman of the Jewish State idea, the modern version of the Wandering Jew, whose constant travels, mostly by air, between country and country and between continent and continent, would have prostrated and undermined the health of any man with a less sturdy constitution and fewer inner resources than those that filled his small and stocky frame. The number of meetings he could pack into a single day, often after an all-night flight, was amazing. His ability to be at his persuasive, sharp, charming, and anecdotal best even in the most exhausting circumstances and faced with the shrewdest, hardest, and most self-willed opponents was nothing short of fabulous. He possessed an uncanny knack of making even his most antagonistic interlocutors enjoy their discussions with him so that they were willing to see him again and again, day after day, and to listen to his renewed arguments while being entertained by his esprit, bons mots, stories, and witticisms.

What Goldmann achieved during the five days of August 6–10 in Washington was to make the American government irrevocably a partner in the Palestine problem and to commit it to its solution through partition and the establishment of a Jewish State in an adequate part of it—the solution that only a few days earlier he himself had to ram down the throat of a reluctant Zionist Executive. Once the U.S. secretaries of state, war, and commerce were won over by him to the partition plan, and, in their capacity of the Cabinet Committee, unanimously recommended it to President Truman, and once the president adopted their recommendation and so informed British Prime Minister Attlee, the

United States, at the time the most influential power in the world, was committed to the course that in due time led to the adoption of the partition resolution by the United Nations.

A nation, unlike a human child, can have many fathers. America speaks proudly and lovingly of its Founding Fathers. Among the founding fathers of Israel, whose ranks include men like Herzl, Weizmann, and Ben-Gurion, Goldmann occupies a special place: more than anybody else it was he who convinced America—the country whose voice counted most in the family of nations—that the Jewish State must be born.

7. Adenauer and the German Reparations: A Documentary Account

Some of the people who have known Goldmann personally have voiced the opinion, in writing or orally, that he was a "bluffer," a man possessed of a strong proclivity to embellish things, and thereby deviate from the truth, out of vanity and desire for ego satisfaction. A brief, casual meeting with a leading statesman, they say, becomes in Goldmann's account of it a sustained relationship and an intimate friendship, and an inconclusive discussion of an issue is transformed in his retrospect into a conversion of his opposite number by Goldmann's persuasiveness from an adversary to a supporter. Therefore, they maintain, everything Goldmann has said or written about his activities and achievements must be taken with a sizable pinch of salt.

It is not my intention to name in print and thus embarrass those who gave me this kind of opinion of Goldmann orally. However, one such statement, which has already been published, bears repetition. Dr. Kurt Blumenfeld (1884–1963), the well-known German Zionist leader and longtime friend of Goldmann, made this remark about him in a letter he wrote on September 18, 1952, to Professor Adolf Reifenberg (1899–1953), of the Hebrew University: "We had a very extensive visit from Nahum Goldmann who gave us and the Lichtheims an extraordinarily interesting report about his German experiences. *His story was this time not only witty but also true.*"[1] Clearly, the italicized sentence implies that usually Goldmann's stories were witty but untrue.

The opinion of those who felt that Goldmann was a bluffer was based on two circumstances. One was that he was an extraordinarily effective raconteur who could tell about his encounters and experiences with famous world figures, at length, in much detail, and with a scintillating humor. This in itself was apt to evoke doubts about his strict veracity.

Those who heard or read his stories, which usually showed his superiority to his interlocutors in grasp, repartee, and ability to find solutions, were often inclined to ask themselves whether he could really have possessed the presence of mind, the ability to formulate so cleverly an impromptu answer while speaking with statesman X, minister Y, or ambassador Z. Was it not rather the case that these stories were subsequently elaborated and embellished by him for stronger effect? Such were questions that almost automatically resulted in doubts of his truthfulness.

The second circumstance is the private nature of Goldmann's meetings with statesmen of many nations. Only in a few cases was a third person present. Thus, for instance, at his first meeting with Konrad Adenauer in London on December 6, 1951, Goldmann was accompanied, according to Adenauer, by the ambassador of Israel to London[2] and, according to Goldmann, by Noah Barou,[3] and at his decisive meeting with Adenauer on June 10, 1952, Felix Shinnar went with him.[4] In general, however, Goldmann preferred to conduct such talks *tête à tête*. In connection with his first meeting with Adenauer, a difference arose between Goldmann and Jacob Blaustein (1892–1970), the leading American Jewish industrialist and philanthropist, who insisted that he, as senior vice-president of the Claims Conference, should conduct the negotiations together with Goldmann. Goldmann objected because Blaustein's participation would have meant that the talks would have to be conducted bilingually, in English and German, with interpreters in between, which would have made them cumbersome. More importantly, Goldmann had been used at all times to negotiate alone, and, with a very few exceptions, had always refused to participate in delegations or to lead them. His manner of negotiating, as he pointed out in 1980, rested on establishing personal contact with his interlocutor, creating a friendly atmosphere, and interjecting Jewish jokes as part of his arguments.[5]

Because this was Goldmann's preference and practice, in most cases only two persons could report on what went on in the meetings: Goldmann and the statesman with whom he met. However, the latter, if he reported at all on the meeting, did so in a memorandum or in memoirs, in a brief, matter-of-fact manner that gave only the barest gist of what had transpired during the course of the often lengthy meetings with Goldmann. Thus, in effect, in most cases, the only source supplying a detailed account of these meetings is Goldmann himself. The unavailability of external corroboration is in itself a circumstance that is calculated to arouse doubts as to the accuracy of the single extant source. The impression is easily created, or feeling evoked, that exaggeration is involved, for the purpose of enhancing the raconteur's image as the skillful negotiator, the masterly marshaler of clinching arguments, the man of wit and esprit, the irresistible charmer.

The question of whether or not such a stricture is justified in the case of Goldmann cannot be answered in general terms. Most of the people with whom he conducted his conversations and negotiations have long since passed away: Mussolini, Tito, Adenauer, Acheson, Judge Proskauer, and many others. The few who are still alive are either inaccessible for the purpose of such verification (for example, King Hassan of Morocco, Ceausescu, and Kissinger) or else played only minor roles in Goldmann's diplomatic activities.

In these circumstances, I looked for a test case that could serve as a touchstone to establish whether the glitter enveloping the Goldmann phenomenon is true gold or not. The way I intended to proceed was, first to try to reconstruct the contacts and relationships between Goldmann and an international statesman without having recourse to what Goldmann himself has written or said about them. Then, having done this, I would show how the picture resulting from this procedure bears out what he himself has to say about the events in question. It so happened that the case where this was most feasible was the second in chronological order of the missions Goldmann undertook in the Gentile world as spokesman of the Jews: the relationship he established with West German Chancellor Konrad Adenauer (1876–1967) and other German officials in connection with the negotiations which led to the German reparations agreement.

The numerous studies on the German reparations make it clear that, though the negotiations which led to the so-called Luxembourg Agreement were conducted on an official and institutional level between German officials on the one hand and Jewish and Israeli representatives on the other, the crux of the whole matter on which hinged their success or failure was the personal relationship Goldmann succeeded in establishing with Adenauer.

As early as 1941, at the Inter-American Conference of twenty-two Jewish communities in the Western hemisphere that was convened by the World Jewish Congress in Baltimore on the eve of the United States' entry into the war, Goldmann broached the subject. Although Germany was at the time at the peak of her power as well as military success and controlled most of Europe from western Russia to the English Channel, Goldmann raised questions predicated on the eventual defeat of

Germany and destruction of the Third Reich, including the ability of the Allies to force the Germans to pay compensation for material damage they caused and to restore property looted by the Nazis to its rightful owners. He said: "Who can doubt that we Jews have every right to international help for European Jewry after the war? If reparations are to be paid, we are the first who have a claim to them."[6]

During the ensuing three years there were, on and off, talks about restitution among the Allies, and Jewish scholars and leaders worked on the specifically Jewish aspects of the problem. The first official Allied declaration on postwar restitution was made on January 5, 1943, by representatives of eighteen Allied governments meeting in London.[7] This was followed in 1943 and 1944 by memoranda and pamphlets written by German-Jewish communal leaders and others living in Palestine, England, and the United States, in which the scope and nature of the Jewish claims against Germany gradually crystallized.[8]

Late in 1944 the World Jewish Congress held its War Emergency Conference in Atlantic City. In his opening address, Goldmann stressed two points: Jewish rights must be restored where they have been abrogated; and, so far as possible, Jewish property must be returned. "It would," he stated, "be adding mockery to tragedy, were non-Jewish individuals and communities to become the heirs to property which, if not legally, certainly morally, belonged to the Jewish community and must be used for rebuilding Jewish life and a Jewish future." The way this problem is settled, he added, will be the real test of the good will and moral sense of the democracies.[9]

Another few years of painful soul-searching had to pass before the government of Israel, led by David Ben-Gurion, reached the conclusion that it was not only their right and duty but also morally right to claim reparations from Germany for the material damage inflicted on the Jewish people by the Nazi regime. However, broad segments of the Israeli population felt otherwise. In many quarters, extremely vehement and bitter feelings were manifested against sitting down at a table to negotiate with Germans. In 1950 it was only five or six years since the German genocide of six million Jews had become public knowledge, and feelings in Israel ran high against all contact with the nation that perpetrated inhuman torture and mass murder. Many people considered the very acceptance of payments in any form from Germany anathema because they felt that such an act would represent an acceptance of blood money and thereby would imply—if not forgiveness of Germany's unspeakable crimes—at least some kind of patching over of the past.

The solution of the political problem these clashing views represented was that the Israeli government decided to move ahead discreetly and indirectly, by addressing demands for German reparations, not to the government of Germany itself, but to the occupying powers, which at that time were still in control of Germany. Subsequently, in the spring of 1950, secret conversations were held between Israeli and German representatives.[10] The most prominent Jewish spokesman at this stage of the negotiations was Noah Barou (1889–1955), chairman of the European board of the World Jewish Congress, who for almost two years conducted talks with Herbert Blankenhorn, director of the German Foreign Office, and others.

On the Israeli side, it was not until July 1951 that a section was set up in the Foreign Ministry to pursue the material claims of the Jewish people against Germany. This office was headed by Felix E. Shinnar.[11] The work of this office, however, continued to be hampered by the prevailing feelings in Israel against contacts with Germany. A typical manifestation of the popular attitude took place when the issue of direct negotiations with Germany came up in the Knesset, on January 7, 1952. Not only did the government's proposal provoke heated discussion in which a wide assortment of parties argued ferociously against it, but at the same time violent street demonstrations broke out, and the press inveighed bitterly against the government. Nevertheless, on January 9 the Knesset approved by a vote of 61 to 50 with 5 abstentions and 4 members absent the government's request for authorization to begin direct negotiations with the Bonn regime.[12]

This official opening of negotiations between the two governments was preceded by almost two years of unofficial, secret, and tentative contacts between Jewish and Israeli officials on the one hand and German officials on the other. Their beginnings dated from the assumption of the office of chancellor of the Federal Republic of Germany by Konrad Adenauer in the fall of 1949. As he wrote in his *Erinnerungen* (Memoirs) in 1966, in his dry, matter-of-fact style: "When I became Chancellor in 1949 I saw in the putting in order of relations with the Jews one of the most important tasks. Our good will could be attested, above all, through material aid. But we had thereby to avoid the impression as if the injustice which had taken place could and should be atoned for through the handing over of material goods. This could be only an external sign of our endeavor to make reparations."[13]

As Adenauer tells the story of the German reparations to which he devotes a chapter of thirty pages in his memoirs, contacts between representatives of Germany and Israel began in the spring of 1950. Then, on March 12, 1951, the government of Israel addressed a note to the occupying powers in Germany asking them to impress upon Germany the need to pay reparations to Israel, not for Jewish property plundered by the Nazis, which is alleged to exceed $6 billion, but for the expenses of $1.5 billion that Israel incurred concerning the resettlement of some 500,000 Jewish refugees.[14]

On September 27, 1951, Adenauer, in a historic speech in the Bundestag, issued an official statement to the effect that the German government was in the position and willing to achieve a solution of the problem of material reparations together with representatives of Jewish world organizations and of the State of Israel in order, as he put it, "to facilitate the way to the psychological cleansing of endless suffering."[15] It was at this point that Goldmann entered into the German-Jewish-Israeli negotiations, immediately assuming the key role in them.

In these circumstances, the government of Israel felt that a representative body of world Jewry should be set up for the purpose of conducting negotiations with Germany about Jewish claims. The suggestion that Jewish world organizations set up a Conference on Jewish Material Claims Against Germany to act on behalf of world Jewry came from Goldmann.[16] At his invitation, representatives of world Zionist and non-Zionist organizations held a series of meetings in October 1951, considered the Adenauer offer, decided to enter into negotiations with Germany, and formed the Conference on Jewish Material Claims Against Germany, chaired by Goldmann. From this point on, he was the Jewish spokesman vis-à-vis Germany, and, as Felix Shinnar, the representative of Israel in the negotiations, said, was "the living spirit" of the Claims Conference.[17]

On December 3, 1951, the government of Israel sent a note to the Federal Republic of Germany detailing its claims, and three days later the first meeting between Goldmann and Adenauer took place in London.[18] This meeting as well as a second one between Goldmann and Adenauer, which took place in February 1952, are described by Adenauer in section 2 of his chapter on "The Luxembourg Agreement: Putting in Order Our Relationship to the Jews." The section is entitled "Meeting with Dr. Goldmann on December 6, 1951, in London." Its full text is as follows:

> I had the wish that it should come as soon as possible to negotiations about the reparations. I considered it desirable that all Jewish interests should be represented by *one* personality. One of the first steps, therefore,

was to ask Israel and the Jewish world organizations to comply with this wish and to agree on one representative.

The difficulties of our situation were recognized, and understanding for them was shown. Dr. Nahum Goldmann was chosen and suggested to me as interlocutor. Dr. Goldmann had in the past lived in Germany, and was now living in New York. He was chairman of the World Jewish Congress, and since October 26, 1951, president of the newly founded Conference on Jewish Material Claims Against Germany. As such he had connections with the Jews in almost every state of the world.

The choice of Dr. Goldmann was a very fortunate solution. Although he was an extremely energetic and skilled representative of those who commissioned him, he understood, on the other hand, also the German difficulties. He devoted himself wholeheartedly to his task, untiringly, tenaciously, and animated by the endeavor to reach an understanding.

The first personal meeting between Dr. Goldmann and me took place on December 6, 1951, in London in the Hotel Claridge. Dr. Goldmann was accompanied, as far as I can remember, by the Israeli ambassador in London, who, however, appeared under an assumed name.[19] His participation in the discussion had to remain unknown. Both men were exposed to great dangers on the part of Jewish organizations which rejected all contact with Germans.

In the conversation, which took place in a very serious and impressive atmosphere, I informed Dr. Goldmann that the Federal Government, as I had already stated in my government declaration on September 27, 1951, was ready to begin negotiations with representatives of Israel and of the Jewish world organizations about a reparation of the damage which arose through the National Socialist regime. I said I considered the time ripe to begin these negotiations. I asked Dr. Goldmann to inform me, in his capacity of chairman of the Conference on Jewish Material Claims Against Germany and also in his capacity of representative of the government of Israel, of the readiness to negotiate.

Dr. Goldmann answered me that the Jewish people could never forget that which had been done to it during the National Socialist period on the German part. A performance of reparations on the part of Germany could be made only in the form of a generous gesture which would have to be judged less by its material value than by its symbolic meaning.

I agreed with Dr. Goldmann. I recognized explicitly the moral obligation of the German people to make reparations, and stated that I considered it a duty of honor of the German people to do its utmost to redress the wrong wrought to the Jewish people.

Dr. Goldmann asked me to acknowledge, in the form of a letter, the recognition of the moral claim of the State of Israel, namely to the effect that the Federal Republic accepted the claims of Israel as they were presented in the Israeli note of March 12, 1951, as the basis of negotiations.

I was prepared to do so, and had on the same day the following letter dispatched to Dr. Goldmann:

December 6, 1951

Dr. Nahum Goldmann
Chairman of the Conference of
Jewish Claims against Germany
London

Dear Dr. Goldmann:

With reference to the declaration which the Federal Government made on Sept. 27, 1951, in the Bundestag and in which it expressed its willingness to enter into negotiations with representatives of the Jewish people and of Israel concerning the reparation of the damages brought about under the Nazi regime, I wish to inform you that the Federal Government feels the time has come for such negotiations to begin. I beg you, in your capacity of chairman of the Conference of Jewish Claims against Germany, to inform both the Conference and the Government of Israel of this readiness.

I wish to add that the Federal Government sees in the problem of reparations above all a moral obligation, and considers it a duty of honor of the German people to do its utmost to redress the wrong wrought to the Jewish people. In this connection the Federal Government will welcome the opportunity to make a contribution to the upbuilding of the State of Israel through shipments of goods. The Federal Government is ready in these negotiations to make the claims advanced by the Government of the State of Israel in its note of March 12, 1951, the basis of the discussions. With the highest esteem,

Yours Sincerely
Adenauer[20]

Before continuing Adenauer's account of the negotiations that led to the Luxembourg Agreement, it is desirable to provide a few illustrations of the difficulties Goldmann encountered on the internal Jewish front, difficulties of which Adenauer could have had little or no inkling. Foregoing again the use of Goldmann's own writings, which contain quite a few references to these inner-Jewish problems, only a few indications given by Israeli and Jewish authors of the struggles that he had to face before practically every one of his meetings with Adenauer and other German officials will be presented.

Felix Shinnar, who represented Israel in the tedious negotiations, which took place in Wassenaar near The Hague, tells about one phase of these disagreements and difficulties. In October 1951 in Jerusalem, Goldmann and George Landauer (1895–1954), a German Zionist leader who was at the time the chairman of the organization of Central European immigrants in Palestine, "had a heated discussion which was not without far-reaching differences of opinion, about the question of the coordination between Israel and the Claims Conference." Shinnar himself was commissioned to work out a proposal, which he did, but his plan was sharply opposed by Goldmann because it "placed into the foreground the prerogatives of Israel as the representative of the Jewish people, with too much emphasis and too self-evidently." Agreement was, however, reached, and on October 26, 1951, the Claims Conference was formally established in New York.[21]

Among the Jewish leaders in the Diaspora the spokesmen of right-wing and religious parties were especially opposed to any contact with the Germans. Joseph B. Schechtman, of New York, chairman of the World Council of Herut-Hatzohar, was a passionate and determined opponent of the planned negotiations. In numerous articles, he pleaded for a total rejection of all traffic with "unclean" and morally "untouchable" Germany. Mizraḥi leaders took a similar position.[22] Because the establishment of the Claims Conference as the unified representative of world Jewry vis-à-vis Germany depended on the consensus of Jewish organizations and party groupings all over the world, these objections could easily have prevented the creation of a body whose purpose was to open negotiations with Germany.

But, even after the Claims Conference was established, Goldmann had a hard fight on his hands with representatives of the world Jewish organizations who were members of it. He called them to a meeting at New York on January 20, 1952, at which the stormy debate that preceded the Knesset vote of Jan. 9 was almost duplicated. At the end, however, they too endorsed the negotiations, and elected an executive committee, chaired by Goldmann. This committee met again in Paris on February 11 in a joint session with the Israeli delegation. An agreement was reached on a global claim of the Claims Conference set at 500 million German marks. At further meetings of the executive committee of the Claims Conference in London on March 16–18, its negotiating team was appointed, consisting of chairman Moses Leavitt, of the American Jewish Joint Distribution Committee, and members Max Easterman, of the World Jewish Congress, Seymour Ruben, of the American Jewish Committee, and Maurice Boukstein, of the Jewish Agency for Palestine. They were to be assisted by Dr. Nehemiah Robinson and other experts. Two days later, the Wassenaar negotiations began.[23]

To return now to Adenauer's account, he next reports that "On January 9, 1952, the parliament of the State of Israel resolved to accept the offer of the Federal Government to begin negotiations. This resolution was officially communicated to me on February 17, 1952, again in the course of a sojourn in London, in a talk with Dr. Goldmann. I underlined, during this second discussion with Dr. Goldmann, that the Federal Government would welcome an early start of the negotiations. We agreed to have the negotiations begin, as far as possible, in the second half of March."[24]

(Some discrepancy exists between this account of Adenauer, according to which the second meeting [after the first of December 6, 1951] between him and Goldmann took place on February 17, 1952, in London, and between Goldmann's *Autobiography*, which states that a meeting between him, Adenauer, German secretary of State for Foreign Affairs Walter Hallstein, and Assistant Secretary Herbert Blankenhorn, occurred on February 4, 1952, in London.[25] Because according to both accounts at this meeting it was agreed that the negotiations should begin in March, one must assume that both refer to the same meeting, though they give different dates.)

Two things become clear from this account by Adenauer. One is that, although Goldmann was accompanied by the Israeli ambassador to London, the latter took no part in the discussion. Adenauer's report makes it appear that the meeting was a dialogue between him and Goldmann, whom he viewed as the representative of both the Claims Conference and the Israeli government. Secondly, Goldmann succeeded in persuading Adenauer to write to him a letter expressing his view that the time has come to begin negotiations between the Jews, Israel, and Germany and that the German Federal Government considered it "a moral duty and a debt of honor of the German people to do its utmost to redress the wrong wrought to the Jewish people." Adenauer says nothing more than that the idea of a letter and its content were suggested by Goldmann; but, because the letter was dated on the very day on which the meeting between the two men took place, the circumstances make it seem likely that Goldmann participated in its drafting.

The German-Israeli negotiations began in Wassenaar on March 20, 1952. As Adenauer records, this "small locality was chosen at the request of the Israelis who feared assassination attempts on the German and

Israeli delegations on the part of right wing radical Jewish associations." And he adds, in his usual dry style, "I myself became the target, on March 27, 1952, in connection with these negotiations, of an assassination attempt with a package of explosives, which cost a human life."[26]

About the Wassenaar negotiations themselves, Adenauer writes that the leader of the German delegation was Professor Franz Böhm and that "the State of Israel and the Claims Conference were represented each by its own delegation. Dr. Goldmann did not participate in these negotiations. He remained in the background, and intervened only when the negotiations threatened to bog down, and it was necessary to overcome difficulties."[27]

After giving a detailed account of the German and the Israeli positions and of the course of the negotiations, Adenauer remarks that "on the Israeli side they were afraid that through the discussions of the experts and men of finance the whole question of the reparations would be reduced to the level of a 'financial cowtrading,' as Dr. Goldmann once expressed himself to me." As for the German position, says Adenauer, "we wanted, precisely because it was a matter of a moral debt, to undertake commitments only in the moment when we knew for certain that we could fulfill them punctually. The German delegation in its negotiations, and in numerous conversations with Dr. Goldmann, repeatedly asked for an understanding of the situation of the Federal Government."[28]

The negotiations became stalled over the total amount of the reparations and the schedule of payments. When a seeming impasse was reached, Goldmann wrote to Adenauer (on May 19, 1952) a letter that Adenauer included in his memoirs:

> On May 21, 1952, I was presented with a letter from Dr. Goldmann in which he informed me of his great concern about the situation that had developed in the meantime. The letter was dated May 19, 1952.
>
> Dr. Goldmann reported about a meeting which had taken place on May 19 between [the German representative Herman Josef] Abs and Dr. [Felix E.] Shinnar, the chief negotiator of the Israeli delegation. . . .
>
> Dr. Goldmann wrote: ". . . The disclosures made by Mr. Abs to the representatives of the Government of Israel contradict in their spirit the declaration of the Federal Government of Sept. 27, 1951; they contradict even more the content of your letter of Dec. 6, 1951, in which you accepted the demand of the State of Israel in the amount of one billion U.S. dollars as the basis of the negotiations.
>
> "If I weigh the proposals of Mr. Abs in the light of these foregoing

declarations, without which it would have never come to the negotiations, I am convinced that the Jewish public will see in them— forgive the harsh word—nothing but an insult. Dr. Shinnar has told this to Mr. Abs spontaneously and instantly. In any case, in the views of Mr. Abs concerning the solution of the problem the willingness to make any kind of real sacrifice for the reparations finds in no way an expression. The thesis of Mr. Abs about the Federal Republic's lack of ability to perform will convince neither the Jewish people nor the world at large, if one takes into account the steadily rising productive power of the German economy, the growing German foreign trade which goes into billions of dollars, and the settlement of the payments burden which has just been made. One cannot solve a problem of the moral significance of the Jewish reparations with the usual methods of commercial negotiations—and bargaining. What impressed me most deeply in the talks with you, Mr. Chancellor, and moved me to recommend that Israel and the Jewish people begin negotiations with the German Federal Republic, was your view of the moral duty of Germany to undertake at least serious material reparations.

"Despite the deep disappointment aroused in all of us by Mr. Abs's disclosure, I cannot as yet give up the conviction that you, Mr. Chancellor, could not endorse such proposals. The contradiction between such proposals and everything you told me in several conversations is so extreme that I cannot imagine that they in any way represent your views. . . .

"In this critical hour of our negotiations I appeal to you, dear Mr. Chancellor, as to the German statesman who has made himself the representative and spokesman of the reparations idea, and request you: lead the negotiations back to the high moral level from which you have hitherto viewed them. Do not allow methods, which are customary in purely commercial issues, to degrade and imperil these negotiations. The present state of uncertainty, the constant delays of a concrete offer which are not in conformity with your letter of Dec. 6, 1951, can no longer continue.

"The Jewish world and Israel have the right to know where they stand. I request you, therefore, to make sure with your whole authority that an offer be most urgently submitted which will make it possible to resume the official negotiations as soon as possible.

"Expecting your reply, on which so much will depend, I remain with deep respect and with the best wishes,

"Yours Sincerely,
Dr. Nahum Goldmann"[29]

The very fact that Adenauer quotes this letter at such length in his memoirs indicates the importance he attached to it. He adds that he was "taken aback by the situation which had developed" and immediately contacted Professor Böhm. Böhm thereupon submitted to him his own proposal, which Adenauer considered suitable to overcoming the difficulties. Adenauer then asked Böhm to get in touch with Goldmann without delay and to present the proposal to him. Because Goldmann in the meantime had left for Paris, Böhm went there, and they met on May 23, 1952. Next day, Böhm submitted to Adenauer a detailed report of this meeting as well as the subsequent meeting, in which at Goldmann's invitation also Giora Josephthal, Felix Shinnar, and Gershon Avner of Israel and Noah Barou of the World Jewish Congress participated. Adenauer included a major part of Böhm's report in his memoirs, from which it is reproduced here:

"I informed Dr. Goldmann," writes Böhm

> that, although I came on behalf of the Federal Chancellor, I was not empowered to bring proposals of the Federal Government. I was only entrusted with presenting the contents of a proposal which I myself had submitted to the Federal Government in the conviction that it would constitute a suitable basis for further negotiations in The Hague. The Federal Government had not yet made a decision about this proposal. But the Chancellor wished to learn unofficially the position of Dr. Goldmann and of the Israeli Government on this proposal, before the Government transmitted its own offer to the Israeli Government.

Then follows Prof. Böhm's proposal, which basically provided for a total payment of DM 3 billion within eight to twelve years, in goods, though many additional details were spelled out.

Professor Böhm reports Goldmann's reaction:

> Dr. Goldmann received this proposal in a decidedly friendly manner. This proposal represented an undoubtedly very serious expression of the reparations intentions, which, as he thought he could say, could count on a positive reception on the part of the Israeli Government. In any case, today's probing would create an atmosphere which, in the eyes of the Government of Israel, would again make the continuation of the negotiations rich in prospects, after the disclosures of last Monday in London had evoked depression and bitterness in the Israeli Government. What impressed him above all was that my proposal offered a closed, total and final solution which actually provided for substantial reparations performances. This, he felt, was a serious basis. From the Israeli point-of-view my proposal contained, of course, some blemishes whose correction should be striven for. He hoped that it would be possible for the Federal Government to present these corrections already in its official offer; otherwise they could be discussed in The Hague.

Then Dr. Goldmann came to speak about the global demand of the Jewish organizations represented by him. He suspected that this demand would have to be subject to quite a considerable cut. Assuming that the Federal Government would acknowledge only 20 to 25 per cent of the amount demanded (that is, a total of ca. 400 to 500 million DM), one would then have to expect very considerable resentment among the Jews, especially among the American Jews (not only against the Federal Government but also against Israel). Therefore he was considering whether it should not be recommended that the Federal Government add the amount it was considering to grant to the Conference on Jewish Material Claims Against Germany to the sum total which would be offered Israel, and leave it to Israel to come to an agreement about the division of the total reparations with the world organizations. In that case Israel alone would be the creditor of the Federal Republic and the receiver of the German payments in goods, but could at the same time undertake contractually to pay the organizations in cash an agreed-upon quota from each German annual delivery to Israel. Thus both sides would be helped. Israel would receive the goods it needed, and the organizations would get money for the support of the needy Jews.

Dr. Goldmann emphasized that he made this suggestion without having consulted Israel and without authorization. But he felt that both the Israeli and the Claims delegations would consent to such a solution, if it should be offered by the Federal Republic. In any case he would make efforts personally to obtain the consent of our negotiating partners for it.[30]

Having thus presented Böhm's report on his discussion in Paris with Goldmann, Adenauer continues:

Böhm declared himself willing to bring up the matter in Bonn, but cautioned that Goldmann's proposal would create additional money transfer problems, which Goldmann acknowledged.

Dr. Goldmann asked Prof. Böhm to inform me that in his view very much depended on the speed with which the decision of the Federal Government would be made. He would welcome it most emphatically if, on the occasion of my sojourn in Paris in connection with the signing of the agreement about the EVG (European Defense Community), I could meet with him and were in the position to give him, already at that time, certain binding explanations about the total frame of the agreement to be entered into. He, Goldmann, was of the opinion that I would endow the German offer of reparations with a special significance if I were to make it the first foreign policy act of the sovereign Federal Republic.

Dr. Goldmann let me know through Prof. Böhm that he was in fundamental agreement with the proposals submitted, and that he considered them a basis for further negotiations. Dr. Goldmann objected, however, to three points, in which, he felt, the Federal Government should, as far as possible, meet the wishes for the State of Israel. These points concerned:

1. The time of compliance: it was too long. The amount fixed should be defrayed at the latest within seven years.

2. The limitation of the delivery of goods: at least one third should be paid in cash.

3. Dr. Goldmann objected to the small initial payments. Since the time of compliance should be shortened, it followed that annually more than 200 million DM should be paid to Israel.

Professor Böhm spoke on the same day to the representatives of the State of Israel. They confirmed their difficulties which Dr. Goldmann had already indicated. . . .

Prior to leaving Paris, Prof. Böhm had another talk with Dr. Goldmann. The latter asked Prof. Böhm, to inform me that it was his conviction that the Government of Israel appreciated the dispatching of my representative to Paris and the content of the offers presented as much as he himself did. If I should come to Paris in the last week of May, he would be at my disposal any time, should I be willing to receive him. If it were possible for me to be accommodating with reference to the points mentioned, then, already at the conclusion of the talks with him, a press release could be issued in which a date for the resumption of the negotiations in Wassenaar could be named. This communiqué would then be the first foreign policy decision of the sovereign Federal Republic, and enter history as such. This gesture would make a deep impression on all Jews.[31]

This suggestion was accepted by Adenauer, and five days later, on May 28, 1952, he and Goldmann met again in Paris. Adenauer records:

On the occasion of my sojourn in Paris for the signing of the EVC (European Defense Community) agreement, I met on May 28 Dr. Goldmann for a talk. I could not yet inform him of a definitive decision, since the cabinet was not yet in a position up to this point in time to discuss the latest development in the Jewish-German negotiations. Dr. Goldmann understood that the consultations of the treaty of Germany and of the agreement about the European Defense Community had fully occupied my Cabinet and me. With a view to the Israeli public opinion we issued the following communiqué about our consultation:

"On May 28, 1951, Federal Chancellor Dr. Adenauer received in Paris the chairman of the Conference of Jewish Claims against Germany, Dr. Nahum Goldmann, for a discussion. In this discussion the Federal Chancellor again gave expression to his and the Federal Government's determination and confidence to carry on the negotiations with Israel and the Jewish organizations to a positive conclusion. The Federal Chancellor and

Dr. Goldmann were in agreement that it was desirable to resume the official negotiations as soon as possible. In order to attain this, another conference was contemplated for the near future in which a concrete proposal will be submitted for the satisfaction of the demands of Israel and the Jewish organizations."[32]

The planned meeting took place on June 10, 1952. Adenauer reports as follows:

> The planned talks between Dr. Goldmann and me were held on June 10, 1952. Apart from Dr. Goldmann, the participants were Dr. Shinnar on the Israeli side, and State Secretary Professor Hallstein, Professor Böhm and Abs, among others, on the German side. These talks brought about the decisive turn, which led ultimately to the final conclusion of an agreement between the State of Israel, the Claims Conference, and the Federal Republic of Germany.
>
> We agreed that the claims of the State of Israel and of the Claims Conference be handled jointly. The Federal Republic, in full agreement with the Claims Conference, would direct its payments *(Leistungen)* to Israel. The satisfaction of the demands expressed by the Claims Conference should be carried out by way of negotiations between the State of Israel and the Claims Conference. As the total amount of the German payments a sum of 3.4 to 3.5 billion DM was considered. About the size of the annual payments we agreed that up to March 31, 1954, 400 million DM will be paid. From April 1, 1954, on ten annual payments of 250 million DM each will be due. . . .
>
> On June 17, the results of the talks of June 10 were intensively discussed in the Cabinet. The Cabinet gave its approval. On the same day I communicated this to Dr. Goldmann and expressed my hope that henceforth a quick and successful conclusion of the negotiations will be reached on the foundations thus created.[33]

After discussing the problems the Federal Republic of Germany had to face when the Arab League protested the German reparations to Israel, Adenauer describes the signing of the agreement in Luxembourg, by Israeli Foreign Minister Sharett in the name of Israel, Goldmann in the name of the Claims Conference, and himself in the name of Germany. The date set for signing was September 10, 1952,

> but in the last minute it was jeopardized by threats of Jewish organizations. Wide circles of the Jewish people refused to accept money or delivery of goods for that which was wrought to the Jewish people on the German

side. Sharett and Dr. Goldmann were in great danger of becoming victims of assassination. We kept the place of signing secret until the last minute, and likewise the precise time. On the day before, we made known that the signing would take place next morning at 10 o'clock in a precisely designated elementary school. On Sept. 9 in the evening Sharett, Dr. Goldmann, and I got together for a last talk in Luxembourg in which we settled details of the act of signing. We agreed to meet next morning at 10 o'clock in the municipal building of the city of Luxembourg.

The Luxembourg agreement was built on the basis of the understanding reached on June 10, 1952. A transfer of payments to Israel in foreign exchange could not be carried out. Already during my first talk with Dr. Goldmann in December 1951 in London we spoke about taking into consideration the possibility of the delivery of goods. According to the agreement now concluded the State of Israel was entitled to buy goods with the DM amounts put at her disposal in the Federal Republic and to export them to Israel. The details were set down in the agreement.[34]

Adenauer's references to and accounts of Goldmann's role in the negotiations leading to the Luxembourg Agreement are complemented by remarks included by Herbert Blankenhorn in his political diary, published in 1980. Blankenhorn was director of the German Foreign Office, and in this capacity he participated in the reparations negotiations. He reports that within a few weeks after the inauguration of the German Federal Government, in October and November 1949, talks took place between Chancellor Adenauer and his collaborators, including Blankenhorn himself, concerning the problem of how it would be possible

to set the relationship of the German people to the Jews and the State of Israel on new foundations. In these talks the idea was again and again put forward that the new German state would regain confidence, respect, and credibility in the world if the Federal Government and the Federal Parliament were to put a distance between themselves and the past by an act of will performed through a free decision, and were to contribute through impressive material reparations to the easing of the incredible amount of mental and material plight suffered [by the Jews], and were to help those who lost everything in the rebuilding of a new existence. It was clear to us that such an act of will could not undo the unspeakable cruelties committed in the past in the name of the German people, nor the endless suffering they caused. But such an act of real reparations would serve the overcoming of the great bitterness evoked among the Jews of the whole world and also among all people of good will by the National Socialist crimes. It would, however, also have the meaning of making the German people conscious of the horrible past and the necessity of a radical return.[35]

After briefly recapitulating the negotiations and describing the scene at the signing of the agreement in Luxembourg, Blankenhorn devotes a few lines to characterizing the Israeli representatives, Moshe Sharett and Felix Shinnar, and then writes about Goldmann:

> On the Jewish side Nahum Goldmann was the dominant figure who found ways out of all difficult situations in the negotiations, and opened up the hearts of his negotiating partners through his calm and his optimism. This was above all the case with the Federal Chancellor who could not resist the charm of this highly cultured, manysided man, and his riveting, cheerful talent to entertain. Born in Lithuania as the son of Zionist parents who moved early to Frankfurt am Main, he spent his youth in the Germany of the Weimar period. Few are his equals in familiarity with the German humanities. As he himself says in his memoirs, Kant, Nietzsche, and Spinoza were his teachers. With all his tenacity and perseverance, Dr. Goldmann is not a man of hard discussions, but rather a man of understanding, of clever tactics, and of reasonable compromise. Filled with the ideas and aims of Zionism, he participated in all phases of the development of the State of Israel, and made efforts again and again to create understanding among his fellow citizens for a proper assessment of the Arab neighbors. Especially in the last years immediately after the great victory in the Six Day War of 1971 [*sic!*] which was so unexpected for Israel, he repeatedly urged in Tel Aviv that a peaceful settlement be brought about as rapidly as possible through corresponding great concessions. His efforts remained without success, which must be ascribed not exclusively to the lack of readiness of the Israelis, but essentially to the game of the world powers which showed neither the interest nor the will which would be necessary to clean up quickly this so dangerous Near Eastern nest of conflict. In the many conversations, which I have conducted with this politically so experienced and well informed man, Dr. Goldmann often expressed his worry that the isolation of Israel which has intensified after the Yom Kippur war of 1973 would make it difficult if not impossible to find the way to a real solution which would satisfy both the Arab and the Israelis. In his remarkable book *Où va Israel* (Paris 1975) he emphatically warned his countrymen against further self-isolation, and gave eloquent expression to the hope of a peaceful development in the Near East.[36]

The picture that emerges from Adenauer's, Böhm's, and Blankenhorn's accounts of Goldmann's role in negotiating with them and other German officials about the reparations to Israel shows Goldmann as the moving spirit of the negotiations. Demonstrating a masterly feeling for the sensibilities of the first postwar German chancellor, he was able to appeal to his highest ambition: to go down in history as the man who led a defeated, execrated, and ostracized Germany, the heir of an odious Nazi legacy, back into the community of nations and made it a respected member of the family of man. Although Adenauer himself was motivated by a strong desire to redress, so far as possible, the wrong wrought to the Jews by the Germans, it was unquestionably Goldmann's achievement to have kept this desire alive throughout the months of tedious negotiations that often deteriorated into haggling, and to strengthen with psychologically effective arguments the chancellor's resolve to satisfy the Israeli and Jewish claims to material reparations even at the price of considerable strain on the German economy and federal budget. As Adenauer's account shows, whenever the negotiations reached an impasse, Goldmann went into action, approached the chancellor in letter or in person, and induced him to put his influence and prestige on the line to overcome the deadlock. That Adenauer was a man of great moral stature cannot be doubted; that Goldmann exerted considerable and decisive influence over him in bringing the reparations to a positive conclusion comes through unmistakably in Adenauer's laconic, dry, and matter-of-fact account.

The chancellor's memoirs also show Goldmann as a man of practical ingenuity, who, more than any other participant in the three-sided negotiations, found solutions to problems, put forward suggestions, and was able to convince the others of their rightness. An example described by Adenauer is Goldmann's proposal, made before he could clear it with the Israeli government, that all the German reparations payments should be made to Israel, and that Israel, on its part, should transfer part of them to the Claims Conference.

Blankenhorn is much less restrained in recording the impression Goldmann made on him. What he writes is nothing short of a homage to a man whose culture, charm, wit, tenacity, and flexibility evidently captivated him as much as it did Chancellor Adenauer.

To complete the story of Goldmann's contacts with Adenauer, accounts of two of their meetings, of which Adenauer makes no mention, are added here. One of them took place at the suggestion of the chancellor on April 20, 1952, as a result of his feelings that a stalemate had been reached in the German-Israeli negotiations. Because this meeting is not mentioned in Adenauer's memoirs, Goldmann's account of it is presented here:

It was clear to me that a deadlock had been reached that could be broken only by the direct intervention of Chancellor Adenauer. Apparently Adenauer shared this feeling, for he wrote inviting me to a meeting. I readily accepted, and on April 20, 1952, I had a long talk with him at his house in Rhoendorf. In the course of our discussion I expressed my deep concern over the long hiatus. "I am afraid," I told him, "that in recent weeks the so-called financial experts have dragged the negotiations down from the high moral level established by the chancellor during early meetings to the level of financial horse-trading. Nothing more injurious could have happened. Agreement is possible only if the German payments to Israel and the Jewish people are regarded as a debt of honor, and this cannot be settled by methods applicable to commercial debts." I described to him the disquiet in Israel and Jewish opinion and the widespread doubt that Germany honestly intended to rise to a truly generous action, and I asked him to arrange for a clarification of the German offer by the beginning of May, when the Zionist General Council was to meet in Israel, principally to discuss the negotiations with Germany. I explained that my position would be greatly eased if I could give the participants some idea of the German offer.

Adenauer assured me emphatically that fears that the German government might be lacking in good faith were quite unfounded. It would be easy enough for the government to assent to all the Jewish claims for the time being, only to sabotage them when the time came. Precisely because it fully recognized the ethical nature of this debt of honor, it wished to assume only such responsibilities as it could fulfill promptly and reliably. This was why its official economic advisers had to be consulted, and that naturally took time. Nevertheless, he appreciated the arguments for expediting the pace and would do all he could to give me some idea of the German offer before I left for Israel. Since essentially it was going to have to be a matter of shipping goods, he would be glad if some Jewish experts, especially Barou and Felix Shinnar, could come to Bonn to discuss technical questions with a committee of specialists appointed for the purpose. I then flew back to New York, while Barou and Shinnar spent several days negotiating in Bonn.[37]

Although little new seems to have transpired at this meeting, it was one of the links in the chain of friendship and mutual respect that was forged between the two men. Adenauer's highly positive impressions of Goldmann have been indicated above. Goldmann, in turn, gives in his 1980 autobiography a detailed pen-picture of Adenauer that expresses his admiration for the man.[38]

The other meeting of which neither Adenauer nor Goldmann makes mention took place several years after the reparations negotiations and is described by Blankenhorn in his diary. Late in 1959 anti-Semitic outbreaks took place in various places in Germany, which prompted Goldmann to ask for a meeting with Adenauer, after which he met also with Blankenhorn. Blankenhorn discusses these meetings in two diary entries:

Bonn, January 18, 1960.
Talk with Goldmann who has come to Bonn by reason of the anti-Semitic machinations, in order to form a personal judgment and to contact the Federal Government and the Federal Chancellor. The meeting with the Federal Chancellor, Goldmann told me, was impressive. The Chancellor takes these things extremely seriously, and he discussed with him in detail the possibilities of preventing such events in the future. Goldmann himself discussed the idea of having a specific commission of internationally recognized German scientists, educators, and politicians, set up by the Federal Chancellor or the Federal Government, to look into the possibility of immunizing the German youth against racial hatred, and to present the results of its deliberations in a report. Apart from that, he suggested to the Chancellor to meet early in February in Bergen-Belsen with some thirty leading representatives of Jewry from all over the world, who will convene at the end of January in Amsterdam for a conference, and to evidence a joint demonstration, a commitment to a real cooperation between Jews and Germans at the graves of those who perished in the concentration camp. The Chancellor reacted positively to both ideas, and Goldmann hoped to receive his definitive consent, at least with regard to the meeting in Belsen.[39]

January 21, 1960
After a brief interruption Goldmann is again in Bonn, and gives a press conference in the Bundeshaus [Federal Parliament] with a large number of German and foreign journalists. At this conference Goldmann finds the proper tone. He consciously avoids bagatellizing things. But he also emphasizes that the overwhelming majority of the German people is undoubtedly not anti-Semitic in its basic position. He explains that it would be a mistake if the German people would make the coming to terms with this problem of great significance an easy matter for itself, and would pass in silence over the frightful horrors committed by a criminal government in the name of the German people.

It is, in fact, insupportable that many of our teachers are simply not equipped to discuss these problems with their pupils. Here the German state is about to miss something quite essential, something decisive for its future life, unless the situation is quickly remedied.

There are today on the international political stage only a few personalities who combine in themselves a sure political discernment, unusual political power to act, and great cultural riches. To them belongs Goldmann, who has acquired a high degree of international respect as cofounder and later president of the Jewish World Congress. Filled with great libertarian ideals, he is able, thanks to his rhetoric talent, to lead his followers from animosities and feelings of hatred, again and again to the decisive constructive problems. Therewith he created a position for the Jews of the Diaspora from which the State of Israel draws, not only financially but also spiritually, quite significant powers.

Unusual is the capacity for work of this man who constantly moves from continent to continent in order to solve the everywhere burning Jewish problems. Unusual is also his inexhaustible "curiosité d'esprit," which keeps him in close contact with all phenomena of intellectual life, and constitutes an essential source of his strength and authority.

His relationship to the State of Israel is very close, and there have been several attempts to induce him to take over the presidency of the state. If he could not find it in himself to do so, the reason for this is, in the first place, that he would not feel happy in the somewhat narrow Israeli circumstances. He needs greater freedom of movement, as it offers itself to him rather in the task of the World Jewish Congress which spans the world. To this must be added that his financial and economic interests in New York, which are a basis of his political independence, have their significance. It is in accordance with his cosmopolitan life style that Goldmann does not belong to the unconditional supporter of a rigid anti-Soviet policy, as Ben-Gurion wishes it. Closer to him is the idea to keep the Jews, and in the first place the Jews of Russia, out of the fangs of the Cold War through an understanding with the Soviet Union. It is not in his nature to hold fast rigidly to a rejection in principle of everything Russian, just as he has never completely given up the thought to overcome the warlike tension between Israel and the Arab world through a reasonable policy of adjustment which takes into account not only the interests of Israel but also certain Arab wishes. I know that he has repeatedly taken up contact with emissaries of Nasser for this purpose, which, however, has never led to concrete results.[40]

After the conclusion of the reparations negotiations, Adenauer mentions Goldmann only once more in his memoirs. Describing his meeting with Ben-Gurion in New York, on March 14, 1960, he writes that he told him: "Out of inner interest I have followed the fate of Israel, and shall continue to do so. Through Nahum Goldmann I am informed about this and that, but I also know that he, Ben Gurion, and Goldmann are not in agreement on everything."[41]

Adenauer's term of office as chancellor came to an end on October

15, 1963. Two and a half years later, in May 1966, at the invitation of the Israeli government, he paid a visit to Israel. The country, he writes in his memoirs, made a deep impression on him. He does not mention that he met Goldmann on that occasion. However, an Honorary Fellowship was conferred at the time upon Adenauer by the Weizmann Institute, which had received some DM 25 million from Germany and from the Volkswagen Foundation for its research work. Adenauer had played an important part in making this German support available to the Weizmann Institute. The first speaker to greet Adenauer at the award ceremony was Goldmann, in his capacity of president of the World Jewish Congress. He said:

> We pay tribute to one of the greatest statesmen and personalities of our generation. There is not one among the leaders of post-war Germany who has shown so much understanding—for the difficulties involved and for the importance of the attempt that is being made, now that the Hitler days are over, to normalize the relations between the Jewish people and the new Germany—as has Dr. Adenauer. He was always aware of the vital moral importance of Germany's efforts to restore normal relations both with the Jewish people and with the State of Israel; the unique system of legislation enabling compensation to be made to the victims of Nazism would never have been possible without the courageous stand that he took in this matter, in respect of which he had so many internal difficulties to overcome. For many years Dr. Adenauer has shown his intense interest in the Weizmann Institute as one of the outward expressions of Israel's contribution to world civilization and science. He has been of assistance to the Institute in a great many respects. He is worthy of every form of recognition that can be shown him—as indeed, Israel is now showing him on the occasion of this visit—and the privilege of being the first to give him an official welcome is one that the Weizmann Institute has richly deserved.[42]

In his acceptance speech, Adenauer said:

> An impression which I shall never forget is the one I experienced when the [German reparations] agreement was signed in Luxembourg, my dear listeners, and I might add that that which ensued would not have ensued if it had not been for the work done by two men on your side. One of them was Mr. Nahum Goldmann, who made it his duty right from the start to contribute towards creating a better atmosphere between Germans and Israelis. I must also mention your representative in the Federal Republic over many years, Mr. Shinnar.[43]

A few days later, Goldmann invited some eighty men and women to a luncheon at the King David Hotel, in Jerusalem, to meet Adenauer. At the luncheon, Goldmann paid tribute in a speech to Adenauer that he concluded as follows: "[Adenauer] is not only the great leader who, after a devastating defeat, restored the position of Germany as a great power, within the shortest possible time, but he has also made every effort to fill his people with a new spirit of democracy and deep respect for moral and spiritual values, which alone constitute an effective guarantee against a revival of the horrors of the past. For all this, Dr. Adenauer deserves both our admiration and our thanks."[44]

This is not the place to give a detailed account of the many efforts Goldmann made, first to establish, and then to intensify and improve, relations—in the first place cultural ones—between Germany and Israel. At every step he took toward this aim, he was attacked both in Israel and in the Diaspora. As Rolf Vogel, who assembled a valuable collection of documents on *The German Path to Israel* (published in German in 1967 and in English in 1969), says: "From the beginning of his conversations with post-war German political figures, Nahum Goldmann had intended through frank discussion to evolve a realistic policy, so far as possible keeping the feelings of the Jewish people out of substantive decisions. During those years Nahum Goldmann was often confronted with bitter criticism in the Jewish organizations. Only through his powerful personality could he get people to follow him."[45]

Less than three months after Adenauer's visit to Israel, the Fifth Plenary Session of the World Jewish Congress in Brussels, on whose agenda Goldmann put the theme "Germans and Jews," invited leading German and Israeli statesmen to participate in the discussion of this highly sensitive subject. After a sharp debate, it was resolved to keep the controversial item on the agenda. The congress was addressed, among others, by Isaac Remba, of Herut-Hatzohar, Professor Gershom Scholem, of Hebrew University, Professor Golo Mann, of Stuttgart University, Professor Salo W. Baron, of Columbia University, and Eugen Gerstenmaier, president of the German Diet. Goldmann presided and made the closing speech.[46] After the assembly, Goldmann was sharply criticized by both leftist and rightist groups in Israel, though, as he stated in an interview with Rolf Vogel in Jerusalem, he felt that the very fact that the relations between Germans and Jews were debated at the assembly of the World Jewish Congress was a major step forward.[47]

When Konrad Adenauer died, on April 19, 1967, Goldmann was the only non-Israeli Jewish statesman to come to Bonn to take leave of the

man with whom he had so many conversations and who was his com-
rade-in-arms in their joint fight for the Luxembourg Agreement. Before
leaving New York for Bonn, Goldmann said:

> In Chancellor Dr. Adenauer, the Jewish people and Israel have lost one
> of their great friends. In the 16 years that I have known him and during
> which I met him very frequently, he has proved again and again his
> inflexible determination to make good as far as possible—at least on the
> material plane—crimes committed by the National Socialists against the
> Jews: this attitude he maintained in the face of much opposition. The
> unique work of indemnification and restoration of property for the victims
> of National Socialism, that found its reflection in the Luxembourg Agree-
> ment and a large number of German laws, would not have been possible
> to achieve in its present form without his unwavering pertinacity and good
> will.
> I have met a large number of the leading statesmen of my generation. I
> considered Konrad Adenauer one of the greatest figures of the post-war
> era, indeed, as a man uniting in one person admirable human qualities
> and remarkable political and statesmanlike talent.
> The Jewish people will never forget his attitude and his achievements
> in the work of indemnification for the crimes of National Socialism, and
> also his most effective cooperation and support in many other most im-
> portant problems arising in connection with Israel and the Jewish people.
> His memory will always be held in reverence by this and future
> generations.[48]

When he arrived in Bonn, on April 23, shortly before four o'clock in
the afternoon, Goldmann went to the Palais Schaumburg and stood for
a minute before Adenauer's coffin. Then he flew straight back to New
York.[49]

Vogel sums up in one brief sentence the role of Goldmann in reaching
the reparations agreement: "Nahum Goldmann was the one who forged
the links."[50] Goldmann himself discussed the significance of the Luxembourg Agreement as follows:

> For Israel, particularly in those difficult financial days, the agreement
> was a downright salvation. When we remember that in recent years the
> greater part of Israel's deficit in foreign exchange has been covered by
> Germany under the agreement, we can see what tremendous importance
> it had for Israel. For hundreds of thousands of Jewish victims of Nazism
> this treaty afforded the opportunity to start a new life and in any case to
> improve their position substantially. Historically speaking—and that may

be its great significance—this treaty created a unique precedent. By signing the treaty, Germany created a new international law on a higher moral level, which may be of the greatest importance in the future for other minority and persecuted groups.[51]

From Adenauer's factual references to Goldmann's role, Professor Böhm's report, and Blankenhorn's words of appreciation of his performance in negotiations and press conferences, it would appear that of the hundreds of statesmen with whom he dealt during the course of his long public career it was his German interlocutors that he most strongly impressed. Why this should be the case is not difficult to understand. First of all, there was the language advantage. Although Goldmann spoke several languages and could with equal facility converse, negotiate, and make speeches in English, French, Yiddish, and Hebrew, his best language, and, in fact the only language he had completely mastered, was German. Having been educated and having lived until his thirty-eighth year in Germany, of all the great literatures in the world he was most thoroughly familiar with that country's. Although cosmopolitan in outlook and equally at home in Paris, London, Geneva, New York, Washington, and Jerusalem, he had the deepest empathy with and understanding of the German character and mentality. When negotiating with Italian, Yugoslav, British, American, and other statesmen, he faced them as a foreigner, a man who in their eyes had somewhat exotic airs. When talking to German statesmen, it was contact between two Germans. Nobody else but a cultured German, such as an Adenauer or a Blankenhorn, could fully appreciate, and be duly impressed by, Goldmann's wide knowledge of German literature, philosophy, and culture. He spoke to Germans in their own language in more sense than one.

In the preceding pages, a documentary picture of Goldmann's role in bringing about the German reparations agreement as seen through the eyes of Adenauer, Böhm, Blankenhorn, and others has been presented. What did Goldmann have to say about his part in the crucial period that elapsed between his creation of the Claims Conference, which was formally established on October 26, 1951, in New York, and the signing of the Reparations Agreement on September 10, 1952, in Luxembourg?

Goldmann gave three accounts of the events and his role in them. The first is contained in his 1969 *Autobiography* (pp. 249–82); the second in his 1978 *The Jewish Paradox* (pp. 121–45); and the third and most detailed in his 1980 *Mein Leben als deutscher Jude* (pp. 371–425), which partly repeats and partly elaborates what he wrote in his *Autobiography*.

In the 1969 and 1980 books, Goldmann opens the chapter on his negotiations with Germany with these words: "My negotiations with German Chancellor Konrad Adenauer and his associates, which culminated in the Luxembourg Agreement of 1952, make up one of the most exciting and successful chapters of my political career."[52] Similarly, in his 1978 book he states, "The obtaining of German reparations after the war was, for me, one of my crucial successes."[53] And he adds a sentence that may contain the clue to his ability to bring the negotiations to a successful conclusion: "After being thrown out of Germany by Adolf Hitler, I returned to speak to Konrad Adenauer almost as an equal!"[54] This feeling of being almost an equal of the German chancellor may have been the basis of the personal relationship and friendship that arose between the two men.

Here was not an expatriate German Jew who came begging at the doors of the mighty men of Germany for alms—even if on a huge scale—for his destitute brethren, but a man radiating calm self-confidence, sure of himself and of the cause he represented, and offering Germany what in fact amounted to a deal: how to redeem itself in the eyes of the world by the simple expedient of undertaking to restore to the Jews what was theirs, either legally or morally or in both ways, and to do this with the full understanding that all Germany could offer was material restitution, which did not even touch upon the inestimably greater and irreparable crime of genocide and of the physical and emotional anguish of those who survived it.

Elsewhere, Goldmann recapitulates his feelings about Adenauer and himself during his negotiations with the chancellor:

> From the day of my first talk with the Chancellor I had a strong feeling of confidence and was convinced that he meant it honestly and had enough authority to prevail. Looking back I can say that this policy, however daring and adventurous it was in the beginning, was entirely worthwhile. Among the many undertakings, in which I participated in the course of my life, there was none in which I could so decisively determine and carry on an issue from the outset, and none which ended with such a clear and indisputable success.[55]

Instantly following this statement, Goldmann says that "this does not mean that others did not contribute to the success of these negotiations" and gives credit to several German political leaders and Jewish officials. Nowhere does he claim that he in any way originated the contacts with Germany. On the contrary, again and again he gives full credit to Noah Barou for having done so.[56] In his 1969 *Autobiography,* Goldmann writes: "In 1950, at the urging of Dr. Barou, I began to occupy myself increasingly with this question [of the German reparations]." And again, "Noah Barou, a wonderful man and a great idealist whose premature death was a severe blow, talked me into taking an active part [in the reparations negotiations] by first of all meeting Adenauer." It was Barou who alone and with great perseverence established contact with the German authorities, met many times with Blankenhorn, and paved the way to the first meeting between Goldmann and Adenauer.[57]

At first, Goldmann insisted on not meeting with Adenauer until the chancellor recognized, in the name of the Federal Republic, Germany's responsibility for the Nazi crimes and formally invited Israel and world Jewry to negotiate restitution. Despite Blankenhorn's urging, he refused to meet Adenauer when the opportunity for an informal get-together presented itself at Bürgenstock on the Vierwaldstätter See, where he and Adenauer happened to be guests in two neighboring hotels.[58]

When finally the first, secret meeting between Goldmann and Adenauer did take place (in London, on December 6, 1951)—it was arranged through Barou and Blankenhorn—Goldmann felt that

> of all the important conversations I have ever conducted, this one was emotionally the most difficult, and politically perhaps the most momentous. I was fully aware what it meant, after the dozen Hitler years and the indescribable crimes committed by the German people against the Jews, for a representative of world Jewry and of Israel—Ben Gurion had authorized me—to meet for the first time with the Chancellor of the German Federal Republic. If ever an encounter deserved to be termed historic, it was this one. At the same time it was clear to me what was at stake. If I was not able to persuade the Chancellor to accept the claims of Israel, I could not with a good conscience advise Ben Gurion to go before the Knesset, just as I could not ask the Claims Conference for an authorization. This, however, would mean that the internal Jewish struggle would continue for months, the prospects of negotiations would steadily diminish, and with them a great chance for Israel and the Jewish people would be lost forever. Thereby I was motivated not only by the thought of the negative economic consequences for Israel which at that time had to struggle hard for its existence, but rather by the moral significance of getting the Jewish demands accepted, for I saw very clearly what such a success would mean for the future.[59]

It is interesting to note that, though Adenauer mentions only the anonymous Israeli ambassador as being present at his first meeting with Goldmann, the latter states that he was accompanied by Barou.[60]

Again, I must refrain here from going into the "internal Jewish struggles" to which Goldmann alludes. Enough to say that he had to fight on several of the internal Jewish fronts simultaneously. He needed to struggle to obtain a mandate from the Claims Conference to negotiate with the Germans in its name, and—as has been seen—to be its sole representative. He had to fight against the Israelis who wished to be the spokesmen not only of Israel but also of the Diaspora. And he had to defend himself and the negotiations against the bitter attacks that were launched in the Israeli and Diaspora press, in the name of several Jewish groups and political formations. Adenauer, as we have seen, refers to the dangers to which the Jewish spokesmen and even he himself were exposed. Elaborating on this point, Goldmann states that for almost half a year he was accompanied on his travels by an Israeli bodyguard twenty-four hours a day, and on his visits to Israel the two rooms on both sides of his hotel room "were inhabited by security men." Finally, after the signing of the Luxembourg Agreement, when Goldmann met Ben-Gurion and the latter asked him "What can Israel do for you?" Goldmann answered, "Call off the bodyguard. It disturbs my whole private life."[61]

Apart from a few added details contained in Goldmann's own account of his meetings with Adenauer and other German officials what his recollections accomplish in comparison with the spare chronicles authored by the latter is to flesh out the rather skeletal sketches written by the Germans. He summarizes or gives in direct quotes what he said to Adenauer and the others, and what they said to him. A few examples will have to suffice.

Before meeting with Adenauer, Goldmann and Barou saw Blankenhorn, and Goldmann made the stipulation that before even embarking on negotiations Germany must accept the Israeli demand of indemnification in the amount of one billion dollars as a starting point. Blankenhorn was taken aback, and exclaimed, "But that's quite impossible. How can the Chancellor make such a commitment without consulting his government?"

Despite this point-blank refusal, at his first meeting with Adenauer Goldmann concluded his 25-minute presentation with these words:

> Until now, Chancellor, I did not know you, but in the twenty-five minutes
> I have been sitting here opposite you, you have impressed me as a man of
> such stature that I can expect you to override conventional regulations. I

ask you to take upon yourself the responsibility of approving the under-taking I have requested, not merely verbally, as I suggested to Blanken-horn, but in the form of a letter.

Blankenhorn, who was present, was visibly distressed by Goldmann's request addressed to the Chancellor after he, Blankenhorn, had made it clear to Goldmann that its fulfillment lay beyond the Chancellor's pow-ers. But Adenauer's reaction was very different from what Blankenhorn had expected, and showed that Goldmann was correct in his estimate of the Chancellor's moral character and stature. Adenauer, moved by Gold-mann's appeal, replied:

> Dr. Goldmann, those who know me know that I am a man of few words, and that I detest high-flown talk. But I must tell you that while you were speaking I felt the wings of world history beating in this room. My desire for restitution is sincere. I regard it as a great moral problem and a debt of honor for the new Germany. You have sized me up correctly. I am prepared to approve the undertaking you request on my own responsibility. If you will give me the draft of such a letter after our talk, I will sign it in the course of the day.[62]

What becomes clear from quotations such as this is that Goldmann clearly possessed a dramatic flair and a strong literary sense. Essentially, his account and Adenauer's are identical. What is missing in Adenauer's version and is supplied in Goldmann's is, apart from dramatic detail, the historical continuity and development. Adenauer indicates; Goldmann narrates. Adenauer states; Goldmann explains. Because of this difference in approach and style, Goldmann's account is considerably longer than Adenauer's: the chancellor devotes twenty-seven pages of his memoirs to "The Luxembourg Agreement and the Ordering of Our Relationship to the Jews" (pp. 132–159), of which more than half are taken up with reprinting such relevant documents as the March 12, 1951, note of Israel to the occupying powers; Adenauer's December 6, 1951, letter to Gold-mann; Professor Böhm's April 23, 1952, report on the negotiations; Goldmann's May 19, 1952, letter to Adenauer; Böhm's May 24, 1952, report to Adenauer on his talk with Goldmann; and the May 28, 1952, press release about the Adenauer-Goldmann meeting in Paris. In Gold-mann's account, the same subject is covered in fifty-five pages, none of which contains documents but all of which are his personal narratives of the event, quotations from memory of conversations, and character pictures, especially of Adenauer.[63]

Goldmann stresses the personal side of his relationship with the Chancellor. He reports that these relations were not only of a purely objective nature, but also assumed always more and more a personal character. For instance, the Chancellor made a point of visiting Goldmann in his New York apartment, on the occasion of Adenauer's first visit to New York, and also received Goldmann repeatedly in his villa in Röhndorf.[64]

The relationship between Goldmann and Adenauer was based, to a high degree, upon mutual sympathy. Goldmann had often felt that the Israeli diplomats, who, of course, had as yet no long experience in this area, underestimated the personal aspect of the relationship with statesmen and politicians. He himself thought that psychology was more important in diplomacy than ideology, because it was the psychology which determined the ideology of individuals, groups, and nations.[65]

At another point Goldmann tells about a long discussion he had with Adenauer about Ignatius of Loyola and Francis of Assisi. Adenauer, with his strict, often rigorous, position, rated Loyola higher than Assisi, whom Goldmann valued more from a religious point-of-view. After an intensive discussion, the two men finally agreed that Ignatius and Francis each possessed his own specific set of character traits in respect of which he outshone the other.[66]

On another occasion, during Adenauer's visit to Israel, he told Goldmann that he had attended a get-together of intellectuals some time before in Cologne. Whenever Adenauer used the word "intellectuals," remarks Goldmann in parentheses, there was always a pinch of irony in his voice. The discussion revolved around the difference between sagacity (*Klugheit*) and intelligence. Those participating in it offered various definitions, none of which satisfied Adenauer. When Adenauer met Goldmann in Israel (the meeting took place in Rehovot), he decided to put the same question to Goldmann, whose intellectual grasp he valued highly. Goldmann's response was that intelligence was almost exclusively a matter of the brain, while sagacity was at least to the same extent also a matter of character. To be sagacious it was not enough to be intelligent and clear-thinking. One also had to possess character traits which enabled one to understand one's adversary, not to consider one's own point-of-view the only valid one, but to be able to appreciate other, diverging, opinions. This answer impressed the Chancellor, and two days later, at a dinner in the home of Israeli Prime Minister Levi Eshkol, Goldmann had occasion to refer back to it. What happened was that Eshkol in his speech made a reference which the ninety-year-old Adenauer considered a slight to Germany, and he became very upset and irate. He refused to be pacified, until Goldmann was asked by Eshkol to go and talk to him. Goldmann then reminded the Chancellor of their conversation about sagacity and intelligence, and urged him to prove that he was not only very intelligent—which was known to everybody—but also very sagacious. Adenauer broke into a smile, and thus "an atmosphere was created which permitted the finding of a formula to eliminate the offence."[67]

As far as understanding others' points of view was concerned, this was an outstanding characteristic of Goldmann himself. In connection with the German negotiations for reparations, of which he was the foremost advocate and for which he was forced to wage a veritable war on several fronts simultaneously, he fully appreciated the opposite position. In his 1978 book, he writes that, before the beginning of his talks with Adenauer, "there was still a big problem: a huge majority of Jewish public opinion was hostile to any contact with the Germans. That is an attitude I understand very well, by the way, and I have often said that if the Jewish people had unanimously agreed to the idea of negotiating for cash reparations from the Germans I would be ashamed of being Jewish. The Jewish people were bound to display their opposition, but its leaders had to take no notice; this is politics."[68]

It is appropriate to conclude this documentary record of the relationship between Goldmann and Adenauer with a résumé of Goldmann's portrait of the German Chancellor. What Goldmann found most impressive in Adenauer was the extraordinary authority which emanated from him. He sensed in Adenauer, as in few other statesmen of his generation, what he called "the mystery of charisma," the magic of the leader's personality. He recalled attending meetings whose atmosphere, the moment Adenauer entered the room, underwent an almost miraculous change. Goldmann had met and had close relations with many great figures, but none of them made such a lasting impression on him as Adenauer, who, he felt, was an unforgettable phenomenon in his "monumental simplicity."[69]

In conclusion, a few words are in place about the global significance of the reparations agreement. On May 5, 1966, Goldmann himself evaluated it as follows:

The [German] legislation of compensation and reparations is a quite singular phenomenon. There is practically no precedent for a government paying out indemnities to the victims of a former regime, to those who are not even citizens of that country. This singular legislation has created new international legal concepts and constituted an important precedent.[70]

In 1980, in the retrospect of almost three decades, Goldmann again emphasized that the Luxembourg Agreement had a significance which transcended its financial aspect. With it, he felt, a precedent was created in the political arena. A mighty nation undertook to redress, as far it was possible, the unspeakable crime it had committed against a weak, defenseless people. It did so without being forced by military threat, merely because it obeyed an ethical imperative, because it respected moral laws, and because it bowed to public opinion. The Luxembourg Agreement therefore represented a great ethical victory, and this, in the last analysis, is its enduring historical meaning.[71]

A student of the German reparations, Nicholas Balabkins, evaluates the historical significance of the Luxembourg Agreement from the global and the Jewish point of view: "In the history of international relations, the Luxembourg Treaty has no counterpart. It is an accord without precedent. It represents a symbol of hope to the entire world and a warning to all lawless and amoral totalitarian governments. To the Jews the Shilumim (reparations) Agreement and the Indemnification Law of 1953 meant that for the first time in two thousand years they had received material compensation for injuries inflicted upon them."[72]

Another scholar, who is also an attorney, feels that the achievement of the Claims Conference "can and must serve as a beacon for future modes of international protection of individual human rights on the international level," and that "the Claims Conference was significant because for the first time in modern international law a group representing individuals successfully defended individual human rights on the international level." As such, the conference can be seen "as a prototype for future procedures in international law."[73]

By 1980 the total paid by Germany to the Jews amounted to about DM 60 billion.[74] Because the Nazis murdered six million Jews, each one they killed cost their heir, the German Federal Republic, DM 10,000. Has the murder of even one person been atoned for by these payments? Of course not. But it made life easier for the individuals who suffered under the Nazi regime but survived, and for Jewry as a whole—the only people singled out by the Third Reich for total extermination.

8. The Meeting with Nasser: Confederation and Neutralization

If one guideline consistently ran through the political and diplomatic life of Nahum Goldmann, it was his unwavering readiness to conduct direct negotiations with anybody, including even the most inveterate opponents of the Jews and Israel. The motivation of this willingness to enter into any lions' den or reach into any viper's nest was his unshakable conviction that in personal contact he always had a better than even chance to wring at least some concession, even from the most inimical interlocutor. This conviction was nurtured and confirmed by each successful round of talks he conducted with Jewish leaders who were opposed to Zionism, with Zionists objecting to his views on the problems and goals of Zionism and Israel, with heads of the most diverse Jewish organizations, and with powerful figures in the international arena of politics and diplomacy.

To be sure, occasions occurred when the chance for Goldmann to pit his wits as negotiator against those of known and sworn opponents of Israel and the Jews eluded him. An example was the trial balloon he launched in the summer of 1979—a long time after he had resigned from his positions of Jewish political leadership—by making it public that he would be willing to meet with the chief of the Palestine Liberation Organization (PLO), Yasir Arafat, if the latter invited him. Fully aware of the "covenant" of the PLO that contained, in effect, the solemn undertaking to destroy Israel, and of the PLO policy of terrorist attacks against the civilian population of Israel, Goldmann nevertheless felt that meeting Arafat personally and telling him "to cease from terror and recognize Israel in borders which would be determined in an agreement on an overall peace"[1] could redound to the benefit of Israel.

Needless to say, this announcement unleashed a furor in Israel, in the

World Jewish Congress (of which Goldmann was one of the founders and longtime president), and in Jewish circles everywhere. The meeting never took place, and thus remained a small-scale replica of a much more momentous sequence of events in which circumstances conspired to abort a meeting between Goldmann and Gamal Abdel Nasser, premier and then president of Egypt from 1954 to his death in 1970, in which both were equally interested. The attempts made by the two men to meet constitute a fascinating example of the frustrations of international diplomacy.

I   One of Goldmann's ideas, which he attempted to realize for a quarter of a century, was the creation of a confederation between Israel and the Arab states. Such a "Near Eastern Confederation"—as he called it—was to comprise Israel, the Arab states, and Turkey. Because each of the member states would have one vote, the Arab states could be sure that in all affairs that would be under the jurisdiction of the confederation Israel would not be able to conduct an individual policy but would need to bow to the collective will. In internal affairs, such as form of government, economy, and immigration, each member state would, of course, be independent.

In chapter 6 above, a detailed account was given of Goldmann's efforts in the summer of 1946 to win support for the establishment of a Jewish State in part of Palestine. During the course of that proselytizing work he gave, on July 17 of that year, a major address to the executives of Hadassah in which, among other things, he argued that the future of the Jews in Palestine depended, not on the British Empire, but on the Arabs. Partition would create a separation between the Jews and the Arabs of Palestine and thus result in an improvement in relations between the two peoples.

"We should start," he said, "by separating from, and immediately cooperating with, the Arabs."

> We could have an economic treaty with Transjordan. . . . We can have a joint development in both countries. . . . And I would go a step further. . . . One of the few legitimate Arab arguments against us—here we can say it—is that they say, "We don't trust the Jews. They will become a spearhead of European imperialism in the Middle East. . . ." I think there is one way to disperse the fear of the Arabs. We should offer the Arabs, if they agree to a Jewish State in part of Palestine—which should be the

larger part of Palestine—that *we will join with them together in a Middle Eastern Federation.* Not in the Arab League, which is nonsense in the twentieth century, but the six Arab states with us together. If Turkey wants to join, let her join. We are ready to join with them in world politics. We will not become representatives of European maneuvers against them, since they can never expect us to become more powerful than six Arab states. This would open the way for mutual good relations. Borders will be opened. Not only will the boycott [of Israel by the Arabs] be abolished, on the contrary, the Arab States will become a hinterland [for the Jewish State]. They certainly don't have to be afraid, since they know we will be out-voted if there is a conflict. If we remain a permanent constitutional member of the Middle Eastern Federation, it can be under the auspices of the United Nations. Such a plan has attraction for the moderate Arabs, for those who feel they cannot get rid of the Jews. . . . No Arab statesman will say it openly today, just as we don't say it openly. Those who know Arab politics know that there are Arabs who will see the point. I think for us it is the only answer to the question that is put to us, "What do you want now?"

During the discussion period that followed Goldmann's address, he reiterated, "We should be part of the Arab world. I have said it for 20 years. . . . If we have status [as a sovereign state] certainly we should become an integral part of the Middle East. . . . [In] our world politics we would work together with them [the Arabs], but on the question of internal policies on immigration, we must be free."[2]

II   Three weeks later (he was in the meantime back in Europe to participate in the meeting of the Jewish Agency Executive in Paris), Goldmann presented his argument for the partition of Palestine to Dean Acheson, at the time acting secretary of state and one of the chief architects of President Truman's foreign policy. The August 7, 1946, meeting between Goldmann and Acheson has been presented in detail above in chapter 6. As far as the plan for a Near Eastern Confederation is concerned, Goldmann reported in his 1969 *Autobiography* that he "submitted to Dean Acheson on behalf of the Zionist Executive" a memorandum that "contained two points of principle: first, the demand for a Jewish state in part of Palestine; second, the participation of that state in a Near Eastern confederation of equal states. This was to be the basis of our relations with the Arab world."[3]

On the very day of the meeting with Goldmann, Acheson prepared a memorandum in which he stated that

He [Goldmann] said that one of the worries of the Arabs was that a Jewish state might be used as a spearhead of Western imperialism. The [Jewish] Agency was prepared to propose to the Arabs that this Jewish state would be willing to join a confederation of the Arab states which would place the Jews in a position where they would always be in a minority and could not possibly be a spearhead for external influence. They would be willing to accept whatever restrictions the other states in their sovereign capacity imposed on relations with the Jewish state, and were convinced of their capacity to work out amicably their common problems.[4]

Five days later (August 12), Acheson cabled Averell Harriman, United States ambassador to the United Kingdom, a detailed account of his meeting with Goldmann, in which he reported that Goldmann had informed him of the August 5 resolution of the Jewish Agency Executive, and then added:

E. In his [Goldmann's] opinion Jewish State would be willing to participate in confederation of Near Eastern states, including Arab States, for purpose of cooperation and under such conditions as should remove fear of Arabs that Jewish state might serve as spearhead for introducing external influences into Near East.

F. In his opinion, more moderate Arabs could be induced not to oppose such a plan.[5]

A comparison of the two accounts given by Acheson of Goldmann's reference to the Jewish State's participation in a Near Eastern Confederation reveals a significant discrepancy. According to Acheson's August 7 memorandum, Goldmann stated that "the [Jewish] Agency was prepared" to propose and join the Near Eastern Confederation; according to Acheson's August 12 cable, Goldmann presented this suggestion merely as his own opinion. Because Acheson's August 7 memorandum conforms to Goldmann's own recollections, it can be accepted as the correct version of what actually took place at that Goldmann-Acheson meeting.

Goldmann's reference to the preparedness of the Jewish Agency to join a Near Eastern Confederation appears to be his interpretation of the position taken at the time by Ben-Gurion, who, in his capacity of chairman of the Jewish Agency Executive, said in his address to the Anglo-American Committee of Inquiry in 1946: "There will be not only peace between us and the Arabs, there will be alliance, there will be friendship. It is an historical necessity, just as much as is a Jewish State. It is a moral, a political, and economic necessity."[6]

This provides a test case of Goldmann's *modus operandi* when it came to putting across an idea or plan in which he strongly believed, even if he lacked any authorization to do so from the body in whose name he spoke and which he represented. The resolution he proposed in Paris to the agency Executive and was adopted by an overwhelming majority does not contain any mention of the confederation plan. The text of the resolution is included in full in both Acheson's August 7, 1946, memorandum and Goldmann's *Autobiography*,[7] and in its crucial second paragraph it speaks only of "the establishment of a viable Jewish state in an adequate area of Palestine." Hence, it must be concluded that the idea of the Near Eastern Confederation, though he knew of Ben-Gurion's readiness to consider an alliance between the future Jewish State and the Arabs, was proposed by Goldmann to Acheson entirely on his own initiative because he felt that this idea was calculated to impress Acheson and persuade him to accept the partition plan.[8] This procedure was characteristic of Goldmann's way of conducting negotiations. As he told me in 1980, "I always acted on my own, and then reported to the Executive the results I achieved."

Goldmann was convinced that the confederation plan would not only facilitate the acceptance of partition by the American government, but that it would actually be the solution of the problem presented by Arab opposition to a Jewish State. In retrospect, he wrote in 1969:

> This would provide for Israel's integration in a Near Eastern confederation of equal states. . . . In a true confederation Israel would retain autonomy in most things, including immigration, but would subscribe to common economic and world political goals. In practice this would mean that the Arabs would inevitably have the upper hand in matters of world politics. Israel would have to reach agreement with the Arab majority over its course in world politics, and would not be able to conduct a policy that conflicted in any marked degree with the declared principles of the Arab world. . . . Israel would become a unit in a larger world political body which would give it a potential influence it can never attain in its present isolation.[9]

III   For many years after the establishment of Israel, Goldmann returned again and again to his plan for a Near Eastern Confederation, in articles, lectures, interviews, and private discussions. He clung to it and tenaciously advocated it, though he never received any encouragement either from Israel or from the Arab states. In 1947 he formulated a corollary of the confederation idea, namely, that the Jewish State should be neutral in respect of power politics, that it should side neither with the West nor with the Eastern Communist countries, and that its safety should be guaranteed by the great powers and the other states of the world, including the Arab countries. He first publicized this idea in an interview he gave to the Associated Press on December 17, 1947.

Goldmann's concept of the neutralization of the future Jewish State came in for early criticism, an example of which is the article published by Maurice Rosenblatt in the American Jewish weekly *The Answer,* under the title "Second Chance: The Neuter State," which said:

> According to the Associated Press, on Dec. 17, Goldmann announced that "Jewish legal experts, working on a draft constitution for the projected Jewish Palestine state . . . have included a clause binding the country to neutrality in any future world conflicts . . . perpetual neutrality would be justified because millions of Jews would still remain scattered in the Eastern World as well as the Western World."

Rosenblatt criticizes this as "a theocratic Jewish state in Palestine with extra-territorial citizenship for Jews all over the world. So begins the first international ghetto, bought and built by Jews. . . . Palestine will be a giant sectarian asylum."[10]

Israel achieved independence in 1948. Seven years later, Goldmann enjoyed an opportunity to take a concrete step toward the realization of his Near Eastern Confederation idea. In 1955 he broached the subject in a talk with Dag Hammarskjöld, secretary-general of the United Nations from 1953 until his death in 1961 in a plane crash. For two years after Hammarskjöld's election as secretary-general, Goldmann avoided meeting him out of consideration for Israeli Prime Minister David Ben-Gurion, whose jealousy, Goldmann felt, would have been aroused by such a meeting. However, in 1955, while Goldmann was in Jerusalem, one morning a United Nations messenger brought him a note from Hammarskjöld, who had stopped over in Jerusalem on his way to Cairo. In the note, Hammarskjöld expressed his surprise that Goldmann had never tried to see him and asked Goldmann to visit him at the former High Commissioner's residence, which served as the UN headquarters in Jerusalem. He would send a UN car to pick up Goldmann at a mutually convenient time.

The meeting took place that same afternoon. Hammarskjöld got straight to the point. He said that a few weeks earlier he had received from Acheson Goldmann's 1946 memorandum that advocated the partition of Palestine. Even before reading it, he knew that Goldmann was one of the staunchest early proponents of partition and a firm advocate of the establishment of a Jewish State. His question to Goldmann was: Now that seven years had passed since the establishment of Israel, did he still believe that partition was the best solution to the Palestine problem?

Goldmann did not answer the question with a straight "yes" or "no." Instead, he said: "As you know, Mr. Secretary General, only half of my memorandum was carried out. The Arabs never accepted or recognized partition. And as for the second part of my memorandum, which suggested the establishment of a Near Eastern Confederation, the Arabs are not ready even to consider the possibility of letting the Jewish State join such a body. Therefore one cannot judge today whether partition was right or not."

Hammarskjöld was satisfied with the answer. Goldmann then made use of the opportunity to ask his help in attempting to realize the second part of his 1946 memorandum. At the time, Nasser was at the height of his popularity as the preeminent leader of the Arab world. His support of a Near Eastern Confederation, in which Israel would be a member, would practically assure its acceptance by the other Arab states. If Nasser would make peace with Israel, Goldmann felt, Nasser's place in history as the great peacemaker of the Middle East would be assured. Having put all this with his not inconsiderable persuasive powers to Hammarskjöld, Goldmann concluded: "Go, talk to Nasser, Mr. Secretary General."

Hammarskjöld, impressed by Goldmann and his common-sense approach, undertook to pass the message to Nasser and asked Goldmann to remain in touch with him. At a subsequent meeting with Goldmann, he reported Nasser's reply. "This," he quoted Nasser as saying,

actually may be a solution. The Zionists did two great injustices to the Arabs. First, they partitioned the small country of Palestine. This the Arabs will steel themselves to accept, because we have vast amounts of land available which will take centuries to develop. The second is that they divided the Arab world. We will never accept Israel as a wedge in the Arab nation. Our plan is to form a bloc stretching from Morocco to Iraq. Unfortunately, at the center of that bloc there is an Israeli state which does not care a rap for our plans. We want to create a policy of non-alignment, and Israel practices a pro-capitalistic policy. We cannot tolerate that.

From a distance of twenty-five years, it is difficult to gauge, let alone reconstruct, how Goldmann could possibly have imagined the realization of his plan of a Near Eastern Confederation. He was not an official spokesman of the Israeli government, nor, for the matter, an unofficial one, and was not in any way entrusted with approaching Hammarskjöld, Nasser, or anybody else, with a scheme that would have decisively influenced Israel's future. As far as is known, neither the prime minister nor the government of Israel gave any indication that, after a mere seven years of independence, they would be even remotely inclined to consider any political development which would, however slightly, impinge upon the absolute sovereignty of the young state. If Goldmann nevertheless proceeded without any Israeli authorization, and, without informing the Israeli government of his intentions, to present his plan to Hammarskjöld and ask him to place it before Nasser, this can be explained in only one way: he was so convinced that a Near Eastern Confederation was the only solution to the Arab-Israeli problem that he felt impelled to act even without advance authorization by Israel—which, he must have suspected, would not be forthcoming. And he must have been equally convinced that, should Nasser be willing to consider the plan in principle, the Israeli government would then also need to give it serious consideration.

In fact, Goldmann kept Ben-Gurion informed about all his talks with Hammarskjöld, and, after he convinced Ben-Gurion that the initiative for his contacts had come from Hammarskjöld and not from him, as Ben-Gurion had at first suspected, he no longer blamed Goldmann for them.[11]

IV Following his first meeting with Hammarskjöld, Goldmann continued to advocate his twin concept of the creation of a Near Eastern Confederation, of which Israel would be a part, and the neutralization of Israel, in a wide variety of public forums. On September 26, 1956, when the Suez Canal problem preoccupied the Western world, he gave a speech to the Foreign Press Association at the Dorchester Hotel in London in which he stressed the need for

> evolving a policy of neutralizing the Middle East, keeping it outside any ideological or power-political bloc, and eventually reaching agreement for the utilization of the tremendous oil resources to everybody's benefit, making the peoples of the Middle East an equal partner and beneficiary of

such economic advancement, and giving them all the help of the West and the East alike in the constructive application of the gains derived from its natural resources. It is this method which should first be applied as a test case to solve the problem of the Suez Canal. If successful, it might well be the basic pattern for a policy of reconstruction in the Middle East, helping the Arab nations as it develops, and curbing fanaticism at the same time.

Then Goldmann went on to discuss the position of Israel in the Middle East:

Israel is a small country but she can play an important part in such a policy. Her share would be much greater than her numerical strength indicates. Geopolitically, she is located in a vital area within the Middle East; geographically she holds the entire center position between the South and the Asian Arab States. Militarily, Israel is much stronger than her population would let appear. She is the Western-most element in the Middle East today, with the technical knowledge of modern civilization at her disposal. Israel's future depends on her integration into the Middle East. Forced as she is today by Arab intransigence to exist as a beleaguered fortress, Israel is bound to remain a source of friction and frustration; admitted as an equal among equals into a partnership of the Middle East, Israel will be able to make available her vast creative powers for the whole area.

Such an integration of Israel is the only way of solving the troublesome problem of Arab-Israeli relations. Without this problem solved, there can be no stability in the Mediterranean area. Its solution will require the acceptance, on the part of the Arabs, of Israel as an equal partner. It will also require the realization on the part of Israel that she forms part of the family of nations in the Middle East, and it will remove her fear of the vast numerical superiority of the Arabs around her frontiers. Only such a transformation and integration will produce a geographical entity in the Middle East, replacing the outmoded Arab League which is based on the concept of racial principles—in stark contradiction to all progressive trends of the twentieth century.

There is a deep historical significance in the fact that Arab and Jewish nationalism emerged almost simultaneously. . . . The simultaneous development of national movements of both the Jewish and the Arab peoples in fact is the basic cause of Arab-Israeli difficulties today. And yet, both Zionism and Arab nationalism may one day grow to be the source of much additional strength for both national movements which are now adversaries. If this conflict is allowed to continue, both groups may one day destroy each other. With relations between the Arab nations and Israel transformed, with their resources channelled into a joint effort, the foundation may be laid for an Arab-Israeli co-operation which might yet bring about the re-birth of the Middle East.[12]

During the same period, Goldmann's assistant, Joseph Golan, who was very active in fostering Arab-Jewish contacts in general, tried to arrange a meeting between Nasser and Goldmann, with the blessing of John Foster Dulles, the American secretary of state, whom Goldmann had consulted.[13] In October 1956 these initiatives were about to bear fruit. As Eric Rouleau, the Middle Eastern expert on the staff of *Le Monde*, who had excellent contacts in Egypt, reported, in the autumn of 1956 Nasser agreed to receive Goldmann:

> In the course of unobtrusive contacts made in various European capitals, and especially in Paris, it was agreed that Dr. Goldmann should go secretly to Cairo. A military plane would come to fetch him from Athens. A villa was being prepared for him in a suburb of Cairo, when Israeli units invaded the Sinai, on October 29, 1956. President Nasser was supposed to have been most upset by this "duplicity." He believed at first, in effect, that Dr. Goldmann had lent himself to a ruse of war, aimed at deceiving his vigilance. It was, in any case, established that Israeli Prime Minister Ben-Gurion, who had been kept informed of the preparations for the planned meeting, prepared simultaneously—in conjunction with the governments of Paris and London—the Suez expedition, one of whose objectives was to overthrow the Nasser regime and to impose on Egypt a peace based on Israeli conditions. The distrust of President Nasser in Dr. Goldmann was dispelled only when he found out that the former president of the World Zionist Organization did not know of the war preparations, and that he was an involuntary instrument of the "activists" of Tel Aviv.[14]

The actual motivations that prompted the government of Israel to launch a preemptive strike against Egypt across the Sinai Peninsula have since often been described, analyzed, and interpreted. In the fall of 1956, the tension between Israel and Egypt increased, Fedayeen raids from Egypt into Israel became more frequent, and on October 24, 1956, a unified command of Arab states under an Egyptian general was established. Israel felt increasingly threatened by these developments and decided that, in order to thwart Egyptian plans for an all-out attack on Israel, it must launch a preemptive strike.

The Sinai Campaign, known in Israel by its code-name Qadesh, began on October 29, and within a hundred hours achieved its objectives. The

Israeli battalions literally overran the peninsula, routed the entire Egyptian force east of the Suez Canal, and halted ten miles from the canal, bowing to a British-French ultimatum, which contravened an earlier understanding concerning Israel's participation in a planned Anglo-French operation in Egypt. The British and French military planners evidently had not anticipated either the speed or the depth of the Israeli penetration across the Sinai. (Goldmann was convinced, and said so on many occasions, that the Sinai Campaign was the greatest mistake and the most foolish political act of Ben-Gurion.)[15]

V   One of the meetings between Goldmann and Hammarskjöld, which took place at the time of that campaign, serves as an illustration of the manner in which Goldmann wielded his favorite negotiating weapon, the interjection of anecdotes and jokes. By the end of the meeting, Goldmann's well-placed humor and banter not only assuaged the secretary-general's wrath over what he viewed as Israel's unprovoked attack on Egypt, but also cemented the friendship between the two men.

As he told me in a 1980 interview, on Sunday, November 4, 1956, at eight in the morning, Goldmann received a phone call from Hammarskjöld: "Can you come to see me right away?" Goldmann said: "Is there anything the matter? Why are you in your office so early on Sunday?"

"Sunday morning is the best time for me to work," answered Hammarskjöld. "Nobody is in, and I can work undisturbed. We must have a fundamental talk." Hammarskjöld at the time was especially resentful of Ben-Gurion. Even before the Sinai Campaign, no love was lost between the two men. Ben-Gurion, "with his great Jewish tact" (as Goldmann put it), used to send cables to Goldmann asking "What does that Nazi [referring to Hammarskjöld] want of me?"

Goldmann dressed hurriedly, and by nine he was in the secretary general's office. He said: "Are you here every Sunday morning?" "Yes," answered Hammarskjöld. "I come here every Sunday and every weekday at seven or seven thirty, because nobody is around till nine, and I can work quietly."

"And when do you go to sleep?" asked Goldmann.

"At twelve or one. And I always get up at five."

"I am reminded," said Goldmann, "of what Thomas Mann wrote about Frederick the Great. His book on the great Prussian starts with the words: 'Frederick the Great was never really married. . . . He needed only four hours of sleep. No wonder that he became a great man.' The same can be said of you.'"[16]

Hammarskjöld laughed. During the course of the ensuing lengthy discussion about the Sinai Campaign and its political implications, Goldmann said, "I too consider this campaign a foolish thing. But quite apart from it, you always blame Ben Gurion and the Israelis. Try to look at Sinai and Egypt from their point-of-view. . . . After all, you are a greater statesman than Ben Gurion. Which, of course, is no *Kunststück* (great trick). Your father was prime minister. Your grandfather was finance minister. You are the descendant of twelve generations of statesmen. Ben Gurion's father was a *Winkeladvocat* (pettifogger) in Plonsk. Give the Israelis one or two generations, and they will learn."

"I would gladly give them all the time they need," said Hammarskjöld, "but the Arabs won't wait so long."

Then he said: "May I ask you a personal question? Whenever I have a good talk with you, after you leave I say to myself, 'Goldmann is not a Jew. He is tolerant, flexible, understands the other fellow's point-of-view. He is quite different.' How come?"

"Dag," answered Goldmann (by that time they were on a first-name basis), "the only explanation can be that one of my ancestresses had an affair with a Hammarskjöld."

This bantering exchange provides insight into Goldmann's approach to difficult situations. Actually, Hammarskjöld's question, though intended as a compliment to Goldmann, betrayed a negative stereotype of the Jew. For Hammarskjöld, the typical Jew was intolerant, inflexible, unable to understand the other fellow's point of view. A Ben-Gurion would have countered by accusing Hammarskjöld of anti-Semitism, or Nazi leanings. Goldmann, too, perceived, of course, beneath the personal compliment its underlying, possibly unconscious, anti-Jewish bias, but chose to ignore it, in fact, to go along with it to the extent of explaining the personality traits discerned in him by Hammarskjöld and considered by him as being atypical and exceptional in a Jew, as being the results of a partially non-Jewish ancestry.

Most interestingly, Hammarskjöld's negative stereotype of the Jews was shared by Goldmann when it came to the Israelis. In his 1978 memoirs, he wrote: "Unlike most Israelis, I am neither fanatical, nor pig-headed, nor convinced that I am always right. I am tolerant, and do not exaggerate the importance of either problems, or of my own activities. The Israelis have the great weakness of thinking that the whole world revolves around them."[17]

Although the Sinai Campaign was a signal victory for Israel, it dealt a blow to the kind of rapprochement between her and the Arabs Goldmann had in mind. Nevertheless, and despite the unfavorable political climate, he did not discontinue his advocacy of a Near Eastern Confederation.

On December 23, 1956, barely six weeks after the Sinai Campaign, in an interview on the Face the Nation program of the CBS TV and radio network, Goldmann said, "Peace . . . should be based on some structure of all the peoples of the Middle East in one big confederation with the Arabs and Israel being part of it. So the Arabs should lose the feeling that Israel is a strange element among the peoples of the Middle East. . . . I personally believe that there won't be peace and security and stability in the Middle East unless there will be some agreement between the West and the East on a kind of neutralization of the Middle East."[18]

As shall be pointed out later, the idea of the neutralization of Israel, broached by Goldmann for the first time during this period, subsequently came to supplant the Near Eastern Confederation in his view of the solution of the Arab-Israeli problem.

VI   About two years after his first meeting with Hammarskjöld in Jerusalem, Goldmann made a second attempt to get word to Nasser, this time through the good offices of Jawaharlal Nehru, Prime Minister of India from 1947 until his death in 1964. Nehru was no great friend of Israel, and to characterize his attitude toward the Jewish State as "ambivalent," as Goldmann does,[19] is to attribute to him more sympathy than he actually possessed for the small Jewish State that happened to have gained independence in the same year as his own India.

Goldmann's meeting with Nehru is one of the few diplomatic encounters concerning which he himself prepared a detailed report.

In January 1957, while Nehru was in New York, Goldmann had submitted to him a memorandum in which he presented his idea of a Near Eastern Confederation. Because no reaction from Nehru was forthcoming, Goldmann felt that a meeting with the Indian prime minister might achieve more results. His idea to meet with Nehru was approved by Ben-Gurion, whereupon Goldmann approached Chester Bowles, who had been American ambassador to India from 1951 to 1953 and was to become undersecretary of state and special representative for Asian, African, and Latin American affairs in 1961. Goldmann knew Bowles well, and asked him to arrange a meeting for him with Nehru.

Bowles was ready to do so, but suggested that the initiative should come, not from him, which would make it an official American move, but from Eleanor Roosevelt, who had played a key role in the United Nations as chairperson of the Commission on Human Rights until 1952. An initiative taken by her, Bowles felt, would not make Nehru suspicious, and he may be more open to any suggestion Goldmann would bring to him. Mrs. Roosevelt spoke to the Indian ambassador in Washington, who in turn informed Nehru that Goldmann would like to see him and was ready to come to New Delhi. A tentative date was fixed, but some time before then the ambassador called Goldmann to inform him that Nehru would be in London in June to attend the British Commonwealth conference, and on that occasion would be ready to receive him.

Before the meeting, Goldmann conferred with Eliahu Elath, who was Israel's ambassador to the Court of St. James from 1950 to 1959. Elath warned him that he should expect to find Nehru extremely reticent and taciturn. "I saw him once for half an hour," Elath said, "and during that time Nehru did not utter a single word. Don't be offended, but be ready to talk all the time you will be with him." It so happened that in his meeting with Goldmann, Nehru had the floor most of the time.

The meeting took place on June 27, 1957, in the afternoon. Nehru's sister, Vijaya Lakshmi Pandit, who was at the time high commissioner for India in London, served tea, and thereafter Goldmann began to explain the ideas of his memorandum. However, Nehru interrupted him and said he had read it several times, knew it almost by heart, and had circulated it to all his ambassadors in the Arab countries while instructing them to make use of every opportunity to sound out the Arab governments on the possibility of coming to some arrangement with Israel.

Then Nehru spoke at length about his experiences at the Bandung Conference of twenty-nine Asian and African nations that had taken place in the period April 18–24, 1955, and of which India was one of the sponsors. The purpose of that conference had been threefold: to build closer relations between the participant nations, to forge a declaration of their neutrality in the cold war, and to speed the end of colonialism. Among the resolutions of the conference was the adoption of Nehru's five principles of peaceful coexistence. Israel was, of course, interested in being invited to Bandung as an Asian state, and Nehru now told Goldmann of his unsuccessful efforts to have such an invitation issued, which had failed because the Arab states threatened to boycott the conference.

Two days before the conference, Nehru said, he had arranged for a

meeting with Nasser and other Arab representatives at which he succeeded in having a draft resolution adopted that would have made it
possible to invite Israel for a planned second Afro-Asian conference.
Nasser, Nehru said, displayed a very reasonable attitude at these discussions. Unfortunately, however, next day the Pakistani and Turkish delegations arrived, and the Palestinians were incensed that Nehru had
discussed the Israeli problem with the Arabs in their absence. They called
for a second meeting with the Arab states which did, in fact, take place
and was attended by Nehru as well as by the Turks. At this meeting, said
Nehru, "I was roundly cursed by the Pakistanis as I had never been in
my life. They blamed me, being a non-Muslim, for discussing Israel with
the Arab States, and submitted a new draft resolution on Israel which
was supported by the Turks."

The result was that Nasser, as he explained to Nehru, felt compelled
to vote for the new resolution because he could not show himself less
concerned about the Arabs than the Pakistanis and the Turks. This was
the story behind the Bandung resolution that supported "the rights of
the Arab people of Palestine and called for the implementation of United
Nations resolutions on Palestine and of the peaceful settlement of the
Palestine question,"[20] and which, in effect, lined up the nations of Africa
and Asia behind the Arabs and against the Jews of Israel.

Nehru then went on to tell Goldmann about his many talks with Arab
leaders about Israel. The most violently anti-Israel were the Syrians,
who, he said, were hysterical when it came to Israel, and almost impossible to talk to. Nevertheless, he said, only ten days earlier he had made
a stopover in Syria on his way from India to London, and told them
bluntly to forget the idea that they would be able to destroy Israel. First
of all, it would take two decades before they would be strong enough to
do it, if at all; and, secondly, not only would America and the Western
world not allow the Arabs to destroy Israel, but he, Nehru, would not
allow it either. "I may not be," he said to them, "a military power, but
I shall use whatever influence I have in the world not to allow the Arabs
to touch Israel. Zionism may originally have been a good or a bad idea.
I was never consulted about the establishment of Israel, nor did I take
an interest in it. But now, after all that had happened to the Jewish
people in the Nazi period, and after the emergence of Israel which is the
only compensation the Jewish people got after that disaster, it is entirely
out of the question that the decent peoples in the world should allow
the Arabs to destroy Israel."

Of all the Arab rulers, Nehru continued, Nasser was the most reasonable one in relation to Israel. Were it not for Nuri as-Said, the Iraqi premier, who was much more violent than Nasser with regard to Israel, Nasser might have already taken some initiative for a rapprochement with Israel. "But whenever I urge him to do it," said Nehru, "Nasser gives me two reasons for hesitating: the possibility that he could be assassinated by the Moslem Brotherhood, and, more importantly, the certainty that Nuri would accuse him publicly of being a traitor to the Arab cause."

Nehru then enlarged on his view that any split in the Arab world was very detrimental for Israel because no Arab leader was willing to do anything for which the other side could denounce him. As for Camille Chamoun, the president of Lebanon, Nehru said, he let loose a bitter anti-Israel tirade that surprised Nehru because he had thought that Lebanon would have reasons to be moderate in its position on Israel. But then, Nehru said, he began to speculate on the possible reasons for Chamoun's anti-Israel stance and thought that as long as a state of war existed between Israel and the Arab states, all the business of the Arab world went through Lebanon, Beirut serving as the main port for the Arab countries. But, once peace was established between Israel and the Arabs and the Jews were able to trade with them, being better business men than the Lebanese, the Jews would displace the Lebanese, and Haifa would replace Beirut. Could this, Nehru asked, be the reason for Chamoun's hard anti-Israel line?

"Yes," Goldmann answered, "there is something to this explanation, but Chamoun himself has always been bitterly anti-Zionist, much more so than Charles Malik and other Lebanese leaders."

Nehru then assured Goldmann that, just as he had been ready in the past to help, he would be ready to do so now, and even more so, in the future. He deemed the basic idea of Goldmann's memorandum of a bloc, or a confederation, between Israel and the Arab states, which would keep out of the cold war and take a neutral position, the only way for a solution. "In your memorandum," he said, "I found for the first time a constructive approach and proposal."

Because Goldmann knew that Nehru had to attend an official dinner and the time he could give him was nearing its end, he said: "Mr. Prime Minister, you did not live up to your reputation during the meeting with me." Surprised, Nehru asked: "What do you mean?" Goldmann said: "I was told by friends that you are a very good listener, but a very reluctant talker; but you have spoken for twenty minutes, as if it were you who had asked me to receive you, whereas, of course, I was the one who asked you for this meeting, which means that I, too, have something to tell you." Nehru laughed and said, "Give me another three minutes, and then the floor is yours."

"I am very happy," said Goldmann, "that you are in accord with the main ideas of my memorandum. I hope that you will begin to think about a more systematic action than mere occasional talks with Arab leaders. Nobody has as much influence as you on some Arab leaders, and especially on Nasser, who owes you so much."

At this point, Nehru remarked that, as a matter of fact, he had received an invitation from Nasser to visit him on his way back from London to India. He had not yet decided whether to accept it, but, he said, "While talking to you I am beginning to make up my mind to do so, and to stay over in Cairo for a day, primarily to talk to Nasser about Israel. . . . Other pending matters, such as the Suez problem, have been fully discussed with Nasser by Krishna Menon who saw him last week. I shall tell Nasser that he has to begin to think of accepting Israel and of finding some way to an agreement. I shall warn him against creating new difficulties with Israel over the canal and the Gulf of Aqaba. I shall suggest to him that he invite you. I shall let you know about my talk with Nasser."

Nehru then asked a number of questions to clarify some points in Goldmann's memorandum. "Do you believe," he asked, "that Israel could actually afford one day to take a neutral position and not remain a satellite of the United States? Would the American Jews not force Israel always to follow the lead of America?"

"First of all," Goldmann replied, "I know many American Jewish leaders who understand that the best position for Israel would be to keep out of the cold war, primarily because three and a half million Jews live in Eastern Europe, and Israel hopes one day to get many of them into her country. There is no people in the world which, by definition and by its structure, is better destined to be neutral than the Jewish people. Secondly, during the first few years of Israel's existence its official policy was non-identification, which is but another term for neutrality. Only in the last few years, when the Arabs continued obstinately to refuse to recognize Israel, to threaten it with destruction, and to build up their military strength, did it become inevitable for Israel to look for allies."

"I understand it," said Nehru, "fear is a very bad guide for a nation. But, speaking of fear, you should know that the Arabs are at least as fearful of Israel as Israel is of the Arab States, and, in view of Israel's superior military strength, probably with better reason. But do you believe that once peace is achieved Israel would return to a position of non-involvement?"

"I cannot," replied Goldmann, "formally commit Israel. Everything I have said is off the record. I am expressing my own personal opinion. But knowing as I do Israel and the Jewish people I believe that once peace and stability are achieved Israel will be glad to maintain a position of non-involvement in the cold war."

Nehru reflected on this for a moment, then looked at Goldmann and said: "I want to ask you a rather difficult question. As the situation is today there is no chance to unite the Middle East into one neutral bloc, primarily because of the Baghdad Pact and Iraq's Western alliance. But suppose that Egypt was ready to make peace with Israel, and form together with her the nucleus of a neutral bloc in the Middle East, would Israel be ready?"

"This is a difficult and far reaching question," replied Goldmann. "I have learned from President Roosevelt that statesmen should not cross bridges until they reach them. This bridge is very far away, so that neither you nor I can even see it. Once Nasser indicates willingness to settle with Israel, the bridge would be in sight, I shall discuss the issue with Israel and give a reply."

Nehru said, "Well, in any case this is an entirely hypothetical question which had just come to my mind."

By this time it was 7:30, and Nehru's invitation was for 8:00. Summing up, he said:

> I was very pleased to have had this talk with you. Please keep in touch with me, don't hesitate to write me about the general development of this problem, or about any suggestion you may feel like making to me, where I could be helpful. I cannot promise you to accept any suggestion you may make, but I shall be glad to be at your disposal. Both my sister, Madame Pandit, and my ambassador in Washington have instructions to convey any message from you to me. Whenever you feel like coming to India you will be welcome. Whenever I am in Europe, and you want to see me, don't hesitate to ask for an appointment. I shall be happy if I can help in settling this difficult and explosive problem.

Goldmann thanked Nehru for his kindness and took his leave. Nehru went down with him to the street, to his car. The interview had lasted forty-five minutes.[21]

VII   Some three weeks later, Goldmann received a phone call from the Indian ambassador in Washington. First the ambassador suggested a personal meeting, but then he said: "Actually, I have only a message for you which I can deliver over the phone. The Prime Minister wants me to tell you that he spoke to Nasser and outlined to him your idea of a Near Eastern Confederation with Israel as a participant. Nasser found it a brilliant idea. He said he had already discussed it with Hammarskjöld. He felt that on this basis an understanding could indeed be reached between the Arabs and Israel. 'But,' he said, 'who is Nahum Goldmann? He cannot deliver the goods. It is Ben-Gurion who makes the decisions, not Goldmann, and we will never talk to Ben-Gurion who is a brutal man, an aggressor, and an imperialist!' "[22]

Despite this rebuff, Goldmann continued to work for confederation and neutralization. On January 15, 1958, in an address to the Jewish Theological Seminary, he emphasized that the central problem of the existence of Israel was her "integration into the Middle East. . . . it is in my opinion, which I am repeating now for years, the central problem of Israel's future, the great test of Israel's statesmanship, because eternally Israel cannot live as a fortress among the Arab world which is becoming stronger from day to day."

A year later, in a lecture at the New School in New York (January 13, 1959), Goldmann stated: "There is only one solution to the problem— a political, if not legal, neutralization of the Middle East. . . . I see no other solution than in the establishment of a federation of Middle Eastern states, with sovereign Israel and sovereign Arab states as equal partners. The Arabs would be the majority in such a federation, but that is the condition of the return of the Jewish people to the Middle East. Israel will retain all rights over its internal affairs, immigration, etc. But in international political matters Israel would have to accommodate herself to some extent to the Arabs. It is inevitable."[23]

During the summer of 1961, in an interview with Philip Gillon of the *Jerusalem Post* (published in the August 11 issue), Goldmann reiterated his by then standard arguments for a neutralized Israel. In a speech to the German Society for Foreign Policy, in Bad Godesberg on January 17, 1962, he outlined the idea that the two superpowers should become the protectors and guarantors of the countries of the Middle East, and then continued:

> Such a West-East guarantee can surely be only an interim solution. It would maintain the present situation, but, of course, the historical conflicts experienced by the two young nationalisms [the Jewish and the Arab] would thereby not be removed. A permanent solution, in my opinion, can only be achieved by the integration of Israel into a confederation of states

of the Near East. No state can today live only for itself. Switzerland will possibly remain the only exception from this rule. Israel as part of a confederation of the Near East has always been the aim of the Zionists. For instance, there is a memorandum dating from 1944 which I submitted to the State Department, in which a Jewish State in a part of Palestine as a member in a Near Eastern confederation is proposed. The former U.S. Secretary of State, Dean Acheson, stated: "You Jews will never have peace with the Arabs if you remain alone." At that time I suggested the confederation, but the Arabs replied with war. And so, although Israel did come into being, the no less needed confederation did not.

The Jewish and Arab nationalisms have a common fate, because they emerged and developed in the same period, and followed a parallel course. This is no coincidence. If history has a deeper meaning, then both nationalisms have only two alternatives: either to fight each other as enemy powers, engaging in always increasing conflicts, with the result that one day they will annihilate each other; or to live together, to coexist, since they stepped on the stage of history in the same epoch, in which case both of them together can, in this confederation, instead of mutually destroying each other, accomplish a great historical achievement, and make the Near East again a great center of human civilization.[24]

Some time after 1962, Goldmann became convinced that the idea of a Near Eastern Confederation was not capable of being realized, given the unabating enmity of the Arabs. He therefore reluctantly shelved the plan, which he had so vigorously advocated for about two decades, and instead turned his attention to the neutralization of Israel, which he had first adumbrated in 1947.

VIII   One of the statesmen of international stature to whom Goldmann presented his idea of a neutralized Israel was Yugoslav president Tito (1892–1980). The friendship between the two men began in 1967, when Goldmann met Tito in Belgrade, on September 27. In May 1968 Tito again invited Goldmann to visit him there. Goldmann was at the time in Paris, and the invitation was conveyed to him over the phone by the Yugoslav ambassador to France. Air traffic out of Paris was in those days paralyzed by the great general strike that began on May 11 and ended only on June 7, so that Goldmann at first replied he was unable to leave the city. However, after a second call from the Yugoslav embassy, he decided to go by car to Brussels and try to take a plane from there. With some difficulty, his chauffeur managed to obtain enough gasoline for the trip, but, upon his arrival in Brussels, a new problem faced him: thousands of other travelers had the same idea, and it was impossible to obtain a seat on a plane.

However, Goldmann had a friend in Brussels, the Countess (Gräfin) Hardenberg, a descendant of Karl August von Hardenberg (1750–1822), chancellor of Prussia from 1810, who was made a prince in 1814 in acknowledgment of his achievements in reorganizing and strengthening the country. (Incidentally, Hardenberg was one of the first German statesmen to advocate, from 1812 on, the emancipation of the Jews.) Countess Hardenberg was chief of protocol of the European Economic Community, and as such wielded enough influence to be able to obtain a seat for Goldmann on a plane to Zurich. From there, no problem existed in taking a flight to Belgrade.

The discussion between Tito and Goldmann inevitably revolved around the Middle East. Tito expressed the view that the situation there was fraught with danger, that both Israel and the Arabs were too well armed, and that a new outbreak of hostilities could come any minute. Goldmann, as was his wont, had an anecdote ready for the occasion.

"Mr. President," he said, "do you like Jewish jokes?"

"Yes," answered Tito, "they are wonderful."

"Well," said Goldmann, "let me tell you a story. Some years ago I went to see Ben-Gurion in his office, and found him in the highest of spirits."

This was unusual, for Ben-Gurion was not a gay man. He was not depressive, but was extremely serious. He took himself very seriously, he was constantly aware of the historical significance of everything he did. In this respect he was the precise opposite of me. But on that occasion he was in the happiest mood. "What's the matter, Ben-Gurion?" I asked, "why are you so happy?" He had a document in his hands. He hesitated for a moment, and then said, "If you promise me not to tell anybody, I'll let you know something before anybody else in Israel knows it." I said, "I promise." So he showed me the paper: it was a list of the first Mystere fighter planes which De Gaulle was giving Israel. And he said, triumphantly, "Now what do you say, Nahum?" I said, "I'll tell you a Jewish story, although you don't have much understanding for humor." He was without any humor, quite un-Jewish in this respect—"A hosid once visited another hosid in a little town. It was raining, the streets were full of mud. The visitor had galoshes, but the other man had none, so his feet, his socks, his trousers got all dirty. The visitor said, 'Moyshe, you are a rich man, can't you afford to spend two rubles to buy yourself galoshes?' 'Sure,' said the other, 'but the rebbe doesn't allow it.' 'Why?' 'The rebbe says, if one has no galoshes, one does not go into mud.' 'So,' I said, 'I am afraid, you, Ben-Gurion, are trying to have too many galoshes!' "

Tito got the point of the story and roared with laughter. This was the beginning of a long friendship between the two men. Throughout the meeting with Goldmann, Tito's interpreter was present. Goldmann spoke English, and she translated for Tito from and into Serbian. She was a handsome young woman, and Goldmann, who had always had a fond eye for female pulchritude, was impressed. At the end of the interview, Tito thanked him for having come and asked him to remain in touch with him, especially because he, Tito, had broken relations with Israel. Inasmuch as Goldmann planned to go on from Belgrade to Israel, via Athens, Tito asked him to call on him again on his way back from Israel and give him his impressions of the country.

Goldmann said, "I shall be glad to, but I have two conditions. One is that we should speak in German. You have a good command of German from the days of your service in the Austrian army. And my way of talking, with my anecdotes, joking remarks, is not good for translation. If you want to say something very important, you may say it in Serbian. And the second condition is that your interpreter should be present, even without doing any translation."

"Why?" asked Tito.

"Because, with all my great admiration for you, it is much nicer to look at her than at you."

"Oh," said Tito, "I have full understanding for this."

Thereafter, whenever Goldmann visited Tito, which he did several times, she was there, in Brioni.[25]

IX The concrete plan of a meeting between Goldmann and Nasser crystallized during the course of a visit Tito paid to Nasser in Aswan, Upper Egypt, on February 23 and 24, 1970.[26] Tito remembered well Goldmann's desire to meet Nasser from his talks with Goldmann. When he brought up the subject, Nasser readily agreed and asked Tito to inform Goldmann through Yugoslav diplomatic channels.

What prompted Nasser at that particular juncture of the Egyptian-Israeli conflict to send an emissary to Goldmann carrying the message that he was willing to meet him in Cairo? The political motivation for this step must be sought in the turn for the worse—from the Egyptian point of view—the war of attrition between Israel and Egypt had taken just a few weeks earlier.

Following the Egyptian defeat by Israel in the Six-Day War of June 1967, Russia amply replaced the war materiel Egypt had lost and re-trained its forces. By the end of 1968, Egypt felt strong enough, not to launch a large-scale attack on Israel, but to embark on a restricted action. Its limited aim would be harassing and weakening Israel, wearing it down, causing it heavy losses even at the cost of suffering several times heavier Egyptian casualties, which Egypt, bolstered by its huge manpower, could easily put up with, and thus bringing Israel to the point where she would feel that the sacrifices demanded by her continued occupation of the Sinai Peninsula outweighed the value that desert had for her security. At that point, Egypt hoped, Israel would be ready to enter into a political settlement satisfactory for Egypt.

The war of attrition, calculated to achieve this aim, was begun by Egypt early in March 1969. For about four months, Egypt was able to impose upon Israel the type of war it wanted: static, protracted, and consisting in the main of artillery activity along the Suez Canal and Egyptian commando raids on the eastern, Israeli-held, shore. Israel countered the latter by occasional, deep, stab-like penetrations into Egypt. Air activity on both sides was limited.

On July 20, 1969, the Israeli Air Force was sent into action, escalating the war and bringing about a breakdown of the Egyptian strategy. Israel, judging that Egypt was "warming up" the front, went on the offensive, using its air power effectively and sending frequent and large-scale commando raids deep into Egyptian territory. Once the Israeli Air Force succeeded in destroying the Egyptian air defense system, the initiative in the war of attrition passed to Israel. In view of this new situation, and bowing to Russian pressure, Nasser decided to postpone indefinitely his plan to cross the canal and to push the Israeli forces back from its east bank. Stalemated in the war of attrition, Egypt indicated its willingness to accept the pattern of the "Rhodes talks" as a formula for indirect contacts with Israel, which led to the Gromyko-Rogers talks at New York in September 1969. These, and subsequent talks in October, resulted in the drafting of the "Rogers Plan," and, in December 1969, in the so-called "Yost Document," both of which were rejected by the Israeli government as running counter to the principal aims of Israeli foreign policy as formulated after the Six-Day War, which comprised: stable and permanent peace; direct negotiations; free navigation; agreed, recognized, and secure boundaries; and solution of the Arab refugee problem within the Arab states after the signing of a peace treaty. The American plans were rejected, albeit for different reasons, by Nasser as well. In view of Egypt's strategic inferiority, Nasser felt that the diplomatic initiative was undesirable because he believed it could lead only to a settlement disadvantageous to Egypt.

On December 9, 1969, Nasser sent a delegation, headed by Anwar Sadat, to Moscow, to obtain improved MIG-21 fighter planes and other sophisticated arms. The Russians, however, refused to make any real commitments. Early in January 1970 Israel decided to carry its raids deep into Egyptian territory. This escalation of the war created in Egypt the belief that Israel intended to use her strategic superiority to impose a political solution to the Israeli-Egyptian conflict by bringing about the overthrow of Nasser and legitimizing the cease-fire lines (that is, the Suez Canal front). When Egypt became convinced it was incapable of confronting Israeli strategic superiority, it decided to turn to Soviet Russia with a call for help.

On January 22, 1970, Nasser himself went to Moscow, asking for a new antiaircraft missile system of the SAM-3 type and for Soviet teams to operate it. Pressing his demand, he made the Russians understand that, if they were not coming to Egypt's aid, he would have to step down, which could have meant the establishment of a pro-Western regime in Egypt. The Soviet positive response to his demand that Russia intervene in the war of attrition, though it was put into effect only on April 18, 1970, enabled Egypt to continue with the war. The first SAM-3 missiles were delivered to Egypt late in February 1970, and in the intervening weeks Russia renewed diplomatic efforts to persuade America to put a stop to the Israeli in-depth raids so as to save the Soviet leadership from having to intervene directly.[27]

Nasser's willingness to meet Goldmann, as the unofficial spokesman of Israel must be viewed against this background. On February 23–24, when he discussed the possibility of such a meeting with Tito, more than a month had passed since his visit to Moscow, during which time the Russians had shown no sign of living up to any promise they gave him with respect to involving themselves directly in the war of attrition on Egypt's side. Nasser may have felt that Moscow had no intention of keeping its word. He therefore must have been in a rather despondent mood and thought that any avenue of reaching a political settlement with Israel was worth exploring. In these circumstances, Tito's reminder that Goldmann was willing to come to Cairo must have been viewed as a most welcome opening by Nasser.

X   In March 1970 the Yugoslav ambassador in Paris telephoned Armand Kaplan, the political director of the Paris office of the World Jewish Congress, and asked him to come to the embassy. There, he said to

Kaplan, "You got finally what you wanted. The *Rais* (i.e., Nasser) sent a message to Marshal Tito through the Yugoslav ambassador in Cairo who came to Belgrade specially for the purpose of delivering it personally, to the effect that Nasser wished to invite Dr. Nahum Goldmann to meet him in Cairo." The ambassador added that Nasser wished the meeting to be kept secret, and the decision to publicize it to be left until after the meeting. Kaplan said to the ambassador that he would, of course, immediately convey the invitation to Goldmann, but added that, because Goldmann was a citizen of Israel, a country with which Egypt was at war, he, Kaplan, assumed that Goldmann would need to inform Mrs. Golda Meir, the prime minister of Israel, before he could respond to Nasser's invitation, and expressed his doubts that Mrs. Meir would approve the meeting.

That same evening, Kaplan went to Goldmann's home in Paris and informed him of what had happened. The message seemed to Goldmann so unbelievable that he asked Kaplan to repeat it three times. Goldmann shared Kaplan's misgivings as to Mrs. Meir, but nevertheless expressed his hope that he might be able to persuade her not to withhold her consent. Goldmann asked Kaplan to tell the Yugoslav ambassador that he would leave instantly for Israel to talk to Mrs. Meir and would let Kaplan know what transpired.

The above account is based on a personal letter written by Kaplan to Goldmann on June 29, 1978. Goldmann's own recollections of these events differ in several details from those of Kaplan (both reported them after a lapse of eight to ten years). As Goldmann told me in an interview in 1980, the idea of a meeting between him and Nasser came up at one of his talks with Tito. Goldmann described to Tito his concept of a neutralized Israel, whereupon Tito said: "You must see Nasser. I will arrange it." A few months passed, and Tito met Nasser in Aswan. Subsequently, the Yugoslav ambassador in Paris telephoned Kaplan and asked him whether or not Goldmann would be in Paris during the next few days because there would be an important message for him from Egypt. Upon receiving Kaplan's positive answer, the ambassador hung up, and after a while called again to ask Kaplan to tell Goldmann that Tito had arranged with Nasser to invite Goldmann, who would learn the details from an Egyptian envoy.

Goldmann was scheduled to leave the next day for Israel. At 11 o'clock at night he received yet another phone call. It was from Eric Rouleau, of *Le Monde*, one of the best French experts on the Middle East and a close friend of Goldmann. Rouleau got straight to the point: a prominent envoy has just arrived from Egypt in order to see Goldmann. He was Colonel Aḥmed Hamrush, one of the group who with Naguib and Nasser had organized the revolution that overthrew King Farouk in 1952. "I understand you are leaving tomorrow. You must see him tonight," said Rouleau.

Goldmann agreed, and about midnight Hamrush arrived. His message was that Tito had arranged with Nasser to invite Goldmann; that he, Hamrush, was authorized by Nasser to extend the invitation; and that Goldmann was invited as a private person, as an individual, not as a representative of Israel, but that Nasser would want him to inform Golda Meir (who had become prime minister of Israel in March 1969, just about a year before the events recounted here). Also, after the meeting had taken place, Nasser was to be free to make it public. The envoy emphasized that Nasser did not want Goldmann to ask for an Israeli government authorization for the meeting, but merely wanted him to inform Mrs. Meir because he did not want her to think that Goldmann did something behind her back, even though he would come as a private individual. Goldmann agreed, and the next morning left for Israel.

A few words should be said here about Colonel Hamrush. Being a man of literary inclinations, he was put in charge of the theaters in Egypt by Nasser and served as editor of *Rōz al-Yūsuf,* the influential literary journal. He authored several books, the latest at the time being his *Miṣr wa-'l-Sūdān, Kifāḥ Mushtarak* ("Egypt and the Sudan: Joint Struggle"), published in 1970 by the Dār al-Hilāl press in Cairo. Hamrush had a leftist orientation and a friendly attitude toward Israel. He subscribed to the ideology that Egypt must be made into a socialist state. He felt that, in order to achieve this, Egypt must first make peace with Israel, for so long as no peace existed between the two countries, the necessity of being prepared for war absorbed all the energies of Egypt. However, he felt that the withdrawal of Israel from all the Arab areas it had occupied was a precondition of any political settlement between Israel and Egypt.[28]

XI   Before describing the painful events that transpired at Israel in March and April 1970, after Goldmann's arrival there, it is necessary to mention that in that very month a critical and rather pessimistic article by Goldmann on the future of Israel was published in the prestigious American journal *Foreign Affairs.* He had written this article more than two years earlier, and its publication at the precise time of his visit to Israel was a pure coincidence. Nevertheless, his efforts to obtain Mrs.

Meir's acquiescence in his visit to Nasser, his talks with Israeli statesmen, his lectures to student groups, and his articles in Israeli newspapers on the subject of the neutralization of Israel, coming as they did right on the heels of his *Foreign Affairs* essay, resulted in a concatenation of circumstances and events that split the Israeli government and public opinion, though anti-Goldmann feelings predominated.

Goldmann's article "The Future of Israel" was the most complete, most carefully thought through, and most candid presentation of his views on the problems facing Zionism, Israel, and the Diaspora as well as their solution. The purpose of the article was to express his deep concern over the dangers threatening the future of Israel and, in consequence, that of the Jews in the Diaspora; and to indicate the steps he believed Israel should take to ensure its own, and the Diaspora's, survival.

Goldmann begins by stating that the Zionist idea had a twofold aim: to enable the Jews suffering from discrimination and persecution to live a decent and meaningful life in their own homeland; and "to ensure the survival of the Jewish people against the threat of disintegration and disappearance in those parts of the world where they enjoy full equality of rights." Although Goldmann stresses that he has "no doubt as to the historical justification and moral validity of Zionism" and believes that "concentration of a large part of the Jewish people in their own national home" is the "only way to solve what has been called for centuries 'the Jewish problem,' " he admits to having "doubts as to whether the establishment of the state of Israel as it is today, a state like all other states in structure and form, was the fullest accomplishment of the Zionist idea."

Throughout their history, the Jews had a unique attachment to their ancient homeland, and today Israel is for the Jewish people, that is for both those in Israel and in the Diaspora, "the only means of survival and the sole guarantee of a creative future." But precisely because of the uniqueness of the Jewish problem and of its Zionist solution, Goldmann doubts whether "a Jewish state no different in structure and character from any other state can be the real implementation of Zionism." Even before the establishment of Israel he had pondered whether the Zionist leadership, engaged in a struggle for a Jewish State in Palestine, should not "ask for a state of a specific character, more in conformity with the special nature of the Jewish people and Jewish history." But the many difficulties that had to be overcome at that juncture made him feel that it would have been "too much to ask at the same time for a unique character for this state." However, the experiences gained in the course of more than two decades since the creation of Israel have led him "to the conviction that to guarantee its survival, and to make sure that it fulfills its raison d'être as the main instrument of Jewish future, one must begin to think of a specific character and form for this state."

The destiny of Israel will be decided by two factors: its relationship to the Arab world, and its relationship with the Jewish Diaspora. Both, Goldmann finds, are unsatisfactory from the point of view of Israel's chances of survival. The Arabs are hostile to Israel. They are gaining in importance economically. Their military strength is on the increase. In the Arab-Israeli conflict, more and more countries side with the Arabs. Even the United States, the only real friend and supporter of Israel, cannot be counted on indefinitely, as shown by the aftermath of the 1956 Sinai Campaign.

As a result of the permanent state of war in which Israel finds itself, the young state "is more admired in the world today for its military brilliance than for its spiritual achievements." This in itself is a negative factor, for it means that "large parts of the progressive world have become disappointed and antagonistic to Israel."

From the Jewish point of view, the fact must be faced that, unless something unexpected occurs such as large-scale persecution of Jews in Western countries, immigration to Israel will remain small, and the majority of the Jewish people will continue to live in the Diaspora. However, active and virulent anti-Semitism is largely a thing of the past; the Jews have become integrated into the political, social, economic, and cultural life of the countries in which they live; and the Jewish religion has largely ceased to be the authoritative force it had been in the past— therefore the danger of assimilation today is greater than it has ever been. Hence, "the existence of Israel as the new center where Jewish civilization can be continued and where new ideas will be created, as a source of challenge and inspiration for Diaspora Jewry, is . . . much more essential for Jewish survival today than was even envisaged by Zionist ideologists before the Nazi period."

Because of the mutual interdependence of Israel and the Diaspora, should the Diaspora lose interest in Israel, "the survival of the state would be nearly impossible." A strengthening of the Diaspora's solidarity with Israel is "the *conditio sine qua non* for the future of Israel." This, however, can be achieved only if the character of Israel can claim the sympathy of world Jewry. Moreover, Israel must be able to attract "the best, most idealistic elements of the young [Jewish] generation, which is in great danger of largely being lost to the Jewish people within a few decades." But an Israel at war, though it can attract thousands of volunteers, ready to go there to fight, does not lure tens of thousands of young immigrants willing to settle in it. One can only try to imagine what could have been created culturally, scientifically, and spiritually by the dynamic genius of Israel in the last twenty years "if its young, gifted, and creative generation with its tremendous energy and élan, not to speak of the billions of dollars, had been concentrated on science, literature, social experiments, and similar tasks, instead of having had to build and maintain, as its greatest and most successful achievement, the brilliant army of the young state."

These considerations lead Goldmann to the conclusion that Israel must not, cannot, become one of the more than a hundred so-called sovereign states as they exist today. Instead of relying on its military and political strength, Israel "should be not merely accepted but guaranteed, de jure and de facto, by all the peoples of the world, including the Arabs, and put under the permanent protection of the whole of mankind." Once neutralized in this manner, Israel "would have to keep itself outside the sphere of power politics. . . . Neutralization may even mean that a permanent symbolic international force may have to be stationed in the state of Israel, so that any attack on it would imply an attack on all the states guaranteeing Israel's existence and neutrality." Israel itself would not be demilitarized until the effectiveness of the international guarantee could be proven.

"Such a neutralization could be the basis for an Arab-Israeli settlement and peace." It would appeal to Arab generosity. It would do away with the Arab fear of Israeli aggression and expansion. It would not be an obstacle to Arab policies.

Although Goldmann admits that he no longer believes, as he did before the establishment of Israel, that the idea of a Jewish-Arab confederation of Middle Eastern states is practicable, he stresses that he does believe in the neutralization of Israel as a realistic possibility. It is politically feasible: "I have reason to hope that the Soviet Union would be ready, in case of a satisfactory agreement, to guarantee the stability and territorial integrity of the countries of the Middle East, together with the United States or with the Big Powers or within the framework of the United Nations." Once this is done, the Arabs would go along, because, for one thing, they could no longer count on Russian help in fighting Israel.

As a neutralized country, Israel would "quickly become a major international cultural center," but, above all, it would become "the natural center of the creativeness of the Jewish people as a whole. It would attract many of the most gifted and idealistic elements" of the Diaspora. It would become "the great new source of Jewish inspiration and challenges, and in the deepest sense of the word the spiritual center of the Jewish people."[29]

It must be left to others to probe into the similarities between the basic concerns voiced in this article by Goldmann and those which had motivated Aḥad Haʿam eighty years earlier, when he found the incipient Jewish settlement in Palestine wanting and expressed his doubts and criticism in a number of articles that have long since become classics in Zionist literature. But, as a mere preliminary indication of the affinity between the two approaches, it can be stated that Aḥad Haʿam, too, viewed Zionism as primarily a means to ensure the continuation of the spiritual creativity of Judaism, the preservation of the "national ego," that is, the collective identity, of the Jewish people. He, too, envisaged that most of the Jews would continue to live in the Diaspora, while the Jewish State in Palestine would be their "spiritual center," creating values that would nourish the Diaspora and ensure its continued existence and unity. However, in comparison to Aḥad Haʿam's concept of the "spiritual center" Goldmann goes much further in observing that the necessity for a permanent armed preparedness is a handicap to the full spiritual development of Israel; and in suggesting that Israel should pay the price of neutralization in order thereby to be able to develop fully its huge creative potential.

XII In discussing the events that transpired in Israel following Goldmann's arrival there on March 23, 1970, it is difficult, if not impossible, to present a coherent account of them. Goldmann's recollections—from a distance of ten years—give one picture; the newspaper reports and articles and the minutes of the Knesset meetings, which are contemporary with the events, give another; and the two do not always mesh. But contradictions exist even between the various on-the-spot reports and accounts, depending on such factors as the reporter's and his paper's or the speaker's political affiliation as well as on the sympathies of the party leaders, whose quoted statements are often at variance with one another.

As Goldmann himself recalled it in 1980, what happened was that, when he arrived in Israel, Golda Meir was not in Jerusalem but in Motza, just outside the city, where she had gone to spend a week in the Arza rest house. The next day, he drove out to see her and reported to her about Nasser's invitation. At first she was incredulous, and Goldmann needed to assure her repeatedly that he was sincere. Once convinced, she said that she would have to inform the cabinet. Goldmann warned her not to do so because, he said, there were no secrets in Israel, and once the cabinet knew about the planned meeting, the next day it would be in the press, which may very well lead Nasser to cancel his invitation or to deny altogether that it had ever been issued.

"I am a democrat," Mrs. Meir insisted. "I don't act on my own."

"Look," said Goldmann, "you have a kitchen cabinet. Inform them, if you must, but don't let it go beyond them. Besides, if the matter is presented to the full cabinet, they will undoubtedly refuse to give their approval, and that will be an official and public rebuff to Nasser."

Finally, Mrs. Meir agreed: "The day after tomorrow I am returning to the city, and the following day I shall let you know." In the meantime, Goldmann discussed the matter with Moshe Dayan and Abba Eban, two of the most influential members of the cabinet. Both were in favor of Goldmann going to see Nasser in view of the fact that the invitation had been issued to him privately. However, Mrs. Meir could not overcome her own reservations, in which one factor may have been that she felt that, if any direct contact was to be established with Nasser, it should be the Israeli prime minister who should meet him, not Goldmann, who had no official position in Israel. She therefore did something that ten years later Goldmann still felt was "a nasty trick." She called a meeting of the cabinet, declared it to be a meeting of the security council, which meant that nothing that transpired at the meeting could be repeated to any outsider, including the press, and informed it that Goldmann had asked for authorization to meet Nasser. As she had expected, this was turned down. Among the negative votes were those of Dayan and Eban, who understood from Mrs. Meir's presentation that Goldmann was asking for governmental authorization to visit Nasser.

When Mrs. Meir informed him of the decision, Goldmann was dismayed. "But you promised not to inform your cabinet!"

"Well, democracy demanded it," was her rejoinder. "You run the country," argued Goldmann, "with your kitchen cabinet, why did precisely this question have to be presented to the full cabinet?"

Instead of continuing to argue about what had been done, Mrs. Meir turned to what she felt needed to be accomplished at that juncture. "I agree with you," she said, "that it would harm Israel if you told Nasser that the cabinet made this refusal. Therefore, I ask you that as a good Israeli patriot you cable Nasser that you refuse to go to see him."

"That I will not do," answered Goldmann. "I am a patriot, but it is you, not I, who did this damage to Israel. I shall inform Nasser that you refused to let me go."

The very next day after the meeting of the Israeli cabinet, the matter, even though discussed under the ban of secrecy, became known, and the Israeli correspondent of *Le Monde,* André Scemama, wanted to cable the story to Paris. The censor held up his cable, whereupon the correspondent said he would fly to Cyprus and file his story from there, or, better still, would phone in the story from Jerusalem, which he could do unhindered because all phone calls could not be controlled. When Goldmann learned about this, he called Jacob Herzog, a good friend of his, and informed him of what was about to happen. Thus Mrs. Meir had no choice but to announce the cabinet decision herself.[30]

XIII From sources other than Goldmann, a fuller story can be pieced together of what transpired in those tense days in Israel late in March and early in April 1970.

Israel was still in the throes of the war of attrition in which, in consequence of the Russian intervention, it was losing the initiative. About the middle of March 1970, indications reached the Israeli government that the president of the World Jewish Congress was about to arrive in Israel with an important political plan. Walter Eytan, Israel's ambassador in Paris, cabled the Foreign Ministry in Jerusalem that Goldmann was carrying in his satchel a political surprise about which he wanted to talk to the prime minister. The Foreign Ministry suggested that Goldmann deliver his message to the Israeli ambassador, but, when the latter met Goldmann, the veteran and experienced Zionist leader kept his surprise for the government.[31]

After his arrival in Israel, Goldmann met several high governmental officials, among them Dr. Jacob Herzog, the prime minister's influential and experienced political adviser, and Moshe Dayan, the minister of defense. The only available information on these meetings are Goldmann's recollections, according to which Dayan supported the plan of the Goldmann-Nasser meeting and said that, if it were up to him, he would not inform the government at all. That is, Dayan said, what Ben-Gurion would have done if he were still prime minister.

The day after his talk with Dayan, on March 24, Goldmann met Prime Minister Meir. When he gave her an account of the manner in which he was contacted in Paris by Nasser's emissary, he could not recall the name of the man who had come to him late at night to tell him of Nasser's willingness to meet him. Mrs. Meir felt the identity of the emissary was important, whereupon Goldmann put through a long-distance call to Paris and was reminded that his name was Colonel Aḥmed Hamrush. As Mrs. Meir subsequently reported to the government and the Knesset, Goldmann informed her that, though he did not have an actual invitation to go to Cairo, the intermediaries who had contacted him in the name of Nasser left no doubt that the Egyptian president was interested in a meeting with him and would receive him willingly, if two conditions were met: one, that the government of Israel should know about the meeting, and that the meeting itself would remain secret unless and until Nasser decided to publicize it.

Mrs. Meir did not like what she heard. She asked, what would Goldmann say to Nasser? Goldmann's reply was that all he would do was to listen to what Nasser would say. This did not seem reasonable to Mrs. Meir. She could not imagine that Nasser would invite Goldmann in order to have him listen to a monologue. She proceeded to act out with Goldmann an imaginary scene between Nasser and him. Playing the role of Nasser, she asked him a series of questions on boundaries, the Arab refugees, the future of Jerusalem, and the like, to demonstrate to him that he could not simply sit and listen to Nasser and say nothing. Goldmann's views on Israeli-Arab relations were much too moderate even for the "doves" in Israel. In fact, during the course of her talk with him Mrs. Meir became convinced that he could not be a suitable spokesman for Israel, not even in an entirely unofficial capacity. Goldmann's argument, "Whoever will be the one to meet with Nasser, any meeting will be to the good. I am, after all, an Israeli," did not sit well with Mrs. Meir.

Although Goldmann knew that his views differed from those of the Israeli government, he argued that his visit to Cairo could be an opening for negotiations. He felt that the Arab-Israeli problem could be solved in a manner similar to that which led to the peace talks in Vietnam. In that Far Eastern issue, it was precisely the American personalities who were sharply critical of the United States policy in Vietnam who were sent, with the knowledge of President Johnson, to talk with the North Vietnamese authorities. They paved the way for the official talks which were taking place at that very moment in Paris between the United States Government and Saigon, on the one hand, and Hanoi and the Vietcong, on the other. Why, then, should not he, Goldmann, be sent to establish the first contact with Nasser? "Just say that you agree," said Goldmann to Mrs. Meir, "and I shall fly tomorrow to Tito, return to Jerusalem, and set out for Cairo."

All this did not convince Mrs. Meir. She was, on the contrary, determined to prevent Goldmann's trip to Cairo, but did not want to do it on her own responsibility. She therefore told Goldmann that she would put the issue before the cabinet. All the arguments of Goldmann were of no avail. In vain did he point out that he did not ask for the "approval" of the government but merely for its "knowledge," that therefore there was no reason to bring the matter before all the twenty-four members of the full cabinet, and that a consultation between the prime minister and a few senior cabinet members was all that was required. Goldmann also informed her that he had already met Jacob Herzog as well as Moshe Dayan and had appointments in the next few days with Abba Eban, the foreign minister, Yigal Allon, the deputy prime minister, and Pinḥas Sapir, the minister of finance. Goldmann also called Mrs. Meir's attention to a certain political damage that could result from Israel's refusal to let him go to Cairo: Nasser could use such a refusal to make the government of Israel appear unwilling to entertain a tentative peace initiative.

But Mrs. Meir remained adamant. As she reported to the Knesset on April 7, she said to him: "I am not used to decide on my own in such matters, in the name of the Government. . . . In matters of state, policy, foreign policy, security—it would never occur to me to make a decision, a determination, without first bringing it to the table of the Government. This is what I said to Dr. Goldmann. I cannot say he was happy with my answer, but I explained to him: 'I have no other way of acting; this is how I act, and I shall not act differently in this matter as well,' And so I did."[32]

Despite this rejection by the prime minister, Goldmann kept his appointments with the other cabinet members. Of his meeting with Foreign Minister Abba Eban on March 29, the latter gave a detailed account to the Knesset on April 7. Goldmann had told him, Eban reported, that he had no invitation from the president of Egypt to travel to Cairo to meet him. However, Goldmann explained to Eban, as he had earlier in more detail to the prime minister, that certain individuals whom he had met and whose identity Goldmann made known to Eban, said that they thought they would succeed in bringing about such a meeting. According to Eban, it would be held

on condition that it should be planned and take place with the knowledge of the Government of Israel, that this consent of the Government of Israel should be made public, but without Goldmann being asked to be a representative linked to the position of the Government or to the principles of its policy. On the contrary, it appears that the persons who had brought up the possibility of this mission recommended Dr. Goldmann as the one to carry it out because his views were not close to those of the Government of Israel, "nonconformist" in English. In other words, the reservations Dr. Goldmann had about the policy of the Government and the Knesset were, in the eyes of these individuals, a main factor which rendered him suitable to being the first Israeli whose utterances President Nasser would hear. What is asked of the Government of Israel is an act of initiative which would ensure it that President Nasser would not hear the position of the Government and the Knesset from the mouth of an Israeli who is familiar with it in all detail and identifies himself with it in his soul, but would meet with a famous interlocutor who is of the opinion—as it is his right to be—that our policy, your policy, Members of the Knesset, is mistaken.[33]

XIV Next day, March 30, the "Goldmann Affair" was discussed at a meeting of the Israeli cabinet. After a lively discussion, when it came to a vote, only two of the members present voted for letting Goldmann go to Cairo. The cabinet decision was prepared by Moshe Dayan and, as Mrs. Meir read it out in the Knesset on April 7, it stated:

The Government discussed the proposal which, according to Dr. Gold-mann, he received from various factors, to go to Egypt for a meeting with President Nasser. According to Dr. Goldmann, President Nasser stipulated that this meeting should take place with the knowledge and approval of the Government of Israel [when reaching this phrase, Mrs. Meir interrupted herself and said, "It says here 'with the knowledge and approval,' but it could be as well 'with the knowledge or approval' "], and that it should be made public. The Government decided that it would respond to all manifestation of readiness on the part of the President of Egypt for a meeting for the clarification of questions vital to Israel and Egypt, if each side is free to choose its representatives. Therefore, in reply to the request of Dr. Goldmann that the Government approve his meeting with the President of Egypt, the Government decided that the answer is negative.[34]

Thus, the Goldmann-Nasser meeting was effectively torpedoed.

Apparently what happened at the cabinet meeting was that, when Mrs. Meir informed her colleagues of her talks with Goldmann, she substituted, either intentionally or inadvertently, the term "approval" for "knowledge." Knowledge by the prime minister, or even by the whole cabinet, simply meant that she (or the cabinet) took cognizance of the planned visit of Goldmann and did not object to it. It did not mean that the cabinet approved it, let alone that it constituted Goldmann as an ad hoc emissary of the Israeli government. Likely, had the expression "knowledge of the Government" been used, the cabinet would not have objected. Approval, of course, was an entirely different matter. It meant, whether so formulated or not, that the government conferred upon Goldmann a quasi-official status, that it gave him its blessing, that it allowed him to speak in its name. This, most members of the government felt, they could not do because Goldmann was neither a member of the government, nor of the Knesset, nor even a permanent resident of Israel. Furthermore, his well-known views were more conciliatory than those of even the most "dovish" in the Israeli government and the Knesset.

When Mrs. Meir informed Goldmann of the decision of the government, which she did on April 1, she asked him to withdraw his suggestion and thus save her the need of having to give him a negative answer. But Goldmann would not let Mrs. Meir, or the government of Israel, off the hook so easily. He explained that he owed an answer to the individuals who had approached him with the suggestion. In addition, there was the matter of a series of articles in *HaAretz*, the influential, independent Tel Aviv daily.

Some time earlier, Goldmann had submitted to Gershon Schocken, editor in chief of *HaAretz*, a series of articles in which he presented the same position and the same arguments as in his article on "The Future of Israel," which was published at that very time in the prestigious American political journal *Foreign Affairs*. Goldmann had asked Schocken to hold publication of his articles until the government of Israel decided on the question of his visit to Cairo. Now that Mrs. Meir let him know that the government had withheld its consent from the visit, Goldmann gave the "go ahead" to Schocken, and the first of his series of articles appeared in the April 2 issue of *HaAretz*, and the sequel was published during the next several days.[35]

Also on April 2 the censor informed the prime minister's office that the story of the cabinet decision had been leaked to the Paris daily *Le Monde*.[36] The dispatch actually was not published in that newspaper until April 5; and, on the same day, it was broadcast over the French radio and television as well as announced in an official statement by the Israeli government.[37] The article in *Le Monde* quoted "circles near to Dr. Nahum Goldmann," but it was suspected that he himself was the origin of the leak.

On April 3 a meeting took place between Goldmann and Arye (Leon) Dulzin, the minister without portfolio in the Israeli government, who at the March 30 cabinet meeting had spoken up most sharply not only against the Goldmann plan but also against Goldmann personally, whom he accused of lack of reliability and inconsistency in reporting events. Their April 3 meeting had been set up about a week earlier for the purpose of discussing economic and financial issues because Goldmann was engaged in the arrangement of financial matters between Israel and Germany that grew out of the Luxembourg Agreement he had concluded with Germany in 1952 (see chapter 7). This time, he wished to report to Dulzin about additional German payments of tens of millions of German marks.

Although Dulzin did not know of the news story, which was cabled by the Israeli correspondent of *Le Monde* to Paris, and Goldmann did not know of Dulzin's attack on him in the cabinet meeting, the planned Cairo visit inevitably came up. Goldmann told Dulzin that he had already received the government's negative reply from Mrs. Meir, and that it was known to him that Eban and Dayan were of a different opinion. Dulzin set the matter straight: Eban had argued strongly against Goldmann's visit, and, as for Dayan, it was he who prepared the government's decision. Goldmann mentioned, as he had when he spoke to Mrs. Meir, that a danger existed that Nasser would use the incident to strike a blow against Israel. Dulzin felt that Nasser would do no such thing because it would not redound to his credit. It was most unlikely that Cairo would disclose the invitation of a Jewish leader to negotiations on a political arrangement. Unless Goldmann himself publicized the affair, who else would? After pondering the question for a moment, Goldmann said—repeating in essence what he had told Mrs. Meir earlier—that he owed a reply to the individuals who initiated the contact, namely the Yugoslav diplomats, and possibly Tito would publicize it.

XV   On April 5, at a scheduled cabinet meeting, Mrs. Meir surprised the members by referring again to the Goldmann Affair and reading out to them from the telegram that the Israeli correspondent of *Le Monde*, André Scemama, sent to his paper. What happened next, according to Dan Margalit's summary of the events, was that Dulzin "jumped up from his seat and told his colleagues of the talk he had with Goldmann, arguing that a comparison between the style of the telegram and what he himself had heard from the mouth of Dr. Goldmann indicated that only Goldmann could have leaked the content of the Government's decision to the man of *Le Monde* in Jerusalem. The errors contained in the telegram were identical with those Goldmann had uttered in his, Dulzin's, presence."[38]

Thus the cabinet was again wrapped up in the Goldmann Affair, and this time it had to decide on the form in which its own version of the events should be made public. Israel Barzilai, of Mapam, the left-wing labor party, who was prevented from being present at the previous cabinet meeting, demanded that the March 30 decision should be reopened for discussion because he wished to oppose it. He reported that, in between the two meetings, he had talked with Goldmann, and, although he had reservations about Goldmann's views as expressed in the articles in *HaAretz* (by April 5 three articles had been printed; three more were to follow on April 6, 8, and 9), he was convinced it would be a mistake to block Goldmann from accepting the Cairo invitation. What had to be done now, argued Barzilai, was to see whether Goldmann's trip could be transformed into a private visit. Barzilai also stated he understood that the minister of defense, Moshe Dayan, was inclined to agree to Goldmann's visit provided it could be described as "a private trip."

Dayan, who arrived late at the meeting, then told his colleagues that Goldmann did not report to him precisely the question of the "approval" on behalf of the government. Dayan was of the opinion that the very fact that the issue was laid on the table of the government required a negative answer. Barzilai subsequently said, "I felt that Moshe [Dayan] was inconsistent. I got the impression that he, too, was curious to know what could be the result of a talk between Goldmann and Nasser."

This time the discussion was shorter. The cabinet members felt that the government must "steal the show" from Cairo and *Le Monde* and quickly publish its own version of the affair. Despite this consensus, nothing concrete was done. And, when Mikhael Arnon, the secretary of the cabinet, held his usual meeting the same day (Sunday, April 5) with the press, he did not mention the Goldmann Affair at all. Several hours later, a reporter phoned Arnon at his home and told him he had learned that the government had decided to make the affair public. He suggested that Arnon may have simply forgotten to include the matter in his briefing. Arnon was not in a position to give a clear reply.

After the French radio broadcast on the Goldmann Affair, still on April 5, the newscasters of the Israeli radio were about to quote the French source and they asked Arnon for his reaction. He asked for a delay of an hour. The time was used to thresh out the matter in urgent phone consultations among the members of the cabinet. When finally the news was broadcast, late at night, many listeners found its brevity and vagueness annoying. Without explaining the motivations behind the decision, the statement merely said that Israel was willing to meet with Egyptian representatives provided each side chose its own spokesman for the talks. Subsequently, the government explained that it did not wish to enter into "personal recrimination and argument" with Goldmann and that it tried to spare his feelings. This, and the formalistic rejection of the Egyptian initiative, sounded, in the ears of many, ridiculous and evasive, coming as it did from a government which for three years had argued that it would not pass up the slightest opening to peace for reasons of prestige and procedure.[39]

It is not easy to establish the motives that led the cabinet to reject the Goldmann initiative. It was a highly complex body, composed of representatives of many different political parties, which had concluded an uneasy truce for the purpose of forming a "Government of National Unity." Yet, despite the apparent cooperation, strong undercurrents of disharmony and competitiveness remained. There were the "doves" and the "hawks"; the Labor groups, including varying shades of leftist orientation; the religious and the nonreligious rightists; and the Liberals, themselves in uneasy union with the Ḥerut (formerly Revisionist) party. Beyond all this, another factor was the typical dislike any establishment has of being interfered with and shown up by an outsider, especially one whose past achievements for the benefit of Israel were so significant that he could not be ignored and who now found a diplomatic opening that the cabinet had sought in vain. And, in the first place, there was, of course, the overriding, patriotic concern about entrusting mediation between Israel and the Arabs to a man with Goldmann's well-known proclivity for seeing the other side's position, being overtly critical of Israel's foreign policy, and voicing the conviction that he could and would do better than the country's elected leadership in representing what he deemed to be the true long-range interests of Israel.

It is more than likely that, quite apart from the semantic difference between "knowledge" and "approval," a major factor in the government's negative decision was the appearance precisely at that time of Goldmann's articles in *Foreign Affairs* and *HaAretz*. In fact, political observers remarked that the timing of the publication of these articles, in addition to the views and proposals contained in them, was connected with his attempt to meet the foremost leader of the Arab world for the purpose of discussing with him the achievement of peace between the

Arabs and Israel. Several commentators felt that Goldmann had clearly shown himself in these articles, as he had formerly during the course of many years of political activity, to be, as one of them put it, not merely a dove, but "a dove without feathers," a man much too ready to agree with the point of view of Israel's opponents, and that therefore he was totally unfitted to act as an intermediary between Israel and the Arabs.

XVI   On April 7, 1970, the government's decision to withhold approval for Goldmann's visit to Cairo was communicated to the Knesset by Foreign Minister Abba Eban. He did this in a long speech, in which he reported what had transpired between him and Goldmann when they met on March 29 (see above) and explained the considerations that impelled the government to deny Goldmann its approval.

When Eban finished, a heated debate ensued. Several members expressed disagreement with the government's decision and sharply criticized it. Golda Meir spoke in its defense. Uri Avneri, the vociferous representative of the miniscule Ha'Olam haZe—Koaḥ Ḥadash party, reported that a short while before he had spoken to Eric Rouleau, "one of those who had worked for the success of this undertaking," and that Rouleau had given him the following facts:

1. The invitation of Dr. Goldmann was decided upon in the course of personal talks between President Tito and President Nasser in Aswan, on February 23 and 24 of this year.
2. This was not the first time that Marshal Tito tried to convince Nasser that he should invite Dr. Goldmann. But Nasser had not believed that such a meeting could take place, since he had been convinced that the hawks in the Government of Israel would explode the secrecy of the meeting even before it took place, and thereby would undermine his, Nasser's, position in the Arab world.
3. Therefore, this time, when President Nasser agreed to the meeting he stipulated that it should not be secret, so that there should be no possibility to accuse him of having established secret contact with Israel, and the Palestinians should not be able to argue that he was selling them out.
4. President Nasser intended to prepare Arab public opinion in the course of two months, and thereafter invite Dr. Goldmann for a talk, publicly and officially. He did not expect official approval of the meeting by the Government of Israel, since he knew that the extremist wing in the Government would prevent such an approval. He only asked of Dr. Gold-

mann that his visit should take place with the knowledge of the Prime
Minister, which would assure it that the Government of Israel would not
sabotage the meeting.

These being the facts of the matter, Avneri concluded, there was
certainly no need at all for Mrs. Meir to bring it before the government
for its approval—unless, that is, she wanted to sabotage this initiative.[40]
This presentation of Rouleau's report by Avneri is essentially identical
with the facts as stated by Rouleau in his article in the April 8, 1970,
issue of *Le Monde* (see below).

Among the others who criticized the government in that Knesset
debate were Eliahu Sasson, of Mapai, a former minister of police; and
Gideon Hausner, of the Independent Liberals, a former attorney general
of the Adolf Eichmann trial fame. At the close of the debate, two motions
of nonconfidence were made, as well as three critical summations of the
government's action. Next afternoon, when these motions were put to
a vote, they were all defeated by overwhelming majorities.

One factor in the decision of the Israeli government and the Knesset
to deny their consent to a Goldmann-Nasser meeting was undoubtedly
the specific situation of the moment on the Israeli-Egyptian front along
the Suez Canal. By the time Goldmann arrived in Israel, late in March
1970, with his plan to meet Nasser, the war of attrition had taken a
definite turn for the worse for Israel. As mentioned above, at the end of
January 1970, Nasser had gone to Moscow to request effective Russian
aid, actually direct Russian intervention, in his war of attrition against
Israel, in which he faced the danger of defeat. Late in February, the
Russians began to deliver SAM-3 missiles to Egypt, and, when the
construction of the missile sites was identified by Israeli reconnaissance
planes, the air force began systematically to bomb them. Despite these
efforts to prevent the deployment of the new Russian missiles, much
superior to the older SAM-2's, by early March it was reported that some
1,500 SAM-3's were delivered, many of them were installed, and numerous Soviet personnel were operating them.

Faced with this Russian presence and determined not to provoke the
Soviets to further and more active intervention, Israel stopped bombing
the Cairo area, which was a main concentration of the Soviet missile
sites, and greatly reduced its in-depth raids into Egypt. Clearly, the direct
Soviet intervention in Egypt forced a defensive attitude upon Israel.[41] In
these circumstances, to open talks with Egypt in any form or manner
would have contravened the principle of never negotiating from a po-

sition of weakness. Goldmann's initiative therefore had to be turned down, whereas only a month or two earlier, when Israel was in a position of being able to impose its strategy on Egypt, it might well have been approved despite the doubts the Israeli cabinet entertained about Goldmann's political views.

Prime Minister Meir herself continued to be highly critical of Goldmann's views as expressed in his *Foreign Affairs* article. At the April 9, 1970, meeting of the Ma'arakh (Alignment), the coalition of the Labor parties that was the dominant political body in the government and the Knesset, Mrs. Meir said: "Never before has such an anti-Zionist article been written by a Jew. When I read it I was shaken. From the article it becomes clear that Goldmann casts doubt upon the very existence of the State of Israel. Even if a real invitation would come from Cairo, how could such a man be sent to Cairo, a man who wrote such an article? In whose name would he speak?"[42]

XVII On April 8, after the cabinet refusal became public knowledge, Goldmann held a press conference in which he stated that, considering the circumstances, had he been a member of the Israeli cabinet, he, too, would have voted against the authorization. He added that, had one been granted him, he would have refused it because he was not prepared to meet with Nasser to support the official Israeli policy.[43]

The government's decision to withhold its consent from the planned meeting between Goldmann and Nasser met with a mixed reception by the Israeli public. The New Left launched a public campaign under the slogan "Let Goldmann Go!—Golda Is Afraid of Peace!" and sent groups of demonstrators to the campus of Tel Aviv University carrying signs thus inscribed. For two days in a row, students demonstrated in Jerusalem and Tel Aviv. On April 6 and 7 they carried placards demanding that the government reconsider and allow Goldmann to travel to Cairo. One sign read: "You have got the phone call you've been waiting for—answer it!" This was a reference to General Dayan's comment after the 1967 war that Israel was waiting for the phone to ring to make peace, but that it never rang.

On April 7, 1970, *HaAretz* published the results of a small-scale public opinion poll in which the question was asked, "Are you for or against a meeting between the president of the World Jewish Congress, Dr. Nahum Goldmann, and the president of Egypt, Gamal Abdel Nasser?" Of the sixty-four persons polled, 63 percent favored such a meeting. The Goldmann Affair also had lively echoes in debates in the press as well as on the radio and television; several editorials attacked the government's decision to reject Goldmann's planned visit to Cairo.

During the next few days, more student demonstrations took place. In front of the prime minister's office and elsewhere, groups of students carried signs reading, "Let Goldmann Go!" "Enough Excuses!" "We Want Nasser-Goldmann Talks!" "Golda, You Cannot Make Peace, Go Away!" "Goldmann to Cairo, Golda to the Kitchen!"[44]

When the police broke up a sit-down demonstration of 250 young people who blocked a main intersection in Jerusalem protesting the government's decision not to support Goldmann's visit to Cairo, and chanting "Golda Must Go!" three persons were hospitalized and two others injured.[45]

Among those who criticized the government were several of the sons of veteran Zionist leaders, who

> gave expression not only to their doubts about the intentions and frankness of the Government, but also a whole world-view and an inner world which was alien and incomprehensible to their fathers. . . . Among them were Yoram Sadeh, Asaf Dayan, Yariv Ben-Aharon, and Sh'muel Shem-Tov, all of them sons of respected ministers, army commanders, party heads, and leaders of the Histadrut.
>
> Most shocking was the letter of the eighth-grade pupils. The Prime Minister told the members of the Government about it in secret. When its content became known, Minister of Education Yigal Allon was asked to meet with those who wrote it. It is not clear whether Allon succeeded in convincing the young critics to change their mind, but it is possible that several moves and changes in his political positions thereafter took place under the influence of the group of youngsters which crowded his office for several hours.[46]

Prominent people, professors, and student's organizations circulated petitions and flooded the government with urgent telegrams expressing amazement at, and disapproval of, the government's decision. Similar sentiments were voiced by some Jewish leaders abroad. One of them, Sir Siegmund Warburg, the well-known London banker, one of the leaders of the "Millionaires' Club" that had been organized by the Israeli government and a major donor to the Jewish Appeal, called on the ambassador of Israel in London, Aharon Remez, informing him that he, Warburg, would wash his hands of all pro-Israel activities and donations. "This was received in Jerusalem with great dismay."[47]

Nor were statements expressing disapproval of Goldmann's views lacking. Dr. Joachim Prinz, of Orange, New Jersey, chairman of the Governing Council of the World Jewish Congress, expressed his disagreement with the recent statements of the president of his organization, Goldmann, to the effect that Israel attracted increasing support from right-wing circles.[48]

Summarizing the events, the political correspondent of *HaAretz*, Dan Margalit, wrote: "After a delay of several months, those near the Prime Minister came to the conclusion that the explosion was inevitable. Under the pressure of the events at the Suez Canal and the fading hopes for a political solution, the moderate wing, which wanted to dissolve the Government of National Unity and became victim of the delusion that the Herut-Liberal Bloc prevented salvation through peace, grew stronger in the Labor Party. Had the government not been caught by the Goldmann Affair, there would have occurred another event which would have developed into a stormy collision. But the practical lesson was different. The Goldmann Affair revealed how remote were the 24 Cabinet Ministers from the broad sectors of the public."[49]

Aware of the seeds of discord sown by his articles and efforts to meet Nasser, Goldmann had cabled Dr. Prinz: "My article in *Foreign Affairs* and likewise the series of articles being published in *HaAretz* are the expression of my personal opinion. The position of the World Jewish Congress as approved in the meeting of its executive committee in Tel Aviv, is unreserved support of Israel whose Government is alone responsible for its foreign policy. I have always agreed and shall always continue to agree with this position. In the World Jewish Congress are comprised Jewish circles, institutions, and communities from all parts of the world, with various views, and therefore it never took a position on Israel's foreign policy."[50]

XVIII   The crisis triggered by the Goldmann Affair in Israeli governmental circles was amply reflected in the press. In fact, for several weeks public opinion was riveted on the affair, and every newspaper included numerous headlines of articles about Goldmann. A few examples illustrate this strong interest in his proposed meeting with Nasser. The April 6, 1970, issue of *Ma'ariv* printed two articles on the Goldmann Affair on the first page: one under a seven-column headline (a page in the paper carried nine columns) reading, "G. Meir Invited Goldmann to Appear Tomorrow Before the Meeting of the Ma'arakh Political Committee and

Executive"; and the second, under a five-column headline, "Tito Stands Behind Goldmann's Initiative." The same page also contained a small one-column note entitled "Cairo Is Silent" (namely about the Goldmann invitation), and on page 2 of the same issue yet another article appeared under a three-column headline reporting that "Dr. Prinz Disagrees with Goldmann Because of the Argument in Goldmann's Article that Israel Attracts the Support of Rightist Circles." Dr. Joachim Prinz was at the time the chairman of the Governing Council of the World Jewish Congress, of which Goldmann was president.

On the same page, a small item tells of the positive reaction of the New Left to the Goldmann initiative. On page 3 a six-column headline reads: "The Government: Goldmann Is Free to Meet With Nasser, in a Personal Capacity—Not In the Name of Israel." Page 8 of the same issue contains two more Goldmann items: an editorial entitled "Was Goldmann Invited to Cairo?" and a cartoon showing Goldmann with a well-traveled, half-open suitcase urging a young boy with a "tembel" hat (representing Israel): "Jump in, and let's go to Egypt!"

Nor was this issue exceptional. In the April 7 issue of *Ma'ariv*, no less than four articles on the first page dealt with various aspects of the Goldmann Affair: Prime Minister Meir's position, Moscow's role, Foreign Minister Abba Eban's statement in the Knesset, and the meeting of the Independent Liberal party concerning the affair. On page 2 a fifth article featured the comments of Moshe Dayan, the minister of defense. On page 3 a sixth article spoke of what he was expected to say in the Knesset on the subject; a seventh dealt with Cairo's denial of Goldmann's invitation; and an eighth consisted of an interview with Goldmann. Page 8 carried a ninth article: a commentary, entitled "If Dr. Goldmann Had Gone [i.e., to Cairo]." And finally page 11 contained an interview with two members of the Knesset, one of whom supported, and the other opposed, the government's decision to withhold its approval from Goldmann's visit to Cairo. All in all, ten articles on the Goldmann Affair appeared in this single issue of *Ma'ariv*, followed by another eight articles in the April 8 issue. In general, *Ma'ariv* took a strongly anti-Goldmann position.

The other Israeli papers took a similar interest in the Goldmann-government controversy and maintained it for several weeks. The English-language *Jerusalem Post*, for instance, published on April 10, 1970, in its *Week-End Magazine*, an article by editorial writer Lea Ben Dor on "The Great Goldmann Gamble" (pages 1 and 9); and a second, by Mark Segal, entitled "Dr. Goldmann Rides Again" (page 3). It carried additional articles on April 30 and May 1. All these articles were either anti-Goldmann or reserved judgment. In between, of course, the day-to-day developments of the affair were reported in detail.[51]

Even before the storm broke over Goldmann's plan to meet Nasser, public opinion in Israel became preoccupied with Goldmann's critical views of Israel and his proposal of Israel's neutralization that appeared in the April 1970 issue of *Foreign Affairs* (see above) and in a series of articles he wrote for the leading Israeli daily, *HaAretz* (published in the April 2, 3, 5, 6, 8, and 9 issues). In these articles, Goldmann presents largely the same argument as in his *Foreign Affairs* essay except that they contain more of an effort to justify his views. In the first *HaAretz* article, entitled "The Foreign Policy of Israel: Nahum Goldmann Breaks His Silence," he says that he knows that most Israelis are opposed to what he will say in these articles, but he reminds his readers that

> with reference to two basic problems in Zionist policy in the last 25 years— the idea of the partition of Palestine and the proposal to embark on negotiations with Germany about reparations—I am sure that, had a public opinion poll been taken, the majority of Zionists both in Israel and in the Diaspora would have taken a negative position. At the time the opposition to these two plans was not only strong but even violent, and included personal attacks, and in the course of the negotiations with Germany there were threats of assassination against me. I permit myself to assume that most of those who opposed my position on those two issues, if they would be asked today, would admit their error. They would recognize that it would have been a catastrophic mistake for the Zionist movement not to propose and accept the partition of Palestine, and for the Jewish people not to reach a reparations agreement with Germany. These considerations encourage me to believe that despite the negation of my present position by the majority, it is possible that I am not entirely mistaken.

XIX Although he had fought long and hard for the acceptance of his plan to meet Nasser, Goldmann bowed to the will of the government of Israel, a decision he later could never forgive himself. In 1980, long after having retired from his position of Jewish and Zionist leadership, he told me that he planned to include a chapter in his memoirs on "Narrischkei-ten die ich gemacht habe" (Foolishnesses I Committed), and that this decision would figure prominently in it.

However, having given up on the plan of meeting Nasser at that juncture did not mean that Goldmann ceased working for Arab-Israeli peace. He met with Palestinian Arab notables in Jerusalem, which brought him yet another disappointment. What he heard from the moderates among the Arab leaders was that the solution of the Palestine problem lay not in the withdrawal of Israel from all the territories she occupied in the 1967 war, but in the adoption of the original 1947 partition plan of the United Nations, that is, in giving up all the areas Israel had taken and annexed after the War of Liberation of 1948. Moreover, they also demanded the readmission of the Arab refugees.[52]

A third disappointment for Goldmann was that between early and late April 1970 the measure of popular support his plan of meeting Nasser had enjoyed initially, rapidly eroded. Public opinion took a sharp turn against him. This was forcefully brought home to him on April 29, when he was scheduled to address students at the Hebrew University, in Jerusalem. For more than half an hour, the crowd prevented him from speaking, and then, because of constant heckling, he could speak for only fifteen minutes and was forced to leave the stage abruptly. It is puzzling, however, to note that though the *Jerusalem Post* campus reporter saw and reported nothing but violent anger at Goldmann on the part of the students, one of those present, in a letter to the editor, criticized the reporter's account as inaccurate and said that Goldmann received "a tremendous applause" from the 2,000 students present.[53] A few days later, the *Jerusalem Post* again reported that Goldmann was "booed off the stage" at Bar Ilan University, in Ramat Gan.[54]

On April 29 Goldmann was invited by the Executive of the World Zionist Organization, which he had headed for more than a decade, to discuss his *Foreign Affairs* article. He tried to explain what his purpose was in publishing the article, stressing that he proposed the neutralization of Israel, but by no means the loss of its sovereignty. All the members of the Executive—chairman Arye Pincus, Arye Dulzin, Mordekhai Bar-On, Mordekhai Kirshblum, Israel Goldstein, and Avraham Schenker—condemned the article with varying degrees of severity. At the end of the four-hour session, the Executive unanimously adopted a resolution expressing "strong reservatior.s" over the article, which, it held, damaged the Zionist cause.[55]

XX Of the dozens of articles that appeared in various Israeli papers condemning Goldmann's plan for the neutralization of Israel, only two will be discussed here: one vituperative, the other objectively critical.

The first, written by the well-known Israeli journalist Y'sha'yahu Ben-Porat, appeared in the *Y'di 'ot Aharonot* of April 10, 1970. Ben-Porat takes Goldmann to task for his "devastating criticism of Israel's unrestrained use of wrong and violent means," for his opinion that the majority of the Jewish people will remain in the Diaspora, and for his view that therefore Israel must become a spiritual center of the Jewish people, and that in every generation the Jewish people had two poles: Israel and the Diaspora. Ben-Porat waxes personally abusive when he says: "For a whole lifetime, Goldmann has followed around the great ones of the world like a shadow; he pushed himself under the protection of foreigners; he has demonstratively disparaged that which 'the Jews do' and admired openly that which 'the Gentiles say.' All this is not connected only with his inclination—so natural and so Jewish in its clearly Exilic meaning—to roam and wander all over the earth and to knock on the doors of the potentates; all this derives from his deep consciousness and reasoned endeavor to endow the Diaspora as it is with a status equal to that of the Jewish State. Ever since the establishment of the state, Goldmann's way has been strewn full of his untiring efforts to secure for world Jewry the right of influencing and deciding the future of the State and its fate, and to justify the continued existence of the Diaspora side by side with Israel."

Next Ben-Porat expresses the suspicion that, possibly, in Goldmann's view, the true substance of the Jewish people is the Diaspora, while the Jewish State is but an almost chance phenomenon, perhaps even a passing one. Ben-Porat further suspects that Goldmann published his article in *Foreign Affairs* in order to serve him as a "visiting card" when he goes to knock on the door of Nasser in Egypt, and that his intention in having a series of articles published in the Israeli daily *HaAretz* at the very time when Ben-Porat's article appeared in *Y'di 'ot Aharonot* was to "punish" the Israeli government for not allowing him to go with its blessing to Egypt.

Ben-Porat's strongest criticism is directed toward Goldmann's idea of a neutralized Israel: "With his eyes directed, as is his wont, in the first place toward the Diaspora, Goldmann warns against the danger of a rift between the Diaspora and Israel which arises from the fact that Israel follows a policy which is liable to be in contradiction to the policy of the countries in which Jews live. Therefore, Israel must be given a character such as to preclude the danger of dual loyalty which hovers over the Jews of the world."

Then, after quoting reproachfully Goldmann's "second conclusion which fits like a glove over his first one"—namely his idea of a neutralized Israel recognized and guaranteed by all the nations of the world, Ben-Porat concludes:

> The matter would be tragic, were it not so very ridiculous. After seventy years of political Zionism, whose aim was to lead the Jews out of the ghetto and to put an end to their debased status among the nations, there arises a Zionist political leader, a heretic supreme, who turns his back on the State, and advises, not us but the world at large, turning to "the Arabs' generosity of heart," to erect in the Land of Israel a new Jewish ghetto whose existence would be assured by the goodwill of the Gentiles. This man of the demeaned Exile has not learned, in fifty years of holding high office, to straighten his back; he was a man of the exile, and a man of the exile he has remained. Perhaps this is why he is a welcome guest in Cairo.
>
> But, truly tragic, and definitely not ridiculous, is the fact that the government of Israel was caught in the trap, and got shamefacedly entangled, in full sight of the world. It should have said to Nasser: "You want Goldmann? Take him. He is yours. But know and remember: His way is not the way of the State of Israel."

(Within eight years, Ben-Porat changed his opinion of Goldmann's policies. This, at least, is the conclusion one reaches upon reading the long series of Ben-Porat's interviews that were published in the July 7, 14, 21, and 28, 1978 issues of the Sabbath supplement of *Y'di'ot Aḥaronot*, which contain not a single word critical of either Goldmann the man or his work. In the introduction to the first interview, Ben-Porat says of the eighty-three-year-old Goldmann:

> Despite his age, Goldmann remains clear-headed, sharp-witted, many-sided, and a charming conversationalist, as he always has been. . . . Although he has withdrawn in the last few years from his former tasks in the Jewish people and in the Zionist movement, he still travels a lot, in connection with meetings with statesmen, or talks and lectures all over the world. As before, Nahum Goldmann continues to personify the image of the wandering Jew in the world. . . . The series of talks published here are not a testimony to the identification of the interviewer with the words of the interviewee. But they definitely testify to the great interest the interviewer found in them, and to the importance he ascribes to them and to the recollections and views of the man who served, only a short time ago, as president of the Zionist movement and as president of the World Jewish Congress.

Reading these lines one wonders that they were written by the same man who only eight years earlier had published an abusive personal attack on Goldmann. One also questions why Goldmann, who must have been aware of Ben-Porat's 1970 article, could agree to be interviewed by him in 1978.)

The second, objectively critical article dealing with Goldmann's essay in *Foreign Affairs* was written by Mordekhai Bar-On and published first in Hebrew in the May 1 and 3 issues of the Tel Aviv daily *Maʿariv*, and subsequently, in an English translation, in *The Jewish Frontier*, of New York (July–August 1970, pp. 12, 15–23). Bar-On, formerly chief education officer of the Israeli Army, was at the time a member of the Jewish Agency Executive and head of its Youth and Halutz Department. The arguments he marshals against Goldmann's neutralization plan are, basically, that the consequences of Goldmann's intention—sincere in themselves—are dangerous; that the demand for a neutralized Israel should be addressed, not to Israel, but to the world because the international orientation of Israel was, to begin with, essentially neutral, and it was the Arabs' intransigence that forced the country to change her stance; and that Goldmann's gloomy analysis and inventory of Israel's shortcomings will bolster the charges of Israel's enemies. The neutralization of Israel can only be regarded by the Arabs as a futile idea to which they will never agree, and the "article will encourage them to intensify the violence of their efforts to speed the anticipated collapse of Israel." Bar-On concludes by saying that the article was "indiscreet, published in an inappropriate organ."

The most unpleasant, indeed painful, aspect of the whole affair from Goldmann's personal point of view was represented by the aspersions several individuals in the Israeli government and press cast on the veracity, or at least the accuracy, of his statements. Minister Without Portfolio Arye Dulzin, at the cabinet meeting discussed earlier, stated that whenever two people talk to Goldmann at one and the same time about a political matter they never hear from him the same story, and when one person talks to him about the same issue twice at long intervals, he always hears two different versions. "I don't believe," said Dulzin, "that there is any substance in this whole thing. Simply, Goldmann has no invitation."[56]

An article in the Tuesday, April 7, issue of *Maʿariv* stated that Foreign Minister Abba Eban argued at the cabinet meeting on the same day that "there is no smell of invitation at all" of Goldmann by Nasser, that he was convinced that Goldmann did not speak with any person authorized by Nasser, and that all this drama involved "an irresponsible exaggeration." The headline stated that contradictions between the stories told by Goldmann to various ministers of state aroused many doubts in the government, that Mrs. Meir threatened to publish the minutes of the talks between her and Goldmann, and that the opinion had crystallized in Jerusalem that Goldmann inflated in an irresponsible manner the contacts he had with unauthorized persons and retracted several details of his stories. The Paris correspondent of *Ma'ariv* wrote in the same issue that most of the people with whom he spoke agreed that the whole affair was exaggerated and inflated, and that one French commentator even said that "Goldmann saw the thoughts of his heart, and turned that which was desirable in his eyes into reality." An editorial comment in the same issue of *Ma'ariv* remarks sarcastically, "Dr. Goldmann got maximum satisfaction. He again is up in the main headlines, gives interviews, scatters about ideas, and has again raised himself, so to speak, to the number one level of Israeli-Diaspora politicians and statesmen—and all this on the basis of a 'duck' *(canard)* which has no legs."

XXI   In the midst of these and similar accusations, not much attention was paid to those reports, articles, and news stories that constituted independent external confirmation of Goldmann's ongoing, albeit indirect, contacts with Nasser that were effected through intermediaries. Thus, one of the several articles about the Goldmann Affair printed in the April 7, 1970, issue of *Ma'ariv* was a news story cabled by Gil Kesari, the paper's Paris correspondent, which asserted that Moscow supported Goldmann's efforts to meet with Nasser. More than a year earlier, Kesari learned in Paris, Goldmann had met Anatoly Dobrynin, the Russian ambassador, in Washington. Dobrynin on that occasion had encouraged him to meet with Nasser and even promised him that the Russians would persuade the Egyptians and obtain their consent to such a meeting. On his way from America to Israel, Goldmann stopped in Paris and enthusiastically described his contact with Dobrynin.

A small item in *HaAretz* of April 8, 1970, reported that, when the Italian press published articles on the refusal of the Israeli government to let Goldmann travel to Egypt, the former mayor of Florence stated that in his talks with Nasser and other Egyptian leaders in 1968 he gained the impression that Nasser valued Goldmann and that he enjoyed a good reputation in Egypt.

More important than these brief items was Eric Rouleau's account, published in the April 8, 1970, issue of the Paris daily *Le Monde.* The first-page article stated that "the possibility of a meeting between Nasser and Goldmann was probably examined in the course of talks which the chief of the United Arab Republic had with Marshal Tito on February 23 and 24 [1970] in Aswan, Upper Egypt." The journalist went on to say that Tito, as well as other foreign personalities, had attempted in years past to bring about such a meeting, but without success. The *Rais* ("Chief")— as Rouleau, following the Egyptians' own usage, refers to Nasser— "who, it is said, appreciates as much as does Marshal Tito the realism and conciliatory spirit of Dr. Goldmann" had reasons to be distrustful because of his experiences in connection with the 1956 attempt to bring about a meeting between him and Goldmann (see above).

Especially after the Six-Day War of 1967, Nasser became convinced that Israel was dominated by "militarists whose basic objective was the annexation of Arab territories by force." Nevertheless, Nasser "was favorably impressed" by the declaration of Prime Minister Meir, reported in the London *Times* of February 18, 1970, to the effect that she "would risk breaking up her government of national unity" if she could be convinced that an Arab country was seriously interested in peace, and five days later "if our information is correct, Nasser let Marshal Tito know that he had no objection to meeting the president of the World Jewish Congress."

Nasser, Rouleau reports, laid down three conditions for the meeting, "in order to avoid the traps into which he feared he could fall. They were: 1) Dr. Goldmann's visit would be public; 2) his guest would have to obtain the authorization of his government to undertake the trip; 3) the president of the World Jewish Congress would express his 'personal views' concerning the means of establishing a 'durable peace' in the Middle East." This formula, says Rouleau, had the merit of not embarrassing any of the parties concerned. Mrs. Meir would not have "to break up her government" prematurely because Goldmann would not be empowered to negotiate or to take soundings in its name. She would have time to learn the results of the Cairo talks before deciding whether they were useful to constitute a basis for "a homogeneous team of 'doves.'" "President Nasser on his part would assert—and rightly so—that he did not violate the resolutions adopted in Khartoum in September 1967 by the Arab heads of state which prohibited direct negotiations with the occupying power (i.e., Israel). The conversations with 'the Jewish pope'—even though he had Israeli nationality—would not have any official character."

Rouleau sees in these three conditions an attempt on Nasser's part to "maneuver the 'hawks,' " who could leak information to the press that would be dangerous, or, at least, embarrassing both to Goldmann and to himself: Goldmann could be publicly disavowed by his government, and Nasser could be suspected of having sought a separate peace with Israel and could appear as the protagonist of a sinister conspiracy against the Palestinians and the other Arab states at war with Israel. Should the leak occur before Nasser had a chance to prepare Arab opinion for the meeting, he could maintain, without uttering a nontruth, that he had not issued an invitation to Goldmann. And this, of course, is precisely what occurred after the Israeli government made public Goldmann's inquiry. "By refusing an illustrious Israeli personality authorization to go to Cairo—which would have been an unprecedented event in the annals of the Israeli-Arab conflict—the government of Mrs. Meir supplied President Nasser with a weighty argument" for his contention that Israel prefers territories to peace.

Rouleau concludes his analysis of the Goldmann Affair by expressing his regret that "this episode has eliminated for a long time all possibility of reaching an amicable arrangement. But is not this precisely the objective of the 'hawks' in both camps?"[57]

XXII   In May 1970 Goldmann flew from Israel to America, and on the 31st he was interviewed on the Meet the Press program of NBC in New York. In reply to a question, he stated that he wrote his *Foreign Affairs* article two and a half years earlier (that is, in December 1967, shortly after the Six-Day War, in which Israel conquered Sinai, the West Bank, and the Golan Heights). He stressed that "first of all Israel has to see to it that it remains strong." He reminded his questioners that he had been advocating the neutralization idea for ten or twelve years, and stated that Ben-Gurion, who had been against it, was now for it because, as long as Russia was not a coguarantor of a final settlement of the Israeli-Arab problem, the Arabs would always hope to be helped by the Soviet Union to destroy Israel. And he said, "As long as there is no real peace . . . Israel cannot concentrate on becoming [not only] a sovereign state absorbing Jews who want to go there [but also] the great spiritual and moral center of the Jewish people, [and cannot] continue the great tradition of Jewish civilization."[58]

A few months later, early in September 1970, Aḥmed Hamrush

brought a new message to Goldmann. President Nasser, said Hamrush, had decided to invite Goldmann in his capacity of president of the World Jewish Congress. The subject of their talk will be only the relations of the Jews and Arabs in the world. This was in part Nasser's response to what he felt was the danger that the Arab-Jewish conflict would spread outside Israel, which he wanted to avoid. The program of Goldmann's visit was outlined by Hamrush. In addition to the meeting with the Egyptian president, Nasser and Goldmann together would appear at a synagogue service in Cairo, and in all probability a joint press conference would also be conducted.

Goldmann's response to this invitation was emphatically positive. At long last, a meeting with Nasser, offering so many possibilities of positive results, was about to be realized. However, he had to tell Colonel Hamrush that, before he could give his official reply, he would need to consult the Executive of the World Jewish Congress. Because its members were scattered all over the world, about a month would be required to convene them. Hamrush duly reported this back to Nasser. Three weeks later, on September 28, 1970, Nasser died of a heart attack.

Ten years later (on January 20, 1980), in recounting these events, Goldmann told me: "I am sure that if Nasser had lived, we would have had peace long ago. He had come to the conclusion that war did not pay, that its price was too high, and that it prevented the development of Egypt. He wanted peace, and, since he had more authority than Sadat, he could have made peace between Israel and all the Arab states."

Nasser's death did not put an end to Goldmann's attempts to seek a way to an understanding between Israel and the Arabs, nor did any of the subsequent military and political developments between Israel and the Arabs induce him to give up or modify his plan for a neutralized Israel, which he had advocated so vigorously in his 1969 *Autobiography.*[59]

Barely four months after Nasser's death, Goldmann again met Tito in Brioni (in January 1971), and discussed with him the problem of Arab-Israeli understanding. On that occasion, at the request of Armand Kaplan, who accompanied Goldmann on that visit, Tito told them the whole story of the invitation Nasser had extended to Goldmann via the Yugoslav ambassador in Cairo, Tito, and the Yugoslav ambassador in Paris.[60]

The next year, in an address at the opening of Brotherhood Week in Münster, on "The Jews and the Nations," Goldmann again expounded the idea. Israel, he said, must be more than a Jewish State, it must be a spiritual center for world Jewry. And, he continued,

In order to make it possible for the Jews of the world to have solidarity with Israel, not as citizens, but religiously, culturally, and economically, Israel must try to keep apart from the power struggle and traffic of the world. Once I suggested to consider that Israel should be the neutral country of the world. My proposition was at the time premature and was often misunderstood. If Switzerland or Austria have a claim to neutrality, Israel has an incomparably greater claim to it, because the majority of neither the Swiss nor the Austrians lives outside their countries. This idea sounds somewhat Utopian; as long as Israel has no peace, some states support Israel, others the Arabs. But once there will be peace—I belong to the optimists and believe that it will come in the near future—Israel must begin to conduct a policy which will place it outside the power play of the states of the world. It must be made possible for every Jew, whether he lives under a democratic government, in a Communist, or a fascist regime, to have solidarity with Israel, in order to safeguard the future of Israel and of the Jewish community in the Diaspora.

Then Goldmann went on to explain that it was the moral duty of the nations of the world to understand the Jewish solidarity with Israel, and that all the nations, including the Arabs, must guarantee the existence of Israel.[61]

XXIII A short time after President Sadat's historic visit to Jerusalem and address to the Knesset, Goldmann gave an interview in Paris to two staff members of the semiofficial Cairo daily *Al-Ahrām,* Makram Muḥammad Aḥmad and ʿAisha ʿAbdel Ghaffar. The interview was published in two installments, in the May 26 and 27, 1978, issues. The headline of the first installment, spreading across five columns, reads: "Goldmann: The Last of 'the Wise Men of Zion,' in an Interview with Al-Ahrām." This is followed by five lines of subheads that spell out the key points of the interview:

"Israel Will Adapt Herself to the New Conditions, Whether With the Presence of Begin Or Without It."
"I Do Not Expect a Coup, But I Do Expect Early Elections."
"The Choice Israel Faces Now Is Between Peace Within Two Years Or a New War."

Lower down on the page, under a picture of Goldmann, appears yet another headline: "What Did I Say to al-Sadat At Our Meeting in Paris?"

The second part of the interview carries the same main heading as the first one, followed by four lines of subheads:

> "Why Did [Mrs. Golda] Meir Prevent Me From Meeting ʿAbd al-Nāṣir Following an Egyptian Offer?"
> "Nobody in Israel Believes in the Existence of a Split in the American-Israeli Relations Because of the Eyes of Begin."

Lower down, under yet another photograph of Goldmann, several more headlines read:

> "What the Arabs Are Saying About the Necessity of Having a Balance of Arms Is Something Necessary for Peace."
> "It is Inevitable that Arab Jerusalem Should Have Her Special Passport and that Her Status Should Be Like That of the Vatican in Rome."

During the course of the interview, Goldmann is quoted as saying:

> Ever since the beginning I have been convinced that the future of Israel and her security depended, above all, on her ability to reach a true understanding with the Arabs so as to become an accepted member in the community of the Middle Eastern states.
> I have never disregarded this truth, (nor) been assailed by any doubt as to its reality which I have recognized for a long time. When the Balfour Declaration was issued I was but eighteen years old[62] and lived in Germany. The enthusiasm of the Jews was enormous everywhere on account of this declaration issued by the British Empire, which recognized the right of the Jews to have a national homeland in the land of Palestine. But I knew that everything would depend on the acceptance by the Arabs of a Jewish state, and I asked, "What will be the reaction of the Arabs?" And they [the Zionist leaders] answered: "The Arabs? They are, until now, nothing more than groups of dispersed Bedouins. . . . You could think of asking Egypt, the only historical entity in the region, but Egypt is under British rule and there is nothing there to cause excitement."

Then the article quotes Goldmann as stating that "we have not invested the necessary energy into initiating a dialogue with the Arabs and to reach jointly a basis of common existence." As for Sadat's peace initiative, it elicited Goldmann's total approval:

> When I met al-Sadat in Paris, only four months ago, I told him: "Had you asked me before the initiative whether you should go to Jerusalem, I

would have answered, 'Immediately!' Going to Jerusalem will mean breaking through the barriers of all the psychological factors which block the solution. But you must not expect great and quick results. The question is encumbered with a huge heritage which weighs down this generation of Israeli leaders. The manifestations of intolerance which the Jews suffered in the Christian West, and above all in Germany, constitute a major element in the psychology of this generation, and therefore the issue requires much patience."

During the course of the interview, Goldmann outlined his views on the crucial question of Israel's security:

The security of Israel depends, above all, on an Israeli-Arab understanding, consolidated by international guarantees. But Begin has no confidence in guarantees. I admit that I find no logic in his attitude. All the peoples of the world live at present in a framework of guarantees. The Germans are happy under an American security guarantee, and all Europe is based on American guarantees. What would be wrong if Israel would enjoy security guarantees from the super-powers? They go about in Israel crying, "The old man [Goldmann] has forgotten what happened in Germany . . . all the guarantees could not save the Jews there." But I answer in advance, "The Arabs and the Jews are of one Semitic family, and despite all our fears, security is a relative thing, and the initiative of Sadat and the response by the Egyptian street are a fine confirmation of the good intentions."

About the PLO Goldmann had this to say:

There is a Palestinian people. It is one of the most intelligent Arab peoples. The number of intellectuals among them probably surpasses that of any other Arab country. It is the right of the Palestinians to decide for themselves what they want. If they consider the P. L. O. their sole representative, Israel must accept a dialogue with the P. L. O. If they want a Palestinian state, there must be no impediment to the establishment of such a state. Such a state could be politically tied to Jordan, and it is possible that in the framework of peace and of new relationships it will have economic ties with Israel. It also could be completely independent; it is up to the Palestinians to decide these things for themselves.

Finally, about the future of Israel, Goldmann said, "King Hassan [of Morocco] told me a few months ago: 'At times I have doubts whether the super-powers want an Arab-Israeli understanding, since, if such an understanding should come about and the enormous capital outlays on armaments—they surpass 30 percent of the total national income of the region—would be devoted entirely to construction, the face of the Middle East would change within two generations, and the Arabs and the Jews together would become, thanks to experience, money, and the power of labor, the true point of liaison between the north and the south, the east and the west.' "

Although this interview did not reveal new elements in Goldmann's thinking about the relationship between Israel and the Arabs and about the future of Israel, the very fact that it was published in *Al-Ahrām,* the most prestigious daily in the entire Arab world, endowed it with special significance because it presented to the Egyptian and Arab readership directly and for the first time the views and ideas of a foremost Jewish leader, who was billed as "the last of the wise men of Zion."

XXIV In the summer of 1979, yet another article by Goldmann, on the neutralization of Israel, was published, this time in the influential Paris monthly *Le Monde Diplomatique.* In this article, in addition to restating his arguments for a neutralized Israel, he presents, for the first time, something like a prescription for the manner in which it could be carried out. A precondition for achieving an understanding with the Arabs, he writes, is a united Arab world: "I have always maintained that, if it is necessary to make war, a division in the Arab world is good for Israel. But if, on the contrary, one wants to achieve peace, such a division is disastrous, because only a united Arab world will have the courage and the authority to accept Israel as a full partner in the Near East."

As early as in the immediate post-World War II years, when the discussion about the establishment of a Jewish State took place, Goldmann writes,

> I dreamt of a neutral Jewish State whose existence and frontiers would be guaranteed by the peoples of the whole world, and especially by the superpowers. Not having been sufficiently firm on this issue is one of the mistakes of my political life. . . . [But] I took into account that it would be difficult enough to convince the two parties of the United Nations membership—which comprised the Communist states as well as the democratic countries—to vote for a Jewish State even without asking them in addition to guarantee its existence and neutrality. . . . At the time I thought that perhaps it would be possible to reach a formula of compromise, e.g., that Israel could join a Near Eastern Confederation. . . .
> To my mind the only efficacious solution will be to start again from the

beginning. I suggest that the United States and the Soviet Union should convoke a Geneva conference with the participation of a maximum of countries, including the greatest possible number of Arab states. The discussion would start out from all the resolutions passed by the U.N. on the subject of the Near East, beginning with that of 1948 which created the Jewish State in Palestine. All the participants will be understood as having accepted these resolutions, that is to say, they will have to be ready to recognize the State of Israel without discussion, but Israel within her pre-1967 borders, perhaps with minor modifications in accordance with resolutions 242 and 338, which can be decided by the conference itself. The recognition of Israel will constitute a *conditio sine qua non* of the participation. The PLO could attend the conference, since, by agreeing to be invited, it would have attested to its will to modify its present charter which demands the liquidation of Israel.

The objective of the conference will be to reach a global regulation in the Near East, guaranteed not only by the U.N.—which would carry the risk of being too weak to be applicable—but, above all, by the two superpowers and by all the other countries willing to participate in it. This guarantee will have to be approved and ratified by the parliaments of the countries concerned, and translated—at least during the first years—into a presence of U.N. forces and other neutral units on the frontiers of Israel. In effect this will signify the permanent neutralization of Israel. In an earlier version of this proposal [in the April 1970 issue of *Foreign Affairs;* see above], I used in part the Swiss precedent, and, in the light of that example, I emphasize that neutralization will not mean the demilitarization of Israel. But it will allow the Israelis to concentrate more fully on questions other than survival and national defense. At the same time, the Arabs will no longer have to fear Israel as a foreign body in this region of the world and an obstacle to their attempt to create a unified Arab bloc. As for the Jews who live outside Israel, and, in particular, the residents of countries in conflict with the Hebrew state, they will be less affected by problems of dual allegiance.

Entirely new in this presentation of Goldmann's neutralization plan is the concept of a similarly guaranteed Palestinian entity:

The same powers which would guarantee Israel, would equally give a guarantee to the existence and the neutrality of a Palestinian entity, whether in relation with Jordan or independently of her, as the interested parties themselves will decide. To the extent to which one can trust any guarantees, this will satisfy the Palestinian claims and will contribute to putting an end to terror, and opening the road to normal and good neighborly relations, which one day can become friendly, between Israel and the Arab states. Also, the neutralization of Israel and the Palestinian entity can ultimately lead to the ambitious project of the elimination of nuclear arms in the whole region.

The violent reactions provoked by this suggestion in certain Israeli circles—which argue that neutralization would be an encroachment upon the sovereignty of Israel and would create a new Jewish ghetto—appear to me unfounded. Neutral Switzerland is certainly not a ghetto; nor can one say that the Federal Republic of Germany is less sovereign because it enjoys the guarantee of the United States and of American troops which are stationed there since the end of World War II.

Goldman concludes his article on a conditionally optimistic note:

> Only a global regulation of the type I am proposing has a chance of bringing about a permanent peace in the Near East. The agreement signed by Begin and Sadat will not be accepted by the Arab states, and Israel will remain a foreign body in this region. A neutral Jewish State, guaranteed by the nations of the world, would not constitute a menace, while the protection of the super-powers would discourage those among the Arabs who dream of destroying Israel.
>
> The cultural and spiritual renaissance which the Zionists have expected in Israel will remain an empty dream unless a true peace is established between Israel and the Arabs. Such an authentic peace can be obtained only by extraordinary means. After thirty years of unfruitful attempts by traditional diplomatic methods, my proposal seems to offer the best possible solution.[63]

XXV   The most complete summary of his views about the neutralization of Israel was given by Goldmann in an article published in the winter 1979–80 issue of the Washington journal *Foreign Policy*. In it he embraces the idea of Aḥad Haʿam that only a spiritual center in a Jewish State could insure Jewish survival and asserts that "a Jewish state that is like all other states is . . . a fundamental distortion of the unique character of the Jewish people in which religion, race, and nation are combined." Bemoaning the lack of progress toward a settlement between Israel and the Arab world, which he deems the overriding problem of Israel's future, and which he attributes mainly to the failure to include the PLO in the negotiations about the crucial issue of Palestinian autonomy, he goes back to his oft-reiterated plan that the existence and security of Israel should be "guaranteed by the two superpowers joined by as many other states as possible" and expresses his conviction that "Israel must be neutral, intervening in controversial issues only when the defense of the Jewish population in any given country requires it." Once a peace treaty is signed, Israel should return, with some modifications, to its pre-1967 borders. Thereafter, "for a number of years it would be necessary to station foreign soldiers around Israel's borders to protect its existence," but these troops could be removed "once the Arab world no longer considered the Jewish state a stranger in its midst, and established relations with it, including trade ties, cultural exchange, and freedom of movement."

The neutralizaton of Israel, as Goldmann envisages it, would not require an end to Jewish immigration. The fundamental principle of Zionism—to create a homeland for those Jews who wish to live a full Jewish life in Israel—can never be abandoned. But the cooperation between Israel and the Arab states would be highly beneficial for all of them, while a neutral Israel would refrain from interfering in international politics and could maintain friendlier and more stable relations with both world Jewry and the Arab countries. A neutralized Israel would make it possible for Jews living under any political regime, whether democratic or communist, to express their political, moral, and sentimental support for Israel. Moreover, a neutralized Israel, abstaining from world political issues, would be acceptable to the Arabs because she would not interfere with the political ambitions of the Islamic states from Morocco to Pakistan. And, as for the Palestinians, who are afraid of Israel's present military superiority, they would favor international military guarantees that would effectively remove this fear, just as these guarantees would eliminate Israel's fear of Arab aggression against her.

Having thus explained the advantages of the neutralization of Israel, Goldmann cautiously refers back to his old and long-abandoned idea of a Near Eastern Confederation: "Should a federation develop between a Palestinian entity and Jordan, or even at a later stage, among the Palestinian entity, Jordan, and Israel, the international guarantees envisaged for Israel could be expanded to apply to the whole area." What Goldmann suggests here is a combination of his two successive plans for the solution of the Arab-Israeli problem: a confederation of Arab states and Israel; and the neutralization of Israel, including international guarantees for her security and the security of the Arab member states of the confederation.[64]

The last formulation of Goldmann's plan for a neutralized Israel is an article published in July 1980 in the influential German paper *Die Zeit* under the title "Aus Sorge für Israel: Plädoyer für einen neutralisierten Staat der Juden" (Out of Concern for Israel: a Plea for a Neutralized State of the Jews). In this article, after a critical review of Israel's foreign policy, which he terms "arrogant," and a discussion of the Camp David agreement, which he judges to be "hopeless," he raises the "very painful and dismaying question" of "whether the realization of the Zionist idea in the form of present-day Israel was the right one, and whether the state will be able to maintain itself for the duration." At the same time, he emphasizes that he "not only has remained a convinced Zionist but considers the Zionist idea one of the boldest, most creative ideas of our century."

His answer to the question posed is that "the creation of a small, overweening, always more and more unpopular Jewish state as the summit of Jewish history and the solution of the Jewish question appears to me a banalization of the unusual Jewish fate, a desecration of the heroic and tragic character of Jewish history."

"Therefore," Goldmann continues, "I have gradually reached the concept of a totally neutralized Israel, guaranteed by many powers of the world—above all also by the Arabs—prevented formally from mixing into world politics, with one single exception: if it would be a question of rescuing an endangered Jewish minority." If such a neutralization were achieved,

> although a strong Israeli army would be necessary for a period of time all guarantees notwithstanding, neutralization would enable Israel, not only financially but also spiritually and creatively, to concentrate on its proper tasks, namely to be a center of inspiration for the Jewish Diaspora, and a substitute for the role played by religion in past centuries. . . . From a Jewish point-of-view a neutralized, internationally guaranteed Israel would comply with the unique character of the Jewish past. It would enable the Jewish people to create a new spiritual and moral center, a source of new inspiration for the Diaspora, and therewith for the safeguarding of the Jewish future.

Goldmann concludes the article with a brief statement of the benefits that would accrue to the Middle East and the world as a whole from such a neutralized Israel.[65]

Between the time he wrote this article and its publication, Goldmann returned to the subject in an interview I had with him in Paris. "I have always been of the opinion," he said that if Israel will be like any other state, it will not survive. Today I am more convinced of this than ever. Israel must be a neutral state, a truly spiritual home for all Jews, in the form of a so-called sovereign state, but guaranteed by the peoples of the world. I blame myself for not having fought for it more energetically. . . .

I have always felt that Israel should not be a member of the United Nations. You cannot be in the United Nations and abstain from voting all the time. Why did Switzerland not join the United Nations? Israel has a hundred times more reasons than Switzerland not to join. Israel would be much better off outside the United Nations. As it is, when the Security Council passes an unreasonable resolution about Israel, under international rules Israel has to abide by it. If Israel were not a member, it would be an entirely different situation. There would not have been so many anti-Israel resolutions.[66]

XXVI   As in 1970, so in 1980, within a week after the publication of his article in *Die Zeit*, violent attacks on Goldmann were launched in the Israeli press.[67] As a rule, he adhered to the self-imposed principle of not responding to such attacks, but this time he made an exception in connection with an article written by Eliahu Salpeter in *HaAretz*, which was, as Goldmann himself stated, a fair and reasonable expression of disagreement with his concepts and position. Goldmann's response is interesting not because of any new argument for the neutralization of Israel marshaled in it, but because of the politico-philosophical ideas it expresses and the psychological observations it makes.

Goldmann considers it an "illusion" that Israel can continue in her political and military isolation and "resist the whole world." He explains that this illusion "is the result of centuries of Galut [Exile]-psychology, during which the Jews did not fundamentally care what the Goyim [Gentiles] thought." Their conviction that they were the Chosen People endowed them with a feeling of great superiority. They looked down upon their persecutors with contempt. "They could afford to take this attitude in the ghetto, because they lived politically on the fringe of political history, though [they occupied] a central position in the moral, religious, and spiritual history of the world." This is the attitude, Goldmann maintains, of Israel to this day, while at the same time she strives to play a role in international politics. "This combination will not be possible in the long run."

Goldmann next argues that precisely because for two thousand years the Jews lacked any power, that is, no state of their own, today in Israel they overvalue sovereignty and would consider it "a violation of Israel's dignity, self-respect, and pride" if she were "dependent on outside guarantees." In fact, he says, in today's world no state is really and totally independent, and "the whole concept of a sovereign state is past history." Not only the small states but even the superpowers are today not really independent. Since the advent of the atomic bomb, "the concept of an independent state which can, de facto if not de jure, do whatever it wants, is an absurdity which threatens the future of mankind. The time will inevitably have to come when the sovereignty of the modern state will have to be abolished and some international rule imposed, either by an organ of the UN or a world court, limiting the individual states' right to declare war."

The neutralization of Israel, as Goldmann sees it, would set an example for the rest of the world in achieving this goal. Although he does not say so, it can be assumed that he must have had in mind, not only the Hebrew prophets' idea of world peace, but also the precedent set by the Jewish people for an international settlement of claims against a powerful nation—Germany—which agreed to make large financial sacrifices, not because it was compelled to do so by force, but because of its own moral considerations. Israel and the Jews set an example in the Luxembourg Agreement, and, Goldmann seems to feel, they must set an example also with regard to the establishment of a truly neutralized state whose existence, safety, and inviolability are guaranteed by the superpowers as well as by most or all other nations of the world.

Goldmann fully understands that "for a stateless and persecuted people the idea of a sovereign state was psychologically a great attraction, and to have achieved it was a source of pride and happiness. . . . But after more than thirty years of a prosaic existence— not only from the point-of-view of what Israel has become, compared with the vision of its founders, but also from the point-of-view of the world situation—is it really such a [source of] pride to be governing a state today?"

Instead, he stresses, just as the Jews have always been a unique and exceptional people, so Israel should strive to become a unique and exceptional state, a model for the many other small states in the world that cannot survive if they must rely on their own power alone. For an indefinite period of transition, while the effectiveness of great-power guarantees for Israel's security and the Arab states' willingness to coexist with Israel as good neighbors are being tested, Israel must maintain a strong army. Thereafter, the time would come in which, relieved of the

strangulation created by its military budget, Israel could become a syn-
thesis of Herzl's concept of a modern Jewish state and Aḥad Ha'am's
idea of the Jewish spiritual center. All the creative energies, all the
intelligence, talent, and genius of the Jewish people could then come
into full play, and an era of undreamt-of cultural creativity would be
ushered in for the benefit of Israel, the Jews, and the world at large. This
is what Goldmann calls his "wonderful dream of a neutralized Israel as
a unique state in world history."[68]

XXVII In 1970 Goldmann had expressed the belief that, despite the
opposition of most Israelis to his position on the neutralization of the
country, it was yet possible that he was "not entirely mistaken" in
advocating this course. And he reminded his readers that he had not
been mistaken in his stand on the partition of Palestine in 1946 and the
negotiations with Germany in 1951, both of which triggered violent
attacks on him at the time but were subsequently accepted and, in fact,
acclaimed, by the Jewish as well as Israeli leadership and public opinion
alike.

In the case of the Near Eastern Confederation and the neutralization
of Israel, the first signs of a shift toward Goldmann's position became
discernible only in the spring of 1981. On March 26, 1981, Labor party
leader Shimon Peres, who at the time was engaged in a preelection
struggle for the office of prime minister of Israel, announced in a television interview that he had conducted secret talks in Morocco and
London with Arab leaders. These talks, he said, had left him more
optimistic about chances for the acceptance of an Israeli initiative for
economic cooperation in the Middle East. He went on to suggest that
the United States, Egypt, Saudi Arabia, Jordan, and Israel should now
consider the establishment of a regional structure to foster economic
cooperation in the Red Sea area and discuss a number of projects that
could benefit all the participating countries.[69] Talks with Arab leaders, a
plan for economic cooperation between Israel and other Middle Eastern
countries, and the suggestion of the establishment of a regional structure
for such cooperation—all these are pages taken out of Goldmann's book.
Evidently by 1981 the Labor party election strategists not only judged
such a plan to be sound policy, but believed it offered definite election
appeal.

As for Goldmann's idea of Israel's neutralization, which he put forward
as early as in 1947 and for which he was most sharply criticized at that

time as well as in 1970 and most recently in 1980, one of its basic features had, by early 1981, become the policy position of both the Begin government and the opposition Labor party. Goldmann's suggestion was that the safety of Israel's borders should be internationally guaranteed, while the nation should, at the same time, continue to maintain a strong army "for a period of time." As the deadline for Israel's final withdrawal from the Sinai drew near, the government made it clear that it would complete its evacuation of the peninsula only if arrangements were made in time for the border between Israel and Egypt to be supervised either by a United Nations peacekeeping force, or, failing that, by a multinational force in which a United States contingent would be one of the constituent units, and this peacekeeping force could be withdrawn only with the consent of both Egypt and Israel.

Although the insistence on such a multinational frontier force is a far cry from the international guarantee for Israel as a whole envisaged by Goldmann, it is a step in the direction of the very concept of a neutralized Israel, relying, at least partly, on an international force for the safety and inviolability of its borders. When Goldmann advocated such a concept, he suffered abuse and vilification. He was accused of wanting to give up an important facet of Israel's sovereignty: her self-reliance in the defense of her borders and territory. And yet, by 1981 a general consensus, in fact, an insistence, had arisen among both the public and the leadership of Israel that the security of the Sinai border must be assured, not only by the vigilance of Israel's own Defense Army, but also by the presence of a multinational force. In 1981 no protest was raised anywhere in Israel against this multinational "security guarantee" of her southwestern border. Nobody felt that such a peacekeeping force would, in any way, impinge on Israel's sovereignty.

Thus both of these basic ideas of Goldmann, which he had for so long advocated, that of cooperation between Israel and her neighbors and that of an international guarantee for the safety of Israel—which in itself is a step toward neutralization—have begun, hesitantly, it is true, and in a piecemeal fashion, to become the policy of the government of Israel and of the major opposition party. These trends are a vindication of Goldmann's political foresight and statesmanship. It would seem that the editors of *Al-Ahrām* were justified in calling him "the last of the wise men of Zion."

Appendixes

Appendix A
David Ben-Gurion to Nahum Goldmann
(original in Hebrew)[1]

London, July 22, 1937

Dear Goldmann,

Before the receipt of this letter you will certainly have read the telegraphic summary of the debate in the two Houses [of the British Parliament]. We are sending you the Hansard, and you can judge for yourself the nature of the discussion. In contrast to the British press which, almost without exception, received the Peel report with full agreement, and even with enthusiasm—in Parliament the partition plan was received with sharp criticism if not with opposition. The Government's motion was not accepted, although the motion of the Labor Party was also rejected. The Government consented to the compromise motion of Churchill-Lloyd George which contains no explicit undertaking to accept the partition plan, but merely allows the Government to come with this proposal before the Mandate Commission [of the League of Nations].

Herbert Samuel was the only one who proposed an alternative plan—a curtailment of immigration so that the Jews should remain a minority, and Palestine become an Arab state, a member in a wider Arab federation. I don't know whether this speech was given with the consent of Samuel's friends, but it is clear that this is the position of all the Yahudim:[2] Warburg, Waley-Cohen, Magnes, and all the rest of the gang. This proposal had no supporters in Parliament. Archibald Sinclair, who in his speech yesterday praised Samuel's address, expressed to me later his regret that he did not pay full attention to Samuel's words on immigration, and admitted that it was impossible for the Jews to accept this proposal.

But the reaction of the press today to the debate—several papers state expressly that the Government failed, and that the partition proposal has been demolished, and, more than that, the information I have of what goes on inside—arouse great anxiety. In the Cabinet there was, to begin with, not much enthusiasm for the establishment of a Jewish state. The Foreign Office, and, it seems, also the War Office, opposed it—each for its own reasons. The Foreign Office, it seems, fears undesirable entanglements from the existence of a Jewish state and the appearance of a Jewish representative in the League of Nations. The War Office, it seems, is afraid of difficulty in the defense of such a state. In any case, it was only with great difficulty that the Cabinet adopted the proposal of the [Peel] Committee. Now there is great resentment in the Cabinet against Ormsby-Gore for having caused them this trouble. There is an increasing inclination to adopt Samuel's proposal. In the afternoon Melchett met with Ormsby-Gore, and I am sending you here the summary of the talk. Therefore, the situation is difficult.

To this must be added the overt opposition of the Yahudim in America and England (and perhaps also in France) to the establishment of a Jewish State. It is known to us that they don't remain idle. Magnes is about to meet the French Foreign Office—and others undoubtedly are trying to subvert, each in his own place. The position of the Mandate Commission can be decisive, and we must now marshal our acts with great caution.

Brodetzky goes this evening to Brussels to meet Orts.[3] The line we have clarified today and decided to take before the Mandate Commission is:

A. The Commission must energetically reject the "palliatives"—as contravening the Mandate and disregarding the international undertakings given to the Jews. Curtailed immigration will not completely satisfy the Arabs who do not want even the presence of the 400,000 Jews who are in the country, and it endangers the National Home (the example of the Assyrians in Iraq!), and robs the Jewish people of its last refuge.

B. The Commission must protest against the decision of the [British] Government to allocate 8,000 [immigration certificates] for eight months—which contravenes both the Mandate and the Proposals of the Royal [Peel] Commission. For the Commission proposed "High level" [immigration] in case there should be no partition; but stated explicitly that if the Government did not accept the partition plan, the immigration must be according to the absorptive capacity of the country, minus the Arab area. After the Government had accepted the partition plan, there was no basis at all to accept a proposal which presented a contradiction to partition. But quite apart from this—the Government cannot make this change in the Mandate (for this is how the Government itself interpreted the Mandate all these years) without the consent of the League of Nations.

I am speaking at length on this point, although this is actually a temporary thing, because nobody knows how long this temporary situation will last. In the meantime the Yishuv will be destroyed.

C. The Commission should not reject the partition plan in its basis. The Commission is not required at this moment to give its approval to the plan—for the issue must come before the assembly of the League of Nations. But the Commission must discuss—for the time being hypothetically and provisionally—the plan by studying its shortcomings, and comment on certain defects, and ask the British Government whether there should be a discussion of corrections, such as in the section dealing with Jerusalem, an adjustment of the borders in the east and the south, the power station and the settlements in the area between the Jarmuk and the Sea of Galilee and the Jordan, the widening of the corridor and its lengthening until the north of the Dead Sea, the placing of the Negev under British Mandate so that the Jews should settle in all or part of it, the assurance of full and true sovereignty to the Jewish state (the cancellation of the building of an independent Jewish port in Tel Aviv, the cancellation of levying port taxes by England, the cancellation or modification of the annual subsidy to the Arab states, the cancellation or shortening of the time of the "provisional" Mandates over the four cities), the carrying out of the "transfer" (of Arabs), etc. *But under no conditions should the Mandate Commission take a negative stand on the partition plan.* The alternative to partition will undoubtedly be curtailed immigration, and changes to our disadvantage in the Mandate. I am sure that the Jewish people will not forgive us—and even those who pretend to object now to partition—if we should cause the great chance which is being given us to establish a Jewish state to come to naught. It is hard for me to imagine a greater national catastrophe than that. One cannot assume that instead of partition they will give us increased immigration. Throughout the year, since the [Arab] riots [in Palestine] began, not a single British voice was heard for this solution of the Palestine problem, which to our mind is the most just and best solution. And more than that: several Jews of influence, not only Samuel, propose a curtailment of immigration. Warburg is negotiating with a certain Shatra and Tannous[4] (who have no value at all among the Arabs) on a curtailment of immigration and on the imposition of minority [status] on the Jews; Smilansky preaches curtailed immigration; and only a mindless person can imagine that, after all this, the British Government will give us increased immigration and arouse against itself not only all the Arabs of Palestine (for many of the Arabs of Palestine would consent to partition, but not one of them would agree to large immigration which would mean a Jewish state in all of Palestine), but also the entire Arab and Moslem world, a great part of the British public opinion—and also the Jewish.

The choice before us is: *partition—or a Jewish minority in an Arab state.*

And we must act accordingly.

I shall stay here for another few days—early next week I shall go to Paris, and from there to Switzerland.

Best regards, yours

D. Ben-Gurion

Appendix B
Chaim Weizmann to Nahum Goldmann, New York.[5]

New York, 23 June 1943

SUBJECT: POLITICAL OFFICE

Dear Dr. Goldmann,

Before I leave this country I think it may be desirable to clarify a number of points in connection with the establishment of the Political Office in Washington under the direction of the Executive.

1. EXECUTIVE AUTHORITY: While it is desirable and even necessary that the Office work in close cooperation with the existing organs of the movement here, it is essential, in my opinion, in order to avoid complications, that the Office should retain a large degree of autonomy and that at the very onset it should be made clear that its primary authority stems from the Executive in London and Jerusalem, and that it is engaged in carrying out the policies laid down by the Executive.

2. JOINT RESPONSIBILITY: You and Mr. Lipsky should be officially in charge of its activities and a clear *modus operandi* should be worked out between you for a proper division of functions. All documents, announcements, communications between here and London and Jerusalem involving policy, should be signed jointly indicating both for internal and external purposes, joint responsibility.

3. NON-ZIONISTS: I suggest the advisability that the Zionist members of the Executive meet at regularly stated intervals with the American Non-Zionist members of the Executive, for purposes of information and exchange of views.

4. THE PANEL:[6] I sincerely hope that the Panel which has been created by the Emergency Committee to cooperate with the members of the Executive will function properly and effectively serve our needs. I would urge, however, that its personnel should be strengthened and that an effort should be made to draw in Dr. Silver as a member of the Panel.

5. ADVISORY COMMITTEE: An Advisory Political Committee should be established in Washington which should meet regularly. We have discussed the names of the personnel on several occasions and there is therefore no need to enumerate them here.

6. FUNCTIONS: The principal function of the Political Office should be to maintain and develop our contacts with the Administration in Washington and other political groups; to keep in close touch with the British Embassy as well as with the Legations of the various Governments in Exile; to initiate and develop systematic political work in Latin American countries; to strengthen our political propaganda in this country in close cooperation with the Public Relations Department of the Emergency Committee.

7. WEISGAL: As heretofore, Meyer Weisgal will continue in charge of the New York office, correlate the various activities and act as the liaison between the

Political Office and the Emergency Committee. He will attend all meetings of the Executive and the Panel and keep me constantly informed of developments; send regular reports to London and do such other work as may be assigned to him by the Political Office or by the Emergency Committee, if the latter meets with your and Weisgal's approval.

8. OTHER PERSONNEL: As far as possible, the personnel which now constitutes the Office of the President should remain intact and become an integral part of the Political Office whether in New York or in Washington. Their functions are clearly defined and can be further clarified by you. I have made arrangements for Dr. Josef Cohn to give only a small part of his time to Rehovoth; he should devote most of his time to research and gathering of material that may be required in connection with the Political Office. He is well equipped for this kind of work.

9. SURVEY COMMISSION: The work of the Survey Commission and of Mr. Emanuel Neumann should be closely tied up and coordinated with the Political Office. I have initiated other activities here along economic lines and they too should, as far as possible, be tied in with the Political Office so as to avoid overlapping and thus create a more or less systematic form of procedure.

10. BUDGET: The Executive in Jerusalem has been asked for an appropriation of $100,000.00. That appropriation has not yet been made. In the meantime I have asked the Keren Hayesod to continue to pay to the Political Office the $3200.00 monthly for its budgetary needs, in accordance with the cable from the Executive. A careful budget should be prepared and an account should be opened in the name of the Political Office or the Jewish Agency whichever may be desirable from a legal point of view. I would suggest that the new account to be opened be signed by you and Mr. Lipsky and countersigned by Mr. Weisgal as the person in charge of the Office.

11. CONFIDENTIAL REPORTS: I have made arrangements for confidential reports to be sent to me regularly through certain existing channels. Weisgal has been apprised of them.

I am sending an identical copy of this letter to Mr. Lipsky.

> Very cordially yours,
> Chaim Weizmann

Appendix C
Memorandum of Conversation,
by Mr. Evan M. Wilson of the Division
of Near Eastern Affairs[7]

[WASHINGTON,] June 20, 1945.
Participants: Dr. Nahum Goldmann, Chairman of the Administrative Committee
of the World Jewish Congress
Mr. Henderson, NEA

Mr. Merriam, NE
Mr. Wilson, NE

Dr. Goldmann called to pay his respects to Mr. Henderson and to apprise the Department of what he described as the grave crisis confronting the Zionist leadership as a result of the continued failure of the British and American Governments to make known a settlement of the Palestine question. He said that for five years and more, the moderate Zionist leaders, such as Dr. Weizmann, Rabbi Wise, and himself, had been urging their people to follow a policy of moderation and not to expect a solution of the Palestine question along Zionist lines before the end of the war in Europe. This advice to their followers had been based on assurances which the Zionist leaders had received from President Roosevelt, Mr. Churchill, and other statesmen to the effect that if the Zionists would only be patient and do nothing to interfere with the war effort, their aims would eventually be realized. Dr. Goldmann said that the Zionist leadership had succeeded to a notable degree in imposing a policy of restraint upon the Jews of the world. There had been some extremists, of course, notably in Palestine itself, but on the whole the Jews had shown great moderation.

Now, he continued, the mood of the Jewish people was turning to one of desperation. They had seen millions of their fellow Jews ruthlessly murdered, their homes destroyed, and their culture completely stamped out, in certain portions of Europe. These developments had naturally brought sorrow to all Jews but there had always been the hope that once the common Nazi enemy was defeated, the Jews would see their aspirations in Palestine realized. It was only owing to the existence of this feeling of confidence in the future that the Zionist leaders had been able to persuade their people to accept in a disciplined manner the terrible misfortunes which had been visited upon world Jewry in the last few days.

Dr. Goldmann continued that the Jewish people were beginning to ask how long they would need to wait, now that the war with Germany was over. They were only too well aware of the vast problems with which any program of rehabilitating the Jews of Europe must cope. Anti-Semitism had remained as the one substantial legacy of the Nazis on the European scene and those Jews who were left in Europe were facing almost insuperable obstacles. In the Jewish community of Palestine there was a new spirit of determination, a readiness to resort to strong measures if necessary, which was rather disturbing. Anything might happen in a community where 60,000 young men were fully trained and ready to take up arms in defense of their rights. In Palestine, as elsewhere, the Zionist leadership had been strongly criticised for following a policy of "appeasement" instead of insisting on the literal fulfillment of Jewish demands. Dr. Goldmann himself had been branded a Quisling while he was in Palestine last year. So strong was the opposition which was developing, that at any time Dr. Weizmann and the other moderates might be ousted in favor of Rabbi Silver and other advocates of a stronger policy. At least seventy per cent of American

Zionists, including the Mizrachi (the religious Zionists), were backing Rabbi Silver strongly and it was not at all certain that the extremists would not prevail. There was also much talk of bringing the Revisionists back into the World Zionist Organization, as Rabbi Silver desired. This had been considered twice recently as a result of a request by the New Zionists that they be admitted to the American Zionist Emergency Council, but Dr. Goldmann and his group had been successful in maintaining the position that the Revisionists should not be re-admitted unless they would first pledge themselves to maintain the discipline of the Council.

In these circumstances, Dr. Goldmann asked, what can the Zionist leaders say to their people? Dr. Weizmann was not a well man and was anxious to resign his leadership. Dr. Goldmann himself had no personal ambitions, but felt it his duty to try to guide his people. Dr. Weizmann had called a meeting of the Smaller Actions Committee of the World Zionist Organization, which would convene in London late in July after the British elections and which would include representatives from Palestine, Great Britain, the United States, and other countries. This meeting would have to decide the course which the Zionist movement would follow. If there were no indications by then of a favorable solution in Palestine, the present leadership would probably resign in favor of Rabbi Silver and his adherents. Dr. Goldmann said that this would be unfortunate, since it would mean that the control would pass to those not averse to violence. There might even be actual bloodshed in Palestine, as no one knew how much longer the young people could be held back if no support were given to their aims.

Dr. Goldmann continued that recently Dr. Weizmann had sought an interview with Mr. Churchill but the Prime Minister was engrossed in his election preparations, and had instead sent his son, Randolph, to see Dr. Weizmann. Randolph Churchill had been at pains to assure Dr. Weizmann that his father was as much of a Zionist as ever. Without some concrete evidence of official support, however, it was difficult for the leadership to continue playing upon that support. In this country, the Zionists had had an appointment with President Truman last week, but it had been cancelled at the last minute. They hoped to see the President after his return from the Pacific Coast for a detailed discussion of the Palestine question as he had promised them.

Dr. Weizmann [*Goldmann?*] referred to his visit to San Francisco during the Conference and said that he had conferred with a number of delegates there, including some from the Arab countries. He had some long talks with Lord Cranborne which the latter would report to Mr. Churchill. Mr. Jan Masaryk had again given assurances, based on a recent visit to Moscow, that the Soviet Union would favor a Jewish State in Palestine. This was in line with what the Zionists had been told by President Roosevelt on his return from Yalta when he had remarked that, to his surprise, Stalin had not appeared opposed to Zionism.

Mr. Henderson here referred to a recent public address by Professor Korovin in Moscow, who had stated that the Soviet Union was supporting the Arabs in Palestine, and he inquired whether Dr. Goldmann had heard of this. Dr. Goldmann showed considerable interest and agreed that there were conflicting indications as to the position of the Soviets in this matter.

In closing, Dr. Goldmann reverted to the crisis facing the Zionist leadership, and said that he could not stress too much the serious nature of the situation. Mr. Henderson thanked Dr. Goldmann for giving us this full account of the present position and assured him that we would bring his views to Mr. Grew's attention and that they would receive very careful consideration.

Appendix D
Memorandum by the Director of the Office of Near Eastern and African Affairs (Henderson) to the Acting Secretary of State (Grew) and Mr. William Phillips, Special Assistant to the Secretary of State.[8]

[WASHINGTON,] June 22, 1945.

If time permits, I believe that you will wish to glance at the attached . . . report which stresses the extent to which the more extreme elements among the Zionists in this country are gaining ground as against the more moderate leaders such as Rabbi Wise and Dr. Nahum Goldmann.

This report, which is based on information from various Jewish sources, takes the position that since the death of President Roosevelt and the end of the war in Europe, many Jews have become disillusioned regarding the policies of the United States and Great Britain, and this has resulted in a "mood of impatience and desperation". Some observers say that the present situation is driving Jewish youth "into the arms of Moscow," while others predict that there will be serious trouble in Palestine unless some concessions are made to the Jews. There is also stated to be a real possibility that the present Zionist leadership in this country under Rabbi Wise and Dr. Goldmann will be replaced by the more militant elements personified by Rabbi Silver.

While some parts of this report may be exaggerated, we have reason to believe that there is considerable truth in the claim that the extreme Zionists are gaining support among Jews both here and abroad. We have just had a talk with Dr. Goldmann, of which we are sending you a memorandum and which bears this out. If such a development should occur and if, as is also likely, there should be disorders in Palestine as a result of some British decision regarding the future of immigration, we might easily be faced with a very difficult situation.

LOY W. HENDERSON

Appendix E
Memorandum of Conversation, by Mr. Evan M. Wilson of
the Division of Near Eastern Affairs[9]

[WASHINGTON,] June 27, 1945.

Participants: Mr. David Ben Gurion—Jewish Agency
Mr. Eliezer Kaplan—Jewish Agency
Dr. Nahum Goldmann—Jewish Agency
Mr. Henderson—NEA
Mr. Merriam—NE
Mr. Wilson—NE

Dr. Goldmann brought Mr. Ben Gurion and Mr. Kaplan in to meet Mr. Henderson and to discuss the Palestine question. Mr. Ben Gurion outlined the Zionist position at some length, going back to the Balfour Declaration and the White Paper and stressing the opposition of the Jews of Palestine to the present policy of the British Government. He declared that unless "this intolerable regime" were modified, there was bound to be trouble, since in his words the Jews could not continue indefinitely to put up with the breach by the administration of its obligations to the Jewish people. What the Jews desire, he said, was to be allowed to set their own house in order without interference from outside elements. For example, they objected to a situation in which their demands in Palestine, which they regarded as legitimate, could not be met because Lord Killearn in Cairo had to appease some Egyptian pasha. The Jews could not, he asserted, recognize that an Egyptian pasha or a Bedouin shaikh, or an Iraqi bey had any rights or interest in the Palestine question. The Arabs of Palestine were, of course, legitimately interested in that country and there was no intention of disturbing them or calling their rights into question. Jews and Arabs had lived there in amity for many years and there was no reason why they should not continue to do so, provided the Arabs elsewhere left them alone.

Dr. Goldmann and Mr. Kaplan both agreed with Mr. Ben Gurion that the claim of any Arabs outside Palestine to any interest in the problem was preposterous.

Mr. Ben Gurion continued that the Jews for the past few years had received promises from Allied leaders which had caused them to believe that they would eventually see the fruition of their aims in Palestine, if only they kept quiet during the European war. Now that that war was over the Jews were beginning to ask what was holding up the implementation of these pledges. Mr. Ben Gurion said that the world must not underestimate the strength of the Jews' feeling on this point. The Jews had no desire to have any trouble with the British Government and they knew perfectly well that if the worst came to worst, they would not last long against the combined might of the British Empire. They would, however, fight if necessary in defense of their rights and the consequences would be on

Great Britain's head if the Jews were provoked into some action which no one wanted to see. In other words, the Jews were determined to have their demands met and if the British should decide otherwise, the fault would be that of the British Government.

In reply to a question from Mr. Henderson as to whether the Arabs were not likely to make trouble in the event that the British should adopt a pro-Zionist solution in Palestine, Mr. Ben Gurion and his companions expressed complete confidence in their ability to deal with the Arabs. Mr. Ben Gurion said that he knew the Arabs well and that they would not really put up any kind of a fight. The Bedouins of the desert were, of course, good fighters but it was well known that they had no interest in the Palestine problem and so the leaders of the Arab States would not be successful in rallying their people to support of the Arab position on Palestine.

Mr. Henderson asked whether it would be correct to say that the immediate objective of the Zionists was to obtain a lowering of the bars to Jewish immigration into Palestine. Mr. Ben Gurion, seconded by Dr. Goldmann and Mr. Kaplan, said that while it was, of course, imperative to reach a settlement on immigration at the earliest possible moment, they were opposed to any attempt to solve the Palestine problem by piecemeal methods. Their position was well known and they had come to the point where they could no longer accept anything less than the granting of all their demands, including the immediate establishment of a Jewish State.

Mr. Henderson thanked Mr. Ben Gurion and his colleagues for giving us their presentation of their views, which he assured them would be carefully noted by the Department.

Appendix F
Memorandum by Dean Acheson on his
meeting with Nahum Goldmann[10]

August 7, 1946

Dr. Goldmann called at his request. He told me that he had been officially designated by the Jewish Agency to come to the United States from their current meeting to bring to the attention of the American Government, through the State Department the following resolution, adopted at a meeting of the Executive on Monday, August 5, 1946:

"1) The Executive of the Jewish Agency regards the British proposals based in the Report of the Committee of Six and as announced by Mr. Morrison in the House of Commons as unacceptable as a basis of discussion.

"2) The Executive is prepared to discuss a proposal for the establishment of a viable Jewish State in an adequate area of Palestine.

"3) As immediate steps for the implementation of Paragraph 2 the Executive puts forward the following demands:—
   "a) the immediate grant of 100,000 certificates and the immediate beginning of the transportation of the 100,000 to Palestine;
   "b) the grant of immediate full autonomy (in appointing its administration and in the economic field) to that area of Palestine to be designated to become a Jewish State;
   "c) the grant of the right of control of immigration to the administration of that area in Palestine designated to be a Jewish State."

Dr. Goldmann told me that paragraph 1 of the Resolution was adopted unanimously and that the remainder of the Resolution was adopted by a vote of ten to one. He reminded me of his conversation with me before leaving for Europe and told me that what he had then said informally he was now authorized to state to me officially and on the record.

He stated that the Executive and all but two per cent of American Jewry, as shown by the recent elections for the Agency, were firmly and finally of opinion that they could not accept the Grady Report, because it continued the Mandate and they were not willing to accept, save only for a short period of two or three years, further British control of a Jewish area in Palestine. They were also unanimous, except for the same unimportant minority, in favor of partitioning. He said that there had been discussion of including certain proposed boundaries for the Jewish State in the Resolution, but that he had dissuaded them from this, leaving the Resolution in its present flexible condition so that negotiations with the Arabs and the British would be practicable.

He said that their representatives were in constant touch with representatives of the Arab states and that he felt sure that such a proposal would be accepted enthusiastically by Trans-Jordan and would be acceptable to Syria and Lebanon. He was not in a position to speak about the other states, but he thought that the matter could be worked out satisfactorily with them.

On the matter of boundaries he said that he would speak frankly. He said that the Jews would ask for the boundaries as established by the Peel Report, plus the Negeb. They would be willing he thought to work out a compromise in Galilee which would be satisfactory. When I pressed him for the reason for including the Negeb in view of its present condition, he said that this was in very considerable part for its effect on Jewish opinion. In respect of the whole of the original mandated territory, including Trans-Jordan, the Grady recommendation gave the Jews four per cent of the area. The boundaries as suggested by him would give a respectable percentage somewhere between thirty and thirty-five per cent, which he thought was defensible. Furthermore, if the Negeb proved not subject to development, that would be the fault of the Jews and not the British.

He said that one of the worries of the Arabs was that a Jewish State might be used as a spearhead of Western imperialism. The Agency was prepared to propose to the Arabs that this Jewish State would be willing to join a confederation with the Arab states which would place the Jews in a position where they would always be in a minority and could not possibly be a spearhead for external influence. They would be willing to accept whatever restriction the other states in their sovereign capacity imposed on relations with the Jewish State and were convinced of their capacity to work out amicably their common problems.

He said that the Agency recognized the desperate position in which the Jews were now placed. If they insisted on the Hutcheson Report and a unitary Palestine, they would not achieve it. Neither the 100,000 nor any other number of Jews would come into Palestine. This would lead to frustration and disorder and the disintegration of the whole Zionist movement. Its only hope lay in some constructive future. It could not survive if its activities were restricted to those of the extremists in Palestine and to Madison Square Garden meetings in New York. They recognized that the U.S. Government might well become disgusted with the whole matter and wash its hands of the affair. The Jews would thus lose their only support. They were willing to accept finally a greatly reduced Jewish State if that meant that they could immediately turn to the problems of transporting the Jews whose place in Europe was becoming more acute both for them and for us every day and that they could also turn to development in Palestine and away from political agitation.

He hoped that this Government could with great expedition discuss the matter with the British Government and urge it to move swiftly in this direction. This might call for a change in the plans of consultation now being prepared in London. He hoped that the American Government would be willing to go forward with financial assistance. He thought that one of the most useful forms which this could take would be in a willingness to finance any movement which Arabs might wish to make from the Jewish area to the Arab area. He stressed that there would be no compulsion about such a movement and he doubted whether it would achieve any substantial proportions, but the fact that it could take place if so desired would furnish a safety valve and a help in this most difficult situation.

After listening carefully to Dr. Goldmann and clarifying some of the points mentioned above, I said to him that one of the problems which had been created for the American Government was that it was most difficult for it to make any constructive suggestion looking toward legislation or financial aid, because the highly charged atmosphere led those members of Congress who were articulate on the subject to denounce any proposal, and the remainder did not or would not support it.

I asked him what Dr. Silver's attitude would be. He said that he had had a telegram from Dr. Silver endorsing partition on the basis outlined above. He thought that the entire Jewish community in the United States would support it.

He told me that tomorrow he was going to make the same statement to the Secretary of the Treasury and the Secretary of War, and that he also had an appointment for the same purpose with the British Ambassador.

At one point in the conversation he stated that the Grady Report was preferable to the Hutcheson Report because it at least looked toward partition. Its fundamental failure and weakness, as brought out in the debates in Parliament, was that the transition to independence was far too indefinite and prolonged, whereas it must be very speedy indeed. He also again stressed the fact that the area must be more substantial even though a considerable part of it might be of problematical value.

I thanked Dr. Goldmann for this full exposition of the views of the Agency and for his very frank statements. I told him that the matter would receive immediate consideration in the Department.

Dean Acheson

Appendix G
Acting Secretary of State Dean Acheson
to the Ambassador in the
United Kingdom (Averell Harriman)[11]

TOP SECRET   WASHINGTON, August 12, 1946–5 p.m.
US URGENT

5973. Section I. Premature leaks from London re contents recommendations incorporated in Morrison Plan gave groups in this country opposed to plan opportunity mobilize so much public sentiment against it that Cabinet Committee and President felt they could not agree accept recommendations at least until they had studied and discussed them in detail. Alternates of Cabinet Committee, American members of Anglo-American Committee, the Cabinet Committee, other members of Cabinet and various interested persons and groups have participated in the discussions. During discussions, it has become clear that it would be unwise for President to give his formal support to Plan in its present form. President feels that in view opposition to Plan, he would not be able to prevail on Congress to agree to financial contributions for its implementation nor to rally sufficient public support to warrant undertaking by this Govt to give plan in its present form moral backing.

Section II. We have now been informed in confidence by Dr. Goldmann, acting behalf of Jewish Agency that on Aug 5, 1946, Executive of that Agency adopted following resolution:

"1) The Executive of the Jewish Agency regards the Brit proposals based on the Report of the Committee of Six and as announced by Mr. Morrison in the House of Commons as unacceptable as a basis of discussion.

"2) The Executive is prepared to discuss a proposal for the establishment of a viable Jewish State in an adequate area of Palestine.

"3) As immediate steps for the implementation of Paragraph 2 the Executive puts forward the following demands:—

"*a*) the immediate grant of 100,000 certificates and the immediate beginning of the transportation of the 100,000 to Palestine;

"*b*) the grant of immediate full autonomy (in appointing its administration and in the economic field) to that area of Palestine to be designated to become a Jewish State;

"*c*) the grant of the right of control of immigration to the administration of that area in Palestine designated to be a Jewish State."

Section III. In discussing this resolution, Dr. Goldmann has orally stated substantially as follows:

A. Executive and most of American Jewry object to Plan primarily because it calls for indefinite continuance Brit control of Jewish area, provides for boundaries which are unacceptable, does not give sufficient degree self-govt for area allotted to Jews, and does not provide for immediate control by Jews of immigration into Jewish area.

B. Executive would be willing accept plan which:

1. would provide for immediate partitioning of Palestine into three areas: Jewish, Arab and the holy places; the Jewish area roughly to include territory assigned to Jews by Peel Report, plus the Negeb; Arab area to include remainder except holy places. (Executive would be willing, however, to negotiate with regard to Galilee);

2. would provide for termination Mandate so far as Jewish area concerned and for setting up of independent Jewish state within set period of not more than two or three years;

3. would permit Jews to set up their own administration and to enjoy considerable home rule in economic matters pending establishment independent Jewish state;

4. would permit Jews, immediately upon adoption of Plan, have full control immigration into their area.

C. He could guarantee support for such a plan on part of Agency and of majority Jews and friends of Zionism in US.

D. If such a plan were carried out, Executive would be willing consider Brit Govt as ally of Jewish State and would support granting to Great Britain of such military establishments in Jewish State as Great Britain might require.

E. In his opinion, Jewish State would be willing to participate in confederation of Near Eastern states, including Arab states, for purpose cooperation and under such conditions as should remove fear of Arabs that Jewish state might serve as spearhead for introducing external influences into Near East.

F. In his opinion, more moderate Arabs could be induced not to oppose such a plan. If it should be decided add Arab area to Trans-Jordan, support of King Abdullah might be obtained since Trans-Jordan might, with addition of some 800,000 Arabs, become viable state.

G. In his opinion, Jewish State could be set up and recognized as independent by Great Britain without detailed review by United Nations in same manner as Trans-Jordan has been set up; naturally when Jewish State would apply for admission to UN it would be subject to scrutiny given all applicants for admission that organization.

H. Immediately upon reaching decision adopt plan immigration 100,000 Jews should commence.

I. Dr. Weizmann was authorized by Executive discuss plan with Brit Govt and Executive hoped without loss of time two Govts might be willing accept it as basis for coming negotiations Brit with Arabs and Jews and that American Govt would give any solution based on it financial support comparable in extent to that suggested in Morrison plan. It hoped in particular American Govt would find it possible give financial assistance facilitate voluntary migration Arabs from Jewish to Arab area. Jews were prepared give every consideration Arab population and would not bring pressure directly or indirectly upon Arabs to leave Jewish territory.

Section IV. Examination Goldmann plan indicates although Executive states in first paragraph resolution that it rejects Morrison plan as basis for discussion, counter-proposals of Executive as elaborated upon by Goldmann might be regarded as certain alterations and extensions in various provisions Morrison plan rather than outlines of an entirely new plan. Counterproposals, for instance, contemplate short definite rather than indefinite transition period, and extension of authority of local govt during such period. According to Goldmann Jews wish their area during period nominate its own ministers subject approval Mandatory; they desire this area should have authority deal with such matters as imports and exports and borrowing money even though they realize creditors would have to be persons or organizations willing rely upon credit of transitory govt. They also insist area have right fully control its own immigration. Boundaries which they apparently have in mind furthermore are much more liberal to Jews than those defined in Morrison proposals. They admit Negeb might be of problematic value but insist it is of great psychological importance in that it added many square miles Jewish area.

Section V. Brit Govt undoubtedly in better position than we to assess kind of reception which such plan would receive from Arabs. In our view this recent development offers hope that Jewish Agency will realistically join in search for practicable solution. As first step we suggest possibility that Brit Govt might let it be known that coming consultations will not be rigidly bound to consideration one plan and the possibility of early creation of viable state of Jewish portion not precluded. If Brit Govt, following consultations with Arabs and Jews, reaches decision which this Govt feels can obtain general public approval this country even though not satisfactory to extremists, this Govt will give it moral support and endeavor back it up with appropriate financial assistance.

Section VI. You are authorized discuss matter with Attlee, Bevin or Acting

Minister Foreign Affairs. Please impress upon them importance of extreme secrecy.

Sent London 5973 rptd Paris 4037 (Secdel 657) for Secretary Byrnes and Ambassador Harriman.

ACHESON

Appendix H
President Truman to the
British Prime Minister (Attlee)[12]

TOP SECRET   WASHINGTON, August 12, 1946–6 p.m.
US URGENT

I appreciate your courtesy in furnishing me information contained urtel Aug. 9.

After further study of recommendations of American and Brit groups and after detailed discussion in which members my cabinet and other advisers participated, I have reluctantly come to conclusion that I can not give formal support to plan in its present form as a joint Anglo-American plan.

The opposition in this country to the plan has become so intense that it is now clear it would be impossible to rally in favor of it sufficient public opinion enable this Govt to give it effective support.

In view critical situation Palestine and of desperate plight of homeless Jews in Europe I believe search for a solution to this difficult problem should continue. I have therefore instructed our Embassy London discuss with you or with appropriate members of Brit Govt certain suggestions which have been made to us and which, I understand, are also being made to you.

Should it be possible to broaden coming conference sufficiently to consider these suggestions, it is my earnest hope conference may make possible decision by your Govt upon a course for which we can obtain necessary support in this country and in the Congress so we can give effective financial help and moral support.

Appendix I
Memorandum by Joseph Proskauer
to John Slawson[13]

August 16, 1946

1. The absolute objective is the immediate immigration of Jews into Palestine.
2. This is tragically vital. After my talk with Patterson I assert that I am ready to do almost anything to achieve it.

3. One obstacle has always been the intransigence of the Jewish Agency.
4. It now comes with a plan that if successful achieves that objective.
5. It asks only a small state—not a Jewish State in the objectionable sense—but a state with a bill of rights for all—not to be called a Jewish State—but empowered to permit immigration.
6. It yields to the Arabs an attractive state.
7. It yields to Great Britain naval and military bases.
8. This is no ideal plan. It has many holes and weaknesses, but if accepted it realizes the main objective. The future can correct errors.
9. I got undisputable evidence that Inverchapel [the British Ambassador in Washington] approved this plan.
10. I got indubitable evidence that the State Dep[artmen]t would back.
11. I got much less convincingly but none the less substantially evidence that it had the backing of important members of the British Cabinet.
12. I got similar evidence that these pro-Jewish members regarded it as hopeless to get immigration precedent to a general Palestine plan.
13. I got less satisfactory evidence that it could be sold to the Arabs.
14. But above all I found our State Dep[artmen]t absolutely sold on it; determined to work for it and regarding it as the only alternative to chaos.
15. I found our State Dep[artmen]t hopeful—not certain—of being able to put it across.
16. I found their view to be that it was the only hopeful plan they had.
17. I did not commit the A[merican] J[ewish] C[ommittee] to it. I had no authority so to do.
18. I did say personally, as I had to, that if our Government felt as it did, I would stand by reserving freedom of action if they failed.
19. Nobody has any other plan that is immediately practicable.
20. If the British come back as you suggested and want more British control and that is reasonable and not the force of the Grady plan, I am in position to urge acceptance of that on the Jewish Agency if we so determine to do.
21. A week or so will tell the story. I repeat, I'm for almost any thing that will save the holocaust that will result unless we immediately start Jewish immigration into Palestine.
22. If the Jewish Agency [. . .] is willing to make these enormous concessions from its former demands, no Jew should block this earnest attempt based on mutual concessions.

Finally, I never gave more concentrated unselfish thought to any matter. Minutes counted in Washington. I hope to God and believe I used them for the salvation of our people.

Joseph M. Proskauer

Notes

Introduction

1. *Encyclopaedia Judaica* (Jerusalem: Keter Publishing House, 1972), 1:2; 7:723–26; Nahum Goldmann, *Mein Leben als deutscher Jude* (München-Wien: Langen Müller, 1980), p. 13.

2. Raphael Patai, *The Jewish Mind* (New York: Scribner's, 1977).

3. Goldmann, *Mein Leben*, p. 13.

4. In his 1980 German autobiography, Goldmann briefly discusses his participation in the sixteenth Zionist Congress and the founding conference of the Jewish Agency. Cf. *Mein Leben*, pp. 185–87, 195.

Chapter 1

1. Nahum Goldmann, *The Autobiography of Nahum Goldmann: Sixty Years of Jewish Life*, trans. Helen Sebba (New York: Holt, Rinehart, and Winston, 1969), p. vii.

2. Ibid., p. 1.

3. Nahum Goldmann, *The Jewish Paradox*, trans. Steve Cox (New York: Fred Jordan Books/Grosset & Dunlap, 1978), p. 12.

4. Goldmann, *Autobiography*, p. 4.

5. Ibid., pp. 2–3.

6. Ibid., p. 4.

7. Ibid., p. 5.

8. Goldmann, *The Jewish Paradox*, p. 13.

9. Goldmann, *Autobiography*, p. 5.

10. Goldmann, *The Jewish Paradox*, p. 12.

11. Goldmann, *Autobiography*, p. 5.

12. Ibid., pp. 6–7.

13. Ibid., pp. 8–9.
14. Ibid., p. 2; Goldmann, *The Jewish Paradox*, p. 11.
15. Taped interview with Goldmann on March 9, 1980.
16. Goldmann, *Autobiography*, p. 3.
17. Loc. cit.; Goldmann, *The Jewish Paradox*, pp. 11–12.
18. Goldmann, *Autobiography*, p. 4.
19. Goldmann, *The Jewish Paradox*, p. 13.
20. Patai, *The Jewish Mind*, pp. 302 ff.
21. Goldmann, *Autobiography*, p. 4.
22. All the quotes in this paragraph are from ibid., p. 7.
23. Ibid., p. 9.

Chapter 2

1. Goldmann, *Autobiography*, pp. 14–16.
2. Ibid., pp. 10–12.
3. Ibid., p. 11.
4. Goldmann, *The Jewish Paradox*, p. 15.
5. Interview with Goldmann on March 9, 1980.
6. Same interview.
7. Goldmann, *Autobiography*, pp. 11–12; *The Jewish Paradox*, p. 15.
8. Interview with Goldmann on March 9, 1980.
9. Goldmann, *Autobiography*, p. 9.
10. In fact, in his 1980 German autobiography Goldmann tells of several mystical experiences he had. Cf. *Mein Leben*, p. 76.
11. Raphael Patai, *The Hebrew Goddess* (New York: Avon Books, 1978), pp. 74, 169 ff.
12. C. G. Jung, *Psychology and Alchemy*, Bollingen Series XX (Princeton, N.J.: Princeton University Press, 1968), p. 11.
13. Interview with Goldmann on March 9, 1980.
14. Goldmann, *Autobiography*, p. 12.
15. Ibid., p. 12.
16. Interview with Goldmann on March 9, 1980.
17. Same interview.
18. Goldmann, *Autobiography*, p. 20.
19. Interview with Goldmann on March 9, 1980.
20. In his 1980 German autobiography, Goldmann states that he compared Joan of Arc with Kassandra. Cf. *Mein Leben*, p. 47.
21. Goldmann, *Autobiography*, p. 12.
22. Ibid., p. 13.
23. Interview with Goldmann on March 9, 1980.
24. Goldmann, *Autobiography*, p. 13.

25. Cf. photograph in J. Dränger, *Nahum Goldmann* (Frankfurt am Main: Europäische Verlagsanstalt, 1959), 1:184.

26. In his 1980 German autobiography, Goldmann is less restrained and speaks repeatedly of his affairs with women, which began at a rather young age. Cf. *Mein Leben*, pp. 67, 76, 91–92, 128.

27. Goldmann, *Autobiography*, pp. 23–24.

28. Interview on March 9, 1980.

29. Goldmann, *Mein Leben*, p. 67.

30. Goldmann, *Autobiography*, p. 21.

31. Ibid., pp. 23, 33.

32. Dränger, *Nahum Goldmann*, 1:86. At the age of sixteen, Goldmann accompanied his father to the Tenth Zionist Congress, which took place on August 5–11, 1911, in Basle, Switzerland.

33. Interview on March 9, 1980. Cf. Goldmann, *Autobiography*, p. 31.

Chapter 3

1. Taped interview with Goldmann in Paris on June 26, 1980. Cf. *Mein Leben*, p. 70.

2. Goldmann, *Autobiography*, p. 36.

3. Interview with Goldmann on June 26, 1980.

4. Same interview.

5. Goldmann, *Autobiography*, p. 38; *Mein Leben*, p. 79.

6. Goldmann, *Mein Leben*, p. 79.

7. Goldmann, *Autobiography*, pp. 43–44.

8. Goldmann, *Mein Leben*, pp. 88–89.

9. Ibid., pp. 89–90.

10. Ibid., p. 90.

11. Ibid., pp. 90–91.

12. Ibid., p. 91.

13. Nahum Goldmann, *Erez Israel: Reisebriefe aus Palästina* (Frankfurt am Main: J. Kauffmann, 1914), p. 5.

14. Ibid., p. 7.

15. Ibid., p. 18.

16. Goldmann, *Erez Israel*, p. 26.

17. Ibid., p. 26.

18. Ibid., p. 28.

19. Ibid., p. 29.

20. Upon his return from Palestine, Goldmann wrote a feuilleton for the *Frankfurter Zeitung* entitled "Eine Reise nach Jerusalem—bete und bettle" (A Visit to Jerusalem—Pray and Beg), which caused quite a furor.

21. Goldmann, *Erez Israel*, pp. 41 ff.

22. Ibid., pp. 42–43.
23. Ibid., p. 77.
24. Cf. Patai, *The Jewish Mind*, pp. 283, 331 ff.
25. Goldmann, *Erez Israel*, p. 77.
26. Ibid., p. 78.
27. Loc. cit.
28. Ibid., p. 80.
29. Goldmann, *Mein Leben*, pp. 128–29.
30. Ibid., p. 96.

Chapter 4

1. Goldmann, *Autobiography*, p. 48; *Mein Leben*, p. 97.
2. Goldmann, *Autobiography*, pp. 50–51; *Mein Leben*, p. 101.
3. Nahum Goldmann, *Der Geist des Militarismus*, Heft 52 in the pamphlet series *Der deutsche Krieg: Politische Flugschriften*, ed. Ernst Jäckh (Stuttgart-Berlin: Deutsche Verlags-Anstalt, 1915), p. 7. All passages quoted are my translations from the German original.
4. Ibid., pp. 8–12.
5. Ibid., pp. 13–14.
6. Ibid., pp. 16–20.
7. Ibid., p. 20.
8. Ibid., pp. 21–38.
9. Ibid., pp. 38–39.
10. Ibid., pp. 39–40.
11. Ibid., pp. 41–42.
12. Goldmann, *Autobiography*, p. 51; *Mein Leben*, p. 103.
13. Interview with Nahum Goldmann by Y'sha'yahu Ben Porat, in *Y'di 'ot Aharonot*, Tel Aviv, July 21, 1978.
14. Goldmann, *Mein Leben*, pp. 109–10.

Chapter 5

1. Goldmann, *Mein Leben*, p. 35.
2. Goldmann, *Autobiography*, p. 75.
3. Ibid., p. 81.
4. Goldmann, *Mein Leben*, p. 149.
5. Ibid., pp. 35–36.
6. Goldmann, *Autobiography*, p. 77.
7. Ibid., p. 76.
8. Ibid., p. 77.

9. Loc. cit.

10. Loc. cit.

11. Ibid., p. 78.

12. Loc. cit.

13. Loc. cit.

14. Loc. cit.

15. Compare Goldmann, *Mein Leben,* pp. 145–47, with his *Autobiography,* pp. 77–79.

16. Goldmann, *Autobiography,* pp. 78–79.

17. Loc. cit.

18. Ibid., p. 80.

19. Nahum Goldmann, *Die drei Forderungen des jüdischen Volkes* (Berlin: Jüdischer Verlag, 1919). All the following quotations are my translations from the German original.

20. Ibid., pp. 3–4.

21. Ibid., pp. 4–5.

22. Ibid., pp. 8–10, 13.

23. Ibid., pp. 14–16.

24. Ibid., pp. 19–20.

25. Ibid., pp. 20, 22.

Chapter 6

1. *The Complete Diaries of Theodor Herzl,* ed. Raphael Patai, trans. Harry Zohn (New York: Herzl Press and Thomas Yoseloff, 1960), 4:1321.

2. *Encyclopaedia of Zionism and Israel* (hereafter cited as EZI), ed. Raphael Patai (New York: Herzl Press and McGraw-Hill, 1971), 2:1128.

3. *Stenographisches Protokoll der Verhandlungen des XVII. Zionistenkongresses* (London: Zentralbureau der Zionistischen Organisation, 1931), pp. 385–86.

4. *Stenographisches Protokoll der Verhandlungen des XVIII. Zionistenkongresses* (London: Zentralbureau der Zionistischen Organisation und Wien: Fiba Verlag, 1934), pp. 558, 631.

5. *Stenographisches Protokoll der Verhandlungen des XIX. Zionistenkongresses* (Wien: Fiba Verlag, 1937), p. 811.

6. Goldmann, *Autobiography,* p. 179.

7. The B'rit Shalom was to be superseded in 1942 by the *Iḥud* ("Union"), which succeeded in attracting a small number of Arabs, several of whom were murdered within the next few years by Arab extremists. The *Iḥud* was also supported by the heads of the leftist Jewish youth movement HaShomer haTzaʿir, whose representatives cast the only opposing votes at the November 10, 1942, meeting of the Inner Actions Committee in Jerusalem, which, by an overwhelming vote of 21 to 4, endorsed the Biltmore program. HaShomer haTzaʿir called instead for a binational Arab-Jewish state in Palestine.

8. *HaQongres haTziyoni ha᷃Esrim. Din v'Ḥeshbon Stenografi,* The Twentieth Zionist Congress: Stenographic Protocol (Jerusalem: The Zionist Organization, n.d.), p. 180.

9. EZI 1:210.

10. Goldmann, *Autobiography,* pp. 179–80.

11. Ibid., p. 180.

12. Ibid., p. 181.

13. Ibid., p. 180.

14. Ibid., p. 221.

15. Ibid., pp. 202, 201, 221.

16. EZI 1:139, 293.

17. Goldmann, *Autobiography,* p. 223.

18. Eliahu Elath, *HaMa'avaq ᷃al haM'dina* (The Struggle for the State) (Tel Aviv: ᷃Am ᷃Oved, 1979), 1:261.

19. Ibid., 1:263–65.

20. *Foreign Relations of the United States, Diplomatic Papers: The Conference of Berlin (The Potsdam Conference)* (Washington: U.S. Government Printing Office, 1960), 1:974–76.

21. *The Story of the Jewish Agency* (New York: Jewish Agency—American Section, 1964), p. 54; Elath, *HaMa'avaq,* 1:265.

22. Elath, *HaMa'avaq,* 1:265, 276.

23. Ibid., 1:250.

24. Eliahu Elath, *Zionism at the UN: A Diary of the First Days* (Philadelphia: Jewish Publication Society of America, 1976), p. 98. Entry of May 11, 1945.

25. Ibid., pp. 115, 117, 131, 178–79, 188–89. On May 30, 1945, after having been at New York in between, Goldmann and Elath dined with Genevieve Tabouis, the well-known French journalist (p. 221). On June 2 Goldmann had meetings with Peter Frazer, of New Zealand, chairman of the Trusteeship Committee (p. 237).

26. Zvi Ganin, *Truman, American Jews, and Israel, 1945–1948* (New York: Holmes and Meier, 1979), p. 27.

27. Nahum Goldmann, Report to the American Zionist Emergency Council, May 30, 1945 (AZEC Papers in the Zionist Archives and Library, New York), as quoted by Ganin, ibid., p. 26.

28. Ganin, ibid., p. 27.

29. *HaAretz,* Tel Aviv, April 4, 1958. In this issue, a large number of documents were printed under the title "On the Way to the State: How Was the Support of the United States for Partition Obtained," and "Dr. N. Goldmann Negotiates with Ernest Bevin: The Agency Will Not Go to the London Conference." The editorial introduction to the documents states that they were put at the paper's disposal by Goldmann. The documents are published here for the first time in English. My translation of these and all other documents from Hebrew and German.

30. Ibid.

31. David B. Sachar, "David K. Niles and United States Policy toward Palestine" (Honors thesis, Harvard University, 1959), p. 24, as quoted by Ganin, *Truman*, p. 60.

32. Elath, *HaMa'avaq*, 1:342.

33. Sachar, "David K. Niles," p. 25; Ganin, *Truman*, pp. 60–61; Elath, *HaMa'avaq*, 1:342.

34. Elath, ibid., 1:363.

35. *HaAretz*, April 4, 1958.

36. Elath, ibid., 1:361; *Foreign Relations of the United States, 1946*, vol. VII, *The Near East and Africa* (Washington: U.S. Government Printing Office, 1949), p. 642.

37. Elath, ibid., 1:377.

38. Ganin, *Truman*, p. 85.

39. Minutes of Hadassah Board, July 31, 1946, pp. 378–79 (copy in the Zionist Archives and Library, New York).

40. *The New York Times*, August 2, 1946.

41. Barnet Litvinov, general ed., *The Letters and Papers of Chaim Weizmann* (New Brunswick, N.J.: Transaction Books, Rutgers University, Jerusalem: Israel Universities Press, 1979), vol. XXII/A, p. xxi; Zvi Ganin, "Tokhnit haḤaluqa uShliḥut Dr. Nahum Goldmann l'Washington, Qayitz 1946" (The Partition Plan and Dr. Nahum Goldmann's Mission to Washington, Summer 1946), in *Ha-Tziyonut: M'assef l'Toldot haT'nuʿa haTziyonit*, Zionism (Papers on the History of the Zionist Movement), (Tel Aviv: Tel Aviv University and HaQibbutz haM'uḥad, 1978), 5:229. On the infighting that took place between Silver and Ben-Gurion over the question of who should represent the Zionist point of view in Washington, cf. the "confidential memorandum" addressed by Rabbi Leon I. Feuer to an unnamed "local Zionist leader," no date, but evidently written in September 1946 (copy in the Zionist Archives and Library, New York).

42. Elath, *HaMa'avaq*, 1:379; *Minutes* of the Meeting of the Jewish Agency Executive in Paris, August 3, 1946, pp. 1–4 (copy in the Central Zionist Archives, Jerusalem).

43. *Minutes*, etc., August 2, p. 1.

44. Ibid., pp. 3–8.

45. Ibid., August 3.

46. Ibid., August 4.

47. Ibid., pp. 6–7.

48. Ibid., August 5, pp. 1–5.

49. Elath, *HaMa'avaq*, 1:380.

50. Ganin, "Tokhnit," p. 235. According to Ganin, the date of the Niles phone call to Goldmann was August 2, and next day a cable was received by Ben-Gurion from Silver in which Silver, too, informed the Executive of the impending meeting on Wednesday, August 7, of the American members of the two committees. Cf. Goldmann, *Autobiography*, p. 234.

51. *Minutes*, etc., August 4.

52. Goldmann, *Autobiography*, p. 233.
53. *Minutes*, etc., August 5, p. 7.
54. Elath, *HaMa'avaq*, 1:381.
55. Silver Archives, Ben-Gurion's cable to Silver, August 5, 1946, and Stephen Wise Archives, Goldmann's letter to Wise, August 5, 1946, as quoted by Ganin, *Truman*, p. 24. Cf. also p. 89 and Goldmann's letter to Ben-Gurion, August 8, 1946.
56. *The New York Times*, August 2, 6, 1946.
57. Ibid., August 3, 1946.
58. Ibid., August 8, 9, 1946; EZI 2:803.
59. EZI 1:31; 2:1034.
60. EZI 2:1034; Rabbi Feuer's memorandum, p. 3 (see note 41).
61. *HaAretz*, April 4, 1958.
62. Goldmann, *Autobiography*, p. 233. This agrees with Goldmann's appointment-book entries for August 6, 1946, which read: "New York. Dr. Silver. Flew to Washington. Bartley Crum. David Niles." All the entries in this appointment book, which Goldmann kept for several years, are extremely brief. Copies of the pages covering the September 7, 1940, to December 12, 1946, period are in the Goldmann file of the Zionist Archives and Library, New York.
63. Ganin, *Truman*, pp. 74, 75, 93, 144, 179.
64. Rabbi Feuer's memorandum, p. 5 (see note 41). Emphases in the original.
65. Elath, *HaMa'avaq*, 1:382.
66. Howard M. Sachar, *A History of Israel* (New York: Knopf, 1976), p. 265.
67. EZI 1:533.
68. Minutes of the Meeting of Hadassah Summer Executive Committee, August 21, 1946, pp. 13, 43 (copy in the Zionist Archives and Library, New York).
69. Goldmann, *Autobiography*, pp. 233–34.
70. Goldmann, *The Jewish Paradox*, p. 33. Cf. *Autobiography*, p. 233.
71. Goldmann, *The Jewish Paradox*, p. 34.
72. Rabbi Feuer's memorandum, pp. 6–7 (see note 41).
73. Ibid., pp. 4, 6, 7.
74. Minutes of the Jewish Agency Executive meeting, Paris, August 5, 1946.
75. Minutes of the Meeting of Hadassah Summer Executive Committee, August 21, 1946, pp. 8, 13, 15; Minutes of the AZEC executive committee meeting of August 7, 1946; Ganin, "Tokhnit," p. 244.
76. Elath, *HaMa'avaq*, 1:384.
77. *HaAretz*, April 4, 1958.
78. Goldmann, *Autobiography*, p. 236.
79. Ibid., p. 234.
80. Goldmann, *The Jewish Paradox*, p. 35.
81. Loc. cit.
82. *HaAretz*, April 4, 1958. According to Goldmann's appointment book entries, he first contacted Proskauer—probably on the phone—on August 7, met

with him on August 8 at 8:30 A.M., went with him to confer with Patterson on the same day at 3:30 P.M., and then met with him again on the same day at 9 P.M.

83. Goldmann, *The Jewish Paradox*, p. 35.

84. Goldmann, *Autobiography*, pp. 234–35; *The Jewish Paradox*, pp. 33–37.

85. *HaAretz*, April 4, 1958.

86. Cf. Proskauer's memorandum in Appendix I; Joseph M. Proskauer, *A Segment of My Times* (New York: Farrar Strauss, 1950), pp. 242–43.

87. Proskauer, *A Segment*, loc. cit.

88. Loc. cit.

89. David Scher, "Joseph Proskauer," in *American Jewish Year Book 73* (1972), pp. 618–28.

90. "American Jewish Committee Report," in *American Jewish Year Book 50* (1948–49), p. 814.

91. Loc. cit.

92. Goldmann, *Autobiography*, p. 235.

93. Probably it is to this meeting that Goldmann's appointment-book entry of August 8 refers: "6:00 Niles."

94. Goldmann, *Autobiography*, p. 235; *The Jewish Paradox*, p. 37.

95. Elath, *HaMa'avaq*, 1:384–85.

96. The above paragraph is my literal translation of the Hebrew text of Goldmann's report to the Executive in Paris on August 13, 1946. The precision of Goldmann's memory and his accuracy in reporting details become evident from a comparison of his presentation with the text of the telegram Acheson sent to the American ambassador in the United Kingdom, Averell Harriman, on August 12, for transmission to the British government (see Appendix G). Despite the sense of urgency Goldmann tried to convey on August 9 to Acheson and Henderson, the telegram was not sent until August 12 at 5:00 P.M. One hour later, in a direct telegram to Prime Minister Attlee, President Truman himself summarized the gist of Acheson's cable (see Appendix H). These telegrams were received in London on August 13 and acknowledged by Attlee on August 15.

97. *HaAretz*, April 4, 1958.

98. In the official collection of State Department documents, *Foreign Relations of the United States, 1946*, vol. VII, *The Near East and Africa* (Washington: U.S. Government Printing Office, 1969), p. 679, this memorandum is referred to in footnote 38 with the remark: "memorandum not printed." However, it is in the Truman Archives and in the State Department files in the U.S. National Archives, no. No1/8-746. The document was published in Ganin, *Truman*, pp. 259–62.

99. Dean Acheson, *Present at the Creation* (New York: William Norton, 1969), pp. 169–92.

100. *HaAretz*, April 4, 1958. This report of Goldmann to the Executive is missing from the files of the Central Zionist Archives, Jerusalem, which contains the minutes of the August 13, 1946, meeting of the Executive in Paris.

101. Elath, *HaMa'avaq*, 1:387.

102. Feuer's memorandum, pp. 10–11 (see note 41); Elath, *HaMa'avaq*, 1:387.

103. Elath, *HaMa'avaq*, 1:388.

104. The reference is to the British proposal for the solution of the Palestine problem that was presented to the House of Commons by Deputy Prime Minister Herbert Morrison on July 31, 1946.

105. The fact is that the Twentieth Zionist Congress, which met in Zurich on August 3–16, 1937, empowered the Executive to negotiate with the British government to clarify the specific terms of the proposal to establish a Jewish State in Palestine.

106. Bevin knew that Goldmann had returned from Washington to Paris on August 12, that is, two days before Goldmann came to see him.

107. Goldmann is referring to the Jordan Valley Authority Plan, which was based on Walter C. Lowdermilk's 1944 book, *Palestine, Land of Promise*.

108. This is a reference to the Peel plan, which envisaged the continuation of the British Mandate over Jaffa and Jerusalem as well as over a corridor connecting the two cities.

109. General Sir Evelyn Barker, the British Army commander in Palestine, made a strongly anti-Semitic remark in the wake of the King David Hotel bombing. Cf. Sachar, *A History of Israel*, p. 274.

110. Field Marshal Viscount Bernard Montgomery was Barker's superior.

111. The above account is a slightly revised version of the first-person narrative of Goldmann that appeared in the April 4, 1958, issue of the Tel Aviv daily *HaAretz*. The report of Goldmann on his talk with Bevin is missing from the files of the Central Zionist Archives, Jerusalem, which contains the Minutes of the August 14, 1946, meeting of the Executive.

112. Source: Goldmann's appointment book, and the Minutes of the meeting of the Jewish Agency Executive on August 15, 1946, in the Central Zionist Archives, Jerusalem.

113. Minutes of the August 14, 1946, meeting of the Executive.

114. Ibid.

115. Litvinov, general ed., *The Letters and Papers of Chaim Weizmann*, XXII/A:182. The text of the letter is accompanied by the note "Letter not sent."

116. Justine Wise Polier and James Waterman Wise, eds., *The Personal Letters of Stephen Wise* (Boston: Beacon Press, 1956), p. 273. Cf. Goldmann's appointment-book entries of August 17, 1946.

117. Goldmann's appointment-book entries of August 17, 1946; Minutes of the meeting of the Jewish Agency Executive, Paris, August 17, 1946, 9 A.M., in the Central Zionist Archives, Jerusalem. Goldmann's report is missing from the Minutes.

118. Minutes, ibid., p. 3.

119. Minutes, ibid., August 18, 1946, pp. 1–5.

120. Interview with Goldmann by Y'sha'yahu Ben-Porat, in *Y'di'ot Aharonot*, Tel Aviv, July 21, 1978.

121. Minutes of the Political Commission of the Jewish Agency Executive, August 21, 1946, 3:30 P.M., pp. 3–4, in the Central Zionist Archives, Jerusalem.

122. *HaAretz*, April 4, 1958. My translation with minor stylistic revisions.

123. Source: Goldmann's appointment-book entries from October 17 to December 4, 1946.

124. Elath, *HaMa'avaq*, 1:406.

125. Ibid., 1:406–7.

126. Ibid., p. 396.

127. Ibid., 1:396–97.

128. *Foreign Relations of the U.S., 1946*, vol. VII, p. 703.

129. Cf. Ganin, *Truman*, pp. 105–6,

130. *Foreign Relations of the U.S., 1946*, vol. VII, pp. 701 ff.

131. Ibid., p. 705 (Report from U.S. Chargé Gallman from London to Secretary of State, October 5, 1946).

132. Elath, *HaMa'avaq*, 1:450.

133. Source: Goldmann's appointment-book entries from October 17 to December 4, 1946.

134. *Foreign Relations of the U.S., 1946*, vol. VII, pp. 722–23.

135. Elath, *HaMa'avaq*, 1:451–52.

136. Minutes of the meeting of the executive committee of the AZEC, September 10, 1946, in the Zionist Archives and Library, New York.

137. Elath, *HaMa'avaq*, 1:435.

138. Protocols of the 22nd Zionist Congress (Jerusalem: The Zionist Executive, n.d.), December 12, 1946.

139. Ganin, *Truman*, p. 116; Elath, *HaMa'avaq*, 1:455. Ganin (quoting John A. Lehrs, American vice-consul in Basle, Report on the Zionist Congress, January 16, 1947, p. 4, note 35, State Department Records 867 No1/1-1647) states that Weizmann, Wise, and Goldmann, the "three casualties of the Silver onslaught," were equally bitter and resentful. Yet, Ganin admits, Goldmann's situation was different from that of the other two, for he remained a member of the Executive. Goldmann felt that, at least until the end of the London Round Table Conference, he had to remain at his post and carry on the struggle for partition. Cf. Ganin, *Truman*, pp. 117–18.

140. Sachar, *A History of Israel*, p. 272.

141. Ganin, *Truman*, pp. 134–35, and sources there.

142. EZI 2:1143, 1144, 1147.

143. Goldmann, *Autobiography*, p. 242.

144. Ibid., p. 234.

145. Ibid., pp. 234–44.

146. Ibid., p. 245.

147. Loc. cit.

Chapter 7

1. Kurt Blumenfeld, *Im Kampf um den Zionismus: Briefe aus fünf Jahrzehnten*, ed. Miriam Sambursky and Jochanan Ginot (Stuttgart: Deutsche Verlags-Anstalt, 1976), p. 242. The quotations from German sources are my translation; emphasis added.

2. Konrad Adenauer, *Erinnerungen, 1953–1955* (Stuttgart: Deutsche Verlags-Anstalt, 1966), p. 137.

3. Goldmann, *Mein Leben*, p. 384.

4. Felix E. Shinnar, *Bericht eines Beauftragten* (Tübingen: Rainer Wunderlich Verlag, 1967), p. 46.

5. Goldmann, *Mein Leben*, p. 389.

6. Goldmann, *Autobiography*, p. 250. Cf. Nicholas Balabkins, *West German Reparations to Israel* (New Brunswick, N.J.: Rutgers University Press, 1971), p. 81.

7. Balabkins, op. cit., pp. 81–82, quoting *U.S. Department of State Bulletin* 8:185 (January 3, 1943):21–22.

8. Ibid., pp. 82–83. Cf. especially Siegfried Moses, *Jewish Postwar Claims* (Tel Aviv: Irgun Olej Merkaz Europa, 1944); F. Gillis and H. Knopf, *The Restoration Claims of the Jewish People* (Tel Aviv: Edition Olympia–M. Feuchtwanger, 1944); Nehemiah Robinson, *Indemnification and Reparations* (New York: Institute for Jewish Affairs of the American Jewish Congress and World Jewish Congress, 1944); Hans Neisser, *The Problem of Reparations* (New York: The American Labor Conference on International Affairs, Studies in Postwar Reconstruction, no. 4, July 1944); Siegfried Goldschmidt, *Legal Claims against Germany* (New York: Dryden Press, for the American Jewish Committee, 1945); Chaim Weizmann, letter to the Allies, dated Sept. 20, 1945, printed in Israel Ministry of Foreign Affairs, *Documents Relating to the Agreement between the Government of Israel and the Government of the Federal Republic of Germany* (Jerusalem: Government Printer, 1953), pp. 9–12; and Nana Sagi, *German Reparations: A History of the Negotiations* (Jerusalem: The Magnes Press–Hebrew University, 1980).

9. World Jewish Congress, War Emergency Conference, *Summary of Proceedings*, Nov. 26–30, 1944, Atlantic City, N.J. (issued by the American Jewish Congress), p. 4.

10. Adenauer, *Erinnerungen*, p. 133.

11. Cf. Shinnar, *Bericht*, p. 20.

12. EZI, s.v. German-Israel Agreement.

13. Adenauer, *Erinnerungen*, p. 132.

14. Ibid., pp. 134–35.

15. Ibid., p. 136.

16. Shinnar, *Bericht*, p. 26.

17. Ibid., p. 27.

18. Adenauer, *Erinnerungen*, p. 137.

19. Goldmann remembered clearly that the man who accompanied him was not the Israeli ambassador, but Dr. Noah Barou. Goldmann to Patai, Paris, January 6, 1981.

20. Adenauer, *Erinnerungen*, pp. 137–39.

21. Shinnar, *Bericht*, p. 27.

22. Cf. material collected in Balabkins, *West German Reparations*, pp. 93–94.

23. Shinnar, *Bericht*, pp. 27 ff.

24. Adenauer, *Erinnerungen*, p. 139.

25. Goldmann, *Autobiography*, p. 262.

26. Adenauer, loc. cit.

27. Loc. cit.

28. Ibid., p. 144.

29. Ibid., pp. 145–47.

30. Ibid., pp. 148–50.

31. Ibid., pp. 149–51.

32. Ibid., pp. 151–52.

33. Ibid., pp. 152–53.

34. Ibid., p. 156.

35. Herbert Blankenhorn, *Verständnis und Verständigung: Blätter eines politischen Tagebuchs, 1949–1979* (Frankfurt a. M.: Propyläen Verlag, 1980), p. 138.

36. Ibid., pp. 141–42.

37. Goldmann, *Autobiography*, pp. 264–65.

38. Goldmann, *Mein Leben*, pp. 414–25.

39. Blankenhorn, *Verständnis*, p. 357.

40. Ibid., pp. 358–60.

41. Konrad Adenauer, *Erinnerungen, 1959–1963* (Stuttgart: Deutsche Verlags-Anstalt, 1968), p. 32.

42. Rolf Vogel, ed., *The German Path to Israel: A Documentation* . . . with a Foreword by Konrad Adenauer (Chester Springs, Pa.: Dufour Editions, 1969), pp. 180–81.

43. Ibid., p. 182.

44. Ibid., p. 186.

45. Ibid., p. 197.

46. Ibid., pp. 197–257.

47. Ibid., p. 258.

48. Ibid., p. 263.

49. Ibid., p. 261.

50. Ibid., p. 115.

51. Ibid., p. 99.

52. Goldmann, *Autobiography*, p. 249; the same in German in *Mein Leben*, p. 371.

53. Goldmann, *The Jewish Paradox*, p. 121.

54. Loc. cit.

55. Goldmann, *Mein Leben*, p. 410.

56. Nahum Goldmann, "A Noble Son of Jewry," in H. F. Infield, ed., *Essays in Jewish Sociology, Labour, and Cooperation in Memory of Dr. Noah Barou (1889–1955)* (London: T. Yoseloff, 1962), pp. 10–15.

57. Goldmann, *Autobiography*, pp. 254–58; cf. p. 216; *The Jewish Paradox*, p. 123; *Mein Leben*, pp. 376, 378–79, 412.

58. Goldmann, *Autobiography*, p. 256; *Mein Leben*, p. 379.

59. Goldmann, *Mein Leben*, pp. 382–83.

60. Ibid., p. 384.

61. Ibid., pp. 380–81.

62. Goldmann, *Autobiography*, p. 260; cf. Goldmann, *The Jewish Paradox*, pp. 126–27; Goldmann, *Mein Leben*, pp. 385–86.

63. Goldmann, *Mein Leben*, pp. 414–25.

64. Ibid., p. 414.

65. Ibid., p. 417.

66. Ibid., p. 419.

67. Goldmann, *Mein Leben*, pp. 420–21. The text of Eshkol's speech and Adenauer's reply is printed in Vogel, ed., *The German Path*, pp. 183–85. A more detailed account of the incident is given in Goldmann, *The Jewish Paradox*, pp. 140–43.

68. Goldmann, *The Jewish Paradox*, p. 124.

69. Goldmann, *Mein Leben*, pp. 424–25.

70. From an address by Goldmann, quoted by German Ambassador Rolf Paul in a speech he delivered in June 1966, at the Israel Industrial Fair, in Tel Aviv. Cf. Vogel, ed., *The German Path*, p. 188.

71. Goldmann, *Mein Leben*, p. 409.

72. Balabkins, *West German Reparations*, p. 154.

73. Dean Silvers, "The Future of International Law as Seen through the Jewish Material Claims Conference against Germany," *Jewish Social Studies* 42:3–4 (Summer–Fall 1980), pp. 215, 216.

74. Goldmann, *Autobiography*, p. 280.

Chapter 8

1. *JTA Daily News Bulletin*, August 24, 1979, p. 1.

2. Minutes of meeting of Hadassah National Board, July 17, 1946, pp. 350–51 (microfilm in the Zionist Archives and Library, New York). Emphasis added.

3. Goldmann, *Autobiography*, p. 287.

4. Memorandum signed by Dean Acheson, in the Truman Archives and in the U.S. National Archives, no. 867 No1/8-746, as quoted by Zvi Ganin, in *HaTziyonut: M'assef l'Toldot haT'nuᶜa haTziyonit v'haYishuv haY'hudi* 5 (1978):260. This seems to be the memorandum that, according to Goldmann's

Autobiography, p. 234, was prepared by Loy Henderson, assistant secretary for the Near East, and initialed by Goldmann. This memorandum is not contained in the source mentioned in the next note.

5. *Foreign Relations of the United States, 1946,* vol. VII, *The Near East and Africa* (Washington: U.S. Government Printing Office, 1969), pp. 680, no. 867 No1/8–1246: telegram.

6. David Ben-Gurion, *Rebirth and Destiny of Israel* (New York: Philosophical Library, 1954), p. 208. In a letter Goldmann addressed to me on December 3, 1980, he wrote: "Ben-Gurion himself was in favor of a confederation. When he presented the Jewish case to the U.N. committee [he means the Anglo-American Committee of Inquiry] dealing with the partition of Palestine, we went even so far—too far in my opinion—to propose an alliance between the future Jewish state and the Arab states."

7. Goldmann, *Autobiography,* pp. 232–33.

8. Ibid., p. 299.

9. Ibid., pp. 299–300.

10. *The Answer* 5:52 (December 26, 1947):5.

11. Goldmann to Patai, Paris, December 3, 1980.

12. Typescript in the Goldmann file, Zionist Archives and Library, New York.

13. Goldmann to Patai, Paris, December 3, 1980.

14. Eric Rouleau, "Scenario of a Meeting that Never Was," *Le Monde,* Paris, April 8, 1956, p. 1.

15. Goldmann to Patai, Paris, December 3, 1980.

16. Goldmann "improved" somewhat on Mann. What Mann actually says in his long essay "Frederick the Great and the Grand Coalition" is that in the summer the Prussian arose at three in the morning, and that "when a man lives separated from his wife and gets up at three o'clock in the morning, he can get a lot done in the course of the day." However, Mann's essay was published in the 1920s, and Goldmann probably read it soon thereafter, that is, some thirty years before his conversation with Hammarskjöld took place. Moreover, by the time he told me about that conversation—in the summer of 1980—another twenty-four years had passed, so that what he actually told me was that which he remembered in 1980 as having said to Hammarskjöld in 1956 about what he remembered at that time from a book he had read in the 1920s. In view of this double lapse of time, a certain inaccuracy in, or embellishment of, the Mann quotation should cause no surprise.

17. Goldmann, *The Jewish Paradox,* p. 56.

18. Goldmann file, Zionist Archives and Library, New York.

19. Goldmann, *Autobiography,* p. 309.

20. *The New York Times,* April 25, 1955.

21. Copy of typescript of Goldmann's first-person report, entitled "Report on Interview with Prime Minister Nehru on Thursday, June 27th, in the afternoon," in the Goldmann file, Zionist Archives and Library, New York.

22. Goldmann file, ibid.

23. Ibid.

24. Ibid.

25. Interview with Goldmann in Paris, July 2, 1980.

26. Eric Rouleau, *Le Monde,* Paris, April 8, 1970, p. 1.

27. The above summary of the war of attrition is based on Yaacov Bar-Siman-Tov, *The Israeli-Egyptian War of Attrition, 1969–1970* (New York: Columbia University Press, 1980), pp. 43–148.

28. Dan Margalit, *Sheder mehaBayit haLavan* (Message from the White House) (Tel Aviv: Otpaz, 1971), p. 85, quoting *HaAretz.* Margalit misspells Hamrush's name as "Harmush."

29. Nahum Goldmann, "The Future of Israel," *Foreign Affairs,* April 1970, pp. 443–59.

30. Interview with Goldmann in Paris, June 26, 27, 1980.

31. Margalit, *Sheder,* p. 84.

32. *Divre haK'nesset* (Knesset Records), April 7, 1970, p. 1586. Cf. the summary of the meeting between Goldmann and Mrs. Meir in Margalit, *Sheder,* pp. 85–88.

33. *Divre haK'nesset,* p. 1573.

34. Ibid., p. 1585.

35. Margalit, *Sheder,* pp. 89–90.

36. *Ma'ariv,* Tel Aviv, April 10, 1970.

37. *Divre haK'nesset,* ibid., Abba Eban's speech.

38. Margalit, *Sheder,* pp. 88–91.

39. The above summary of the events of the period March 30–April 5 is based partly on Margalit, *Sheder,* pp. 88–92.

40. *Divre haK'nesset,* p. 1593.

41. Bar-Siman-Tov, *The Israeli-Egyptian War,* pp. 149–51.

42. *Ma'ariv,* Tel Aviv, April 10, 1970.

43. Goldmann to Patai, Paris, December 3, 1980.

44. *The New York Times,* April 7, 9, 10, 1970; *Le Monde,* April 8, 1970.

45. *Jerusalem Post,* April 9, 1970; *Le Monde,* April 8, 1970 (news story by the paper's Israeli correspondent André Scemama).

46. Margalit, *Sheder,* pp. 96, 102.

47. *Ma'ariv,* April 10, 1970.

48. Ibid., p. 2.

49. Margalit, *Sheder,* pp. 96–97.

50. *Ma'ariv,* April 6, 1970, p. 2.

51. *Jerusalem Post,* April 8, 10, 19, May 1, 3, 6, 7, etc.

52. Margalit, *Sheder,* p. 95.

53. *Jerusalem Post,* April 30, May 6, 1970.

54. Ibid., May 7, 1970.

55. Ibid., April 30, 1970.

56. Margalit, *Sheder,* p. 88.

57. Eric Rouleau, *Le Monde,* April 8, 1970.

58. Typescript in the Goldmann file, Zionist Archives and Library, New York.

59. Goldmann, *Autobiography,* pp. 301–7.

60. Armand Kaplan to Goldmann, Paris, June 29, 1978, p. 2 (copy sent by Goldmann to Patai). According to this letter, in early 1967 Goldmann was "possessed with the dream or hope to meet Nasser," and "in July, 1967, I [Kaplan] met for the first time in Paris Mr. Vejvoda, then Yugoslav Ambassador, and brought up the idea—which for me was wishful thinking." In the next paragraph of his letter, Kaplan says that "in Spring 1969, at one of my dinners at Vejvoda's house, I had a long conversation with him during which I brought up 'the idea' of a meeting between you [Goldmann] and Nasser. Since I knew the very close relationship between Tito and Nasser, it was quite natural for me to convey to Vejvoda he should indulge Tito with the idea." Apart from the contradiction in the two dates—July 1967 and spring 1969—on which Kaplan says he "brought up the idea" of a Goldmann-Nasser meeting in a talk with the Yugoslav ambassador, it appears from this letter that, though Goldmann had made efforts to interest Nasser in his Near Eastern Confederation concept as early as 1955 (through Dag Hammarskjöld) and 1957 (through Nehru), he became seized with the idea of a personal meeting between him and Nasser only in early 1967.

61. Nahum Goldmann, "Die Juden und die Völker," in *Beiheft,* vol. 2, 1972, of the Jüdischer Weltkongress und Deutscher Koordinierungsrat der Gesellschaften für Christlich-Jüdische Zusammenarbeit, Köln, 1972.

62. In fact, Goldmann was twenty-two years old in November 1917, when the Balfour Declaration was issued.

63. Nahum Goldmann, *Le Monde Diplomatique,* August 1974, pp. 1, 17.

64. *Foreign Policy,* Washington, D.C., Winter 1979–80, no. 37, pp. 133–41.

65. *Die Zeit,* July 11, 1980.

66. Interview with Goldmann in Paris, July 2, 1980.

67. One of them, written by the well-known Israeli novelist Aharon Meged, takes Goldmann to task for, among other things, criticizing and warning Israel of the dangers she faces. See *The Jewish Week—American Examiner,* August 17, 1980. The strictures seem unfair, coming as they do from the pen of an author who in "his most ambitious work," the novel *HaHay ʿal haMet* (1965; in English, *The Living on the Dead,* 1970), "describes in unflattering terms modern Israeli society, and makes the accusation that the great expectations of the first pioneers have not been fulfilled by their successors." Cf. *Encyclopaedia Judaica,* 1972, s.v. Meged, Aharon.

68. First published in *HaAretz,* and then in an English translation in *The Jewish Week—American Examiner,* October 26, 1980.

69. *JTA Daily News Bulletin,* New York, March 27, 1981.

Appendixes

1. Source: David Ben-Gurion, *Zikhronot* (Memoirs), vol. IV (Tel Aviv: ʿAm ʿOved, 1976), pp. 314–16. My translation from the Hebrew.

2. Derogatory term designating assimilant, upper-class Jews.

3. Pierre Orts was chairman of the Permanent Mandates Commission of the League of Nations.

4. Fuad Shatra was an American of Lebanese descent, who, in the 1930s, headed the Arab National League in the United States. ʿIzzat Tannous was an Arab physician and politician, a leader of the Husayni party in Palestine, who, in the 1930s, was head of the Arab office in London. In May–June 1937 Shatra and Tannous established contact with non-Zionist Jews in the United States seeking to reach an Arab-Jewish agreement.

5. Source: Litvinov, general ed., *The Letters and Papers of Chaim Weizmann,* XXI/A:40–42.

6. The Emergency Committee had determined that the panel should comprise: the president of the Jewish Agency as chairman; members of the Political Department of the Jewish Agency and the Zionist Executive resident or sojourning in the United States; the chairman of the American Zionist Emergency Committee; and not more than seven others. This panel, also called the Political Committee, would be collectively responsible for all Zionist political activities in the United States, would render monthly reports to the Office Committee of the AZEC, and was authorized to assign specific tasks to ad hoc subcommittees. Ibid., p. 41, note 3.

7. Source: *Foreign Relations of the United States, 1946,* vol. VII, pp. 710–12.

8. Source: Ibid., pp. 712–13.

9. Source: Ibid., pp. 713–15.

10. Source: State Department files in the U.S. National Archives, no. 867 No1/ 8-746) (copy in the Truman Archives, Missouri).

11. Source: as in note 7, pp. 679–82.

12. Source: as in note 7, p. 682.

13. Source: Archives of the American Jewish Committee, New York.

Index

Index

About the Author

Raphael Patai is an anthropologist specializing in the Middle East. He received the Ph.D. from the University of Budapest and the Hebrew University of Jerusalem. He taught at the Hebrew University and, from 1947 on, at several American universities. He is the author of many books, including *The Hebrew Goddess, The Arab Mind, The Myth of the Jewish Race* (with Jennifer Wing), *The Jewish Mind, The Messiah Texts, Gates to the Old City, The Vanished Worlds of Jewry, On Jewish Folklore,* and *The Seed of Abraham: Jews and Arabs in Contact and Conflict.* He edited *The Complete Diaries of Theodor Herzl, The Herzl Year Books,* and *The Encyclopaedia of Zionism and Israel.*